Lecture Notes in Computer Science   14730

Founding Editors

Gerhard Goos
Juris Hartmanis

The series Lecture Notes in Computer Science (LNCS), including its subseries Lecture Notes in Artificial Intelligence (LNAI) and Lecture Notes in Bioinformatics (LNBI), has established itself as a medium for the publication of new developments in computer science and information technology research, teaching, and education.

LNCS enjoys close cooperation with the computer science R & D community, the series counts many renowned academics among its volume editors and paper authors, and collaborates with prestigious societies. Its mission is to serve this international community by providing an invaluable service, mainly focused on the publication of conference and workshop proceedings and postproceedings. LNCS commenced publication in 1973.

Xiaowen Fang
Editor

HCI in Games

6th International Conference, HCI-Games 2024
Held as Part of the 26th HCI International Conference, HCII 2024
Washington, DC, USA, June 29 – July 4, 2024
Proceedings, Part I

 Springer

Editor
Xiaowen Fang
DePaul University
Chicago, IL, USA

ISSN 0302-9743   ISSN 1611-3349 (electronic)
Lecture Notes in Computer Science
ISBN 978-3-031-60691-5   ISBN 978-3-031-60692-2 (eBook)
https://doi.org/10.1007/978-3-031-60692-2

This Springer imprint is published by the registered company Springer Nature Switzerland AG
The registered company address is: Gewerbestrasse 11, 6330 Cham, Switzerland

If disposing of this product, please recycle the paper.

Foreword

This year we celebrate 40 years since the establishment of the HCI International (HCII) Conference, which has been a hub for presenting groundbreaking research and novel ideas and collaboration for people from all over the world.

The HCII conference was founded in 1984 by Prof. Gavriel Salvendy (Purdue University, USA, Tsinghua University, P.R. China, and University of Central Florida, USA) and the first event of the series, "1st USA-Japan Conference on Human-Computer Interaction", was held in Honolulu, Hawaii, USA, 18–20 August. Since then, HCI International is held jointly with several Thematic Areas and Affiliated Conferences, with each one under the auspices of a distinguished international Program Board and under one management and one registration. Twenty-six HCI International Conferences have been organized so far (every two years until 2013, and annually thereafter).

Over the years, this conference has served as a platform for scholars, researchers, industry experts and students to exchange ideas, connect, and address challenges in the ever-evolving HCI field. Throughout these 40 years, the conference has evolved itself, adapting to new technologies and emerging trends, while staying committed to its core mission of advancing knowledge and driving change.

As we celebrate this milestone anniversary, we reflect on the contributions of its founding members and appreciate the commitment of its current and past Affiliated Conference Program Board Chairs and members. We are also thankful to all past conference attendees who have shaped this community into what it is today.

The 26th International Conference on Human-Computer Interaction, HCI International 2024 (HCII 2024), was held as a 'hybrid' event at the Washington Hilton Hotel, Washington, DC, USA, during 29 June – 4 July 2024. It incorporated the 21 thematic areas and affiliated conferences listed below.

A total of 5108 individuals from academia, research institutes, industry, and government agencies from 85 countries submitted contributions, and 1271 papers and 309 posters were included in the volumes of the proceedings that were published just before the start of the conference, these are listed below. The contributions thoroughly cover the entire field of human-computer interaction, addressing major advances in knowledge and effective use of computers in a variety of application areas. These papers provide academics, researchers, engineers, scientists, practitioners and students with state-of-the-art information on the most recent advances in HCI.

The HCI International (HCII) conference also offers the option of presenting 'Late Breaking Work', and this applies both for papers and posters, with corresponding volumes of proceedings that will be published after the conference. Full papers will be included in the 'HCII 2024 - Late Breaking Papers' volumes of the proceedings to be published in the Springer LNCS series, while 'Poster Extended Abstracts' will be included as short research papers in the 'HCII 2024 - Late Breaking Posters' volumes to be published in the Springer CCIS series.

I would like to thank the Program Board Chairs and the members of the Program Boards of all thematic areas and affiliated conferences for their contribution towards the high scientific quality and overall success of the HCI International 2024 conference. Their manifold support in terms of paper reviewing (single-blind review process, with a minimum of two reviews per submission), session organization and their willingness to act as goodwill ambassadors for the conference is most highly appreciated.

This conference would not have been possible without the continuous and unwavering support and advice of Gavriel Salvendy, founder, General Chair Emeritus, and Scientific Advisor. For his outstanding efforts, I would like to express my sincere appreciation to Abbas Moallem, Communications Chair and Editor of HCI International News.

July 2024   Constantine Stephanidis

HCI International 2024 Thematic Areas and Affiliated Conferences

- HCI: Human-Computer Interaction Thematic Area
- HIMI: Human Interface and the Management of Information Thematic Area
- EPCE: 21st International Conference on Engineering Psychology and Cognitive Ergonomics
- AC: 18th International Conference on Augmented Cognition
- UAHCI: 18th International Conference on Universal Access in Human-Computer Interaction
- CCD: 16th International Conference on Cross-Cultural Design
- SCSM: 16th International Conference on Social Computing and Social Media
- VAMR: 16th International Conference on Virtual, Augmented and Mixed Reality
- DHM: 15th International Conference on Digital Human Modeling & Applications in Health, Safety, Ergonomics & Risk Management
- DUXU: 13th International Conference on Design, User Experience and Usability
- C&C: 12th International Conference on Culture and Computing
- DAPI: 12th International Conference on Distributed, Ambient and Pervasive Interactions
- HCIBGO: 11th International Conference on HCI in Business, Government and Organizations
- LCT: 11th International Conference on Learning and Collaboration Technologies
- ITAP: 10th International Conference on Human Aspects of IT for the Aged Population
- AIS: 6th International Conference on Adaptive Instructional Systems
- HCI-CPT: 6th International Conference on HCI for Cybersecurity, Privacy and Trust
- HCI-Games: 6th International Conference on HCI in Games
- MobiTAS: 6th International Conference on HCI in Mobility, Transport and Automotive Systems
- AI-HCI: 5th International Conference on Artificial Intelligence in HCI
- MOBILE: 5th International Conference on Human-Centered Design, Operation and Evaluation of Mobile Communications

List of Conference Proceedings Volumes Appearing Before the Conference

1. LNCS 14684, Human-Computer Interaction: Part I, edited by Masaaki Kurosu and Ayako Hashizume
2. LNCS 14685, Human-Computer Interaction: Part II, edited by Masaaki Kurosu and Ayako Hashizume
3. LNCS 14686, Human-Computer Interaction: Part III, edited by Masaaki Kurosu and Ayako Hashizume
4. LNCS 14687, Human-Computer Interaction: Part IV, edited by Masaaki Kurosu and Ayako Hashizume
5. LNCS 14688, Human-Computer Interaction: Part V, edited by Masaaki Kurosu and Ayako Hashizume
6. LNCS 14689, Human Interface and the Management of Information: Part I, edited by Hirohiko Mori and Yumi Asahi
7. LNCS 14690, Human Interface and the Management of Information: Part II, edited by Hirohiko Mori and Yumi Asahi
8. LNCS 14691, Human Interface and the Management of Information: Part III, edited by Hirohiko Mori and Yumi Asahi
9. LNAI 14692, Engineering Psychology and Cognitive Ergonomics: Part I, edited by Don Harris and Wen-Chin Li
10. LNAI 14693, Engineering Psychology and Cognitive Ergonomics: Part II, edited by Don Harris and Wen-Chin Li
11. LNAI 14694, Augmented Cognition, Part I, edited by Dylan D. Schmorrow and Cali M. Fidopiastis
12. LNAI 14695, Augmented Cognition, Part II, edited by Dylan D. Schmorrow and Cali M. Fidopiastis
13. LNCS 14696, Universal Access in Human-Computer Interaction: Part I, edited by Margherita Antona and Constantine Stephanidis
14. LNCS 14697, Universal Access in Human-Computer Interaction: Part II, edited by Margherita Antona and Constantine Stephanidis
15. LNCS 14698, Universal Access in Human-Computer Interaction: Part III, edited by Margherita Antona and Constantine Stephanidis
16. LNCS 14699, Cross-Cultural Design: Part I, edited by Pei-Luen Patrick Rau
17. LNCS 14700, Cross-Cultural Design: Part II, edited by Pei-Luen Patrick Rau
18. LNCS 14701, Cross-Cultural Design: Part III, edited by Pei-Luen Patrick Rau
19. LNCS 14702, Cross-Cultural Design: Part IV, edited by Pei-Luen Patrick Rau
20. LNCS 14703, Social Computing and Social Media: Part I, edited by Adela Coman and Simona Vasilache
21. LNCS 14704, Social Computing and Social Media: Part II, edited by Adela Coman and Simona Vasilache
22. LNCS 14705, Social Computing and Social Media: Part III, edited by Adela Coman and Simona Vasilache

23. LNCS 14706, Virtual, Augmented and Mixed Reality: Part I, edited by Jessie Y. C. Chen and Gino Fragomeni
24. LNCS 14707, Virtual, Augmented and Mixed Reality: Part II, edited by Jessie Y. C. Chen and Gino Fragomeni
25. LNCS 14708, Virtual, Augmented and Mixed Reality: Part III, edited by Jessie Y. C. Chen and Gino Fragomeni
26. LNCS 14709, Digital Human Modeling and Applications in Health, Safety, Ergonomics and Risk Management: Part I, edited by Vincent G. Duffy
27. LNCS 14710, Digital Human Modeling and Applications in Health, Safety, Ergonomics and Risk Management: Part II, edited by Vincent G. Duffy
28. LNCS 14711, Digital Human Modeling and Applications in Health, Safety, Ergonomics and Risk Management: Part III, edited by Vincent G. Duffy
29. LNCS 14712, Design, User Experience, and Usability: Part I, edited by Aaron Marcus, Elizabeth Rosenzweig and Marcelo M. Soares
30. LNCS 14713, Design, User Experience, and Usability: Part II, edited by Aaron Marcus, Elizabeth Rosenzweig and Marcelo M. Soares
31. LNCS 14714, Design, User Experience, and Usability: Part III, edited by Aaron Marcus, Elizabeth Rosenzweig and Marcelo M. Soares
32. LNCS 14715, Design, User Experience, and Usability: Part IV, edited by Aaron Marcus, Elizabeth Rosenzweig and Marcelo M. Soares
33. LNCS 14716, Design, User Experience, and Usability: Part V, edited by Aaron Marcus, Elizabeth Rosenzweig and Marcelo M. Soares
34. LNCS 14717, Culture and Computing, edited by Matthias Rauterberg
35. LNCS 14718, Distributed, Ambient and Pervasive Interactions: Part I, edited by Norbert A. Streitz and Shin'ichi Konomi
36. LNCS 14719, Distributed, Ambient and Pervasive Interactions: Part II, edited by Norbert A. Streitz and Shin'ichi Konomi
37. LNCS 14720, HCI in Business, Government and Organizations: Part I, edited by Fiona Fui-Hoon Nah and Keng Leng Siau
38. LNCS 14721, HCI in Business, Government and Organizations: Part II, edited by Fiona Fui-Hoon Nah and Keng Leng Siau
39. LNCS 14722, Learning and Collaboration Technologies: Part I, edited by Panayiotis Zaphiris and Andri Ioannou
40. LNCS 14723, Learning and Collaboration Technologies: Part II, edited by Panayiotis Zaphiris and Andri Ioannou
41. LNCS 14724, Learning and Collaboration Technologies: Part III, edited by Panayiotis Zaphiris and Andri Ioannou
42. LNCS 14725, Human Aspects of IT for the Aged Population: Part I, edited by Qin Gao and Jia Zhou
43. LNCS 14726, Human Aspects of IT for the Aged Population: Part II, edited by Qin Gao and Jia Zhou
44. LNCS 14727, Adaptive Instructional System, edited by Robert A. Sottilare and Jessica Schwarz
45. LNCS 14728, HCI for Cybersecurity, Privacy and Trust: Part I, edited by Abbas Moallem
46. LNCS 14729, HCI for Cybersecurity, Privacy and Trust: Part II, edited by Abbas Moallem

https://2024.hci.international/proceedings

Preface

Computer games have grown beyond simple entertainment activities. Researchers and practitioners have attempted to utilize games in many innovative ways, such as educational games, therapeutic games, simulation games, and gamification of utilitarian applications. Although a lot of attention has been given to investigate the positive impact of games in recent years, prior research has only studied isolated fragments of a game system. More research on games is needed to develop and utilize games for the benefit of society.

At a high level, a game system has three basic elements: system input, process, and system output. System input concerns the external factors impacting the game system. It may include but is not limited to, player personalities and motivations to play games. The process is about game mechanism and play experience. System output includes the effects of gameplay. There is no doubt that users are involved in all three elements. Human-Computer Interaction (HCI) plays a critical role in the study of games. By examining player characteristics, interactions during gameplay, and behavioral implications of gameplay, HCI professionals can help design and develop better games for society.

The 6th International Conference on HCI in Games (HCI-Games 2024), an affiliated conference of the HCI International Conference, was intended to help, promote, and encourage research in this field by providing a forum for interaction and exchanges among researchers, academics, and practitioners in the fields of HCI and games. The conference addressed HCI principles, methods, and tools for better games. Papers included in the proceedings have actively explored the area of game design from various viewpoints including gamification, empathy, playfulness, affordances, mobile gaming, and tutorial design. Furthermore, papers have contributed state-of-the-art research on player experience and engagement, addressing attainable game experiences, aesthetics, meaning, and toxicity, as well as user studies on player behavior and perspectives. The impact of games in learning and education has also been actively explored, with research focusing on the user experience of immersive games and embodied experiences and exploring various application domains of serious games such as language learning, environmental awareness, physical therapy and rehabilitation, cultural heritage, and art. Finally, as AI technologies continue to advance, their transformative impact on game experience has been studied, from producing game content with natural language to designing game characters and intelligent agents or creating adaptive games and evaluating game experiences.

Two volumes of the HCII 2024 proceedings are dedicated to this year's edition of the HCI-Games Conference. The first focuses on topics related to Game Design and Gamification, Game-Based Learning, and Games and Artificial Intelligence, while the second focuses on topics related to Advancing Education Through Serious Games, and Player Experience and Engagement.

The papers in these volumes were accepted for publication after a minimum of two single-blind reviews from the members of the HCI-Games Program Board or, in some cases, from members of the Program Boards of other affiliated conferences. I would like to thank all of them for their invaluable contribution, support, and efforts.

July 2024   Xiaowen Fang

6th International Conference on HCI in Games
(HCI-Games 2024)

Program Board Chair: **Xiaowen Fang**, *DePaul University, USA*

- Amir Zaib Abbasi, *King Fahd University of Petroleum & Minerals, Saudi Arabia*
- Saeed Abo-oleet, *Najran University, Saudi Arabia*
- Barbara Caci, *University of Palermo, Italy*
- Benjamin Ultan Cowley, *University of Helsinki, Finland*
- Khaldoon Dhou, *Texas A&M University-Central Texas, USA*
- Reza Hadi Mogavi, *University of Waterloo, Canada*
- Kevin Keeker, *Sony Interactive Entertainment Europe, USA*
- Daniel Riha, *Charles University, Czech Republic*
- Owen Schaffer, *Elmhurst University, USA*
- Jason Schklar, *UX is Fine, USA*
- Chaoguang Wang, *Bournemouth University, UK*
- Hanan Makki Zakari, *Ministry of Communications and Information Technology, Saudi Arabia*
- Fan Zhao, *Florida Gulf Coast University, USA*
- Miaoqi Zhu, *Sony Pictures Entertainment, USA*

The full list with the Program Board Chairs and the members of the Program Boards of all thematic areas and affiliated conferences of HCII 2024 is available online at:

http://www.hci.international/board-members-2024.php

HCI International 2025 Conference

The 27th International Conference on Human-Computer Interaction, HCI International 2025, will be held jointly with the affiliated conferences at the Swedish Exhibition & Congress Centre and Gothia Towers Hotel, Gothenburg, Sweden, June 22–27, 2025. It will cover a broad spectrum of themes related to Human-Computer Interaction, including theoretical issues, methods, tools, processes, and case studies in HCI design, as well as novel interaction techniques, interfaces, and applications. The proceedings will be published by Springer. More information will become available on the conference website: https://2025.hci.international/.

General Chair
Prof. Constantine Stephanidis
University of Crete and ICS-FORTH
Heraklion, Crete, Greece
Email: general_chair@2025.hci.international

https://2025.hci.international/

Contents – Part I

Game-Based Learning

Games and Artificial Intelligence

Contents – Part II

Player Experience and Engagement

Game Design and Gamification

Lost in Gamification Design: A Scientometric Analysis

Simone Bassanelli[1,2]([⊠]) [iD], Federica Gini[1,2] [iD], Antonio Bucchiarone[1] [iD],
Federico Bonetti[1] [iD], Eftychia Roumelioti[1] [iD], and Annapaola Marconi[1] [iD]

[1] Fondazione Bruno Kessler, 38122 Trento (TN), Italy
{sbassanelli,fgini,bucchiarone,fbonetti,eroumelioti,marconi}@fbk.eu
[2] University of Trento, 38122 Trento (TN), Italy

Abstract. Gamification represents a solution to motivate and engage users by introducing elements and characteristics of video games in non-playful activities. To help designers in the definition of these gamified systems, researchers are developing a consistent amount of gamification design frameworks. Through the current scientometric review, we analyzed a total of 1,751 results and 64,109 unique references and identified the most impactful publications in the domain of gamification design frameworks, the most relevant authors, and how research trends have changed over time. On the basis of the analysis, we also provide four suggestions for the future agenda. As a pioneering scientometric examination of the gamification design frameworks literature, this study will appeal to a diverse audience including academic researchers at various stages of their careers, graduate students, and professors seeking to discern research trends, pertinent subjects, major publications, and key scholars within the field.

Keywords: Gamification design · Design framework · Scientometrics

1 Introduction

Studies have shown video games to be a highly motivating activity [1–3]. Gamification adopts characteristic features of video games, also referred to as "game elements", to improve users' motivation and engagement towards certain activities and to promote learning or other positive behaviors, such as adopting environmentally friendly habits [4,5]. Game elements can be, for example, points, badges, leaderboards, levels, and many others [4]. According to the literature, the application of gamification has been sparing during the last decade, and it is mostly employed in education, health, and crowdsourcing [6,7]. Initially, designers adopted a "one-size-fits-all" approach [8], but quickly switched to the personalization of gameful systems, because (1) gamification produced mixed results in terms of effectiveness, and (2) there is more and more evidence of cultural, demographic, and contextual differences in the appreciation of game elements [6,9–12]. Moreover, the process of gamification design often demands

X. Fang (Ed.): HCII 2024, LNCS 14730, pp. 3–21, 2024.
https://doi.org/10.1007/978-3-031-60692-2_1

significant investments in time and finances, sometimes surpassing the expected benefits [13]. Thus, a large number of design frameworks have been developed in the last few years to guide designers in the creation of gameful systems, and as a result, enhance the effectiveness of gameful systems.

Recent works [14–16] underscore a diverse array of scrutinized frameworks, ranging from highly theoretical constructs to more conceptual viewpoints, encompassing perspectives on gamification from various domains of interest; as result, generic frameworks and frameworks related to specific application domains, such as education, health care, and business can be identified in the literature but hardly related to each other. Moreover, many of them tend to emphasize ad-hoc experiences rather than formal design processes, adding to the intricacy of the gamification field. In addition to the range of domains they cover, design frameworks differ in the factors they consider (e.g., social elements and interaction, players' taxonomies, rules of the game), and the measured variables (e.g., game analytics, metrics associated with users' performance) [16]. Finally, Rauschenberger et al. [17] point out the insufficient validation of gamification design frameworks, reporting that only three out of ten educational frameworks have been validated. Thereby, while gamification design frameworks hold considerable potential, they often face issues of low reliability due to a lack of standardization, limited validation, and difficulties in supporting the entire design process, including playtesting and evaluation. Addressing these challenges is crucial for advancing gamification design [6]. However, to proceed, it is necessary to have an overview of the relevant literature, knowing the structure, and its documents, authors, and keywords of reference.

Scientometrics is the study of how the literature is structured around a topic, map the scientific citations, and understand the impact of publications in a specific research field [18]. The current scientometric review aims to provide a comprehensive summary of the structure and content of the literature that affected the development of gamification design frameworks. We want to systematically describe the major trends and changes in the literature, focusing on the most important documents, authors, and keywords. To achieve this goal, we have formulated the following research questions:

RQ1. What are the most influential documents in relation to the design of gameful systems?
RQ2. Who are the most influential authors in relation to the design of gameful systems?
RQ3. How have research trends changed over time in relation to the design of gameful systems?

The paper is structured into five main sections. In Sect. 2 we explain the methodology we adopted for the literature search and the scientometric analysis, including a description of the metrics; we then report the results in Sect. 3. In Sect. 4, we describe and discuss the main findings according to the research questions previously defined. We present the conclusions to our work in Sect. 5.

Finally, in Sect. 6 we present a research agenda derived from the trends identified in the paper.

2 Methods

The methodology adopted in our study is mainly composed of two macro-steps: (1) the literature search and (2) the data analysis and visualization. The following sections present all the details needed to understand the study protocol used and possibly replicate it.

2.1 Literature Search and Settings

The analyses were based on 1,751 publications about gamification design frameworks and models published between January 1, 2012, and December 16, 2022. The Scopus database[1] was used to download 66,880 unique references. The time range of publications depended uniquely on Scopus' availability, and no a priori temporal exclusion criteria were applied. Out of a group of 1,826 documents, we discarded the results that were not written in English and the duplicates, leaving us with a sample of 1,751. The search code used was the following.

```
(TITLE-ABS-KEY (gamif*) AND TITLE-ABS-KEY (design AND framework)
OR TITLE-ABS-KEY (design AND model))
```

We chose the search term `gamif*` because they include all possible forms that come from the root. For example, `gamif*` includes all forms of gamification and the verb gamify. The coverage of books, book chapters, reference books, and scientific publications was the reason for choosing Scopus over other databases [19]. The data from the Scopus database were converted to a CiteSpace-friendly format with the information related to each of the 1,751 publications retrieved. At this point, we used the CiteSpace software[2] (version 6.1.R4) to analyze the data. Of the total references cited, 64,109 of the 66,880 (95%) were considered valid. Due to mistakes in the data that CiteSpace cannot fix, a small number of references were lost. This percentage of unprocessed references can be considered a negligible loss of data [20].

Using CiteSpace, we conducted an analysis of networks without setting any time limits. We divided the time frame into annual slices and evaluated three different criteria for selecting nodes in the networks: Top N, Top N%, and g-index. The Top N method chooses the N articles that are most often cited and uses this information to make a network for each time slice. The Top N% method includes the top N% of most frequently cited articles in each time slice to form the network. The g-index is a variation of the h-index[3] that allows one to assess the global citation performance of a group of articles. It is the "(unique) largest

---

[1] https://www.scopus.com/.
[2] http://cluster.cis.drexel.edu/~cchen/citespace/.
[3] https://en.wikipedia.org/wiki/H-index.

number such that the top g articles received (together) at least g^2 citations" [21]. We compared networks created using the Top N method with N set to 25, the Top N% method with N set to 5 and 10, and the g-index method with a scaling factor of 10 and 25. In summary, we chose to use the networks generated with the Top N and a scaling factor of 25 for our Document co-citation analysis (DCA), author co-citation analysis (ACA), and keyword co-occurrence analysis as they produced the best overall results in terms of structural metrics, number of nodes and links, and consistency in cluster structure for DCA. The chosen network for each analysis refers to the largest connected component (LCC), which is the largest sub-network where it is possible to reach any node from any other node [20]. In this case, the LCC included 890 nodes (71% of the whole network).

2.2   Analysis

DCA was performed to examine the frequency with which multiple documents have been cited together in later publications [22]. The study of co-citation networks focuses on interpreting the nature of clusters of co-cited documents [23]. If two documents receive high co-citations, they can be thematically connected. ACA was conducted to evaluate the frequency of co-citation among authors. This methodology enables the identification of complex interconnections among authors, by analyzing patterns of co-citation [22]. Keywords co-occurrence analysis was carried out to detect the most influential keywords and their evolution over time; it can provide information about the core content of the articles [24]. Analysis of keywords and their co-occurrence can help us find hot and cutting-edge topics [25].

2.3   Metrics

To examine the properties of the networks and clusters, several temporal and structural metrics of co-citation were adopted. The parameters considered to detect the structural quality of the network were betweenness centrality, modularity Q index, and average silhouette; while citation burstness, and sigma (Σ) were considered temporal and hybrid metrics [26]. *Betweenness centrality* measures the extent to which the node is part of a path that connects other nodes in the network [23]. The higher its value, the more well-connected and central a node/publication is within the network [27]. *Modularity Q index* is a measure of the extent to which a network can be divided into distinct modules or clusters. The higher its value (from 0 to 1), the more divisible or distinct the network clusters are; values close to 0 indicate that the network does not have clear boundaries between its clusters [23]. The *Silhouette* score is a measure of the homogeneity of a cluster. Higher values represent greater cluster homogeneity, values close to zero indicate that the objects in a cluster are on or very close to the boundary between two neighboring clusters, and negative values, on the other hand, indicate that cluster elements may have been assigned to the wrong cluster [23,26]. *Burstness* refers to a sudden increase in the number of citations for a node over a short time within a larger time frame [23]. This can be an indication of a temporary surge in interest or attention towards the node, which may be a document, journal, or author. *Sigma* (Σ) reflects the impact of the node on the network and by extension, higher values are suggestive of the publication's novelty and significance [23,28]. It is calculated using the equation $\Sigma = (centrality + 1)^{burstness}$.

2.4 Clustering

To identify clusters of documents for DCA, we used the clustering function in CiteSpace. This algorithm creates clusters of publications by considering the strength of connections between cited and citing documents. The cluster labels are selected from noun phrases and index terms using three different algorithms: Log-Likelihood Ratio (LLR), Mutual Information (MI), and Latent Semantic Indexing (LSI) [29]. These algorithms use different methods to identify the themes of the clusters. For example, LSI uses document matrices, while LLR and MI identify cluster themes by indexing noun phrases in the abstracts of citing articles [23]. We applied all three algorithms to label the clusters automatically and ultimately decided to use the LLR algorithm for comparison based on its ability to provide unique labels with sufficient coverage. The clusters obtained through the LLR algorithm were numbered in descending order based on their cluster size, as recommended by the software creator [29].

3 Results

Within this section, we present the outcomes based on the utilized metrics for every CiteSpace analysis.

3.1 Document Co-citation Analysis

The DCA analysis was used to answer **RQ1**, providing insight into the most influential documents on the design of gameful systems. The DCA provided a network with 1,243 nodes and 24,911 links, showing a modularity Q index of 0.8614 and an average silhouette metric of 0.9369, suggesting that the network was sufficiently divisible into clusters (according to the Q index) and that each cluster was highly consistent (according to the silhouette index) (Fig. 1).

The DCA resulted in 17 co-citation clusters, sorted from the largest in size (cluster #0 = "gamification background", size = 183, silhouette = 0.759, mean year = 2007) to the smallest (cluster #26 = "online community", size = 15, silhouette = 0.991, mean year = 2006). Since some of the clusters identified through the DCA were not substantial enough, others were too heterogeneous and others had been created by a few citing papers, we chose to present in detail only 4 of the major clusters generated through the "generate narrative" command (Table 1). Furthermore, in alignment with the recommendations of Aryadoust et al. [30], which stress the significance of evaluating the contents within each cluster and to differentiate them, we have decided to adopt a new

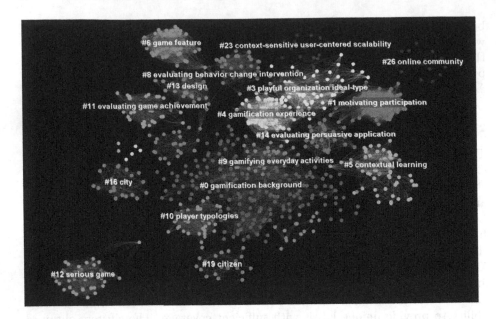

Fig. 1. Cluster view of the document co-citation analysis (DCA) generated using CiteSpace Version 6.1.R6. Modularity Q = 0.8614; average silhouette = 0.9369. Colored shades indicate the different clusters.

Table 1. Cluster labels computed via document co-citation analysis (DCA).

Cluster ID	Cluster label	Size	Silhouette	Mean (year)	Begin	End	Duration
0	gamification background	227	0.759	2007	1938	2020	82
1	motivating participation	81	0.991	2003	1954	2012	58
3	gamification experience	66	0.955	2003	1967	2012	45
4	contextual learning	63	0.980	2002	1980	2012	32

nomenclature for cluster #3, replacing the term "gamification background" with "gamification experience" to identify the cluster more accurately.

Among the reported clusters, the duration ranged from 32 to 82 years, presenting a partial overlap. In this section, each of the clusters presented is described qualitatively, in descending order of their size. They are described in terms of citing papers and cited papers. Citing papers that contribute to each cluster can be characterized by their coverage (number of references in the cluster cited by that paper) and global citing score (GCS: the total number of citations of that paper according to Scopus).

Cluster #0, "gamification background", is the first cluster in terms of size (size = 183, silhouette = 0.759). It comprises the following top citing papers: Teh et al. [31] (coverage = 29; GCS = 10), Herzig et al. [32] (coverage = 22; GCS = 30), and Nah et al., [33] (coverage = 12; GCS = 59). These papers mainly focus on how to use motivational elements to increase user participation in theory, learning, and business. Specifically, Teh et al. [31] report the need in gameful systems design to tap into intrinsic motivations by framing tasks in ways that evoke positive attitudes through challenge and friendly competition. The LLR label of the cluster, "gamification background", points to the importance of gamification background, hence how gamification can be a useful approach to motivate users in different contexts. As a result, the most cited papers in this cluster mainly present the theoretical aspect of gamification effectiveness [4,34–36], how to correctly design gameful systems [37–39], game design elements effectiveness to foster motivation [40,41], the difficulty to use game design technique and what issues need to be addressed [6,42], and how to implement game-based learning in the classroom [43–45].

Cluster #1, "motivating participation", is the second cluster in size (size = 81, silhouette = 0.991). It is mainly composed of two citing papers that focus on the use of gamification to increase users' motivation through persuasion. Specifically, Vasileva et al. [46] (coverage = 81; GCS = 145) present a paper with an overview of different approaches to motivate users to participate, and Oja and Riekki [47] (coverage = 31; GCS = 7) present a framework that facilitates creation and evaluation of persuasive systems based on different theories to change users' behavior desirably. The LLR label of the cluster, "motivating participation", refers to how important is to provide the right stimuli to foster users' motivation. As a result, the majority of the cited papers present some background about persuasion techniques [48,49], intrinsic motivation and self-determination theory [50,51] and how gamification can increase user motivation [4,52].

Cluster #3, "gamification experience" (size = 66, silhouette = 0.955), is composed of three main citing papers: Marache-Francisco and Brangier [53] (coverage = 62; GCS = 16), Oja and Riekki [47] (coverage = 29; GCS = 7), and Holman et al. [54] (coverage = 5; GCS = 37). The most citing document, "The Gamification Experience: UXD with a Gamification Background" [53], is a book chapter in which the authors provide a categorization of gamification elements through HCI design concepts. The authors refer to three different dimensions: sensory-motor modalities, motivation elements, and cognitive process support elements. The documents cited with the highest citation frequency deal mainly with game design, engagement and flow [55–58].

Cluster #4, "contextual learning" (size = 63, silhouette = 0.980), comprehends a list of cited papers that refer to game-based learning, contextual learning, student behavior [59–62]. The citing documents with the greatest coverage in this cluster are Li et al. [63] (coverage = 41; GCS = 170), and Bidarra te al. [64] (coverage = 24; GCS = 20). These papers mainly focus on the use of gamification and a game-based approach for contextual learning.

Through DCA, we computed the major 10 citation bursts (see Table 2). The publications of Koivisto and Hamari [6], Seaborn and Fels [34], and Sailer et al. [40] have the strongest burst of the network, with a strength of 22.50, 22.29 and 20.96 respectively. The publication of Hamari et al. [42] is the burst with the longest duration over time (6 years). The oldest burst in the network started in 2014 [36], while the newests started in 2019 [6,37,40]. Among our network, the publications of McGonigal [36], Kapp [44] and Zichermann and Cunningham [38] have a sigma value higher than the other publications (10.98, 3.31 and 2.01 respectively), followed by Deterding and colleagues [4,52] (1.86 and 1.68 respectively), Schell [56] (1.64), and Reeves and Read [58] (1.50). The other documents present lower values. Instead, regarding the values for the betweenness centrality, publications range from 0 to 0.21. The only document that stands apart is McGonigal [36] with a betweenness centrality value of 0.21.

Table 2. List of the top 10 documents for burst strength, estimated via document co-citation analysis (DCA).

Reference	Frequency	Burst Strength	Burst Begin	Burst End	Centrality	Sigma	Cluster ID
Koivisto and Hamari [6]	57	22.50	2019	2022	0.00	1.02	0
Seaborn and Fels [34]	111	22.29	2017	2022	0.01	1.25	0
Sailer et al. [40]	62	20.96	2019	2022	0.00	1.07	0
Hamari et al. [42]	52	13.33	2016	2022	0.01	1.09	0
Deterding et al. [4]	120	12.66	2016	2020	0.05	1.86	0
McGonigal [36]	50	12.56	2014	2016	0.21	10.98	3
Dicheva et al. [41]	55	11.47	2017	2022	0.00	1.02	0
Werbach et al. [37]	112	10.55	2019	2022	0.03	1.42	0
Kapp [44]	97	10.38	2016	2020	0.12	3.31	0
Robson et al. [35]	40	9.38	2017	2022	0.00	1.03	0

3.2 Author Co-citation Analysis

By analyzing author co-citation analysis, we can find influential authors in the field of gamification design frameworks (**RQ2**). The network obtained through the ACA contains 344 nodes and 7,940 collaboration links, showing a modularity Q index of 0.5785, and an average silhouette metric of 0.8943 (Fig. 2). The network has a wide range of collaborations, which reflects the interdisciplinary nature of gamification and the several domains in which it is applied. Table 3 presents the top 10 authors according to the citation frequency. The largest node represents Deterding S. with a frequency of 647 and a centrality value of 0.45, followed by Hamari J. with a citation frequency of 399 and a centrality of 0.01, and Werbach K., with a citation frequency of 213 and a centrality value of 0. Table 4 depicts the top 10 authors according to citation burst, or the number of citations for an author over a short period. The author with the highest burst strength is Koivisto J. (strength = 17.34, centrality = 0.01), whose burstness started in 2020 and ended in 2022, followed by Sailer M. (strength = 16.47, centrality = 0.00) and Landers R. M. (strength = 14.24, centrality = 0.00). However, the citation burst of some authors ended in 2022, which is the year the literature search was conducted, suggesting that their burst strength is likely to continue for the foreseeable future.

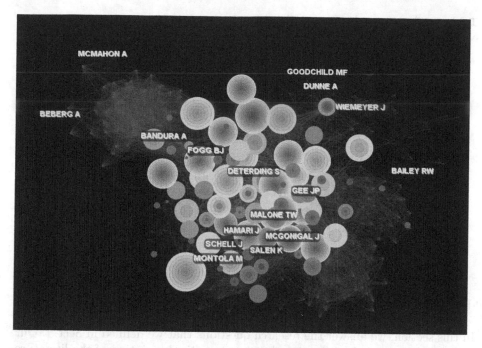

Fig. 2. Overview of the author co-citation analysis (ACA) generated using CiteSpace Version 6.1.R6. Modularity Q = 0.5785; average silhouette = 0.8943. Colored rings refer to the nodes with high burstness.

3.3 Keyword Co-occurrence Analysis

The keyword co-occurrence analysis is an important aid in explaining the structure of scientific knowledge and discovering research trends [65]. Through the keyword co-occurrence analysis, we aimed to answer **RQ3** and identify how research trends changed over time. The detection of keywords refers to the words that are frequently used or that are used in a shorter period. The keyword co-occurrence analysis provided a network with 218 nodes and 2,365 links, showing a modularity Q index of 0.5305 and a weighted mean silhouette of 0.87. Table 5 lists the top 10 keywords with the strongest bursts. In terms of burst strength, the top-ranked keyword is "education" with a burst of 15.64, followed by "software engineering" with a burst of 10.07, "teaching" with a burst of 8.15, "design" with a burst of 8.06 and "application program" with a burst of 7.87. "Design" has the earliest burst begin, while "application program", "survey", and "artificial intelligence" have the latest burst begin. The "survey" burst ends in 2022 because it was the date of our search. It is legitimate to think that it could continue in the future years, increasing the duration time.

Table 3. Top 10 cited authors ordered by citation frequency via author co-citation analysis (ACA).

Authors	Frequency	Centrality
Deterding S	647	0.45
Hamari J	399	0.01
Werbach K	213	0.00
Zichermann G	189	0.11
Ryan R. M	189	0.03
Kapp K. M	175	0.01
Csikszentmihalyi M	159	0.10
Seaborn K	155	0.00
Deci E. L	150	0.07
Huotari K.	145	0.01

4   Discussion

In this section, we answer the research questions that we defined in Sect. 1. Our final aim is to provide a structured and systematic description of the literature related to the design frameworks developed and used in the gamification domain.

4.1   (RQ1) What Are the Most Influential Documents in Relation to the Design of Gameful Systems?

To answer this question, we focused on DCA only, since it contains all the information needed to respond. Our analysis is mainly based on two different approaches: (1) we looked at the documents with the higher sigma values, burst strength, and betweenness centrality since burstness reflects sudden research interest in a limited period, betweenness centrality reflects the influence on the network and sigma is a combination of these two measures [26], and on the other hand, (2) we considered the top cited and citing documents contained in the presented clusters.

Considering the three metrics and the frequency, the papers that have attracted the most research attention and that have influenced the literature network are those by Seaborn and Fels [34] (burst strength = 22.29, sigma = 1.25), Koivisto and Hamari [6] (burst strength = 22.50, sigma = 1.02), Sailer et al. [40] (burst strength = 20.96, sigma = 1.07), and McGonigal [36] (burst strength = 12.56, sigma = 10.98). In detail, Seaborn and Fels [34] aim to examine the current theoretical underpinnings of gamification, as well as to compare and contrast gamification with related methodologies such as alternate reality games, games with a purpose, and gameful design. "The rise of motivational information systems: A review of gamification research" [6] consists of a large systematic review of 819 empirical studies that employed gamification which reports

Table 4. Top 10 author bursts computed via author co-citation analysis (ACA).

Cited authors	Burst strength	Begin	End	Span	Centrality	Frequency
Koivisto J	17.34	2020	2022	2	0.01	111
Sailer M	16.47	2020	2022	2	0.00	113
Landers R. N	14.24	2019	2022	3	0.00	79
Gee J. P	14.20	2014	2016	2	0.01	32
Dicehv C	14.03	2020	2022	2	0.00	32
Malone T. W	14.01	2011	2017	6	0.09	46
McGonigal J	13.29	2013	2017	4	0.14	100
Mora A	13.21	2018	2022	4	0.00	63
Schell J	12.97	2013	2016	3	0.01	30
Mekler E. D	12.21	2017	2019	2	0.00	32

Table 5. Top 10 keyword bursts computed via keyword analysis.

Keywords	Strength	Begin	End	Duration
education	15.64	2015	2017	2
software engineering	10.07	2015	2017	2
teaching	8.15	2016	2018	2
design	8.06	2013	2015	2
application program	7.87	2019	2020	1
information use	7.78	2018	2019	1
survey	7.06	2019	2022	1
artificial intelligence	6.84	2019	2020	1
article	6.59	2018	2020	2
computer game	6.51	2017	2019	2

a critical overview of gamification application and a detailed future research agenda that suggests future directions for gamification research; "How gamification motivates: An experimental study of the effects of specific game design elements on psychological need satisfaction" [40] consists of a randomized controlled study in an online simulation environment with different configurations of game design elements. In "Reality Is Broken: Why Games Make Us Better and How They Can Change the World" [36], the author argues that games have the power to make people happier, more productive, and more creative and that games can be used to solve real-world problems. Moreover, the author suggests that games are inherently more engaging and motivating than other forms of media and that people are naturally drawn to the kind of challenges and feedback that games provide. According to the sigma value, this work can be considered a milestone that significantly impacted shaping the literature on gamification design, promoting the development of new design frameworks [23, 28]. However, the citation peak (or the burstness) of the cited papers ended in 2016 (burst started in 2014 and ended in 2016), suggesting that this document had been influential for some years for design frameworks in gamification, but has recently been overlooked. The burst of the other above-mentioned papers began in a relatively more recent year (2017 and 2019) and may not have ended yet (bursts ended in 2022, which is the year the literature search was conducted). Considering the citation frequencies, the most important documents are Deterding et al. [4] (citation frequency = 120), Werbach et al. [37] (citation frequency = 112) and Seaborn and Fels [34] (citation frequency = 111). Interestingly, these documents are also considered among the most important according to the metrics.

All the above-mentioned documents, except McGonigal [36], are representative of cluster #0 (gamification background), which collects the most important documents pertaining to both theoretical and practical information on gamification theory and background. Due to this, the cluster results are broader and more heterogeneous than the others, reflecting the trend in the gamification design framework production to remain anchored to a few theoretical papers and struggle to build a comprehensive network. Cluster #1 (motivating participation), albeit presenting a smaller number of documents, presents a collection of articles related to the self-determination theory and persuasion techniques, providing insight into how important this part of the literature is in the design phase of gameful systems and the creation of design frameworks. Clusters #3 (gamification experience) and #4 (contextual learning) have a lower impact on the overall network; however, their analysis suggests that it is important to use specific frameworks for contextual learning, which is a teaching and learning approach that emphasizes the importance of understanding the context in which new information is presented [66].

Overall, the field of gamification design frameworks and models appears to have been shaped initially by documents that focus on persuasion techniques, and generically on gamification definition and background. Lately, there seems to have been a shift in reference documents, giving increasing importance to methodological and critical references.

4.2 (RQ2) Who Are the Most Influential Authors in Relation to the Design of Gameful systems?

To address this research question, we rely on the results of the ACA. Table 3 and Table 4 give an overview of the most influential authors according to citation frequency and burst strength.

Considering the burst strength, Koivisto J. is the author who attracted the most research attention over a period (burst strength = 17.34). The author's burst is probably due to the paper "The rise of motivational information systems: A review of gamification research" [6], which is considered one of the most influential documents according to the DCA analysis. Since the burst ended in 2022, it is legitimate to think that the burst might continue in the foreseeable future. According to the burst strength, the second influential author is Sailer M. The burst is probably related to the paper "How gamification motivates: An experimental study of the effects of specific game design elements on psychological need satisfaction" [40], which is one of the most influential documents according to the DCA. According to the burst timing, the authors with the earlier burst are Malone T. W. (2011 to 2017), Schell J. (2013 to 2016), McGonigal J. (2013 to 2017), and Gee J. P. (2014 to 2016). Their works mainly focus on teaching and learning mechanics used by video game developers and how these game design elements can be used in education. Meanwhile, authors belonging to later bursts include Koivisto J. (2020 to 2022), Sailer M. (2020 to 2022), Dichev C. (2020 to 2022), Mora A. (2018 to 2022), and Landers R. N. (2019 to 2022). Their works mainly focus on critical reviews about gamification design and application, what are the main issues, and how to face them to design and use properly gameful systems. Taking into account the frequency, Deterding S. (647), Hamari J. (399), Werbach K. (213) Zichermann G. (189), and Ryan R. M. (189) are considered the most influential authors of the network. It is not surprising since these authors produced some papers that are considered a cornerstone in the field of gamification [4,37–39,42,52,67], and their articles have helped shape what is the current literature on gamification. Interestingly, these authors do not present a citation burst because a highly cited paper may not be identified with a citation burst if its citation counts over the years are relatively stable.

Overall, the ACA results suggest that initially the structure of the literature about gamification design frameworks and models has been based on the analysis of game design and how to implement game design elements in educational contexts. According to the previous section, there seems to have been a shift in reference documents, and the authors have placed more emphasis on critical reviews and research agendas [6,68].

4.3 (RQ3) How Have Research Trends Changed over Time in Relation to the Design Of gameful Systems?

To answer this question, we rely on an overview of the keyword's change over time and on the DCA and ACA burst strength time shift. The research trends in the field of gamification design have been analyzed by examining the burst strength of keywords and the burst of the most influential documents. A timeline of these trends was extrapolated from this analysis. Results indicate that there has been a shift in the focus of researchers over time.

According to the analysis of the keywords, the first trends that appeared in the field of gamification design frameworks were "design" (beginning year = 2013), "education" (2015), and "software engineering" (2015). This timeline might reflect the initial interest in the definition and design of gameful systems (for examples see [38, 67, 69]) and their first application in education, especially in the field of software engineering and computer science (see [44, 70] for examples). Later, the keywords show a change towards "teaching", "application program", "information use" and "artificial intelligence", indicating that the trend has not totally changed, but there has been a growing interest in information use techniques, mainly automated, to provide adaptation of gameful systems. According to the DCA and ACA mentioned above, results indicate how the trend in the literature was initially based on articles and authors that focused on persuasion techniques and the usefulness of gamification (both in a generic and specific way), and that later the main trend was to question the elements of game design hitherto considered, to create new design methodologies that are effective.

Overall, these results seem to suggest that trends have changed considerably over time, first describing broad motivational intervention designs, and generic design techniques, then attracting more and more resources in the direction of a new critical approach toward gamification, suggesting that there are no models or frameworks for the design of gameful systems that are widely used, or that are a reference for the production of further design frameworks or models.

5   Conclusions

Gamification, as the application of game elements in non-playful contexts to motivate and engage users has became more and more adopted in the last decade [6], along with the increased number of gamification frameworks born with the intent of guiding designers in the definition of gameful systems [16]. In the current scientometric review, we aimed to explore the structure of the references related to gamification design frameworks and models. Through Scopus, and then CiteSpace, we analyzed a final number of 1,751 publications and 64,109 unique references to identify the most influential documents (**RQ1**), authors (**RQ2**), and the main trends (**RQ3**). Through a DCA we were able to select the most impactful publications [6, 34, 36, 40] (**RQ1**), by ordering the results by burst strength, sigma (Σ), and citation frequency. We performed an ACA to answer to **RQ2** and identify the authors that contributed more to the research on gamification design frameworks, sorting the authors by the burst strength. Based on the years of interest, we found two distinct sets of authors. Through the analysis of keyword change over time, and the burst strength time shift in both DCA and ACA we noticed a change in the trend of research interests in the study of gamification design frameworks. As for the analysis of the keywords, the results indicate a moderately increased interest in the use of automated techniques to design adaptive gamified systems, which have lately been replaced by an increasing interest in surveys. Also, from the results of the DCA and ACA, we observed a shift of emphasis from the implementation of game elements in education, to critical reviews and research agendas (**RQ3**).

In conclusion, methodological papers about gamification, game design, and persuasive design techniques have influenced the production of gamification design frameworks for nearly a decade. Indeed, the largest cluster is the one related to gamification background, followed by another one containing work related to motivating participation and persuasion. Then, due to the appearance of numerous inconsistent results associated with the use of gamification, the research interest appears to have changed towards conducting critical studies and reviews [6,34,42]. In line with other findings in the literature [26], the current trend seems to be questioning current methodologies to design new reliable techniques and frameworks. According to our results, the most relevant trends, regardless of the time window, are related to education and teaching, a result that indicates both the fruitfulness and importance of such a topic.

A rather new and relatively under-explored research avenue emerges that consists of automating gamification and content creation. This research direction has been gaining traction in recent years and will arguably face new opportunities and challenges thanks to the popularization of large generative AI models. We report suggestions for future research in this area in the next section.

6 Future Agenda

There is a large number of gamification design frameworks that appear in the literature [16], but none of the frameworks are widely used by the community. Also, the results of the current review show a shift of focus from generic design techniques and motivational intervention design, to a more critical approach to gamification design and its successful elements. Therefore, we suggest that researchers carefully examine and analyze the (numerous) solutions available in the literature before starting the development of new design frameworks. Given the results of the scientometric review, especially in relation to the keyword and research trend analysis discussed above, we define four future directions as the research agenda in the field.

1. Make full use of/systematization of existing gamification frameworks. We suggest that researchers in the field of gamification explore the already existing works to employ them directly or systematize them into more comprehensive frameworks. This would contribute to reducing the number of frameworks and enhance their quality to establish a more reliable common ground for researchers and practitioners. **2. Synthesis of critical perspectives and practical insights.** As the focus shifts towards a more critical approach to gamification design, future research should strive to synthesize critical perspectives emerging from the literature. Combining these critical analysis with practical insights derived from successful gamification implementations can lead to the development or adaptation of frameworks that not only address theoretical concerns but also resonate with the practical requirements of designers and stakeholders. **3. Artificial intelligence and automated design**. We also suggest exploring the rather young field of automated techniques and artificial intelligence in gameful systems, a field that has been gaining traction lately and has promising implications in terms of adaptation, as opposed to the one-size-fits-all approaches. In particular, with the emergence of generative AI based on large models, such as ChatGPT and Stable Diffusion, we expect automatic content generation to become an integral part of automation and adaptation in gamification and serious game design. We therefore recommend researching techniques and defining design guidelines and frameworks including the use of such tools. **4. Ethical considerations in gamification.** With the integration of automated techniques and AI, ethical considerations become paramount. Future research should proactively address the ethical implications of gamification design, ensuring that the forthcoming use of AI for user engagement is not only effective but also responsible, respectful, and aligned with ethical standards.

References

1. Rigby, S., Ryan, R.M.: Glued to games: How video games draw us in and hold us spellbound: How video games draw us in and hold us spellbound. AbC-CLIo (2011)
2. Deterding, S.: Situated motivational affordances of game elements: a conceptual model. In: Gamification: Using Game Design Elements in Non-Gaming Contexts, A Workshop at CHI, vol. 10 (2011)
3. Halbrook, Y.J., O'Donnell, A.T., Msetfi, R.M.: When and how video games can be good: a review of the positive effects of video games on well-being. Perspect. Psychol. Sci. **14**(6), 1096–1104 (2019)
4. Deterding, S., Dixon, D., Khaled, R., Nacke, L.: From game design elements to gamefulness: defining gamification. In: Proceedings of the 15th International Academic MindTrek Conference: Envisioning Future Media Environments, pp. 9–15 (2011)
5. Hamari, J.G., Ritzer, G., Rojek, C.: The blackwell encyclopedia of sociology (2019)
6. Koivisto, J., Hamari, J.: The rise of motivational information systems: a review of gamification research. Int. J. Inf. Manage. **45**, 191–210 (2019)
7. Morschheuser, B., Maedche, A., Walter, D.: Designing cooperative gamification: conceptualization and prototypical implementation. In: Proceedings of the 2017 ACM Conference on Computer Supported Cooperative Work and Social Computing, pp. 2410–2421 (2017)
8. Böckle, M., Micheel, I., Bick, M., Novak, J.: A design framework for adaptive gamification applications In: Proceedings of the 51st Hawaii International Conference on System Sciences (2018)
9. Klock, A.C.T., Gasparini, I., Pimenta, M.S., Hamari, J.: Tailored gamification: a review of literature. Int. J. Hum. Comput. Stud. **144**, 102495 (2020)
10. Koivisto, J., Hamari, J.: Demographic differences in perceived benefits from gamification. Comput. Hum. Behav. **35**, 179–188 (2014)
11. Tondello, G.F., Wehbe, R.R., Diamond, L., Busch, M., Marczewski, A., Nacke, L.E.: The gamification user types HEXAD scale. In: Proceedings of the 2016 Annual Symposium on Computer-Human Interaction in Play, pp. 229–243 (2016)

12. Codish, D., Ravid, G.: Gender moderation in gamification: does one size fit all? (2017)
13. O'Donovan, S., Gain, J., Marais, P.: A case study in the gamification of a university-level games development course. In: Proceedings of the South African Institute for Computer Scientists and Information Technologists Conference, pp. 242–251 (2013)
14. Bassanelli, S., Bucchiarone, A.: Gamidoc: a tool for designing and evaluating gamified solutions. In: Extended Abstracts of the 2022 Annual Symposium on Computer-Human Interaction in Play, pp. 203–208 (2022)
15. Kölln, K.: Maybe we don't need a new gamification framework after all. In: Extended Abstracts of the 2022 Annual Symposium on Computer-Human Interaction in Play, pp. 384–387 (2022)
16. Mora, A., Riera, D., González, C., Arnedo-Moreno, J.: Gamification: a systematic review of design frameworks. J. Comput. High. Educ. **29**, 516–548 (2017)
17. Rauschenberger, M., Willems, A., Ternieden, M., Thomaschewski, J.: Towards the use of gamification frameworks in learning environments. J. Interact. Learn. Res. **30**(2), 147–165 (2019)
18. Leydesdorff, L., Milojević, S.: Scientometrics (2012). arXiv preprint arXiv:1208.4566
19. Huang, C.-K., et al.: Comparison of bibliographic data sources: implications for the robustness of university rankings. Quant. Sci. Stud. **1**(2), 445–478 (2020)
20. Chen, C.: CiteSpace: a practical guide for mapping scientific literature. Nova Science Publishers Hauppauge, NY (2016)
21. Egghe, L.: Theory and practise of the g-index. Scientometrics **69**(1), 131–152 (2006)
22. Chen, C., Song, I.-Y., Yuan, X., Zhang, J.: The thematic and citation landscape of data and knowledge engineering (1985–2007). Data Knowl. Eng. **67**(2), 234–259 (2008)
23. Chen, C., Ibekwe-SanJuan, F., Hou, J.: The structure and dynamics of cocitation clusters: a multiple-perspective cocitation analysis. J. Am. Soc. Inform. Sci. Technol. **61**(7), 1386–1409 (2010)
24. Chen, X., Liu, Y.: Visualization analysis of high-speed railway research based on CiteSpace. Transp. Policy **85**, 1–17 (2020)
25. Xie, P.: Study of international anticancer research trends via co-word and document co-citation visualization analysis. Scientometrics **105**(1), 611–622 (2015)
26. Bassanelli, S., Vasta, N., Bucchiarone, A., Marconi, A.: Gamification for behavior change: a scientometric review. Acta Physiol. (Oxf) **228**, 103657 (2022)
27. Gaggero, G., Bonassi, A., Dellantonio, S., Pastore, L., Aryadoust, V., Esposito, G.: A scientometric review of alexithymia: mapping thematic and disciplinary shifts in half a century of research. Front. Psych. **11**, 1405 (2020)
28. Chen, C., Chen, Y., Horowitz, M., Hou, H., Liu, Z., Pellegrino, D.: Towards an explanatory and computational theory of scientific discovery. J. Informet. **3**(3), 191–209 (2009)
29. Chen, C.: The CiteSpace manual. College of Computing and Informatics **1**, 1–84 (2014)
30. Aryadoust, V., Zakaria, A., Lim, M.H., Chen, C.: An extensive knowledge mapping review of measurement and validity in language assessment and SLA research. Front. Psychol. **11**, 1941 (2021)
31. Teh, N., Schuff, D., Johnson, S., Geddes, D.: Can work be fun? Improving task motivation and help-seeking through game mechanics (2013)
32. Herzig, P., Jugel, K., Momm, C., Ameling, M., Schill, A.: GaML-a modeling language for gamification. In: 2013 IEEE/ACM 6th International Conference on Utility and Cloud Computing, pp. 494–499, IEEE (2013)

33. Nah, F.F.-H., Telaprolu, V.R., Rallapalli, S., Venkata, P.R.: Gamification of education using computer games. In: Yamamoto, S. (ed.) HIMI 2013. LNCS, vol. 8018, pp. 99–107. Springer, Heidelberg (2013). https://doi.org/10.1007/978-3-642-39226-9_12
34. Seaborn, K., Fels, D.I.: Gamification in theory and action: a survey. Int. J. Hum. Comput. Stud. **74**, 14–31 (2015)
35. Robson, K., Plangger, K., Kietzmann, J.H., McCarthy, I., Pitt, L.: Is it all a game? Understanding the principles of gamification. Bus. Horiz. **58**(4), 411–420 (2015)
36. McGonigal, J.: Reality is broken: Why games make us better and how they can change the world. Penguin (2011)
37. Werbach, K., Hunter, D., Dixon, W.: For the win: How Game Thinking can Revolutionize Your Business, vol. 1. Wharton Digital Press Philadelphia (2012)
38. Zichermann, G., Cunningham, C.: Gamification by design: Implementing game mechanics in web and mobile apps. O'Reilly Media, Inc. (2011)
39. Huotari, K., Hamari, J.: A definition for gamification: anchoring gamification in the service marketing literature. Electron. Mark. **27**(1), 21–31 (2017)
40. Sailer, M., Hense, J.U., Mayr, S.K., Mandl, H.: How gamification motivates: an experimental study of the effects of specific game design elements on psychological need satisfaction. Comput. Hum. Behav. **69**, 371–380 (2017)
41. Dicheva, D., Dichev, C., Irwin, K., Jones, E.J., Cassel, L.B., Clarke, P.J.: Can game elements make computer science courses more attractive?. In: Proceedings of the 50th ACM Technical Symposium on Computer Science Education, SIGCSE 2019, pp. 1245 (2019)
42. Hamari, J., Koivisto, J., Sarsa, H.: Does gamification work?–A literature review of empirical studies on gamification. In: 2014 47th Hawaii International Conference on System Sciences, pp. 3025–3034. IEEE (2014)
43. Domínguez, A., Saenz-de Navarrete, J., De-Marcos, L., Fernández-Sanz, L., Pagés, C., Martínez-Herráiz, J.-J.: Gamifying learning experiences: practical implications and outcomes. Comput. Educ. **63**, 380–392 (2013)
44. Kapp, K.M.: The gamification of Learning and Instruction: Game-based Methods and Strategies for Training and Education. Wiley, San Francisco (2012)
45. Hanus, M.D., Fox, J.: Assessing the effects of gamification in the classroom: a longitudinal study on intrinsic motivation, social comparison, satisfaction, effort, and academic performance. Comput. Educ. **80**, 152–161 (2015)
46. Vassileva, J.: Motivating participation in social computing applications: a user modeling perspective. User Model. User-Adap. Inter. **22**(1), 177–201 (2012)
47. Oja, M., Riekki, J.: Ubiquitous framework for creating and evaluating persuasive applications and games. In: Rautiainen, M., et al. (eds.) GPC 2011. LNCS, vol. 7096, pp. 133–140. Springer, Heidelberg (2012). https://doi.org/10.1007/978-3-642-27916-4_15
48. Cheng, R., Vassileva, J.: User motivation and persuasion strategy for peer-to-peer communities. In: Proceedings of the 38th Annual Hawaii International Conference on System Sciences, pp. 193a–193a. IEEE (2005)
49. Fogg, B.J.: Persuasive technology: using computers to change what we think and do. Ubiquity **2002**(December), 2 (2002)
50. Deci, E.L., et al.: i ryan, rm (1985). Intrinsic motivation and self-determination in human behavior, vol. 1 (1985)
51. Reiss, S.: Multifaceted nature of intrinsic motivation: the theory of 16 basic desires. Rev. Gen. Psychol. **8**(3), 179–193 (2004)

52. Deterding, S., Sicart, M., Nacke, L., O'Hara, K., Dixon, D.: Gamification. Using game-design elements in non-gaming contexts. In: CHI'11 Extended Abstracts on Human Factors in Computing Systems, pp. 2425–2428 (2011)
53. Marache-Francisco, C., Brangier, E.: The gamification experience: UXD with a gamification background. In: Emerging Research and Trends in Interactivity and the Human-Computer Interface, pp. 205–223, IGI Global (2014)
54. Holman, C., Aguilar, S., Fishman, B.: GradeCraft: what can we learn from a game-inspired learning management system?. In: Proceedings of the Third International Conference on Learning Analytics and Knowledge, pp. 260–264 (2013)
55. Adams, E.: Fundamentals of Game Design. Pearson Education, Boca Raton (2014)
56. Schell, J.: The Art of Game Design: A Book of Lenses. CRC Press, Boston (2008)
57. Csikszentmihalyi, M., Csikzentmihaly, M.: Flow: The Psychology of Optimal Experience, vol. 1990. Harper & Row New York (1990)
58. Reeves, B., Read, J.L.: Total Engagement: How Games and Virtual Worlds are Changing the Way People Work and Businesses Compete. Harvard Business Press, Boston (2009)
59. Prensky, M.: Digital game-based learning. Comput. Entertainment (CIE) 1(1), 21–21 (2003)
60. Gee, J.P.: What video games have to teach us about learning and literacy. Comput. Entertainment (CIE) 1(1), 20–20 (2003)
61. Brown, J.S., Collins, A., Duguid, P.: Situated cognition and the culture of learning. Educ. Res. 18(1), 32–42 (1989)
62. Weisberg, M.: Student attitudes and behaviors towards digital textbooks. Publ. Res. Q. 27(2), 188–196 (2011)
63. Li, W., Grossman, T., Fitzmaurice, G.: GamiCAD: a gamified tutorial system for first time autoCAD users. In: Proceedings of the 25th Annual ACM Symposium on User Interface Software and Technology, pp. 103–112 (2012)
64. Bidarra, J., Figueiredo, M., Natálio, C.: Interactive design and gamification of eBooks for mobile and contextual learning. Int. J. Interact. Mob. Technol. (iJIM), 9(3), 24–32 (2015)
65. Su, X., Li, X., Kang, Y.: A bibliometric analysis of research on intangible cultural heritage using CiteSpace. SAGE Open 9(2), 2158244019840119 (2019)
66. Mahendra, I.: Contextual learning approach and performance assessment in mathematics learning. Int. Res. J. Manage. IT Soc. Sci. 3(3), 7–15 (2016)
67. Deterding, S., Björk, S.L., Nacke, L.E., Dixon, D., Lawley, E.: Designing gamification: creating gameful and playful experiences. In: CHI'13 Extended Abstracts on Human Factors in Computing Systems, pp. 3263–3266 (2013)
68. Landers, R.N., Auer, E.M., Collmus, A.B., Armstrong, M.B.: Gamification science, its history and future: definitions and a research agenda. Simul. Gaming 49(3), 315–337 (2018)
69. Deterding, S.: Gamification: designing for motivation. Interactions 19(4), 14–17 (2012)
70. Barata, G., Gama, S., Jorge, J., Gonçalves, D.: Engaging engineering students with gamification. In: 2013 5th International Conference on Games and Virtual Worlds for Serious Applications (VS-GAMES), pp. 1–8. IEEE (2013)

Personalize Mobile Game Interface Design

Yuchen Gui[1] and Fan Zhao[2(✉)]

[1] School of Digital Media, Savannah College of Art and Design, Savannah, GA, USA
yucgui20@student.scad.edu
[2] Florida Gulf Coast University, 10501 FGCU Blvd. South, Fort Myers, FL 33967, USA
fzhao@fgcu.edu

Abstract. Previous studies on mobile games have predominantly concentrated on the pre-adoption phase, neglecting post-adoption behaviors. Furthermore, existing research has often treated game players as a collective entity concerning their gaming needs and emotions, with minimal exploration of distinctions among player levels. To address these gaps, our study delves into mobile game design by considering the perspectives of distinct levels of game players. We aim to identify pivotal factors for personalizing mobile game design based on the specific levels of the players. The finding s from a preliminary study recognized simplicity and learnability as key factors influencing the enjoyment of mobile game players, subsequently affecting their intention to persistently engage with the game.

Keywords: Game Design · UX · Mobile Game Interface

1 Introduction

With the increasing prevalence of mobile devices, they have become an essential tool for social activities and entertainment in our daily lives. As smartphones gain wider coverage, mobile games are emerging as the preferred choice for leisure activities. These gaming applications are designed to be played on small handheld computing devices like smartphones and tablets, equipped with wireless communication functionality. Projections from a new Data.ai report indicate that mobile gaming revenue is expected to experience a 4% year-over-year increase, reaching $111.4 billion in 2024 [1].

The substantial growth of the mobile game market is attributed not only to the widespread use of smartphones but also to the simplified development process of mobile games. Developers can easily leverage and adopt game engines such as Unity, Unreal, or Godot to create and publish mobile games on online application stores enabling players to easily download and engage with the games. Therefore, early studies investigated factors influencing download decisions, initial engagement, and game acceptance, especially from game marketing perspective, such as app store rankings, reviews, and advertising effectiveness [2, 3].

Conversely, according to Chernobai [4], rapid expansion has swiftly transformed into a quickly downturn. For instance, the game Pokémon Go experienced a decline from approximately 45 million players to around 30 million just in a month. Notably, 64%

X. Fang (Ed.): HCII 2024, LNCS 14730, pp. 22–31, 2024.
https://doi.org/10.1007/978-3-031-60692-2_2

of games entering the Top 50 remain in that position for five days or less. Furthermore, the time span from a game's launch until downloads begin to decrease has shortened in recent years, with the average lifespan of a top 50 grossing game in the U.S. App Store currently standing at 27.75 days. Hence, there is a notable research shift dedicated to comprehending the factors influencing users' behaviors and sustained usage in the post-adoption phase [5]. However, the mobile gaming industry is currently grappling with challenges related to player retention, as 61% of users delete the game within 24 h of downloading it [6], which implies that these users promptly discontinued playing the game shortly after installing it. From the game learning perspective, Passalacqua et al. [7] highlighted the significance of game learnability in elucidating this phenomenon, proposing that game tutorials could influence players' state of flow, consequently affecting their intentions to continue playing the game. Yet, few studies have attempted to explain this phenomenon from the perspectives of user interface (UI) and user experience (UX). This paper aims to provide an explanation for the phenomenon and enhance user intention to continue playing the game.

2 Literature Review

2.1 UI/UX

The success of mobile apps relies on intuitive, elegant graphical user interfaces (GUIs) that incorporate effective design principles for both user experience (UX) and user interface (UI) [8]. Concerning GUIs, various elements can be modified, including but not limited to structure, navigation, layout, font style attributes, font size, buttons, color, lists, information density, support, and alignment [9]. UI/UX design in mobile games is crucial because players are influenced by how the game looks and how it feels to play it. Games must draw attention by the look and hold the attention with the game's overall experience. A well-designed interface ensures visual appeal and contributes to smooth navigation, creating control and satisfaction for the players. It serves as the bridge between the player and the virtual world, enhancing the overall gaming experience.

User interface design is one of the most important aspects to any application, but it matters much more for mobile games. It allows players to understand and comprehend a games flows and objectives. Interfaces allow a player to follow the guidelines set by the developer to partake in the gameplay. UIs can let a player know a glance what something is or what it could be based on other UIs they have interacted with. Having a proper UI in mobile games can make the difference of if a player will remain interested in the game as well. A frustrating UI can make a world of difference. If the UI is unresponsive/unintuitive than players will quit the game or uninstall it outright.

Alben [10] outlines eight criteria essential for effective UX interaction design and the creation of high-quality user experiences. These criteria encompass aesthetic experience, manageable, understanding of users, learnable usable, needed, mutable, effective design processes, and appropriate.

According to Fanfarelli et al. [11], there are three overarching UX categories for user perceptions, identified as usability, adaptability, and efficiency. These criteria, though interrelated, provide a useful framework for understanding major themes within UX. It emphasizes the subjective nature of user experience, focusing on users' thoughts and feelings rather than objective facts.

The first category, usability, concerns users' perceptions of a product's structure and design. It questions whether the design is straightforward, intuitive, and easy to navigate. Usability includes physical and virtual properties, considering factors like the size of a mobile device and the organization of an online user registration page. Poor usability in healthcare products may lead to frustration or annoyance, acting as barriers to long-term user interactions.

Adaptability examines users' perceptions of a product's value over time, considering whether the product remains helpful as users' needs and environments change. For instance, a hospital's time tracking application illustrates how a product may work well for small numbers of users but become cumbersome as the user base grows. The adaptability perspective can be analyzed through Garrett's five planes [12], considering the product's strategy, skeleton, structure, and surface.

Efficiency is not limited to information processing but focuses on a product's ability to meet the designer's or audience's needs. It aligns with Alben's categories [10] of "needed" and "appropriate" and emphasizes a product's effectiveness in serving its intended purpose. For instance, a versatile coffee maker highlights that a well-designed product may still lack efficiency if it does not fulfill its primary function promptly and intuitively. It is important to address organizational needs across different dimensions of the games and applications.

2.2 Game Usability

In accordance with the DeLone and McLean Model of Information Systems Success [13], the system's usability stands out as a crucial determinant of overall system quality. Usability, in this context, encompasses factors such as efficiency, satisfaction, effectiveness, learnability, memorability, cognitive load, error prevention capability, ease of use, and the ability to facilitate enjoyable interactions within the system [14, 15]. This description pertains to the quality of user interfaces when viewed from the user's perspective. Consequently, when implementing an e-Learning system, one of the paramount considerations should be the quality of its user interface (UI).

Learnability, a crucial aspect of mobile app usability, refers to how easily and quickly users can understand and effectively use the app [15]. It encompasses both initial acquisition of basic functions and mastery of advanced features. A highly learnable app allows users to quickly navigate, complete tasks, and achieve their goals with minimal confusion or frustration. Intuitive design plays a key role, where interface elements like icons, labels, and layout are familiar and consistent. Consistent use of established design patterns, clear terminology, and well-placed tutorials can further enhance clarity. Additionally, discoverability is important, ensuring users can easily find features and understand their purpose. This involves logical information architecture, readily available search functionality, and appropriate contextual cues. By prioritizing discoverability and intuitive design, apps can empower users to learn independently and confidently, fostering long-term engagement and satisfaction [16].

Simplicity refers to the effortlessness with which users can interact with and navigate the app [17]. Unlike complexity, which often overwhelms and frustrates, simplicity fosters clarity and ease of use, leading to a pleasant and efficient user experience. Several key pillars support a simple app. Focus on core functionalities is paramount, prioritizing tasks crucial to the app's purpose [18]. Eliminating unnecessary features or superfluous options reduces cognitive load and streamlines the user journey. Furthermore, intuitive design plays a pivotal role. Consistent layouts, familiar interaction patterns, and clear visual cues all contribute to an environment where users can intuitively understand how to achieve their goals without expending excessive mental effort. By prioritizing these principles, app developers can ensure a smooth and intuitive experience for users of all tech backgrounds, fostering higher engagement and increased satisfaction.

2.3 Cognitive Load Theory

Cognitive Load theory is based on learning happening only when the cognitive capacities of learners' working memory are not overloaded. A student learning a complex underlying systems and processes of a computer simulation is difficult for them when they have low prior knowledge. Simulations have been shown to overwhelm a student because of all the tasks required to do a simulation. There are a few hands-on tasks that a student must do to perform the simulation like reading directions, handling equipment, and collaborating with your group in some cases [19]. The extra load has a negative impact on the expected learning outcome as the student becomes more focused on the other tasks.

Another factor to consider is that students may have an issue adjusting to the device the simulation is on and this could also increase the cognitive load. Those students will withdraw from the simulations. Confusion has been negatively correlated with germane cognitive load [20]. Germane cognitive load deals with putting new information in long term memory. Then if they are in a group the workload for the simulation changes and other students will have to pick up the work from the low adapting students [19]. This can create a cyclical effect because those students now feel like the cognitive workload is greater to them. This makes simulation not seem to help with learning, but it can be fixed by having each student work individually so that they don't increase the workload of others. The low adapting student will also ask for help since they cannot rely on another student finishing their simulation.

Cognitive load can be improved by including spoken text with simulations. Learners using a computer simulation need time to repeatedly read the procedures for a simulation. When doing a simulation, it is best to have written texts of conditions to reference. There are many different tasks that a student must do during this type of exercise and having spoken instruction highlights the negative effects of the dual processes at work, auditory and visual [21].

3   Research Model and Game Design

3.1   Research Model

Learnability is a critical aspect of mobile app usability, focusing on how easily users can understand and become proficient in using the application [15]. A highly learnable mobile app provides an intuitive and user-friendly interface that allows users to quickly grasp its functionalities without the need for extensive guidance or training. Key elements contributing to learnability include clear and well-designed navigation, easily identifiable icons, and straightforward menu structures. By offering a logical and predictable user experience, learnable mobile apps empower users to explore and learn the app's features with minimal effort.

In addition to design considerations, informative onboarding processes and well-crafted tutorials play a significant role in enhancing the learnability of a mobile app [16]. Providing users with concise and engaging introductions to the app's core features during onboarding helps set expectations and familiarize users with the interface. Tutorials that guide users through essential actions and functionalities further contribute to the app's learnability, ensuring that users can quickly adapt to and proficiently use the app. A learnable mobile app not only facilitates a positive initial experience but also encourages sustained engagement as users continue to discover and master its capabilities over time. Thus, we propose the following hypothesis:

Hypothesis 1 (H1). Learnability will positively influence perceived enjoyment.

Simplicity in mobile app usability is a fundamental attribute that significantly influences the overall user experience [18]. A simple mobile app design is characterized by clarity and ease of navigation, minimizing unnecessary complexity and ensuring users can effortlessly accomplish their tasks. From an interface standpoint, simplicity involves a clean and uncluttered layout, with intuitive placement of key features and controls. Clear and concise language in instructions or prompts further enhances simplicity, aiding users in understanding and interacting with the app without confusion. Figure 1 shows a comparison of two mobile game interfaces. Clearly, the interface on the left is simpler and more straightforward, making it easier to understand, while the one on the right is overly complex and confusing.

Fig. 1. Simplicity Comparison

Moreover, simplicity extends to the overall flow and functionality of the mobile app [22]. A simple app ensures that users can quickly grasp how to navigate through various screens, perform actions, and access essential information. The simplicity of mobile app usability is closely tied to efficiency, as users can achieve their goals without unnecessary steps or complications. Striking the right balance between providing necessary features and maintaining a straightforward design is crucial, as simplicity contributes not only to user satisfaction but also to increased engagement and the likelihood of continued app usage. Hence, the following hypothesis was posited:

Hypothesis 2 (H2). Simplicity will positively influence perceived enjoyment.

Numerous studies have explored the behavioral impacts of enjoyment in relation to continuous use intention of diverse information systems [23]. Mobile game enjoyment is a pivotal factor influencing user engagement and continuous use intention [24]. Enjoyment in the context of mobile gaming refers to the positive emotional experiences, satisfaction, and amusement users derive from playing a game. It encompasses various elements such as engaging gameplay, appealing graphics, immersive storytelling, and the overall entertainment value provided by the game. Therefore, we propose the following hypothesis. Please see Fig. 2 for our research model.

Hypothesis 3 (H3). Perceived enjoyment will positively influence continuous use intention of playing mobile games.

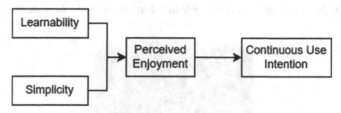

Fig. 2. Research Model

3.2 Game Design

In this study, we created a mobile game called "Greek Gods," enabling players to engage in battles with various ancient Greek deities. Players can enhance their fighting capabilities, acquire superior equipment, and aim to ascend to the top position among all the gods by strategically advancing their avatar. We created two interface designs with identical game features, functions, and tasks. The first design (Design A) features a simplified and easily learnable initial interface that gradually becomes more complex as the avatar's level increases (see Fig. 3). In contrast, the second design (Design B) presents a complicated initial interface incorporating all necessary features and functions, remaining unchanged as the avatar's level progresses (see Fig. 4).

In our preliminary study, we hired 20 volunteers (junior students in an US university). These 20 participants were randomly allocated into two groups, each consisting of 10 students. Group 1 engaged in playing the mobile game featuring Design A, while Group 2 experienced the game with Design B. All participants were tasked with playing the game for a duration of 2 h spread across 2 days. Subsequently, we requested them to fill out a survey regarding their experience with the game they had played.

Fig. 3. Left: Simple and Learnable initial interface; Right: final interface

Fig. 4. Game interface no change during the game

4   Results and Discussion

The results of the analysis are shown in Fig. 5. Both simplicity and learnability have positive and significant direct effects on perceived enjoyment in the SEM model. Simplicity had the strongest direct effect on perceived enjoyment, suggesting that simplicity played a more significant role in user enjoyment than learnability. While its effect on enjoyment was smaller, learnability is still important to consider when we design a mobile game. Easier-to-learn interfaces can still contribute to positive user experiences. This suggests that users in the simple interface group found the game more enjoyable than those in the complicated interface group. Perceived enjoyment has a strong and significant positive direct effect on continuous use intention. This indicates that users who enjoyed the game more are more likely to intend to use it again in the future.

This study highlights the importance of both simplicity and learnability in mobile game design. Focusing on clear, intuitive interfaces that are easy to grasp and navigate can lead to increased user enjoyment and ultimately, higher engagement. While both interface types appear to influence continuous use intention through enjoyment, simplicity seems to have a stronger overall impact. This suggests that developers may benefit from prioritizing simplicity when designing mobile games, especially for broader audiences.

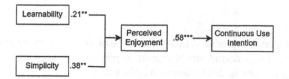

Fig. 5. SEM results

Furthermore, the findings of this study substantiated our initial idea that tailoring mobile game interface design to the individual levels of players enhances their perception of the intention to sustain gameplay. Consequently, it is imperative to take into account the varied perspectives of different levels of game players in the design of mobile games, with a specific focus on simplifying the user interface (UI) to enhance the overall user experience (UX).

5 Conclusions

As smart device technologies advance and smartphones become more widespread, users now expect more than just the functions of mobile applications. In contemporary application design and development for a mobile game, designers need to anticipate not only the functionalities of the game to meet essential user needs but also aim for UI and UX, especially some usability factors, such as simplicity and learnability of the game. This study explores the realm of mobile game design by taking into account the viewpoints of diverse levels of game players. Our objective is to pinpoint essential elements for tailoring mobile game design according to the specific levels of players. The results of our initial investigation revealed that simplicity and learnability are fundamental factors that impact the enjoyment of mobile game players, consequently influencing their intention to consistently participate in the game.

The findings of this research contribute valuable insights to the current demand for understanding player retention in the mobile gaming context. It underscores the significance of user interface (UI) and user experience (UX) as key factors influencing players' enjoyment, as well as continuous-use intentions in gaming. The practical application of these results is particularly relevant given the frequent abandonment of games shortly after download. Specifically, emphasizing simplicity and learnability in game design for players with less experience in easily comprehensible games enhances perceived enjoyment and fosters continuous-use intentions. On a broader scale, this research lays the foundation for exploring a player's initial interaction with a game using different interfaces, potentially opening up new avenues for the development of future adapted, effective, and enjoyable mobile game interfaces.

References

1. McEvoy, S.: Report: US predicted to account for 40% of growth in mobile gaming revenue in 2024. https://www.gamesindustry.biz/report-us-predicted-to-account-for-40-of-growth-in-mobile-gaming-revenue-in-2024. Accessed 2024 Feb 12
2. Kumar, V., Mittal, S.: Mobile marketing campaigns: practices, challenges and opportunities. Int. J. Bus. Innovation Res. **21**(4), 523–539 (2020)
3. Molinillo, S., Japutra, A., Liébana-Cabanillas, F.: Impact of perceived value on casual mobile game loyalty: the moderating effect of intensity of playing. J. Consum. Behav. **19**(5), 493–504 (2020)
4. Chernobai, B.: Behind the lifecycle of the mobile game. https://www.gamedeveloper.com/business/behind-the-lifecycle-of-the-mobile-game#close-modal. Accessed 2024 Feb 11
5. Wang, W., Hang, H.: Exploring the eudaimonic game experience through purchasing functional and nonfunctional items in MMORPGs. Psychol. Mark. **38**(10), 1847–1862 (2021)
6. Wurmser, Y.: Mobile App Installs 2019. https://www.insiderintelligence.com/content/mobile-app-installs-2019. Accessed 2024 Feb 11
7. Passalacqua, M., Morin, R., Sénécal, S., Nacke, L.E., Léger, P.M.: Demystifying the first-time experience of mobile games: the presence of a tutorial has a positive impact on non-expert players' flow and continuous-use intentions. Multimodal Technol. Interact. **4**(3), 41–53 (2020)
8. Moran, K., Li, B., Bernal-Cárdenas, C., Jelf, D., Poshyvanyk, D.: Automated reporting of GUI design violations for mobile apps. In: Proceedings of the 40th International Conference on Software Engineering, pp. 165–175 (2018)
9. Alves, T., Natálio, J., Henriques-Calado, J., Gama, S.: Incorporating personality in user interface design: a review. Pers. Individ. Differ. **155**, 109709 (2020)
10. Alben, L.: Defining the criteria for effective interaction design: quality of experience. Interactions **3**(3), 11–15 (1996)
11. Fanfarelli, J.R., McDaniel, R., Crossley, C.: Adapting UX to the design of healthcare games and applications. Entertainment Comput. **28**, 21–31 (2018)
12. Garrett, J.: The elements of user experience: User-centered design for the web and beyond, 2nd edn. New Riders Publishing, Berkeley, CA (2011)
13. DeLone, W.H., McLean, E.R.: The DeLone and McLean model of information systems success: a ten-year update. J. Manag. Inf. Syst. **19**(4), 9–30 (2003)
14. Nielsen, J.: Usability engineering. Morgan Kaufmann, CA (1994)
15. Weichbroth, P.: Usability of mobile applications: a systematic literature study. IEEE Access **8**, 55563–55577 (2020)
16. Parsazadeh, N., Ali, R., Rezaei, M.: A framework for cooperative and interactive mobile learning to improve online information evaluation skills. Comput. Educ. **120**, 75–89 (2018)
17. Chintapalli, V.V., Tao, W., Meng, Z., Zhang, K., Kong, J., Ge, Y.: A comparative study of spreadsheet applications on mobile devices. Mob. Inf. Syst. **2016**, 1–10 (2016)
18. Henshall, C., Davey, Z., Jacelon, C., Martin, C.: A usability study to test the effectiveness, efficiency and simplicity of a newly developed Internet-based exercise-focused health app for lung cancer survivors (iEXHALE): protocol paper. Health Inform. J. **26**(2), 1431–1442 (2020)
19. Krüger, J.T., Höffler, T.N., Wahl, M., Knickmeier, K., Parchmann, I.: Two comparative studies of computer simulations and experiments as learning tools in school and out-of-school education. Instr. Sci. **50**(2), 169–197 (2022)
20. Magana, A.J., Hwang, J., Feng, S., Rebello, S., Zu, T., Kao, D.: Emotional and cognitive effects of learning with computer simulations and computer videogames. J. Comput. Assist. Learn. **38**(3), 875–891 (2022)

21. Liu, T.C., Lin, Y.C., Hsu, C.Y., Hsu, C.Y., Paas, F.: Learning from animations and computer simulations: modality and reverse modality effects. Br. J. Edu. Technol. **52**(1), 304–317 (2021)

22. Clapp, S.R., Karwowski, W., Hancock, P.A.: Simplicity and predictability: a phenomenological study of psychological flow in transactional workers. Front. Psychol. **14**, 1137930 (2023)

23. Yan, M., Filieri, R., Gorton, M.: Continuance intention of online technologies: a systematic literature review. Int. J. Inf. Manage. **58**, 102315 (2021)

24. Singh, S., Singh, N., Kalinić, Z., Liébana-Cabanillas, F.J.: Assessing determinants influencing continued use of live streaming services: an extended perceived value theory of streaming addiction. Expert Syst. Appl. **168**, 114241 (2021)

Long-Term Gamification: A Survey

Lei Huang[1]([✉]), Chao Deng[1], Jennifer Hoffman[1], Reza Hadi Mogavi[2],
Justin Juho Kim[3], and Pan Hui[3,4,5]

[1] Research and Development, Accessible Meta Group, Michigan, USA
{lhuang,cdeng,jhoffman}@accessiblemeta.org
[2] HCI Games Group, Games Institute, and Stratford School of Interaction Design
and Business, University of Waterloo, Ontario, Canada
rhadimog@uwaterloo.ca
[3] Hong Kong University of Science and Technology, Hong Kong SAR, China
jjkimab@connect.ust.hk
[4] Hong Kong University of Science and Technology (Guangzhou), Guangzhou, China
panhui@ust.hk
[5] University of Helsinki, Helsinki, Finland

Abstract. In addressing the challenge of sustaining user engagement
in gamified systems, this survey explores the long-term effects of gamification strategies. It emerges that success hinges on a nuanced blend
of design elements, tailored personalization, evolving challenges, collaborative features, story-driven content, and dynamic updates. These factors are found to foster a deep-rooted sense of ownership, skill development, community belonging, and continuous discovery, all of which are
crucial for keeping users engaged over time. This paper contributes by
providing an early analysis of longitudinal studies, offering a valuable
roadmap for developing enduring gamification experiences within the
fields of human-computer interaction and gamification. Our paper advocates for further research examining long-term gamification in a more
systematic and thorough manner.

Keywords: Long-Term Engagement · Gamification · User
Motivation · Design Principles · Survey · Literature Review

1 Introduction

Gamification, defined as the application of game design elements in non-game
contexts [7,8], has emerged as a powerful strategy for boosting user engagement,
motivation, and behavior change [41]. Employing features such as points, badges,
leaderboards, and challenges [16,18,35], gamification taps into the innate psychological allure of games (and game elements) to render otherwise mundane
tasks more enjoyable and compelling. This technique has been effectively implemented across a diverse array of domains, including education, corporate, health,
and consumer sectors [13,15,21,31,37].

Although initial engagement spikes are commonly observed when gamification is introduced, the main challenge lies in sustaining long-term engagement

X. Fang (Ed.): HCII 2024, LNCS 14730, pp. 32–43, 2024.
https://doi.org/10.1007/978-3-031-60692-2_3

and preventing user fatigue [22,42]. In educational environments, for example, this prolonged engagement can lead to improved learning outcomes [6], while in the corporate sphere, it may result in consistent employee productivity and enhanced customer loyalty [20,28].

Sustaining high levels of engagement is a crucial aspect of successful performance in various domains [12,14,15,17]. However, numerous gamification initiatives encounter a diminution in user motivation as initial enthusiasm wanes, jeopardizing the long-term goals that gamification endeavors to achieve [14,15,30]. This highlights the imperative for strategies that are deliberately crafted to encourage lasting engagement.

In response to this imperative, the concept of long-term gamification emerges [22,24]. It emphasizes strategic design that engages individuals beyond the initial and ephemeral impact of gamification effects [43]. Such design demands a sophisticated grasp of user motivation and the enduring attractiveness of game elements [15].

Despite the vast body of research celebrating gamification's immediate (and passing) victories [1,29], there is a notable paucity of review studies (especially in the field of Human-Computer Interaction (HCI)) looking into how these effects can be sustained over extended periods [43]. This survey aims to bridge this gap by *consolidating the existing knowledge on the long-term efficacy of gamification*.

This study meticulously reviews empirical research evaluating the enduring impact of gamification. We include only those studies that employ longitudinal methods, spanning from several weeks to months, as they are pivotal for determining the sustainability of user engagement with gamified systems. Research with a timeframe of less than two weeks is systematically excluded for providing limited insight into engagement longevity.

By concentrating on this specific corpus of research, our paper distills and compiles the gamification strategies and design principles that have demonstrably encouraged sustained user involvement, thereby furnishing valuable guidance for crafting more efficacious and lasting gamified experiences.

In summary, our findings indicate that long-term engagement in gamified systems is enhanced by strategies that include *customization and personalization, adaptive progression dynamics, integrated social connectivity, narrative immersion,* and *the regular introduction of new content and updates*. These elements contribute to a feeling of *ownership, competency, community,* and *ongoing novelty*, which are essential for maintaining user interest and activity over extended periods.

Following this introduction, the subsequent sections of the paper will review the methodology, go over the main findings, discuss their implications, and make recommendations for future research.

2   Survey Method

The sequential stages of our literature review on long-term gamification are depicted in Fig. 1. The proliferation of research on long-term gamification can

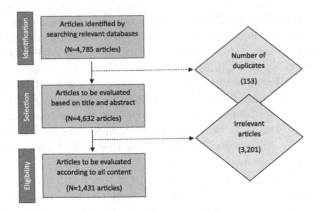

Fig. 1. Stages of the Literature Review Process

be attributed to the widespread adoption and interdisciplinary nature of gamification in various fields. Our multi-step review commenced with the establishment of precise search criteria targeting *empirical studies* that explored the sustainability of *long-term gamification* through *longitudinal research* designs.

We focused our search on well-regarded scientific literature databases, including the ACM Digital Library, IEEE Xplore, PubMed, and Springer. Keywords were carefully chosen to encapsulate our research scope, employing a combination of "Gamificaton" AND ("Long-term" OR "Enduring" OR "Sustained" OR "Prolonged"). The search was confined to research articles published in English from January 2010 through December 2023. The number of pertinent articles retrieved from each database using our selected keywords is reported in Table 1. The subsequent examination of our data reveals a relatively predominant presence of discussions surrounding long-term gamification within the domains of health (38.98%) and education (24.13%). A total of 89 research papers were included in the final selection through the process of snowball sampling.

The preliminary aggregation of studies underwent a meticulous screening process, where inclusion and exclusion criteria were applied to *titles* and *abstracts* to refine the selection. Inclusion necessitated that studies (1) explicitly address gamification, (2) report on user engagement over a minimum duration of two weeks, (3) be conducted in a longitudinal style, (4) have a clear definition of engagement, and (5) entail empirical evaluation via quantitative or qualitative methods. Studies that fell short of these criteria, particularly those examining only short-term effects or lacking clear definitions and measures of user engagement, were excluded. Screening was conducted independently by pairs of our research team members to ensure methodological rigor and reliability. Any inconsistencies encountered were reconciled through group discussion or by consulting a third team member when needed.

Following the screening phase, our meticulous data extraction procedure began. We diligently recorded and reviewed critical information from the

Table 1. The Number of Relevant Articles Retrieved from Each Database

Repository	Number of Papers
ACM Digital Library	2,696
Springer	1,779
PubMed	199
IEEE Xplore	111

studies that were selected, focusing on the design of the gamification interventions, the game mechanics and dynamics used, motivational incentives for users, the impact on user engagement, and any reported challenges or limitations. This detailed extraction enabled us to build a comprehensive understanding of the factors that contribute to gamification's long-term effectiveness.

3 Main Findings

Our examination of the existing body of literature uncovers significant understandings regarding the determinants that facilitate the continuation of user engagement in gamified environments. The subsections below discuss the pivotal strategies identified as effective for maintaining user engagement over time. These strategies are closely linked to fulfilling users' psychological needs and motivations, which are essential for nurturing consistent user behavior. We discuss the interplay between customization and personalization with the sense of ownership, the balance achieved through adaptive progression dynamics with the feeling of competency, the creation of community via integrated social connectivity, the sustained interest provided by narrative immersion, and the fresh appeal offered by the regular introduction of new content and updates. Each of these strategies plays a significant role in preventing user dropout and ensuring a lasting, engaged user base.

3.1 Customization and Personalization

The incorporation of game elements into a system or activity should not be approached with a one-size-fits-all mentality as there is little chance that it will effectively achieve desired objectives [14]. The efficacy of gamification design relies heavily on its ability to instill a strong sense of relevance and purpose within participants [35]. To attain this crucial aspect, a thorough comprehension of the target audience and their motivations is essential [15]. Implementing customization and personalization strategies can aid in this understanding and ultimately lead to more successful outcomes [3,33]. Furthermore, the selection of appropriate game mechanics and elements must align with the core goals and values of the system or activity [13,14]. By establishing a sense of significance and meaningfulness, individuals are more likely to sustain their engagement and motivation over an extended period of time.

The use of the terms "customization" and "personalization" has been a subject of confusion and interchangeability, especially in the context of marketing and technology. However, it is important to note that these two concepts have distinct meanings and should not be used interchangeably [39]. The process of customization is primarily initiated by the user, whereas personalization is primarily carried out by the system or designer. The concept of customization pertains to the process of affording users the ability to modify or adjust a product or service to meet their specific requirements or preferences. In contrast, personalization involves tailoring a product or service based on the distinct qualities and behaviors of an individual consumer. Hence, while both concepts involve catering to the specific requirements of customers, they differ in terms of the level of individualization and control.

Through customization and personalization, users are given the opportunity to showcase their individuality and unique identities within the gamified environment [39,44]. This can greatly heighten their sense of ownership as they feel a deeper connection to the experience and believe that their actions have a direct impact. Customization options can range from aesthetic decisions, such as selecting avatars and themes, to more practical choices like setting personalized goals and selecting specific tasks [4,15]. These personal touches enhance engagement and foster a stronger sense of control over the user's experience [46].

Customization can also encompass how progress and feedback are presented. Personalized dashboards and progress reports that reflect individual user's goals and milestones can motivate users by providing a clear vision of their achievements and the path ahead [1,10].

In regard to our discourse on customization and personalization, it has been determined that demographic variables could also play a significant role in individuals' response to gamification, particularly over a prolonged period of time [27].

Hammerschall proposed a framework for gamifying educational processes that aims to promote sustained engagement. This framework is based on two well-established theoretical models, namely the Self-Determination Theory (SDT) and the Transtheoretical Model of Change (TTM) [19]. The core principles of SDT, which include autonomy, relatedness, and competence, are integrated into the framework in order to enhance intrinsic motivation. Additionally, the framework aligns with the TTM, which focuses on the stages of behavior change, to support students in their long-term engagement with learning activities. Therefore, this framework incorporates both social and individual elements to create a holistic approach that fosters student engagement.

Kazhamiakin and colleagues conduct an investigation into the potential of gamification in promoting long-term engagement and inducing behavioral changes in the context of Smart Cities [25]. To achieve this objective, they propose a novel gamification framework that emphasizes the importance of integrating behavioral modifications into sustainable practices. This framework includes provisions for adapting Smart City policies and goals, as well as for seamless integration of diverse services. Additionally, it caters to multiple stakeholders and enables the inclusion of playable elements at different levels and time frames. The authors also introduce the concept of personalized challenges, which are tailored to the individual player's profile, preferences, usage history, and game progress. This approach ensures that the gameplay experience is personalized and contextualized for each player, with meaningful objectives and rewards.

In a study conducted by Zhao [50], a gamified fitness system was introduced, incorporating personalized recommendations. The experiment spanned 60 days and yielded notable enhancements in long-term engagement, motivation, and satisfaction towards physical activities, achieved through dynamic player modeling. The implementation of customization was found to be pivotal in driving continual user engagement and adherence to exercise regimes.

3.2 Integrated Social Connectivity

Integrated social connectivity could potentially enhance the effectiveness and longevity of gamification efforts by tapping into the fundamental human desire for interaction and community [23,46]. The integration of social features within gamified systems not only fosters a sense of community but also promotes sustained user engagement through competition, collaboration, and sharing of experiences [15].

Building on this foundation, research into the social network structure of gamified e-learning courses offers further insights. Specifically, a study by de-Marcos et al. [32] revealed that gamification significantly influences social interaction and collaboration among students. This gamification led to a small-world network phenomenon, where most students were closely connected, thus facilitating better academic performance and engagement throughout the semester. This evidence underscores the potential of integrated social connectivity to bolster learning experiences.

While integrated social connectivity shows promise in fostering engagement and community, sustaining these effects poses a significant challenge. This necessitates a deeper understanding of user engagement and the evolving dynamics within gamified environments.

For instance, Xu et al. [49] explore the complexities of designing group-based competition mechanisms in health games for youth. Through an empirical study of a pervasive health game deployed in the real world over a long period, they identified five distinctive player types based on their motivation, behavior, and influence on others. These insights are crucial for game designers to consider when integrating group-based mechanics to maximize the effectiveness of interventions. This highlights a critical message: while gamification holds potential benefits, its successful long-term application necessitates a nuanced understanding of user dynamics.

The insights from Xu et al. emphasize the importance of tailoring gamification to diverse user motivations and behaviors, a principle that becomes even more critical when we consider the sustainability of behavioral changes in other contexts. For instance, further complicating the design of effective gamified systems, a study on an app-based intervention aimed at reducing household electricity consumption utilized gamified elements linked to smart meters [47]. Initially, significant reductions in electricity use among participants were observed. However, one year after the intervention, the positive behavior change was not maintained, despite participants reporting more efficient behavior and perceiving *continued impact in their community*.

3.3 Narrative Immersion

The utilization of a semantic layer, like a scenario, theme, or story, can significantly amplify the effectiveness and coherence of a gamification event [11,45]. By infusing the experience with a storytelling component, participants are presented with a more captivating and enduring interaction, which ultimately leads to a higher level of overall gratification [38,45]. However, despite the evident advantages of narrative game elements, there is a shortage of gamification experiences that thoroughly incorporate such elements, as many tend to prioritize the triad of Point, Badge, and Leaderboard over narrative elements [9,45].

The use of gamified narratives has been found to be highly effective in eliciting emotions among users [34], resulting in the creation of engaging and memorable experiences that keep them continuously engaged. The emotional investment of users is a crucial factor in ensuring their continued participation, highlighting the importance of incorporating gamified elements that can effectively foster this emotional connection [15]. In this sense, characters hold a significant role within these narratives, acting as companions or mentors and further strengthening users' connection to the evolving story [26]. This emotional and psychological attachment to characters in gamified narratives enhances user motivation and engagement, making it a crucial component in the success of these systems [15].

Allowing users to influence the narrative direction could also enhance their investment and personalizes the experience [46,48]. This sense of agency contributes to a more engaging and immersive experience, as evidenced by the positive associations between user interactions with gamification features and intrinsic need satisfaction [1,46]. Aligning the narrative with user progression and milestones maintains a sense of advancement and purpose. This alignment is critical for sustaining user interest over time, necessitating the introduction of new story arcs or challenges that resonate with the ongoing narrative.

3.4 Regular Introduction of New Content and Updates

The inclusion of new content and the implementation of updates are paramount in creating a sustainable and engaging gamified environment. Regular updates serve to maintain user interest and mitigate the risk of monotony and disinterest over time [15].

In the study conducted by Zhao et al., the significance of continuous content updates and feature enhancements in fostering and maintaining user engagement with wearable-based exergames was investigated [51]. Over a 70-day period, participants utilized a wearable activity tracker in conjunction with a gamified exercise application, revealing a decline in user engagement over time. However, this decline was found to be reversible with the introduction of periodic updates to the game, indicating that regular content and feature refreshment can revitalize user interest and motivation. This finding emphasizes the vital importance of ongoing development and content renewal in sustaining the attractiveness and efficacy of gamified systems.

Darejeh and Salim's systematic review explores the breadth of gamification strategies and their effect on user engagement within software [5]. The authors highlight the critical role of incorporating user feedback throughout the design process in creating an effective gamification approach. Thus, continual solicitation of user feedback should serve as the foundation for constant improvements and enhancements to a gamified system [15].

To summarize, refining each of these strategies is crucial in creating engaging and motivating gamified experiences that can sustain user interest over the long term. At present, the majority of studies published do not devote sufficient attention to long-term gamification and only provide a brief overview of the potential effects of their findings on long-term gamification. Therefore, additional research is required to comprehensively investigate the efficacy of long-term gamification and its influence on user engagement in a more methodical, controlled, and targeted manner.

4 Conclusion and Directions for Future Work

In conclusion, the longevity of user engagement in gamified systems is not a serendipitous outcome but the result of carefully crafted strategies that resonate with the users' evolving needs [15]. This survey contributes a comprehensive analysis that serves as both a reflection on past practices and a guide for future gamification endeavors in HCI.

As we consider the future, it is imperative for researchers to concentrate on developing frameworks that incorporate the psychological foundations of motivation with the tangible elements of game design for sustainable implementation. There is a fertile ground for interdisciplinary exploration that utilizes cutting-edge psychological theories, data analysis techniques, and adaptive technologies to construct gamification models that dynamically respond to user progress and input [13,14,40].

Future research should also explore the longitudinal effects of incorporating gamification in various populations and contexts, with a specific focus on cultural disparities in motivation and engagement [36]. Furthermore, the ethical implications of gamification, such as user autonomy and consent, demand further examination to ensure that gamification tactics empower rather than manipulate individuals [2,13].

The HCI community finds itself on the brink of a new era in gamification research, where the sustained involvement and welfare of the user are paramount to design [13,15]. The findings derived from this survey provide a framework for designing impactful and sustainable gamified interventions that could potentially engage users more effectively.

Acknowledgement. This research was supported in part by a grant from the Guangzhou Municipal Nansha District Science and Technology Bureau under Contract No.2022ZD01 and the MetaHKUST project from the Hong Kong University of Science and Technology (Guangzhou).

References

1. Anderson, A., Huttenlocher, D., Kleinberg, J., Leskovec, J.: Steering user behavior with badges. In: Proceedings of the 22nd International Conference on World Wide Web, pp. 95–106. WWW '13, Association for Computing Machinery, New York, NY, USA (2013). https://doi.org/10.1145/2488388.2488398
2. Andrade, F.R.H., Mizoguchi, R., Isotani, S.: The Bright and Dark Sides of Gamification. In: Micarelli, A., Stamper, J., Panourgia, K. (eds.) ITS 2016. LNCS, vol. 9684, pp. 176–186. Springer, Cham (2016). https://doi.org/10.1007/978-3-319-39583-8_17
3. Barata, G., Gama, S., Jorge, J., Gonçalves, D.: Studying student differentiation in gamified education: a long-term study. Comput. Hum. Behav. **71**, 550–585 (2017). https://doi.org/10.1016/j.chb.2016.08.049
4. Chen, L., Baird, A., Straub, D.: The impact of hierarchical privilege levels and non-hierarchical incentives on continued contribution in online Q&A communities: a motivational model of gamification goals. Decis. Support Syst. **153**, 113667 (2022). https://doi.org/10.1016/j.dss.2021.113667
5. Darejeh, A., Salim, S.S.: Gamification solutions to enhance software user engagement: a systematic review. Int. J. Hum.-Comput. Interact. **32**(8), 613–642 (2016). https://doi.org/10.1080/10447318.2016.1183330
6. Denny, P., McDonald, F., Empson, R., Kelly, P., Petersen, A.: Empirical support for a causal relationship between gamification and learning outcomes. In: Proceedings of the 2018 CHI Conference on Human Factors in Computing Systems, pp. 1–13. CHI '18, Association for Computing Machinery, New York, NY, USA (2018). https://doi.org/10.1145/3173574.3173885
7. Deterding, S., Dixon, D., Khaled, R., Nacke, L.: From game design elements to gamefulness: defining "gamification". In: Proceedings of the 15th International Academic MindTrek Conference: Envisioning Future Media Environments, pp. 9–15. MindTrek '11, Association for Computing Machinery, New York, NY, USA (2011). https://doi.org/10.1145/2181037.2181040
8. Deterding, S., Sicart, M., Nacke, L., O'Hara, K., Dixon, D.: Gamification. Using game-design elements in non-gaming contexts. In: CHI '11 Extended Abstracts on Human Factors in Computing Systems, pp. 2425–2428. CHI EA '11, Association for Computing Machinery, New York, NY, USA (2011). https://doi.org/10.1145/1979742.1979575
9. Durin, F., Lee, R., Bade, A., On, C.K., Hamzah, N.: Impact of implementing game elements in gamifying educational environment: a study. J. Phys. Conf. Ser. **1358**(1), 012064 (2019). https://doi.org/10.1088/1742-6596/1358/1/012064
10. Fortes Tondello, G.: Dynamic personalization of gameful interactive systems (2019)
11. Grobelny, J., Smierzchalska, J., Czapkowski, K.: Narrative gamification as a method of increasing sales performance: a field experimental study (2018)
12. Hadi Mogavi, R., et al.: Your favorite gameplay speaks volumes about you: Predicting user behavior and hexad type. In: Fang, X. (ed.) HCI in Games, pp. 210–228. Springer Nature Switzerland, Cham (2023). https://doi.org/10.1007/978-3-031-35979-8_17

13. Hadi Mogavi, R., Guo, B., Zhang, Y., Haq, E.U., Hui, P., Ma, X.: When gamification spoils your learning: a qualitative case study of gamification misuse in a language-learning app. In: Proceedings of the Ninth ACM Conference on Learning @ Scale, pp. 175–188. L@S '22, Association for Computing Machinery, New York, NY, USA (2022). https://doi.org/10.1145/3491140.3528274

14. Hadi Mogavi, R., Haq, E.U., Gujar, S., Hui, P., Ma, X.: More gamification is not always better: a case study of promotional gamification in a question answering website. In: Proceedings of the ACM on Human-Computer Interaction, vol. 6, no. CSCW2 (2022). https://doi.org/10.1145/3555553

15. Hadi Mogavi, R., Zhang, Y., Haq, E.U., Wu, Y., Hui, P., Ma, X.: What do users think of promotional gamification schemes? A qualitative case study in a question answering website. In: Proceedings of the ACM on Human-Computer Interaction, vol. 6, no. CSCW2 (2022). https://doi.org/10.1145/3555124

16. Hamari, J.: Transforming homo economicus into homo ludens: a field experiment on gamification in a utilitarian peer-to-peer trading service. Electron. Commer. Res. Appl. 12(4), 236–245 (2013). https://doi.org/10.1016/j.elerap.2013.01.004

17. Hamari, J.: Do badges increase user activity? A field experiment on the effects of gamification. Comput. Hum. Behav. 71, 469–478 (2017). https://doi.org/10.1016/j.chb.2015.03.036

18. Hamari, J., Koivisto, J., Sarsa, H.: Does gamification work? – A literature review of empirical studies on gamification. In: 2014 47th Hawaii International Conference on System Sciences. IEEE (2014).https://doi.org/10.1109/hicss.2014.377

19. Hammerschall, U.: A gamification framework for long-term engagement in education based on self determination theory and the transtheoretical model of change. In: 2019 IEEE Global Engineering Education Conference (EDUCON). IEEE (2019). https://doi.org/10.1109/educon.2019.8725251

20. Hwang, J., Choi, L.: Having fun while receiving rewards?: Exploration of gamification in loyalty programs for consumer loyalty. J. Bus. Res. 106, 365–376 (2020). https://doi.org/10.1016/j.jbusres.2019.01.031

21. Kappen, D.L., Nacke, L.E.: The kaleidoscope of effective gamification: deconstructing gamification in business applications. In: Proceedings of the First International Conference on Gameful Design, Research, and Applications, pp. 119–122. Gamification '13, Association for Computing Machinery, New York, NY, USA (2013). https://doi.org/10.1145/2583008.2583029

22. Katsumata, K., et al.: Motivating long-term dietary habit modification through mobile MR gamification (demo). In: Proceedings of the 17th Annual International Conference on Mobile Systems, Applications, and Services, pp. 671–672. MobiSys '19, Association for Computing Machinery, New York, NY, USA (2019). https://doi.org/10.1145/3307334.3328575

23. Kayali, F., Luckner, N., Purgathofer, P., Spiel, K., Fitzpatrick, G.: Design considerations towards long-term engagement in games for health. In: Proceedings of the 13th International Conference on the Foundations of Digital Games. FDG '18, Association for Computing Machinery, New York, NY, USA (2018). https://doi.org/10.1145/3235765.3235789

24. Kazhamiakin, R., Marconi, A., Martinelli, A., Pistore, M., Valetto, G.: A gamification framework for the long-term engagement of smart citizens. In: 2016 IEEE International Smart Cities Conference (ISC2). IEEE (2016). https://doi.org/10.1109/isc2.2016.7580746

25. Kazhamiakin, R., Marconi, A., Martinelli, A., Pistore, M., Valetto, G.: A gamification framework for the long-term engagement of smart citizens. In: 2016 IEEE International Smart Cities Conference (ISC2). IEEE (2016). https://doi.org/10.1109/isc2.2016.7580746

26. Kit, C.W., Zolkepli, I.A.: The role of narrative elements in gamification towards value co-creation: a case of mobile app users in Malaysia, pp. 203–227. IGI Global (2020). https://doi.org/10.4018/978-1-7998-1566-2.ch011

27. Koivisto, J., Hamari, J.: Demographic differences in perceived benefits from gamification. Comput. Hum. Behav. **35**, 179–188 (2014). https://doi.org/10.1016/j.chb.2014.03.007

28. Krath, J.: Gamification for sustainable employee behavior: extended abstract for the chi play 2021 doctoral consortium. In: Extended Abstracts of the 2021 Annual Symposium on Computer-Human Interaction in Play, pp. 411–414. CHI PLAY '21, Association for Computing Machinery, New York, NY, USA (2021). https://doi.org/10.1145/3450337.3483523

29. Kusmierczyk, T., Gomez-Rodriguez, M.: On the causal effect of badges. In: Proceedings of the 2018 World Wide Web Conference, pp. 659–668. WWW '18, International World Wide Web Conferences Steering Committee, Republic and Canton of Geneva, CHE (2018). https://doi.org/10.1145/3178876.3186147

30. Loria, E., Nacke, L.E., Marconi, A.: On social contagion in gamification: the power of influencers in a location-based gameful system. In: Proceedings of the ACM on Human-Computer Interaction, vol. 5, no. (CHI PLAY) (2021). https://doi.org/10.1145/3474670

31. Majuri, J., Koivisto, J., Hamari, J.: Gamification of education and learning: a review of empirical literature. In: Proceedings of the 2nd International GamiFIN Conference, GamiFIN 2018. CEUR-WS (2018)

32. de Marcos, L., et al.: Social network analysis of a gamified e-learning course: small-world phenomenon and network metrics as predictors of academic performance. Comput. Hum. Behav. **60**, 312–321 (2016). https://doi.org/10.1016/j.chb.2016.02.052

33. Mora, A., Tondello, G.F., Calvet, L., González, C., Arnedo-Moreno, J., Nacke, L.E.: The quest for a better tailoring of gameful design: an analysis of player type preferences. In: Proceedings of the XX International Conference on Human Computer Interaction. Interacción '19, Association for Computing Machinery, New York, NY, USA (2019). https://doi.org/10.1145/3335595.3335625

34. Mullins, J.K., Sabherwal, R.: Gamification: a cognitive-emotional view. J. Bus. Res. **106**, 304–314 (2020). https://doi.org/10.1016/j.jbusres.2018.09.023

35. Nicholson, S.: A RECIPE for meaningful gamification. In: Reiners, T., Wood, L.C. (eds.) Gamification in Education and Business, pp. 1–20. Springer, Cham (2015). https://doi.org/10.1007/978-3-319-10208-5_1

36. Oliveira, N., Muller, M., Andrade, N., Reinecke, K.: The exchange in stackExchange: divergences between stack overflow and its culturally diverse participants. In: Proceedings of the ACM on Human-Computer Interaction, vol. 2, no. CSCW (2018). https://doi.org/10.1145/3274399

37. Orji, R., Nacke, L.E., Di Marco, C.: Towards personality-driven persuasive health games and gamified systems. In: Proceedings of the 2017 CHI Conference on Human Factors in Computing Systems, pp. 1015–1027. CHI '17, Association for Computing Machinery, New York, NY, USA (2017). https://doi.org/10.1145/3025453.3025577

38. Pujolà, J.T., Argüello, A.: Stories or scenarios: implementing narratives in gamified language teaching. GamiLearn (2019)

39. Rodrigues, L., et al.: Personalization improves gamification: evidence from a mixed-methods study. In: Proceedings of the ACM on Human-Computer Interaction, vol. 5, no. CHI PLAY (2021). https://doi.org/10.1145/3474714
40. Rodrigues, L., Toda, A.M., Palomino, P.T., Oliveira, W., Isotani, S.: Personalized gamification: a literature review of outcomes, experiments, and approaches. In: Eighth International Conference on Technological Ecosystems for Enhancing Multiculturality, pp. 699–706. TEEM'20, Association for Computing Machinery, New York, NY, USA (2021). https://doi.org/10.1145/3434780.3436665
41. Seaborn, K., Fels, D.I.: Gamification in theory and action: a survey. Int. J. Hum.-Comput. Stud. **74**, 14–31 (2015). https://doi.org/10.1016/j.ijhcs.2014.09.006
42. Senior, J.: Vocabulary taught via mobile application gamification: receptive, productive and long-term usability of words taught using quizlet and quizlet live. In: 2022 International Conference on Business Analytics for Technology and Security (ICBATS). IEEE (2022). https://doi.org/10.1109/icbats54253.2022.9759019
43. Stepanovic, S., Mettler, T.: Gamification applied for health promotion: does it really foster long-term engagement? A scoping review. In: Proceedings of the 26th European Conference on Information Systems, pp. 1–16. AIS (2018)
44. Tondello, G.F., Mora, A., Nacke, L.E.: Elements of gameful design emerging from user preferences. In: Proceedings of the Annual Symposium on Computer-Human Interaction in Play. CHI PLAY '17, ACM (2017). https://doi.org/10.1145/3116595.3116627
45. Trinidad, M., Calderon, A., Ruiz, M.: GoRace: a multi-context and narrative-based gamification suite to overcome gamification technological challenges. IEEE Access **9**, 65882–65905 (2021). https://doi.org/10.1109/access.2021.3076291
46. Tyack, A., Mekler, E.D.: Self-determination theory in HCI games research: current uses and open questions. In: Proceedings of the 2020 CHI Conference on Human Factors in Computing Systems, pp. 1–22. CHI '20, Association for Computing Machinery, New York, NY, USA (2020). https://doi.org/10.1145/3313831.3376723
47. Wemyss, D., Cellina, F., Lobsiger-Kägi, E., de Luca, V., Castri, R.: Does it last? Long-term impacts of an app-based behavior change intervention on household electricity savings in Switzerland. Energy Res. Soc. Sci. **47**, 16–27 (2019). https://doi.org/10.1016/j.erss.2018.08.018
48. Xi, N., Hamari, J.: Does gamification satisfy needs? A study on the relationship between gamification features and intrinsic need satisfaction. Int. J. Inf. Manag. **46**, 210–221 (2019). https://doi.org/10.1016/j.ijinfomgt.2018.12.002
49. Xu, Y., et al.: This is not a one-horse race: understanding player types in multi-player pervasive health games for youth. In: Proceedings of the ACM 2012 Conference on Computer Supported Cooperative Work, pp. 843–852. CSCW '12, Association for Computing Machinery, New York, NY, USA (2012). https://doi.org/10.1145/2145204.2145330
50. Zhao, Z., Arya, A., Orji, R., Chan, G.: Effects of a personalized fitness recommender system using gamification and continuous player modeling: system design and long-term validation study. JMIR Serious Games **8**(4), e19968 (2020). https://doi.org/10.2196/19968
51. Zhao, Z., Arya, A., Whitehead, A., Chan, G., Etemad, S.A.: Keeping users engaged through feature updates: a long-term study of using wearable-based exergames. In: Proceedings of the 2017 CHI Conference on Human Factors in Computing Systems, pp. 1053–1064. CHI '17, Association for Computing Machinery, New York, NY, USA (2017). https://doi.org/10.1145/3025453.3025982

Experiential Affordance: Explore Gamification in Dating Apps Advertisements

Javzmaa Jadamba, Anna Maria Wen, and Dongjing Kang[✉]

School of Media and Communication, Shanghai Jiao Tong University, Shanghai, China
{jjavzmaa,annamariawen,dongjingkang}@sjtu.edu.cn

Abstract. Human-computer interaction, digital advertising, and communication research have identified gamified cues as a key factor impacting consumer responses to effective advergames. Guided by four key gamification principles, we used qualitative content analysis to examine the video advertisements of top-ten dating apps in the global market. Four distinct themes were identified: 1) the desire for a relationship as the primary motivator, 2) the use of gamified affordances such as swiping, in-app games, and group functions, 3) the immersive multi-sensory experience that emphasizes both emotional and visual aspects in promoting the app affordances, and 4) the acquisition of knowledge about key app features and interface characteristics. The results offer insights into the impact of gamification in dating app ads, contribute to a broader understanding of gamification in non-game industries, and provide practical implications for marketing professionals and ad developers.

Keywords: dating app advertisement · gamification · experiential affordance · human factors

1 Introduction

In today's ever-changing social landscape, dating apps like Tinder, Bumble, and Grindr have significantly shaped modern relationships [1]. These platforms have evolved beyond their original purpose of matchmaking and have incorporated gamification elements - a technique that involves using game design elements in non-game contexts [2]. The goal of this integration is to improve user engagement and their overall experience [2–8]. This study explores the role of gamified affordances in dating apps, focusing on how gamification principles are incorporated into the promotional advertisement of dating applications. Affordances generally refers to action possibilities that the interface features provide for certain interactions [41].

The use of gamification strategies in dating applications has revolutionized the user experience, creating dynamic ecosystems that captivate and retain user interest. From swiping mechanisms to reward-based incentives, these strategies have significantly altered the way users engage with these platforms [9]. Thus, there is a growing need to further investigate the use of gamification on user engagement in the interdisciplinary fields of human-computer interaction, digital advertising, and communication.

X. Fang (Ed.): HCII 2024, LNCS 14730, pp. 44–54, 2024.
https://doi.org/10.1007/978-3-031-60692-2_4

To gain insight into the ways dating apps incorporate gamification and how users respond to it, we first identified four key principles of gamification that are significant in digital advertising: the source of motivation, engagement, sensory experience, and learning. Then we collected the video advertisements of the top ten most downloaded dating apps as the field of analysis. Based on the four principles of gamification, we conducted a qualitative content analysis of these videos. This study aims to inform the gamified design and marketing strategies of dating application advertisements and sheds light on the changing dynamics of social relationships in the digital age. As such, it contributes to the larger conversation surrounding gamification, technology, and social connectivity.

2 Literature Review: Gamification

The integration of game elements and design from gaming into different contexts has been a longstanding topic in the field of human-computer interaction (HCI). Since the early 1980s, there have been continuous efforts to formulate principles for creating engaging interfaces inspired by games [10, 11]. This endeavor has evolved into what we now recognize as gamification, progressing through various stages of development. Gamification is the use of gaming methods and instruments of rewards in nongame settings [12]. Deterding et al. define 'gamification' as 'the use of game design elements in non-game contexts' [13]. The term gamification appeared in Google Trends for the first time in 2010, and since then, it has been gaining increasing interest [14]. Introduced in 2002 by Nick Pelling, gamification initially related to the application of game-like accelerated user interface design on commercial electronic devices such as ATMs, vending machines, and mobile phones [15]. With the purpose of making electronic transactions both enjoyable and fast, it was understood as an attempt to enhance user interactions with physical devices rather than digital interfaces or platforms [15]. Pelling's initial use of the term is widely recognized as a starting point for discussions around applying game elements in non-game contexts. The idea has evolved since then and gained prominence within the *serious games* movement, where researchers, scholars, and practitioners have created comprehensive games to impart training, education, and persuasion [16].

During the mid-2000s, the intersection of web technologies, digital business models, and online and location-based gaming gave rise to the most recent form of gamification, an industry practice defined as "the use of game design elements in non-game contexts" [13]. Among its early examples are mobile applications like FourSquare [17] and platforms like StackOverflow, which started integrating design features such as point scores, badges, or leaderboards from social network games and meta-gaming systems like Xbox Live to encourage user engagement [18]. The initial wave of research on gamification revolved around the question of whether gamification works, focusing on creating definitions, frameworks, and conducting studies on its technical aspects and user effects. Disseminated across various disciplines, these effect studies spanned fields including human-computer interaction, computer science, informatics, game studies, psychology, and others. The prevailing empirical studies published in that timeframe consistently revealed positive outcomes concerning specific motivational aspects of gamification implementations, underscoring its effectiveness and benefits, particularly in the context of education and intra-organizational systems [19].

Understood as the select incorporation of game elements into an interactive system without a fully-fledged game as the end product [16, 20], gamification in the digital world is the strategic attempt to enhance systems, services, organizations, and activities by creating similar experiences to those experienced when playing games to motivate and engage users [2]. It is used to describe the features of an interactive system that aim to motivate and engage end-users through the use of game elements and mechanics. Based on prior research, the gamification approach has a positive impact on customer attitudes and purchase intentions [21]. It elevates the importance of incentives, influencing cognitive and emotional responses [22], such as customer awareness, brand attitude, and brand recall, ultimately establishing a distinctive interaction between the brand and its customers [23]. Overall, existing research in the interdisciplinary fields of HCI, digital advertising, and communication has well-explored gamification in dating apps. However, limited study has been done on how gamification principles play out in dating app advertisements.

2.1 Contextualization of Four Key Elements in Gamification in App Advertisements

The research on gamification has become an increasingly popular topic of investigation and is now a cross-disciplinary field with a mature understanding of theory-driven empirical studies, design methods, and application areas [18]. Until recently, gamification discussions were primarily held within the HCI. Understanding how gamification aligns with existing knowledge in service literature is beneficial for both industry professionals and academics, as there are significant similarities in the objectives and strategies of gamification and marketing. The conceptualization of gamification in the business sector has predominantly been guided by Zichermann and colleagues. According to Zichermann and Linder [24], gamification is a method to enhance branding initiatives by incorporating game elements and mechanics. Deterding and colleagous [13] defined it as "an informal umbrella term for the use of video game elements in non-gaming systems to improve user experience (UX) and user engagement." [13]. Gamification. Using game-design elements in non-gaming contexts. In *CHI'11 extended abstracts on human factors in computing systems* (pp. 2425–2428). In their definition of gamification, Huotari and Hamari [25] highlight the role of gamification in invoking the same psychological experiences as games (generally) do.

To contextualize gamification within the field of digital advertising, we identified four key gamification principles that could be appropriate to analyze dating app advertisements. The first principle, motivation, encompasses both internal and external factors. Internal motivation refers to personal interests, playfulness, autonomy, mastery, and purpose, while external motivation involves various types of rewards. Motivational aspects within information systems have garnered significant interest in recent years [2]. Motivational appeal of information systems has always been one of the central factors in study of gamification [3–7]. By creating a "gameful experience" that evokes positive emotions and motivations similar to those found in enjoyable games and has the potential to increase motivation [2, 26]. According to Garris and colleagues [27], the process of motivation is characterized by a game cycle that triggers a perpetual loop of user assessments (such as satisfaction), actions (gameplay), and responses. This game cycle underscores the significance of a vital sequence of interrelated elements: (a) To promote desirable behaviors in learners, (b) they must first undergo pleasant emotional or cognitive encounters, (c) which arise from their interaction with and reaction to feedback from gameplay [27]. Reward mechanisms provide a sense of fun by fostering intrinsically rewarding experiences and are equally or more important than the extrinsic rewards that are distributed [28].

Second, engagement, explores how the interactive features, feedback mechanism, and personalization that encourage further action or continuous improvement are presented in the advertisement. O'Brien and Toms [29] developed a comprehensive definition of user engagement that encompasses factors like challenge, aesthetic appeal, feedback, interactivity, novelty, perceived control over time, awareness, motivation, interest, and affect. Lehmann and colleagues [30] study "Models of User Engagement" provides further insight into user engagement and effective measurement techniques for online services. User engagement reflects the quality of a user's experience, highlighting positive interactions that encourage platform utilization. For instance, Tinder strategically employs gamification tactics, like user engagement, to attract and retain users without disrupting their experience [31]. These tactics steer user behavior, including engagement and other practices, in a more manageable direction [32].

The third principle, experiential content, refers to multi-sensory stimulations and gamified experiences that can enhance engagement by providing context, meaning, and a sense of purpose [33, 34]. Through the integration of behavioral psychology and predictive algorithms, companies can now anticipate consumer preferences before they are even consciously acknowledged [35]. Digital platforms and apps have harnessed game structures observed in casino environments to create compulsive and addictive features that provide engaging multi-sensory experiences for users [36]. Social media's "digital slot machine logic" as an "intimate closed loop architecture of obsession, loss of self, and auto-gratification" [36], which echoes Schüll's [37] argument that game designers aspire to create a "total machine" where play adapts to every player's speed and preference. For instance, digital gambling venues have been designed to enhance user comfort and blood circulation, reflecting the improved circulation of capital and extended play [37], while cultivating the illusion of control and autonomy through choice [37]. As a result, the gamified elements suspend time and space, and the coordinates of the body are more readily submitted [33]. Gamblers seek a subjective experience that leads to a state of self-forgetting, an irresistible momentum that feels like being "played by the machine" [36].

Lastly, the learning principle includes knowing how to use some features of the app and/or knowing what they could obtain if becoming a user [20, 38]. The gamified elements have been often seen as the reinforcement of learning in higher education [39]. They could also provide relevant insight in digital advertising industry. Viewers can be seen as "learners" when they are motivated in getting the role (a user) in the game. Guided by these four gamification principles, we raised two research questions (RQ):

- RQ 1: What game elements are used in dating app advertisements?
- RQ 2: How are gamification principles incorporated into the promotional advertisement of dating applications?

2.2   Methodology: Qualitative Content Analysis

We collected video ads for the top 10 most downloaded apps worldwide in 2023, including Tinder, Bumble, and Badoo, among others (see Fig. 1 for the full list from Statista, 2023). The selection criteria of the video include: 1) the promotional video feature contains at least one prominent technological affordance; 2) the video incorporates game-like elements. Two of the top 10 apps, Momo and TanTan, are geared toward Asian/Chinese audiences, while the remaining options should be culturally universal for English-speaking markets.

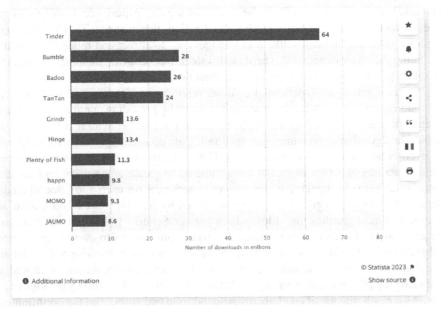

Leading dating apps worldwide in 2022, by downloads
(in millions)

Fig. 1. .

To analyze the ten dating app advertising videos (see Appendix), we utilized a qualitative content analysis method [40]. Our analysis began with open coding, focusing on finding content that highlights gamified elements and affordances. Second, we performed theoretical coding based on the gamification principles. Last, three coders discussed which codes from open coding are the most important and central theoretical codes. Through the process, we refined and elevated the codes to four thematic categories: 1) explicit external motivation for seeking a relationship, 2) engaging gamified affordances such as swiping and in-app games, 3) immersive multi-sensory experiences that highlight emotional and visual elements, and 4) learning outcomes that include understanding key features and interface characteristics of the app.

3   Analysis/Results

Theme 1: Explicit External Motivation of Seeking for a Relationship. One of the primary drives for users to start using a dating app is the to fullfil the desire to find a compatible partner, which can be fueled by various *external motivators* such as validation from peers, personal initiative, or even game-plays [6, 7]. For example, the Tinder video advertisement offers a "find a match" feature that allows users' friends to assess someone's compatibility based on their perception of their friend and choose the most suitable match. Another external motivation presented in all the videos is the common featurer: to receive rewards in various forms, such as playing games with a match to get to know them better and engage in a playful environment, all while pursuing the initial motivation of finding a suitable partner. In some dating app advertisements, users can earn scores that serve as a form of reward. For instance, in Bumble, users can invite their match to a virtual "night together" and play different games while video calling. Each game played results in different rewards. Finally, Grindr offers a "boost me" function that increases users' chances of meeting more people. One of the fundamental principles of gamification is the identification of sources of motivation [2, 26], which can be categorized into internal and external factors.

The internal motivation is derived from a set of intrinsic factors such as interests, playfulness, desire for autonomy, mastery, and purpose [28]. On the other hand, external motivations primarily stem from various forms of rewards [27]. One of the primary reasons for seeking a compatible partner is a fundamental drive that is inherently linked to the desired outcome while engaging in various gamified features. Additionally, a reward system is employed in diverse ways, whereby users earn various incentives such as high scores during gameplay or finding a match that aligns with their preferences. The current theme centers on the clear external incentives for users to participate, spurred by the aspiration to discover a suitable companion and shaped by elements such as affirmation from friends, individual drive, and game-like attributes that provide benefits such as achieving a high score or fulfilling preferences in a match.

Theme 2: Engaging Gamified Affordances such as Swiping, in-app Games, and Group Functions. Most dating apps offer a swipe function for users to accept or reject potential matches. Advertisements often highlight this feature as an interactive interface that allows users to make decisions based on their assessments. Comparatively, Tinder emphasizes the simplicity of "just a swipe," while Bumble introduces a more comprehensive feature called Trivia Night, enabling users to invite matches to play a game or chat. *Engaging with a match* leads to further assessment, and in Bumble's case, a pop-up function suggests icebreakers to help start conversations. Second, *personalization* is also a key element in these ads, with users personalizing their "bios" to find suitable matches, assessing others' bios to match preferences, and receiving friend suggestions based on compatibility assessments. It reflected the principle of engagement that encompasses interactive features, feedback mechanisms, personalization, and incentive structures that promote sustained actions and continuous improvement [29]. This principle underscores the importance of fostering user motivation and involvement through immersive and dynamic experiences that are tailored to individual preferences and needs [30]. Third, in the promotional videos, the *swiping feature* found on dating apps is presented as a gamified element that captivates users by providing immediate feedback as they read through potential matches' personalized bios. These bios are a crucial aspect of dating app profiles, as they are tailored to each user's individual preferences and needs. For example, in the Tinder advertisement, a user's friends may ask personalized questions that highlight important characteristics for their friend. The focal point of the theme is to integrate interactive and game-like features, like swiping, group activities, and in-app games, in dating applications to encourage user participation, interest, and customized communication for improved and lively engagement.

Theme 3: Immersive Multi-sensory Experience Highlighting Emotional and Visual Experience. Dating app advertisements often highlight *immersive and multi-sensory* experiences in its app affordances. Primarily, vivid colors like red and pink are featured in Tinder advertisements, while Bumble ads often have a yellow and pink color scheme. The colors chosen for each ad are meant to evoke different emotions depending on the plot. Secondly, *emotional* and sexual arousal elements (often in nonverbal expressions) are a central part of these ads including sexy vocalics, anticipating nonverbals of excitement, and romantic setting. For example, a male user in a Tinder ad expresses his passion with a sexy vocalics, saying, "Lauren, you got my heart soaring (tone up)." Anticipating excitement is also emphasized in various ways, such as the nervousness of waiting for peer-approval, assessing potential matches, playing games with matches, or changing profile pictures and expecting feedback. Creating a romantic setting through colors, words, and physical settings for sexual arousal is a prominent characteristics in the video ads. In the Hinge advertising video, the scene of meeting someone was situated in a dimmed light, cozy environment, and nice music create a romantic atmosphere. Thus, the multi-sensory experience in its app affordance is a crucial factor for boosting user engagement by imbuing a sense of context, purpose, and meaning into multi-sensory gamified experiences [33, 36]. Overall, the advertisement videos intend to create an environment for users to feel immersive by highlighting their visual and emotional experiences. It were also the external and internal motivations that could draw users into the game environment and further them.

Theme 4: Learning Outcomes Including Knowing how to Use the Key Feature of the App, and Knowing the Content of the App Interface Characteristics. The gamification principle of learning aims to engege users/viewers to *know what* the app's features, content, and characteristics and to *know how* to use them in the advertising videos. For example, the Tinder ad strategically introduced how friends could select a match and assess compatibility based on their perceptions of potential partners. And the Bumble ad introduced the "Trivia game" feature and encouraged users to become familiar with the interface's various components, such as the functions to text, live videos, and chat. Other platform features such as "like" and "match" were also highlighted in most of the ads. Grindr's "Boost Me" gamified function was introduced to help users gain more attention from the community.

Besides introducing the affordances of the apps, demonstrating in a teacherly manner about how to use the app has been identified in all the videos. To coach viewers how to become mindful users, Plenty of Fish's promotional video encouraged users to learn how to date online with mutual respect and not to use inappropriate words or pickup lines such as mutual respect and no dick pics. In gamification, learning how to use the app's features and understanding what benefits come with using the app are crucial outcomes.

Overall, knowing what and knowing how are two basic principles in a gamified environment [20]. In our analysis, users may watch dating apps with a purpose, learning the different features the app offers, and mimicking the behaviors in the videos on how to use them.

4 Conclusion

Overall, we identified key gamified elements in the world's top ten dating app advertisements and explored how the four gamification principles are incorporated into promotional videos. Among the four themes, gamified strategies enhancing multisensory experiences stood out as being most significant in motivating users, engaging further interaction, and reinforcing continuous learning.

The results hope to shed light on the impact of gamification in dating app advertisements, with a focus on how it influences user motivation, engagement, and learning outcomes. By leveraging these insights, developers can create more compelling advertisement highlighting the gamified affordances that stimulate multi-sensory experiences that not only attract but also retain users. As technology evolves, it's important to understand how gamification affects app companies to design user-centered, culturally specific, and/or universal dating apps. The study also offers practical implications for HCI and digital advertising professionals looking to optimize their strategies for user acquisition and retention and contributes to a larger understanding of gamification in non-game industries. Ultimately, these findings invite further research and experimentation in the dynamic realm of HCI, digital advertising, and communication, driving innovation and growth in the field.

Appendix

No	Company	Ad Message	Video Link
1	Tinder	Just a swipe	https://www.youtube.com/watch?v=Vx8FbRC7nHI
2	Bumble	Got game?	https://www.youtube.com/watch?v=0LWXiNfkpZg
3	Badoo	There is an other way to date	https://www.youtube.com/watch?v=Q_MkZq0QQ1U
4	TanTan	Destiny	https://www.youtube.com/watch?v=slCYN9SLG4A
5	Grindr	Boost me	https://m.youtube.com/watch?v=rE8VtdWChGQ
6	Hinge	Designed to Be Deleted	https://m.youtube.com/watch?v=kTe0HoDlBoA
7	Plenty of Fish	Makes Date More Welcoming	https://www.youtube.com/watch?v=YoPIJNzRHuI

(continued)

(continued)

No	Company	Ad Message	Video Link
8	Happn	Find the crush in the place you love	https://m.youtube.com/watch?v=xStM5xOq_2g
9	MOMO	Be an animal	https://www.youtube.com/watch?v=7UemlF47ZNI
10	JAUMO	A World of New Friends	https://www.youtube.com/watch?v=VT_gti_2prc

References

1. Tankovska, H.: Dating apps: most downloaded worldwide 2021. Statista. Published February 23, 2021. https://www.statista.com/statistics/1200234/most-popular-dating-apps-worldwide-by-number-of-downloads/
2. Koivisto, J., Hamari, J.: The rise of motivational information systems: a review of gamification research. Int. J. Inf. Manage. **45**, 191–210 (2019)
3. Marlow, S.L., Salas, E., Landon, L.B., Presnell, B.: Eliciting teamwork with game attributes: a systematic review and research agenda. Comput. Hum. Behav. **55**, 413–423 (2016)
4. Meske, C., Brockmann, T., Wilms, K., Stieglitz, S.: Social Collaboration and Gamification. Gamification: Using Game Elements in Serious Contexts, pp. 93–109 (2017)
5. Morschheuser, B., Hamari, J., Koivisto, J., Maedche, A.: Gamified crowdsourcing: conceptualization, literature review, and future agenda. Int. J. Hum. Comput. Stud. **106**, 26–43 (2017)
6. Suh, A., Wagner, C.: How gamification of an enterprise collaboration system increases knowledge contribution: an affordance approach. J. Knowl. Manag. **21**(2), 416–431 (2017)
7. Friedrich, J., Becker, M., Kramer, F., Wirth, M., Schneider, M.: Incentive design and gamification for knowledge management. J. Bus. Res. **106**, 341–352 (2020)
8. Hamari, J., Xi, N., Legaki, Z., Morschheuser, B.: Gamification. In: Hawaii International Conference on System Sciences, pp. 1105 (2023)
9. Ronkainen, T.: Principles of increasing user engagement and habit formation in social network platforms: An exploratory literature review (2023)
10. Malone, T.W.: What makes things fun to learn? Stanford University, A study of intrinsically motivating computer games (1980)
11. Malone, T.W.: Heuristics for designing enjoyable user interfaces: lessons from computer games. In: Proceedings of the 1982 Conference on Human Factors in Computing Systems, pp. 63–68 (1982)
12. Robson, K., Plangger, K., Kietzmann, J.H., McCarthy, I., Pitt, L.: Is it all a game? Understanding the principles of gamification. Bus. Horiz. **58**(4), 411–420 (2015)
13. Deterding, S., Sicart, M., Nacke, L., O'Hara, K., Dixon, D.: Gamification. Using game-design elements in non-gaming contexts. In: CHI'11 Extended Abstracts on Human Factors in Computing Systems, pp. 2425–2428 (2011)
14. Gamification at Google Trends. Google Trends. http://www.google.com/trends/explore#q=gamification. Accessed 13 Dec 2023
15. Pelling, N.: The (Short) Prehistory of "Gamification." Funding Startups (& Other Impossibilities) blog. Retrieved: December 13, 2023. http://nanodome.wordpress.com/2011/08/09/the-short-prehistory-of-gamification/ (2011, August 9)

16. Deterding, S.: Gamification: designing for motivation. Interactions **19**(4), 14–17 (2012). https://doi.org/10.1145/2212877.2212883
17. Burke, B.: Gamify: How Gamification Motivates People to do Extraordinary Things. Routledge, London (2016).https://doi.org/10.4324/9781315230344
18. Nacke, L.E., Deterding, S.: The maturing of gamification research. Comput. Hum. Behav. **71**, 450–454 (2017)
19. Hamari, J., Koivisto, J., Sarsa, H.: Does gamification work?–A literature review of empirical studies on gamification. In: 2014 47th Hawaii International Conference on System Sciences, pp. 3025–3034. IEEE (2014)
20. Kang, D.: Game-based learning and instructional effectiveness in organizational communication classrooms. In: Stephanidis, C., Harris, D., Li, W.-C., Schmorrow, D.D., Fidopiastis, C.M., Zaphiris, P., Ioannou, A., Fang, X., Sottilare, R.A., Schwarz, J. (eds.) HCII 2020. LNCS, vol. 12425, pp. 700–707. Springer, Cham (2020). https://doi.org/10.1007/978-3-030-60128-7_51
21. Bittner, J.V., Shipper, J.: Motivational effects and age differences of gamification in product advertising. J. Consum. Mark. **31**(5), 391–400 (2014)
22. Vanwesenbeeck, I., Walrave, M., Ponnet, K.: Children and advergames: the role of product involvement, prior brand attitude, persuasion knowledge and game attitude in purchase intentions and changing attitudes. Int. J. Advert. **36**(4), 520–541 (2017)
23. Sreejesh, S., Anusree, M.R.: Effects of cognition demand, mode of interactivity and brand anthropomorphism on gamers' brand attention and memory in advergames. Comput. Hum. Behav. **70**, 575–588 (2017)
24. Zichermann, G., Linder, J.: Game-based marketing: inspire customer loyalty through rewards, challenges, and contests. John Wiley & Sons (2010)
25. Huotari, K., Hamari, J.: Defining gamification: a service marketing perspective. In: Proceeding of the 16th International Academic MindTrek Conference, pp. 17–22 (2012)
26. Högberg, J., Ramberg, M.O., Gustafsson, A., Wästlund, E.: Creating brand engagement through in-store gamified customer experiences. J. Retail. Consum. Serv. **50**, 122–130 (2019)
27. Garris, R., Ahlers, R., Driskell, J.E.: Games, motivation, and learning: a research and practice model. Simul. Gaming **33**(4), 441–467 (2002)
28. Wang, H., Sun, C.T.: Game Reward Systems: Gaming Experiences and Social Meanings. In: DiGRA Conference, vol. 114 (2011)
29. O'Brien, H.L., Toms, E.G.: What is user engagement? A conceptual framework for defining user engagement with technology. J. Am. Soc. Inform. Sci. Technol. **59**(6), 938–955 (2008)
30. Lehmann, J., Lalmas, M., Yom-Tov, E., Dupret, G.: Models of user engagement. In: Masthoff, J., Mobasher, B., Desmarais, M.C., Nkambou, R. (eds.) UMAP 2012. LNCS, vol. 7379, pp. 164–175. Springer, Heidelberg (2012). https://doi.org/10.1007/978-3-642-31454-4_14
31. Solovyeva, O., Laskin, A.V.: Gamification, tinder effect, and tinder fatigue: dating as a CMC experience. In: The Emerald Handbook of Computer-Mediated Communication and Social Media, pp. 197–211. Emerald Publishing Limited (2022)
32. Nicholson, S.: A recipe for meaningful gamification. In: Reiners, T., Wood, L.C. (eds.) Gamification in education and business, pp. 1–20. Springer, Cham (2015). https://doi.org/10.1007/978-3-319-10208-5_1
33. Mackinnon, L.: Love, games and gamification: gambling and gaming as techniques of modern romantic love. Theory Cult. Soc. **39**(6), 121–137 (2022)
34. Wu, B., Liu, P., Xu, X.: An evolutionary analysis of low-carbon strategies based on the government–enterprise game in the complex network context. J. Clean. Prod. **141**, 168–179 (2017)
35. Plonsky, O., et al.: Predicting human decisions with behavioral theories and machine learning (2019). arXiv preprint arXiv:1904.06866

36. Zuboff, S.: We Make Them Dance': Surveillance Capitalism, the Rise of Instrumentarian Power, and the Threat to Human Rights. Human Rights in the Age of Platforms, pp. 3–51 (2019)
37. Schull, N.D.: Digital gambling: the coincidence of desire and design. Ann. Am. Acad. Pol. Soc. Sci. **597**(1), 65–81 (2005)
38. Lederman, N.G.: Students' and teachers' understanding of the nature of science: a reassessment. Sch. Sci. Math. **86**(2), 91–99 (1986)
39. Tan Ai Lin, D., Ganapathy, M., Kaur, M.: Kahoot! It: Gamification in higher education. Pertanika J. Soc. Sci. Humanit. **26**(1), 565–582 (2018)
40. Forman, J., Damschroder, L.: Qualitative content analysis. In: Empirical Methods for Bioethics: A Primer, pp. 39–62 (2007). Emerald Group Publishing Limited
41. Norman, D.A.: Affordance, conventions, and design. Interactions **6**(3), 38–43 (1999). https://doi.org/10.1145/301153.301168

Optimizing Tutorial Design for Video Card Games Based on Cognitive Load Theory: Measuring Game Complexity

Chengyi Li, Chengjie Dai, and Wai Kin (Victor) Chan(✉)

Tsinghua Shenzhen International Graduate School, Shenzhen 518055, China
{lichengy21,dcj21}@mails.tsinghua.edu.cn, chanw@sz.tsinghua.edu.cn

Abstract. In this study, we delineated the theoretical underpinnings of game tutorial design within the contemporary domain of game design, emphasizing the genesis and evolution of Cognitive Load Theory (CLT). Upon this theoretical framework, we investigated the incorporation of CLT into the explicit design of game tutorials, introducing an innovative approach for the quantification of knowledge and task complexity in card games. This approach is designed to evaluate the cognitive load (CL) potentially imposed on players by game levels.A custom game was developed for this purpose, wherein several participants were engaged in experimental sessions followed by a comprehensive analysis of the data gathered. The outcomes were promising, indicating that tutorials crafted in alignment with CLT principles not only significantly mitigated the cognitive load experienced by players but also augmented their learning efficiency. Such results underscore the tangible applicability of CLT in game design, especially concerning tutorial development. Through the quantification of game complexity to modulate the cognitive load, our study not only promoted player learning and engagement but also pre-empted the risk of exceeding their cognitive limits.

Keywords: Video Card Games · Cognitive Load Theory · Tutorial Design · Game Design · Level Design

1 Introduction

The game tutorials are often the first part of a game which player will meet first, and an effective tutorial design could be very crucial for retaining these new player. Video card games employ a variety of instructional styles, including hints, help tips, manuals, and challenges. However, the effectiveness of these styles remains unclear. Therefore, designers often rely on theirself intuition, personal experience or existing examples, and extensive user testing when they creating tutorials. Andersen et al. conducted an experiment with 45,000 players and found that tutorials significantly increase the playing time and progress of players in complex games [1].

© The Author(s), under exclusive license to Springer Nature Switzerland AG 2024
X. Fang (Ed.): HCII 2024, LNCS 14730, pp. 55–67, 2024.
https://doi.org/10.1007/978-3-031-60692-2_5

There is no universal theory in academia regarding the design of game tutorials, but there is considerable research on game design itself, especially theories related to game difficulty. For instance, studies on Dynamic Difficulty Adjustment (DDA) quantify player levels and adjust the difficulty when player playing game [25], and use Video Game Description Language (VGDL) to define task lists for automatic tutorial generation [9]. In 2007, Jenova Chen applied the theory of flow to gaming [2], attempting to explain the pleasure players derive from games and the relationship between their skills and game difficulty.

The theory of flow was developed by Mihaly in the mid-1970 s, with the aim of explaining happiness [7]. He introduced the concept of flow, which later became a cornerstone of positive psychology. In a state of flow, individuals experience intense focus, maximizing performance and enjoyment in an activity, hence it is also referred to as the optimal experience. The key to flow theory lies in balancing the challenges of a game with the player's abilities. When the challenge exceeds ability, the player may feel anxious; if the challenge is too low, they might feel bored.

Challenge is an essential component of games, and many players derive enjoyment from it [25]. Based on Csikszentmihalyi's model of difficulty adaptation and flow theory [6], this model shows how task difficulty is directly related to the performer's perception. As games become increasingly diverse and complex, the importance of game tutorials has become more apparent. However, previous research has not fundamentally defined game difficulty, often describing it using player scores. Defining challenge in games is a difficult task and has been rarely addressed in past research. This study aims to introduce Cognitive Load Theory (CLT) to describe the cognitive load (CL) of new players when encountering new games. This provides a basis for quantifying the difficulty level of new players and guiding the instructional design of games. Sweller's CLT explains the cognitive state of learners when acquiring new knowledge, focusing on the involved mental effort [19]. It elucidates how people process information, transform it into memory, and then into skills [8]. CLT links general cognition with domain-specific knowledge and skills, which is crucial for understanding how players learn to play new games.

In gaming, CLT specifically identifies the root of learning difficulties, focusing on the transfer of biologically secondary information which is from the external environment to working memory, and then to long-term memory. The quantity, complexity, and interrelatedness of information significantly affect CL during this process [21]. The theory allows for the quantification of learning difficulties in new games using subjective methods like the Paas scale, as well as objective methods of physiological assessment [20,22]. This study proposes an indirect measurement approach for video games, combining objective information analysis to handled the complexity in game to reduce CL of player.

2 Underpinning Theory

2.1 Theory Background

As early as the 1950 s, researchers primarily focused on the processes and limitations of human information processing. Among these, Miller's research proposed the limits of human information processing, namely that human working memory capacity is limited and can only remember about 7 elements [11]; Newell and Simon's research explored the process of human problem-solving and proposed the production system model [12]; Peterson and Peterson's research focused on the retention of short-term memory, finding that humans can only maintain short-term memory for about 20 s [14]. These studies laid the foundation for the development of CLT.

At the beginning of 21 century, Sweller and other researchers proposed the basic CLT, which posits that the capacity of human working memory is limited, and learning effectiveness is impacted when the learning task exceeds this capacity. They then embarked on research into strategies for reducing CL, including step-by-step learning and demonstrative learning [19]. Kirschner and others proposed the Collaborative CLT, which explores CL issues in multi-person collaborative learning [10]. During collaborative learning, learners need to process information from different sources simultaneously, increasing their CL. Therefore, to reduce CL, collaborative learning requires strategies such as task division, information sharing, and communication coordination. These strategies can help learners reduce the amount of information they need to process, thereby lowering CL and enhancing learning effectiveness. Additionally, there are other related studies exploring the application of CLT in educational technology, like the research by Chen et al. [3]. Based on these findings, Chen et al. proposed several design principles for educational technology that can reduce CL and enhance learning effectiveness. These principles include providing exemplars, reducing element interactivity, and spaced learning.

Subsequently, Sweller and others explored the application of CLT in adaptive learning [23]. In addition, the 4-Component Instructional Design model which is called 4C/ID is an effective method designed for those very complex learning [5], aimed at simultaneously developing knowledge, skills, and methodologies to acquire complex skills and professional competencies. This model was initially developed in the late 1980 s by Jeroen and others, focusing on integrating knowledge, skills, and methodologies; coordinating some different component skills, then transferring what is learned from school to daily life and work.

CL refers to the amount of mental processing resources that people must use while performing a task, describing the "pressure" the brain endures while processing information. This theory divides CL into three types: intrinsic CL, extraneous CL, and germane CL. Intrinsic CL is the CL inherent in the complexity of the learning material itself. Extraneous CL is caused by the way instructional materials are presented or by the teaching methods used. Germane CL is related to the cognitive effort involved in constructing knowledge and understanding concepts. How game designers handle these types of CL during the novice tutorial phase affects players' interest and enjoyment of the game. In the gaming process, too high or too low CL for players can lead to a mismatch between difficulty and ability, preventing players from entering a state of flow and causing them to feel frustrated or bored. Therefore, in game design, designers need to reasonably arrange game content and tutorials to help players learn to play. How to measure players' CL and the complexity of game content is precisely what this study aims to elucidate.

2.2   Measure CL and Complexity

In the theory of CL, measuring CL is a significant area of research. It is a means of quantifying the CL of learners and can be used as a basis to assist in assessing the relationship between CL and learning effectiveness. Sweller proposed a self-report method, where learners assess the magnitude of CL based on their feelings and experiences [18]. Another method is the physiological indicator method, which assesses CL by measuring the physiological responses of learners, such as heart rate and skin conductance [18]. There is also a behavioral indicator method, which assesses CL by observing the behavior of learners, such as reaction time and error rate. These methods can be used to assess the level of CL of learning tasks and to provide guidance for instructional design [18]. Overall, measuring CL is an important aspect of instructional design because it can help educators create effective and efficient learning environments, enhancing learners' cognitive processing and information retention. Similarly, this also provides important insights for game designers.

On the other hand, complexity in games is a major source of CL for players, and complexity is primarily divided into knowledge complexity and task complexity [4]. Knowledge complexity refers to the quantity and type of information or knowledge elements related to a specific task. These elements can be concepts, facts, principles, procedures, etc. Knowledge complexity is usually related to the amount of information learners need to process, having a direct impact on their CL. Task complexity, however, is more related to the interactivity of elements during task execution. It refers to the degree of interaction between elements when completing a task. Tasks with high task complexity typically require learners to process multiple interrelated elements simultaneously, increasing intrinsic CL. Task complexity differs from knowledge complexity as it focuses more on the dynamic process of task execution and the interaction between elements. In the context of the card games studied in this research, sources of knowledge complexity include rules, card elements, enemies, etc., while task complexity includes their combinations, content of levels, and the organization of the interface. These two concepts are key to understanding and assessing the complexity of game content for players and are crucial for designing effective instructional strategies and enhancing teaching effectiveness.

3   How to Build a Good Tutorial

3.1   Measure CL After Play Game

In the field of psychology, the measurement of CL primarily relies on two methodologies: physiological tools and psychological measurement tools. Physiological tools, such as pupillometry [17], assess CL by observing and analyzing the pupil's response to changes in cognitive stress. On the other hand, psychological measurement tools, like the Paas scale [4], are based on individuals' subjective assessments of task difficulty and perceived CL. The Paas scale enables players to rate their CL after completing specific tasks, thereby offering a rapid and effective method for measuring CL. Compared to physiological measurement methods, the advantage of the Paas scale lies in its simplicity and direct feedback on user experience. Research indicates a strong positive correlation between pupillometry and the Paas scale in measuring CL [24]. Both methods are effective in measuring CL, and their results corroborate each other to a certain extent. Given the simplicity and intuitiveness of the Paas scale, this study opts to use the Paas scale [23] as the tool for measuring CL, particularly in evaluating the CL levels of players during gameplay.

3.2   Measure Knowledge Complexity in Game

In quantifying knowledge complexity, we employ the concept of information entropy from information theory. This concept was first introduced by Claude Shannon in 1948 and extensively explored in his paper [15]. He defined information entropy as the average amount of information in a system, a method to measure the uncertainty or randomness of information in the system [16]. Shannon provided a formula for the information content of a specific message :

$$I = -\ln p \tag{1}$$

which the I is the information content of message, and p is the probability of occurrence of every single message.Then sum all I, we can get the information entropy. Events that are less likely to occur have a higher information content because they provide more "new" or "uncertain" information. This definitions laid the foundation for the development of information theory, profoundly influencing various disciplines, from communication engineering to biology. To assess the information content of a sentence, it is necessary to consider the probability of each word in the sentence. The occurrence of a rare word in a sentence may increase the sentence's information content. However, directly applying Shannon's formula to assess the information content of natural language sentences is complex, as the structure, grammar, context, and nuances of a sentence all influence its information content. Here, we will use the N-Gram model for a simplistic assessment of information content. This model can be used to assess the information content of a sentence. Specifically, the information content of a sentence can be obtained by calculating the probability of the entire sentence and using Shannon's information entropy for representation:

$$H(W) = -\sum_{w\in W} P(w) \log P(w) \tag{2}$$

where W represents a set of sentences or words, and $P(w)$ is the probability of word w in the corpus [13]. The source of the corpus is the game currently being played by the player (Table 1).

Table 1. Examples of Information Entropy Calculation

Order	Information Entropy	Original Text
1	3.88	A magician proud of his heritage. He left his hometown as if fleeing that day
2	3.00	The weather is nice today, I want to go out for a walk
3	4.22	Deal 1 damage to a minion. If "Death Coil" kills the minion, draw a card
4	4.33	CLT is a theory of cognitive psychology about how people acquire and process information, especially in learning environments

3.3   Measure Task Complexity in Game

According to CLT, task complexity is closely related to the element interactivity during task execution. In the context of card games, this complexity can be understood as the diversity and intricacy of challenges that players encounter throughout the game. This includes not only the complexity of game rules and strategies but also the complexity of the decision-making process. In card games, this is typically manifested in the strategic choices of different card combinations, the prediction of opponent players' behaviors, and the capability to handle random events in the game. As a type of strategy game, card games possess their own complete state space. Quantifying this state space can effectively describe the game's task complexity. For a specific game scenario, all possible states can be determined through enumeration, denoting these state numbers as W. Among all possible states, they can generally be divided into two outcomes based on the nature of the game: victory and defeat, corresponding to state numbers W_1 and W_2, respectively. Based on this, the complexity (or entropy) of the game can be defined as:

$$S = \ln W_1 + \ln W_2 \tag{3}$$

In practical application, different games can define various classifications of state numbers according to their uniqueness. However, to maintain consistency and comparability, a game should follow a uniform standard when quantifying its complexity. This is a key point emphasized by CLT, which is that the measurement of task complexity should be a relative rather than an absolute standard

[4]. For instance, we can compare the difficulty of solving different linear equations, but we should not directly compare the difficulty of physics and chemistry problems, as they belong to different domains of knowledge and modes of thinking.

3.4 Tutorial Design Principles for Card Games

Under the guidance of CLT, a series of principles for the design and validation of card game tutorials can be established. These principles aim to optimize the learning experience by aligning the game's complexity with the cognitive abilities of players.

Spiral Increase in Game Knowledge and Task Complexity. The complexity of game knowledge and tasks should exhibit a spiral increase. Especially in the initial stages of learning, the focus should be predominantly on knowledge complexity. This approach lays a solid foundation for players, ensuring they are not overwhelmed by the game mechanics and strategic complexities at the outset. As players gradually become familiar with the basic knowledge, the complexity of tasks can be incrementally increased, thereby adding strategic depth and decision-making challenges.

Task Level Division Based on Game Content Modules. Task levels should be reasonably divided according to the content modules within the game, following the principle of a spiral increase in complexity. This involves distinguishing the skill modules and level arrangements that players need to master within the game and organizing them in an order of increasing difficulty, thus forming a step-by-step learning path. Such division not only aids players in gradually mastering every aspect of the game but also ensures a balanced CL throughout the learning process.

Difficulty Adjustment Using CL Questionnaires. Employing CL questionnaires for comparative analysis to adjust the difficulty design of game levels is crucial. This includes using structured questionnaires at different stages of gameplay to assess players' CL. Analyzing this questionnaire data allows for the identification of parts of the game that may be excessively challenging or too simplistic. Based on this analysis, adjustments can be made to the game's difficulty settings, ensuring each level is appropriately challenging without being overly difficult or too easy. This method not only enhances the learning experience but also helps maintain high player engagement.

In conclusion, these principles derived from CLT provide a framework for creating a more effective and engaging learning environment in card games, ensuring that players not only enjoy the game but also develop a comprehensive understanding and mastery of its mechanics and strategies.

4   Experiment in Self-made Game

4.1   Tutorial Design

The primary practical subject of this study is the self-developed game "Card Flow." We created a brief tutorial for this game using the methods described in the previous chapters. The tutorial lasts between 15 to 25 min, mainly introducing the game's combat rules and key elements such as cards, skills, and enemies. The game is structured in independent levels, and the tutorial includes five levels. In each level, the complexity of knowledge is calculated as follows: the text set of all elements that may appear in the level, including cards, skills, enemies, events, and tutorial instructions, is collated. After deduplication and cleansing, the knowledge complexity of the level is calculated using the formula presented earlier.

The complexity of tasks is calculated by tree search, which evaluates the game's state space. We employed the Monte Carlo tree search method, thoroughly exploring every possible game state space given sufficient computational resources. The total number of distinct spaces is then counted and converted into the task complexity of the level using the formula mentioned earlier.

In the preliminary experiment, we gathered some approximate empirical data. In "Card Flow", a knowledge complexity below 5 is considered simple, between 5 and 6 is of medium complexity, and above 6 is very complex. Task complexity, derived from the logarithm of the state space count, is deemed simple if it's below 4.5, medium between 4.5 and 6.5, and very complex if above 6.5. The specific content of the five levels is as follows (Fig. 1).

Fig. 1. Self-made Game.

Level 1: Introduction to Game Basic Mechanics. This level contains two instructional guides to help players understand the game's elements and learn the basic combat rules. It includes six cards involving enemies and player cards, and one player skill. The calculated knowledge complexity is 4.18, and the task complexity is 3.8.

Level 2: Introduction to Common Card Mechanics. This level features one instructional guide, which introduces players to the special mechanics of cards, explaining the operational principles and effects of these special mechanics. It includes five cards involving enemies and player cards, and one player skill. The calculated knowledge complexity is 4.72, and the task complexity is 4.21.

Level 3: Combat Training 1. This level has no instructional guides and increases the difficulty and number of elements to challenge players and reinforce learning outcomes. It includes ten cards involving enemies and player cards, and one player skill. The calculated knowledge complexity is 5.45, and the task complexity is 4.74.

Level 4: Introduction to New Skills and Enemy Mechanics. This level contains two instructional guides for introducing new skill mechanics and enemy mechanics to players. It includes nine cards involving enemies and player cards, and two player skills. The calculated knowledge complexity is 5.85, and the task complexity is 5.04.

Level 5: Combat Training 2. This level, without instructional guides, increases the combat difficulty and element quantity, primarily aiming to consolidate the players' previously learned skills. It includes ten cards involving enemies and player cards, and two player skills. The calculated knowledge complexity is 5.63, and the task complexity is 5.6 (Fig. 2).

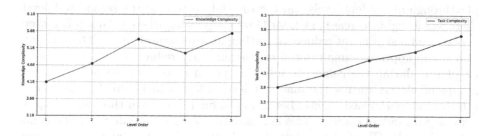

Fig. 2. Knowledge and Task Complexity of Levels.

4.2 Experiment

In the experiment, all participants played two different test levels to assess their gaming proficiency. All participants first played Test Level A, and based on their scores, they were randomly assigned to ensure approximately equal skill levels across two groups. Depending on the group, one set of players played random game content, while the other played the game tutorial we developed. We invited 20 players for this experiment, with 10 in Group A, who played random content, and 10 in Group B, who played the game tutorial. In the test levels, players' gaming proficiency was evaluated using a scoring system. In this game, both players and enemies have a concept of health points, so we defined the scoring criteria for the levels as follows:

$$S = (1 - EnemyHp/EnemyMaxHp + PlayerHp/PlayerMaxHp) * 50 \quad (4)$$

We first tested all players using Test Level A, which was completely unrelated to the levels used in subsequent experiments. The number of elements in Test Levels A and B was roughly the same, and extensive testing with a search tree AI ensured that their difficulties were also nearly identical. After obtaining the test scores, we divided the players into two groups of approximately equal skill levels. Subsequently, players filled out a CL questionnaire to determine the CL imposed by Test Level A (Fig. 3). Next, we had the players from both Group A and Group B experience our game for 20 min. Group A players experienced random levels, while Group B players went through the tutorial we developed. After this, both groups played Test Level B, received scores, and then filled out the CL questionnaire again to assess their CL from both the game experience and Test Level B (Fig. 4). The experimental results revealed that players who went through our tutorial showed a 10.1% improvement in performance in Test Level B compared to those who played random levels. Furthermore, their CL rating was 29.1% lower. The following graph represents the results of the CL questionnaire survey completed by the players. It is evident that players experienced a generally high level of CL during the first test level, which had a considerable negative impact on their enjoyment and interest in the game. During the playthrough of random levels and the tutorial, as well as the second test level, there was a slight decrease in CL for Group A players, whereas Group B players experienced a significant reduction, settling at a reasonable level. This suggests that an appropriate game tutorial can significantly reduce the CL experienced by players during the game.The following graph reveals the scores of the two groups of players during the final test level. Players in Group B, who played the tutorial, performed slightly better in the final level than those in Group A, who played random content. This indicates that an appropriate tutorial can not only reduce the CL of players but also help them learn to play the game more effectively (Fig. 5 and Table 2).

Table 2. Experiment Data Overview

Group	Test-A Score	Test-B Score	Test-A CL	Play&Test-B CL
A	40.4	64.85	6.6	5.5
B	40.5	71.4	6.9	3.9

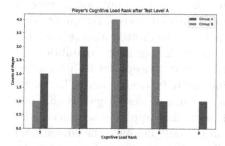

Fig. 3. Player's CL Rank after Test Level A.

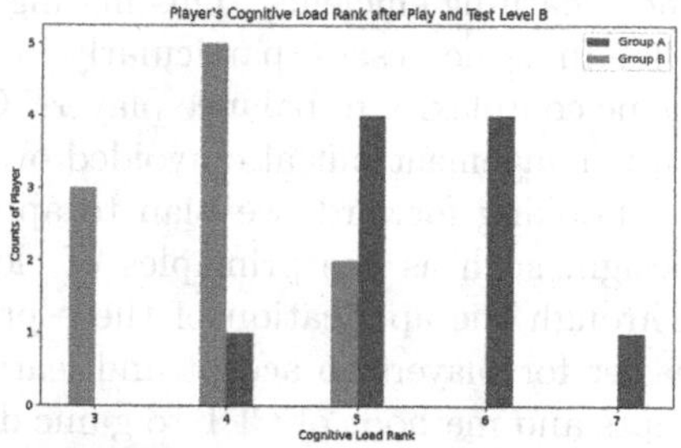

Fig. 4. Player's CL Rank after Play and Test Level B.

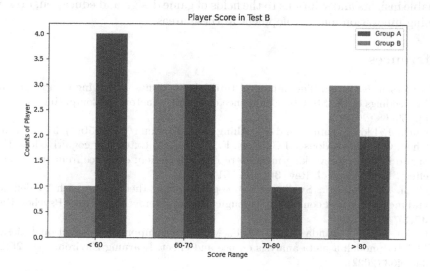

Fig. 5. Player Score in Test B.

5   Discussion

We outlined the theoretical foundations of game tutorial design in the current field of game design, with a focus on the origins of CL, and studied it's developments. Building upon this foundation, we explored how to integrate CLT into the specific design of game tutorials, proposing a new method for quantifying knowledge complexity and task complexity in card games. This method aims to assess the level of CL that game levels may impose on players.

We developed a self-made game, inviting several players to participate in experiments and conducted an in-depth analysis of the experimental data. Encouragingly, the results showed that tutorials designed based on the principles of CLT not only effectively reduced the CL on players but also enhanced their learning efficiency. This finding validates the practical application value of CLT in game design, particularly in the area of tutorial design. By quantifying game complexity to balance players' CL, we not only facilitated players' learning and engagement but also avoided overburdening their cognitive capabilities.

Looking forward, we plan to apply more related concepts of CLT in game design, such as the principles of element interactivity design and CL effects. Through the application of these principles, we aim to design games that are easier for players to accept and learn. We believe that applying advanced concepts and methods of CLT to game design can not only enhance the educational value of games but also strengthen the overall gaming experience for players. An effective gaming experience is one that challenges players while avoiding excessive burdens, thereby achieving ideal learning outcomes and player satisfaction. We hope that through continuous research and practice, we can contribute more valuable insights and solutions to the fields of game design and education, driving ongoing innovation and development in these areas.

References

1. Andersen, E., et al.: The impact of tutorials on games of varying complexity. In: Proceedings of the SIGCHI Conference on Human Factors in Computing Systems, pp. 59–68 (2012)
2. Chen, J.: Flow in games (and everything else). Commun. ACM **50**(4), 31–34 (2007)
3. Chen, O., Castro-Alonso, J.C., Paas, F., Sweller, J.: Extending cognitive load theory to incorporate working memory resource depletion: evidence from the spacing effect. Educ. Psychol. Rev. **30**, 483–501 (2018)
4. Chen, O., Paas, F., Sweller, J.: A cognitive load theory approach to defining and measuring task complexity through element interactivity. Educ. Psychol. Rev. **35**(2), 63 (2023)
5. Costa, J.M., Miranda, G.L., Melo, M.: Four-component instructional design (4C/ID) model: a meta-analysis on use and effect. Learning Environ. Res. **25**(2), 445–463 (2022)
6. CSikszentmih, A., Flow, M.: The Psychology of Optimal Experience (2008)
7. Debold, E.: Flow with soul. Retrieved on January **9**, 2005 (2002)
8. Geary, D.C.: Principles of evolutionary educational psychology. Learn. Individ. Differ. **12**(4), 317–345 (2002)
9. Green, M., Khalifa, A., Barros, G., Togellius, J.: Press space to fire: automatic video game tutorial generation. In: Proceedings of the AAAI Conference on Artificial Intelligence and Interactive Digital Entertainment, vol. 13, pp. 75–80 (2017)
10. Kirschner, P.A., Sweller, J., Kirschner, F., Zambrano R., J.: From cognitive load theory to collaborative cognitive load theory. Inter. J. Comput.-Support. Collaborative Learn. **13**(2), 213–233 (2018). https://doi.org/10.1007/s11412-018-9277-y

11. Miller, G.A.: The magical number seven, plus or minus two: some limits on our capacity for processing information. Psychol. Rev. **63**(2), 81 (1956)
12. Newell, A., Simon, H.A., et al.: Human Problem Solving, vol. 104. Prentice-hall Englewood Cliffs, NJ (1972)
13. Parsing, C.: Speech and Language Processing. Power Point Slides (2009)
14. Peterson, L., Peterson, M.J.: Short-term retention of individual verbal items. J. Exp. Psychol. **58**(3), 193 (1959)
15. Shannon, C.E.: A mathematical theory of communication. Bell Syst. Tech. J. **27**(3), 379–423 (1948)
16. Shannon, C.E.: A mathematical theory of communication. ACM SIGMOBILE Mob. Comput. Commun. Rev. **5**(1), 3–55 (2001)
17. Strauch, C., Wang, C.A., Einhäuser, W., Van der Stigchel, S., Naber, M.: Pupillometry as an integrated readout of distinct attentional networks. Trends Neurosci. **45**(8), 635–647 (2022)
18. Sweller, J.: Cognitive Load Theory: Recent Theoretical Advances, Cambridge University Press (2010)
19. Sweller, J.: Cognitive load theory. In: Psychology of Learning and Motivation, Academic Press, vol. 55, pp. 37–76. Elsevier (2011)
20. Sweller, J.: Measuring cognitive load. Perspect. Med. Educ. **7**, 1–2 (2018)
21. Sweller, J.: Cognitive load theory and educational technology. Educ. Tech. Res. Dev. **68**(1), 1–16 (2020)
22. Sweller, J., Ayres, P., Kalyuga, S., Sweller, J., Ayres, P., Kalyuga, S.: Measuring cognitive load. Cognitive Load Theory, pp. 71–85 (2011)
23. Sweller, J., van Merriënboer, J.J., Paas, F.: Cognitive architecture and instructional design: 20 years later. Educ. Psychol. Rev. **31**, 261–292 (2019)
24. Szulewski, A., Gegenfurtner, A., Howes, D.W., Sivilotti, M.L., van Merriënboer, J.J.: Measuring physician cognitive load: validity evidence for a physiologic and a psychometric tool. Adv. Health Sci. Educ. **22**, 951–968 (2017)
25. Zohaib, M., et al.: Dynamic difficulty adjustment (DDA) in computer games: a review. Adv. Hum. Comput. Interact. **2018**, 1–12 (2018)

Who is the GOAT (Greatest of All Time) Formula One Racer—Hamilton, Schumacher, Verstappen, Vettel, or Some Other Driver, Perhaps Fangio? Statistical Analyses Provide Answers and Information for Game Designers

Hermann Prossinger[1,2] , Silvia Boschetti[3] , Tomáš Hladký[3] , Daniel Říha[3] ,
Violetta Prossinger-Beck[4], Thomas Beck[5], and Jakub Binter[2(✉)]

[1] Department of Evolutionary Biology, University of Vienna, Vienna, Austria
`hermann.prossinger@univie.ac.at`
[2] Faculty of Social and Economic Studies, University of Jan Evangelista Purkyně,
Usti Nad Labem, Czech Republic
`jakub.binter@ujep.cz`
[3] Faculty of Humanities, Charles University, Prague, Czech Republic
[4] Technical University, Dresden, Germany
[5] Seestrasse 14, Dresden, Germany

Abstract. The debate about who is the GOAT (the "Greatest Of All Time") is not restricted to Formula One competition. There are several possible criteria, other than the number of World Championships won. We approach this issue of attempting to identify the GOAT (assuming that there is only one), by looking at the race performance of 12 drivers who participated in Grand Prix races since 1950.

(a) Unquestionably, the more race participation, the greater the chance of accumulating wins and therefore improving a driver's ranking towards being the GOAT. (b) A similar line of argument occurs for the ranking via podiums. (c) The system of awarding points for ranks after the race has changed five times since 1950. Comparing points accrued by different drivers therefore necessitates reassigning points to achieve comparability. We also consider how rankings change if other point systems are used.

(d) Bayesian statistical analysis allows not only the evaluation of who is eligible for GOAT without using a point system (via Beta and Dirichlet distributions) but can also estimate the probability that two contenders' performances differ only by chance.

Formula One also takes place in video games, particularly in tournaments. Here we provide evidence that avoiding point systems to identify winners of the tournament is advisable.

We provide suspense by not revealing who is the GOAT in this Abstract. We provide the names of one or several GOATs (there might be several) in this publication.

Keywords: Formula One · Dirichlet Distribution · Confusion Matrix

© The Author(s), under exclusive license to Springer Nature Switzerland AG 2024
X. Fang (Ed.): HCII 2024, LNCS 14730, pp. 68–80, 2024.
https://doi.org/10.1007/978-3-031-60692-2_6

1 Introduction: The Challenge

1.1 Ranking Issues

After Liberty Media acquired the Formula One Group in 2017, the popularity of watching and interest in the competition increased greatly; it has become a multi-billion-(US)-dollar business. In 2022, the worldwide viewership was 1.54 billion (AR1, 2023)—with more than 70 million watching adults (older than 15 years and younger than 65 years; Dyvik, 2023) per race (if we assume that every adult so defined watched every race). This is 61% of the viewership of the 115 million for the NFL Super Bowl 2023 (Stoll, 2023)—the latter taking place only once per year, however, while the Formula One races 22–23 times—or roughly once every fortnight. The debate about who is the GOAT ("The Greatest Of All Time") of Formula One drivers is ongoing and will, arguably, continue. The debate reached its current nadir in 2021, when the contested decision at the last Grand Prix in Abu Dhabi by Race Director Michael Masi to let the lapped 'stragglers' 'unlap' during the safety car phase enabled Verstappen (who had fresher tires) to overtake Hamilton at Turn 5 several hundred meters before the chequered flag was waved, marking him the winner. Had Hamilton not been overtaken, he would have won a record-breaking 8th World Championship; instead, Verstappen won his 1st. This outcome infuriated Hamilton and his fans and made the argument about the GOAT far more acrimonious than it had been before—and it hadn't been civil even then. If Hamilton had won his 8th World Championship, he would have been the uncontested leader in the Winners of the World Championship list; with Masi's decision, he remained tied with Michael Schumacher at seven World Championships each.

We use this ongoing debate to investigate the issue of how to (statistically) determine who is the GOAT. We limit ourselves (obviously) to those drivers who, since the beginning of Formula One racing (in 1946, although this date is contested; noncontroversial is the year 1950), are candidates: arguably at most 12, listed in Table 1. The awarded points for the rank at the end of the race have not been constant over the 78 years of racing (Table 2), so we need to investigate whether rankings change when the awarded points are consistently applied over more than a ¾ of a century (note: "… Of *All* Time").

There are, however, other ways to assess driver performance without relying on point systems. Most useful, as we argue in this paper, is to compare the Dirichlet distributions of podium places (thereby making the awarding of points obsolete). But we also include other statistical approaches. Another issue that we investigate is the fact that the number of races in a given year has varied enormously. In 1950, 'only' six Grand Prix were held, and the Indianapolis 500 was included to determine the World Champion of that year. In 2023, 22 Grand Prix were held (the one scheduled for Imola was cancelled, due to flooding)—more than 3× as many. If a point system is used, then the sheer number of points awarded most recently with the current system (Max Verstappen won a stupendous 575 points in 2023) cannot be compared with the earlier competitions (Juan Manuel Fangio, in 1951, won the World Championship with 47 points). The 2023 champion (Max Verstappen) won 12.2× as many points as did the 1951 champion (Manuel Fangio). Sophisticated statistical methods are called for to level the playing field.

1.2 The Gaming Industry

One industry that is amongst the fastest growing is the gaming industry. There were an estimated 3.3 billion active gamers in 2023, an increase of 1 billion in the last 8 years. 37% of the gamers play racing games.

Two of the most played racing games on streaming platforms involve F1; namely F1 22 and F1 22 Manager. There are many variants of F1 games, but some only function on specific devices, while some function on many devices (but not all). For some, mobile phones are included as devices. Moreover, some gamers focus on specific games and specific platforms, while others drive whatever has (virtual) wheels—regardless of platform.

The inferences of how to rank winners and runners-up in VR and XR Formula One video gaming tournaments involving many competitors and many races make the conclusions we draw in this investigation exciting and inferential.

2 Materials: Formula One Race Results

We compare the race results for the 12 drivers listed in Table 1, which includes the time ranges of their participation in the Formula One competition (albeit occasionally with gaps) and lists many multiple winners of the World Championship.

3 Methods

3.1 Conventional Rules and Questionable Comparisons

Since 2010, points have been awarded according to the final ranking at the end of the race (Table 2). Since 2022, a driver completing the fastest lap is awarded an additional point, but only if the driver completes the race within the top ten positions. These points will not be included in the discussion we present here, as they do not contribute to the investigation of GOAT. To be able to make meaningful comparisons, we also list, in Table 1, the performances that do not depend on the point awarding system applicable at the time when the races took place (with one exception: the number of World Championships).

3.2 Rigorous Statistical Comparisons of Point Systems

The post-2010-point system is not the only way to compare the top performance of the drivers competing for being GOAT. We first supply a critique of the shortcomings of using a point system and then show how competition for GOAT changes as other statistical methods as well as other point systems are introduced.

Table 1. Selected performances and achievements of 12 drivers, some occasionally considered eligible for GOAT. Only one of the column entries (namely, the World Championship one) depends on the point system used at the time the championship rank was awarded. The last two columns show considerable variation as to possible criteria for awarding GOAT. *Podiums* are the places 1st, 2nd, or 3rd at the end of the race. Some drivers, who do not qualify for GOAT, are included in this list for statistical comparison purposes. We note that for both the ratios of wins to starts and podiums to starts, Juan Fangio is best, and therefore is—arguably—the GOAT (assuming these two criteria are the only applicable ones). Also note that Lewis Hamilton has $1.7\times$ as many entries as does Max Verstappen, so Verstappen's 29.2% wins per start far outweighs Hamilton's—31.0% further fueling the Hamilton/Verstappen GOAT debate.

Driver	1st year	Last year	Starts	Poles	3rd	2nd	1st (*Wins*)	World Champ	$\frac{Wins}{Starts}$ (%)	$\frac{Podiums}{Starts}$ (%)
Fernando Alonso	2001	present	377	22	34	40	32	2	8.5	28.1
Jim Clark	1960	1968	72	33	6	1	25	2	34.7	44.4
Juan Manuel Fangio	1950	1958	49	29	1	10	24	5	49.0	71.4
Lewis Hamilton	2007	present	332	104	38	56	102	7	30.7	59.0
Niki Lauda	1971	1985	173	24	9	20	25	3	14.5	31.2
Nigel Mansell	1980	1995	186	32	11	17	31	1	16.7	31.7
Alain Prost	1980	1993	198	33	20	35	51	4	25.8	53.5
Michael Schumacher	1991	2012	306	68	21	43	91	7	29.7	50.7
Ayrton Senna	1984	1994	162	65	16	23	41	3	25.3	49.4
Jackie Stewart	1965	1973	99	17	5	11	27	3	27.3	43.4
Max Verstappen	2001	present	185	32	16	28	54	3	29.2	53.0
Sebastian Vettel	1960	2022	299	57	33	36	53	4	17.7	40.8

3.3 Ranking Based on Bayesian Statistics

(a) In Bayesian statistical methods, probability is a random variable s ($0 \leq s \leq 1$). The likelihood function $\mathcal{L}(s)$ informs the most likely probability and its uncertainty. If a driver has won the World Championship n times and had m unsuccessful attempts, the likelihood function is the *pdf* (probability density function) of a Beta distribution, viz.

$$\mathcal{L}(s) = c \times s^n \times (1 - s)^m$$

where the constant c ensures that $\int_0^1 \mathcal{L}(s)ds = 1$. In Fig. 3, we show the 12 likelihood functions and describe in the figure caption the inferences that can be drawn from these. We note that the exponent n depends on the points awarding system, m does not

(b) One investigation that does not involve a point system is to compare the podium achievements. The number of races a driver participated in does influence the number of possible podiums, but the Bayesian methods mitigate this to a certain degree (as Fig. 4 shows).

Assume that a driver, during his career, has achieved n_1 wins, n_2 second places, and n_3 third places. The probabilities for each of these are s_1, s_2, and s_3. Then the likelihood function is the *pdf* of a Dirichlet distribution

$$\mathcal{L}(s_1, s_2) = c \times s_1^{n_1} \times s_2^{n_2} \times (1 - (s_1 + s_2))^{n_3}$$

(because $s_1 + s_2 + s_3 = 1$) and the constant c is again determined by integration.

The two modes (wins and second place) of this likelihood function are

$$m_{win} = \frac{n_1}{n_1 + n_2 + n_3} \text{ and } m_{2nd} = \frac{n_2}{n_1 + n_2 + n_3}.$$

To determine whether the modes are significantly different, we use a Monte Carlo method. For driver A, $pdf_A = pdf\left(Dir(n_1^A, n_2^A, n_3^A), s_1, s_2\right)$ and for driver B, $pdf_B = pdf\left(Dir(n_1^B, n_2^B, n_3^B), s_1, s_2\right)$. We generate N_{ran} random vectors $\{s_1, s_2\}_k k = 1 \ldots N_{ran}$. For each vector, we test whether

$$pdf\left(Dir\left(n_1^A, n_2^A, n_3^A\right), \{s_1, s_2\}_k\right) > pdf\left(Dir\left(n_1^B, n_2^B, n_3^B\right), \{s_1, s_2\}_k\right).$$

We tally n_{true}^A and $n_{false}^A = N_{ran} - n_{true}^A$. We repeat these calculations for driver B and find n_{true}^B and $n_{false}^B = N_{ran} - n_{true}^B$. (Note that the random vectors generated with pdf_A will differ from those generated with pdf_B.)

We construct the confusion matrix

$$\frac{1}{N_{ran}} \begin{pmatrix} n_{true}^A & n_{false}^A \\ n_{false}^B & n_{true}^B \end{pmatrix}.$$

If the off-diagonal entries are very small, then the modes are significantly different. The ratios $\frac{n_{false}^A}{N_{ran}}$ and $\frac{n_{false}^B}{N_{ran}}$ (the off-diagonal entries) are the significance levels; both must be small in the case of a significant result.

We present two examples from the world of European association football (soccer in US-American parlance).

(i) In the English *Premier League*, after 21 rounds in 2023/24, the wins, losses, and ties for Liverpool were $\left(n_1^A \ n_2^A \ n_3^A\right) = \left(14 \ 1 \ 6, \right)$ and for Manchester United, they were $\left(n_1^B \ n_2^B \ n_3^B\right) = \left(10 \ 9 \ 2\right)$. We twice generate $N_{ran} = 50000$ random numbers (once for Liverpool and once for Manchester United) and obtain the following confusion matrix $\begin{pmatrix} 99.1 & 0.9 \\ 0.8 & 99.2 \end{pmatrix}$%. The higher ranking for Liverpool (14 wins and 1 loss) is *significantly* superior to Manchester United's ranking (10 wins and 9 losses). (Sorry, ManU fans!)

(ii) In Spain, the rivalry between Real Madrid and FC Barcelona is legendary. After 20 rounds in the *Primera Division* in the season 2023/24, the Madrid performances were $\left(n_1^A \, n_2^A \, n_3^A \right) = \left(16 \, 1 \, 3 \right)$, and for Barcelona, they were $\left(n_1^B \, n_2^B \, n_3^B \right) = \left(13 \, 2 \, 5 \right)$. The confusion matrix $\begin{pmatrix} 78.4 & 21.6 \\ 19.0 & 81.0 \end{pmatrix}\%$ shows that the rankings of these two teams are not significantly different. Indeed, after 20 rounds, they are ranked 2nd and 3rd with 51 and 44 league points, respectively (when using the current point-awarding system of *win* $\rightarrow$ 3, *tie* $\rightarrow$ 1 and *loss* $\rightarrow$ 0). This example shows that a point system is both arbitrary (and must be agreed on) and statistically questionable. The point system is necessary for fans, because, among other reasons, it enables them to follow their favorite team's performance easily.

Table 2. The points awarded for the rank of a driver upon completion of the race. Blanks indicate where no points were awarded. The year in the top row is the year in which the point system that replaced the previous one was adopted. The last three columns are not Formula One point systems. 'motoGP' are the points currently awarded in the motorcycle Grand Prix system; 'PrimesA' and 'PrimesB' are artificially constructed; they are sequences of primes that are mapped into the set of the first 15 ranks and first 5 ranks, respectively.

Rank	1950	1960	1991	2003	2010	motoGP	PrimesA	PrimesB
1st	8	8	10	10	25	25	67	47
2nd	6	6	6	8	18	20	61	41
3rd	4	4	4	6	15	16	59	31
4th	3	3	3	5	12	13	53	23
5th	2	2	2	4	10	11	47	17
6th		1	1	3	8	10	43	
7th				2	6	9	41	
8th				1	4	8	37	
9th					2	7	31	
10th					1	6	29	
11th						5	23	
12th						4	19	
13th						3	17	
14th						2	13	
15th						1	11	

4 Findings

(a) If we calculate the fractions of World Championships wins versus starts (Fig. 1), Fangio is the GOAT. However, winning the World Championship depends on the points award system. Remarkably, Stewart and Clark rank as 2nd and 3rd.

(b) If we compare rankings according to different point systems (Fig. 2), we find that Fangio is GOAT in all Formula One point-awarding systems, and also in MotoGP. Only in one case of an artificially constructed point awarding system is Fangio outranked by Hamilton. Figure 2 also shows that Verstappen is always 3rd, but there is no consistency for the remaining 8 drivers.

(c) The Beta distributions (which also rely on the point system when the driver won the World Championship), show that Fangio is the GOAT. However, the other drivers cluster, with Hamilton's 2nd and Schumacher's 3rd not significantly different. Furthermore, if Verstappen wins two more World Championships (irrespective of the number of starts), then he will overtake both Hamilton and Schumacher (details available from the author).

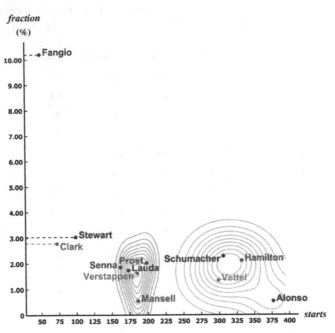

Fig. 1. A graph showing the distribution of fractions of starts that resulted in winning the Formula One World Championship. We observe that Schumacher needed considerably fewer starts (306) to achieve his seven World Championships than did Hamilton (332), so Hamilton's fraction is somewhat less than Schumacher's. We observe that the 2nd highest fraction is Stewart's, and Clark's fraction is 3rd highest. In this analysis method, we obtain the surprising result that both Stewart and Clark are significantly better than the conventionally expected Schuhmacher and Hamilton. Fangio is in a class by himself; the first indication that he qualifies for the title GOAT. The contour lines indicate the clustering of two batches of drivers. The probability density functions generating these contours are KDEs (Kernel Density Estimates) using an Epanechnikov kernel.

(d) The confusion matrices derived from the 12 likelihood functions for podium achievements are often not significantly different (Fig. 4). However, some are significantly
different for the drivers Alonso, Clark, Hamilton/Verstappen, and Fangio (Table 3).
In particular, the likelihood functions for the pair Hamilton/Verstappen are not *significantly* different. Interestingly, this insignificance sheds an unfortunate light on
and perhaps should avoid fuelling the acrimony in the debate about who is the GOAT:
Hamilton or Verstappen. Indeed, neither is. It is Fangio! We note that this finding
does not depend on any point-awarding system.

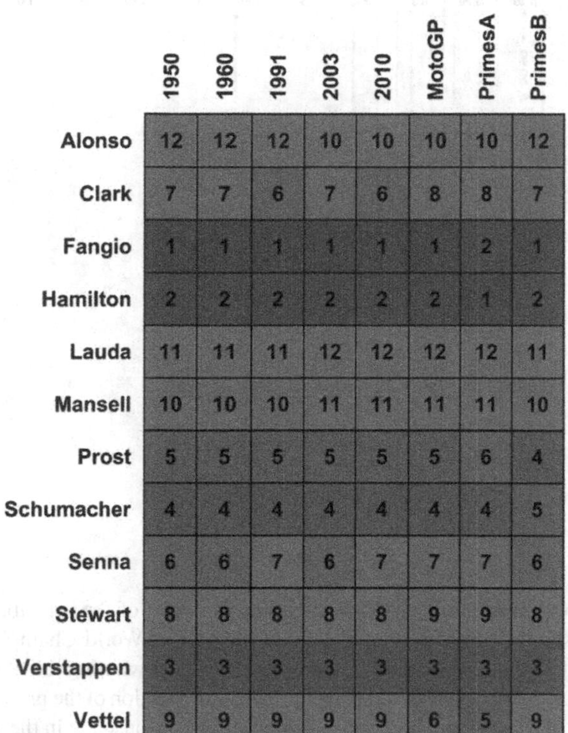

	1950	1960	1991	2003	2010	MotoGP	PrimesA	PrimesB
Alonso	12	12	12	10	10	10	10	12
Clark	7	7	6	7	6	8	8	7
Fangio	1	1	1	1	1	1	2	1
Hamilton	2	2	2	2	2	2	1	2
Lauda	11	11	11	12	12	12	12	11
Mansell	10	10	10	11	11	11	11	10
Prost	5	5	5	5	5	5	6	4
Schumacher	4	4	4	4	4	4	4	5
Senna	6	6	7	6	7	7	7	6
Stewart	8	8	8	8	8	9	9	8
Verstappen	3	3	3	3	3	3	3	3
Vettel	9	9	9	9	9	6	5	9

Fig. 2. A heat map showing the ranking of the drivers investigated in the manuscript as a function
of the point award system (Table 2). Because the points awarded for the places achieved at the
end of the race varied historically, it is not possible to directly compare the points achieved as
published in commonly distributed tables. This heat map demonstrates how the point-awarding
system changes the rankings; we have included other ranking systems (Table 2) to further document
(and accentuate) the effect.

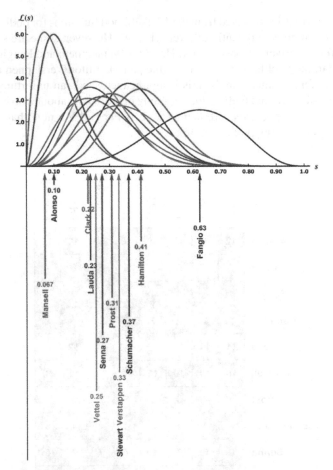

Fig. 3. The likelihood functions $\mathcal{L}(s)$ of the Beta distributions of the probability s of winning a World Championship in Formula One. If n is the number of World Championships won and m is the number of failed attempts (with probability $(1 - s)$) at winning the championship, then $\mathcal{L}(s) = const \times s^n \times (1 - s)^m$. Note that the likelihood $\mathcal{L}$ is a function of the probability $0 \le s \le 1$. We observe that the likelihood functions cluster: Mansell and Alonso are in the 1st cluster; Clark, Lauda, Vettel, and Senna are in the 2nd cluster; Verstappen, Schumacher, Stewart, and Hamilton are in the 3rd cluster. Fangio is in his own cluster and, consequently, had a much higher probability of winning a World Championship for each attempt. (It is indeed spectacular that his probability of winning a World Championship is almost $^2/_3$.) The numbers at the bases of the arrows are the (rounded) most likely probabilities for each driver investigated in this manuscript. Stewart and Verstappen currently have the same most likely probabilities.

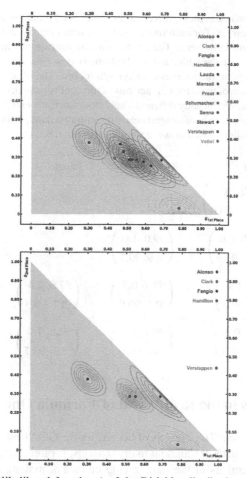

Fig. 4. The *pdf*s (the likelihood functions) of the Dirichlet distributions of the podium performances for (above) all 12 drivers investigated in this paper and (below) the five drivers Alonso, Clark, Fangio, Hamilton, and Verstappen. The contours of constant likelihood of the *pdf*s of the Dirichlet distributions are in steps of $\frac{1}{7}\mathcal{L}_{max}$ (where the maximum likelihood is different for different drivers). Podium distributions are in Table 1. The *pdf*s of the Dirichlet distributions are only defined over the triangle (shown in light gray), because the 3rd probability is constrained: $s_3 = 1 - (s_1 + s_2)$, where s_k is the probability of achieving k^{th} ($k = 1 \ldots 3$) rank after the race. The colored, black-rimmed points are the positions of the maximum likelihood for each driver's podium performance. In (above), we observe that most drivers' *pdf*s overlap considerably (except for Clark's), so there are no pair-wise significant differences between their podium achievements. In (below), we observe that (i) the achievements of Alonso, Hamilton, Clark, and Fangio are significantly different, while those of Hamilton versus Verstappen are not, evidenced in Table 3. (See text for details about the confusion matrices.) (ii) We observe that Clark has a better podium performance than does Alonso (maximum likelihood is further to the right and 1st rank counts more than 2nd rank). We also observe that the maximum likelihood shifts from Hamilton to Verstappen to Fangio are the direction of increasingly better podium probabilities. (Their 2nd place probabilities are very close to constant, but their 1st place probabilities increase from Hamilton to Verstappen to Fangio.) Interestingly, Verstappen's podium performance is better than Hamilton's (but not significantly, Table 3), despite Verstappen having completed only slightly more than half Hamilton's completed races (56%; 185 versus 332; Table 1). Again, as in many other comparisons, Fangio is the GOAT

Table 3. The confusion matrices for the drivers whose likelihood functions are displayed in Fig. 4 (below). Entries are in percent. For each row in each confusion matrix, 25000 random numbers were generated (details are in the text). The top rows in the confusion matrix are the entries for the driver in the columns of the table, and the bottom rows are the drivers in the row of the table. Note that the confusion matrix is not always symmetric. The off-diagonal entries are the significance levels. The sum of the entries in each row of the confusion matrix is 100%. We observe that all drivers listed have significantly different likelihood functions except for Hamilton versus Verstappen. These two therefore have insignificantly different podium performances, while for all the other pairings, the podium differences are significantly different.

	Alonso	Clark	Fangio	Hamilton
Clark	$\begin{pmatrix} 100.0 & 0.0 \\ 0.0 & 100.0 \end{pmatrix}$			
Fangio	$\begin{pmatrix} 100.0 & 0.0 \\ 0.1 & 99.9 \end{pmatrix}$	$\begin{pmatrix} 99.0 & 1.0 \\ 0.9 & 99.1 \end{pmatrix}$		
Hamilton	$\begin{pmatrix} 99.6 & 0.4 \\ 0.3 & 99.7 \end{pmatrix}$	$\begin{pmatrix} 99.7 & 0.3 \\ 0.1 & 99.9 \end{pmatrix}$	$\begin{pmatrix} 97.6 & 2.4 \\ 0.7 & 99.3 \end{pmatrix}$	
Verstappen	$\begin{pmatrix} 99.7 & 0.3 \\ 0.5 & 99.5 \end{pmatrix}$	$\begin{pmatrix} 99.1 & 0.9 \\ 0.4 & 99.6 \end{pmatrix}$	$\begin{pmatrix} 92.6 & 7.4 \\ 3.3 & 96.7 \end{pmatrix}$	$\begin{pmatrix} 80.4 & 9.6 \\ 38.9 & 61.1 \end{pmatrix}$

5 Complications in the Real World of Formula One

(a) Teammate dominance: The chances of becoming the GOAT increase if a driver can dominate his teammates throughout many seasons. It rarely happens that drivers of equal skill are members of the same racing car team, making it difficult to make a neutral comparison. For example, Schumacher's dominance over Barrichello and Verstappen's over Perez didn't matter much. It did, though, when Senna gave away a world title to Prost and Hamilton to Rosberg.

(b) Performing in an inferior car under challenging conditions: Senna and Schumacher are remembered for their outstanding performance in wet weather conditions, despite (partially) damaged cars.

(c) Willingness to take risks: In the days of Fangio, participating in a Grand Prix posed a high risk of fatal incidents, with security not being the highest concern then.

(d) Team development: Having a driver's seat in an inferior car and being able to improve the car's performance throughout multiple seasons is something Schumacher was able to achieve with Ferrari, whereas Vettel failed in that very same task.

(e) Being favored by rule changes: The interval of rule changes, especially those involving significant design changes, can mean a team dropping in performance after almost winning a title. On multiple occasions, teams were able to maintain their dominance (Schumacher's titles with Ferrari, Vettel's with Red Bull, and Verstappen's with Red Bull).

6 Conclusion

WIKIPEDIA lists, under the heading "Formula One video games", 176 of them—the earliest dating from 1976 and the most recent ones released in 2023. To our knowledge, all these video games adhere to the rules/regulations and point-scoring systems in existence at the time the video games were released.

Our analyses show that it is possible to rank winners and runners-up without entering a controversy about whether a point awarding system is fair or not. The Dirichlet distributions are defined for an arbitrary number of rankings at the end of races, albeit the ranks 1st, 2nd, and 3rd are arguably the most sensible.

We do not propose altering the Formula One rules and regulations for the actual Formula One Grand Prix World Championship—Liberty Media would rightfully worry about losing many more than only some of its vast viewership.

Based on the outcomes of the analyses we present here, we propose deleting scoring systems for future video game tournaments, allowing for a fairer assessment of the skills of the gamers.

We note that the above-described approach (of using Dirichlet distributions of podium places) remains applicable even for the cases when players switch devices, and platforms, and are active for different periods. It should not be overlooked that the same statistical methodology we present here can be applied to any online server community to rank their gamers within a tournament. In addition, if Bayesian methods are used, outcomes from different tournaments and platforms are possible, even if the point systems vary from platform to platform or from tournament to tournament. This is a considerable bonus for the gaming industry.

Also, gamer preferences, their performance, and their desired device usage can be used to tailor the game design, programmed mechanics of the virtual race cars, and display graphics. Certain player segments and device types, based on comparisons of immersion, are issues. Some players can transfer easily across multiple devices and game formats. Such data can be used to identify common growing pain issues during beta phases of a new game in development, areas for its improvement, and deal with potential bugs and/or glitches. As part of this analysis mainly considers gaming as an entertainment enterprise we provide descriptions for gamer-oriented designs. If adopted by the gaming industry, the revenues generated by this approach would increase.

The title of this presentation asked a question. Irrespective of game design issues, we are in a position to answer it. Based on the four ranking analyses we have performed here, Fangio is the GOAT!

Ethics Statement. All awarded points and ranks over the entire history of Formula One are publicly available. This data was used.

Conflict of Interest. The authors declare no conflict of interest.

References

Autoracing.com (2023) F1: 2022 TV viewership hits 1.54 billion. AR1 Staff Posting, (2023)

Dyvik, E.H.: World Population by Age and Region, Statista (2023). https://www.statista.com/sta tistics/265759/world-population-by-age-and-region/

Gehmacher, W., Clooney, G.: How boring can a Formula One Video Game be? Sky Sports, London, UK (2020)

Stoll, J.: How many people watch the Super Bowl? Statista (2023). https://www.statista.com/sta tistics/216526/super-bowl-us-tv-viewership/

The Impact of Playfulness Trait on Attitude and Intention Towards Gamified Health Behavior

Yang Qiu[1,2]([⊠]), Toh Hsiang Benny Tan[1], Chan Hua Nicholas Vun[2], and Zhiqi Shen[2]

[1] Joint NTU-WeBank Research Centre on FinTech, Nanyang Technological University, Singapore, Singapore
{qiuyang,bennytanth}@ntu.edu.sg
[2] School of Computer Science and Engineering, Nanyang Technological University, Singapore, Singapore
{aschvun,zqshen}@ntu.edu.sg

Abstract. Despite the growing use of gamification in healthcare to encourage positive health behaviors, its overall effectiveness is still uncertain. This study explores the hypothesis that individual differences in playfulness - a predisposition to engage enjoyably with situations - might significantly influence an individual's attitude and intention towards gamified health practices. To test this, a survey was conducted, focusing on three hypotheses: the positive impact of playfulness on attitudes towards gamified health behaviors, its influence on behavioral intentions, and the interaction between attitudes and intentions. Data analysis was conducted using Partial Least Squares based Structural Equation Modeling (PLS-SEM), involving 297 participants. The results highlighted a significant positive correlation between playfulness and both attitudes and intentions towards gamified health interventions, indicating that individuals with more pronounced playfulness traits are likely to be more receptive to these interventions. This finding emphasizes the importance of factoring in the playfulness trait when designing and implementing gamification solutions in healthcare settings.

Keywords: gamification · playfulness · healthcare · attitude · behavior intention

1 Introduction

Gamification began its rise to prominence during the latter part of 2010, bolstered by successful business cases, public exposure and the increasing influence of gaming in everyday culture [1]. It was soon introduced into the healthcare sector as a potential strategy to encourage positive health behaviors. However, despite a decade of advancements, the ability of gamification to consistently elicit desired health behavior outcomes is still unconclusive [2]. Tailored gamification, aims to enhance the effectiveness by taking into account characteristic differences between individuals such as demographics, player typology, or motivation [3]. This study seeks to contribute to existing literature in this area by bringing scholarly attention to an understudied characteristic: playfulness as a personal trait.

X. Fang (Ed.): HCII 2024, LNCS 14730, pp. 81–97, 2024.
https://doi.org/10.1007/978-3-031-60692-2_7

The trait of playfulness has been studied in psychology as a personal characteristic predisposition, that makes the individual more likely to engage in a situation or environment and find it more enjoyable or entertaining [4, 5, 6, 7]. It has been defined as: "the predisposition to frame (or reframe) a situation in such a way as to provide oneself (and possibly others) with amusement, humor, and/or entertainment" [4].

Playfulness has not been extensively studied in gamification research. Since its inception, definitions of gamification have revolved around the concept of games rather than play [8]. It is regarded as the design strategy of using game design elements for gamefulness, which denotes the experiential and behavioral qualities for gaming, while the term playfulness denotes the experiential and behavioral qualities of playing [8]. While playfulness was identified as a largely underexplored concept in the field of gamification for health behavior change earlier in 2013 [9], even after a decade, this substantial research gap remains unaddressed. In studies involving the concept of playfulness, it is commonly presented as a sub-construct of gamefulness, measured as perceived playfulness, and used to describe the fun aspect of the gamified system [10].

A focused discussion on playfulness comes from the framework of meaningful gamification and its concept of playification. Introduced in 2012 as a parallel concept to gamification, playification aimed to incorporate the playfulness and playful elements missing from traditional gamification approaches [11]. Playification was meant to shift gamification researchers' focus onto a more playful, less regulated, and more spontaneous way of integrating playful elements in non-play environments [11–12]. However, the concept advocates for user empowerment and autonomy, to such an extent that even the essentiality of play where a user interacts with the gamification should be optional for it to be genuine [11]. Such stance did not gain widespread acceptance to date.

As gamification research keeps evolving and attracting broader attention, there is a tendency in the research field to include playfulness into the discussion of gamification. Game study scholars have argued for gamefulness as an extension of playfulness, tying to bring the two concepts together rather than viewing them as opposing types of play [13]. In The gameful world, Deterding sees a gameful world that the ludification of culture is driving towards and has included play form and play rhetoric as two rhetoric of the gameful world [1]. In Landers' attempts to replace 'gamefulness' with three distinct terms, playfulness as a trait, along with other user characteristics, was hypothesized to potentially moderate the effectiveness of gamification in creating gameful experiences [14].

At first glance, the expression of playfulness and health behaviors may not seem compatible. Many if not most health behaviors require extra efforts and are less pleasant compared to the alternatives. Some of which is even accompanied with severe pain and discomfort. Approaching these behaviors with a playful mindset seems difficult, since the expression of playfulness requires certain environmental conditions such as a feeling of safety. However, playfulness can be engaged in almost any situation [15]. In existing studies of playfulness in healthcare, playfulness is found to be positively related to one's health behavior in three ways: Firstly, it can promote health behaviors via positive affect: Playful personalities give rise to feeling playful more frequently which is associated itself with experiencing a pleasant and positive feeling. The experienced positive affect may also act against (emotional) distress, which may be a hindering factor for engaging in health behavior [16]. Secondly, playfulness can so provide action orientated tendencies toward curiosity, exploration, or physical activities [17–19]. Thirdly, a playful person may be more interested in engaging in health-promoting activities and pursue a more active way of life [16, 20, 21].

The existing research gaps concerning playfulness in gamification, combined with the potential synergies between the playfulness trait and health behaviors, have motivated this study.

2 Hypothesis

This study seeks to investigate the potential impact of the playfulness trait on an individuals' attitudes and behavioral intentions within the context of healthcare gamification through the validation of three core hypotheses.

Playfulness as an inherent trait is characterized by an individual's innate inclination towards spontaneous and enjoyable activities. Individuals with a pronounced playfulness trait are more lighthearted, fun-seeking and more pursuing an active way of life [16, 22]. Within the healthcare domain, evidence suggests that individuals with a pronounced playfulness trait exhibit a more favorable attitude towards features of mobile health monitoring applications [23].

Gamification seeks to incorporate elements of play and game into traditionally routine or challenging tasks. The primary intention of introducing these elements is to make the activity more engaging. Individuals with a pronounced playfulness trait are likely to be more receptive to these game elements, aligning with their intrinsic inclination. Thus, it is plausible to hypothesize that individuals with a pronounced playfulness trait would exhibit a more favorable disposition towards gamified health behaviors. Similarly, varying levels of the playfulness trait could potentially account for varying attitudes towards the same gamified system observed in prior studies. For instance, while some participants enjoyed outdoor physical activity with Pokémon Go, seeing it as an exhilarating experience [24], others believed it should remain purely a recreational game and not an exercise tool [25]. Similarly, while some appraised gamified systems as being fun and engaging, others felt that the gamification undermined the task, trivialized it and made it less meaningful [26]. Thus, the first hypothesis proposed by this study is:

H0: There is a positive impact of playfulness trait on attitude.

The playfulness trait is also expected to show a direct positive influence on behavioral intention. Gamified health behaviors embody attributes of both playful activities and serious health actions. From the perspective of play, the playfulness trait inherently promotes playful activities. When viewed from a health standpoint, playfulness has been demonstrated to enhance positive affect towards health behaviors and foster proactive tendencies towards physical activities [16, 18]. Consequently, it is postulated that the playfulness trait can directly influence intentions towards gamified health behaviors. The study's second hypothesis is articulated as:

H1: There is a positive impact of playfulness trait on gamified health behavior intention.

The significant influence of attitude on behavioral intention is well-established and widely recognized, with one prominent exampling being the Theory of Planned Behavior (TPB) [27]. This relationship has been hypothesized and validated across various domains, including within the realm of gamification. Consequently, the final hypothesis of this study is articulated as:

H2: There is a positive impact of attitude on gamified health behavior intention.

The research model of this study is presented in Fig. 1.

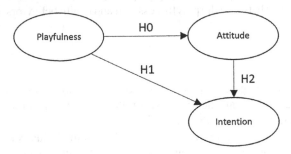

Fig. 1. Research model.

3 Methodology

To test the proposed hypotheses, a cross-sectional descriptive survey was conducted. Since the aim of this study is to confirm the influence of playfulness on gamified health behavior intention, a cross-sectional survey capturing data at a single point in time without the need for prolonged and resource-intensive follow-ups was chosen for its efficiency and cost-effectiveness. This design is also able to facilitate a broad snapshot of populations, enhancing generalizability.

3.1 Sample and Data Collection

The survey was designed for the general adult population without specific characteristics in mind. Hosted on the Survey Monkey online platform for a duration of one month, participants were recruited with the following criteria: (a) aged between 18 to 65, and (b) proficient in reading and comprehending English. Respondents were compensated for their time, and of the 403 responses received during the survey's active window, 297 were deemed valid and used for analysis.

3.2 Instrument

The instrument created for this study comprises 24 items (see Appendix). This included 19 items to assess playfulness trait, 3 items to assess attitude, and 2 items to evaluate behavior intention. All measurements utilized a 7-point Likert scale, spanning from strongly disagree to strongly agree.

To measure playfulness, the 19 item Adult playfulness trait scale (APTS) developed by Shen et al. [28] which models playfulness trait as a third-order latent structure was adopted. It comprises five primary constructs: *fun belief*, *initiative*, *reactivity*, *uninhibitedness*, and *spontaneity*. Additionally, a secondary construct, *fun-Seeking motivation*, is used to amalgamate *fun belief*, *initiative*, and *reactivity*. The multi-facet structure is deemed to fit well with other literature in playfulness research and has been confirmed and validated in multiple studies [29]. APTS was originally developed in English. All of its items were adopted in this study without alteration.

The attitude questionnaire employed in this research encompasses three distinct items. Traditionally, attitude assessments have focused on specific systems or behaviors. This study, however, deviates from this norm. Instead of targeting a particular system or behavior, it emphasizes the broader theme of "gamified health behavior". Recognizing that this might be an unfamiliar concept to many, especially to those not acquainted with gamification applications, the questionnaire's three items were designed to assess participants' receptivity and attitude towards the idea of incorporating elements of play and games into health behaviors, specifically in diet management and physical activity. Attitude refers to a predisposition to evaluate some object in a favorable or unfavorable manner [30]. The phrasing of the items was carefully chosen to encapsulate this definition.

In order to measure behavior intention towards gamified health behavior, two new items were developed. Given that this study does not focus on specific systems already in use by the participants, the items measured intention to use via a hypothetical scenario.

To offer a context grounded in healthcare gamification, the measurement items for both attitude and behavioral intention were contextualized within the healthcare domain. Given that the study aims at the general population and does not focus on a specific illness, we selected fitness maintenance as the overarching healthcare theme. Two universally relevant health behaviors, diet management and physical exercise, were highlighted. These behaviors were chosen for their broad applicability making them relatable for a wide spectrum of participants.

3.3 Data Analysis

This study employs Structure Equation Modeling (SEM) for data analysis. SEM encompasses a suite of statistical methodologies that facilitate the measurement and analysis of relationships between latent variables, both independent and dependent. There are two major approaches in SEM: Covariance Based SEM (CB-SEM) and Partial Least Squares SEM (PLS-SEM). CB-SEM prioritizes the fitting of a theoretical model to the observed covariance matrix and is especially apt when the primary focus is on theory testing. In contrast, PLS-SEM emphasizes the explanation of variance and is more accommodating of smaller sample sizes and non-normal data. Its strength lies in theory development and predictive analysis. Both approaches were employed in this study with different focuses.

Preliminary Analysis. Survey data from the 297 participants was analysed with IBM SPSS Statistics 26. The dataset was first examined for its normality. Both Shapiro-Wilk test and Kolmogorov-Smirnov (K-S) test concluded that the data has a non-normal distribution (all items $p < .001$). In the preliminary analysis to assess the suitability of the data for factor analysis, the Kaiser-Meyer-Olkin (KMO) Measure of Sampling Adequacy was determined to be .909. This value, being close to 1, denotes that the patterns of correlations amongst variables are relatively compact, suggesting that factor analysis should yield distinct and reliable factors. Furthermore, the Bartlett's Test of Sphericity was significant ($\chi 2(253) = 3194.182$, p < .000), implying that the observed correlation matrix significantly deviates from an identity matrix. These two metrics showed that the dataset is appropriate for the subsequent factor analysis.

Confirmatory Factor Analysis of APTS. A Confirmatory Factor Analysis (CFA) was conducted to ascertain if the gathered data fit the predetermined model. To this end, a maximum likelihood-based CFA was executed on the APTS using Covariance-based Structural Equation Modeling (CB-SEM) in IBM SPSS Amos 26. Since the data appears non-normally distributed, bootstrapping was used to provide more accurate standard errors and confidence intervals in CB-SEM. Four criteria were employed to assess the model fit, root mean square error of approximation (RMSEA), comparative fit index (CFI), Tucker-Lewis Index (TLI) and Standardized Root Mean Square Residual (SRMR).

For RMSEA, values below .08 indicate an adequate fit, while values below .05 are indicative of a good fit [31]. For CFI, a value greater than .90 is considered to be adequate (Bentler, 1990), while values exceeding .95 are indicative of a good fit [32]. For TLI, values greater than .90 are indicative of an adequate fit, while those exceeding .95 denote a good fit [32]. For SRMR, values at or below .08 reflect a reasonably good fit [32].

Partial Least Squares Structural Equation Modeling (PLS-SEM). A Partial Least Squares Structural Equation Modeling (PLS-SEM) was conducted in SmartPLS4 to test the hypotheses. The model assessment was conducted in a two-step approach [33]: a measurement model analysis followed by a structural model analysis.

Factor loadings were examined to establish indicator reliability, a threshold of 0.7 is employed, although values just above 0.60 might be deemed acceptable, especially if the variable holds significant theoretical importance, as outlined by Hair et al. [34].

Construct reliability was examined through Cronbach's Alpha and Composite Reliability (rho_c) metrics. While both should ideally exceed 0.70 for internal consistency, for Cronbach's Alpha, values over 0.60 can also be seen as acceptable [35]. Convergent validity was then evaluated by calculating the Average Variance Extracted (AVE), where values above 0.50 are considered adequate.

For assessing discriminant validity, Heterotrait-monotrait ratio (HTMT) and the Fornell-Larcker Criterion were employed. Ideally, the HTMT ratio should not exceed 0.85. Per the Fornell-Larcker Criterion, the square root of the AVE for each construct should surpass its correlations with other constructs.

To inspect potential multicollinearity issues among measurement items, Variance Inflation Factor (VIF) was calculated. Values below 5 are indicative of acceptable multicollinearity levels.

After all the items and constructs were validated, A structural model was constructed to test the hypotheses. First, the variance inflation factor (VIF) was calculated for each construct in the path to ensure no multicollinearity issues. Subsequently, to test the hypnotized relationships between the constructs, a path analysis using the bootstrapping method was performed. The magnitude and direction of the connections between constructs were determined using standardized path coefficients. A close to 1 path coefficient indicates strong tie between the linked variables. A value near 0 implied limited or non-existent relationships. The statistical significance of a path coefficient, shown by p-values, either supports or contradicts the initial hypothesis.

Explanatory Power, Effect Size and Predictive Relevance. For PLS interpretation, explanatory power (R-square) values below 0.19 are viewed as very weak, those between 0.19 and 0.33 as weak, between 0.34 and 0.67 as moderate, and any value exceeding 0.67 as substantial [36]. Effect size (F-square) under 0.2 signify no effect, those ranging from 0.02 to 0.14 are small, between 0.15 and 0.34 are medium, and any value above 0.35 is indicative of a large effect based on Cohen's conventions [37]. A predictive relevance (Q-square) value under 0 suggest imprecise prediction, a zero value indicates prediction incapability, and any value over 0 signifies predictive relevance.

4 Results

4.1 Participants

Socio-demographic characteristics of the 297 participants is shown in Table 1. Males dominate the sample, comprising 68.4% (203 participants). During sampling, efforts were made to try to achieve a balanced age distribution across groups. A significant majority, 79.8% (237 participants), have attained higher education levels.

4.2 Confirmatory Factor Analysis of APTS

A CFA was performed on a third order APTS model as it was originally proposed. The original model exhibited a less than ideal model fit with CFI merely above 0.9 (0.906) and a TLI below 0.9 (0.889). Upon a careful examination of the factors and referencing the modification indices, two adjustments were made. First, an item under *uninhibitedness* was removed due to a low factor loading (0.340). Secondly, based on the modification indices, there was a notable correlation between the error variances of

Table 1. Participant characteristics.

Characteristic	Sample (N = 297)
Gender	
Male	203 (68.4%)
Female	94 (31.6%)
Age (year)	
18–34	92 (31.0%)
35–44	88 (29.6%)
45–54	77 (25.9%)
55–65	40 (13.5%)
Educational level	
Secondary education or lower	60 (20.2%)
Higher education	237 (79.8%)

two items categorized under *spontaneity*. These items, "I often do things on the spur of the moment" and "I often do unplanned things," appear to have overlapping meaning. Consequently, a covariance was introduced between their variances (see Fig. 2). A test performed after the adjustment showed a relatively good model fit, shown in Table 2. To avoid overfitting, no further adjustments were made to the model.

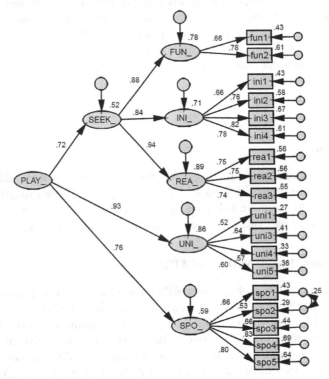

Fig. 2. Adjusted CFA model of APTS.

Table 2. Fit indices of the adjusted model.

ChiSqr	df	ChiSqr/df	RMSEA	SRMR	TLI	CFI	AIC
290.342	124	2.341	0.607	0.55	0.907	0.925	384.342

4.3 PLS-SEM of the Research Model

Measurement model was constructed based on the research model of this study. Reliability and validity of the latent constructs in the model were first examined.

Reliability and Validity. Reliability related indexes are detailed in Table 3. In terms of indicator reliability, majority of the items showed a factor loading above 0.70. Three items (UNI1, UNI4, SPO2) were slightly below the threshold but were close enough to be considered acceptable.

Table 3. Evaluation indices of the measurement mode.

Constructs	Items	Factor loadings	CA	CR (rho_c)	AVE	VIF
Fun belief	FUN1	0.853	0.676	0.860	0.755	1.352
	FUN2	0.884				1.352
Initiative	INI1	0.726	0.838	0.891	0.673	1.558
	INI2	0.822				1.946
	INI3	0.874				2.359
	INI4	0.852				2.036
Reactivity	REA1	0.821	0.790	0.877	0.704	1.625
	REA2	0.839				1.616
	REA3	0.857				1.769
Uninhibitedness	UNI1	0.642	0.668	0.800	0.501	1.177
	UNI3	0.793				1.347
	UNI4	0.670				1.268
	UNI5	0.718				1.341
Spontaneity	SPO1	0.761	0.834	0.878	0.594	1.657
	SPO2	0.626				1.549
	SPO3	0.734				1.749
	SPO4	0.854				2.294
	SPO5	0.856				2.064
Attitude	ATT1	0.828	0.779	0.872	0.694	1.630
	ATT2	0.864				1.850
	ATT3	0.805				1.499
Intention	INT1	0.889	0.740	0.885	0.794	1.528
	INT2	0.893				1.528

For internal consistency assessment, a majority of the constructs showcased CA values above 0.70 with *fun belief* and *uninhibitedness* slightly below the benchmark. The two constructs with values greater than 0.60 were retained due to their theoretical significance. All CR values are above the threshold, signifying a good composite reliability.

Variance Inflation Factor (VIF) was examined for each construct to evaluate potential multicollinearity issues. All constructs in this study displayed VIF values well below the threshold, signifying no multicollinearity issues among the constructs.

Convergent validity was assessed using the Average Variance Extracted (AVE). An AVE value of 0.50 or above is desirable as it indicates that, on average, a construct explains more than half of the variance of its indicators. All constructs achieved AVE values above the benchmark, underlining the satisfactory convergent validity of the measurement model.

Results of discriminant validity with the Heterotrait-Monotrait ratio (HTMT) and the Fornell-Larcker Criterion are presented in Tables 4 and 5, respectively.

Table 4. Heterotrait-monotrait ratio (HTMT).

	Att	Fun	Ini	Int	Rea	Spo	Uni
Attitude							
Fun belief	0.640						
Initiative	0.756	0.780					
Intention	0.790	0.799	0.536				
Reactivity	0.750	0.857	0.783	0.734			
Spontaneity	0.442	0.419	0.509	0.385	0.494		
Uninhibitedness	0.568	0.512	0.657	0.416	0.657	0.744	

Table 5. Fornell-Larcker Criterion test.

	Att	Fun	Ini	Int	Rea	Spo	Uni
Attitude	**0.833**						
Fun belief	0.465	**0.869**					
Initiative	0.620	0.579	**0.821**				
Intention	0.600	0.567	0.429	**0.891**			
Reactivity	0.588	0.629	0.639	0.562	**0.839**		
Spontaneity	0.388	0.339	0.438	0.330	0.419	**0.771**	
Uninhibitedness	0.409	0.350	0.489	0.304	0.475	0.561	**0.708**

The results revealed HTMT values below the recommended threshold for all construct pairs, suggesting distinctiveness among them. Result from the Fornell-Larcker Criterion test indicates that the square root of the Average Variance Extracted (AVE) for each construct (diagonal values) was greater than its correlations with other constructs (off-diagonal values). For instance, *attitude*'s square root of AVE (0.833) surpassed its correlations with other constructs, such as 0.465 with *fun belief*. This pattern was consistent across all constructs, affirming the discriminant validity of the constructs in the model.

Since the model involves higher-order constructs (HOC), their validity was also assessed. The disjoint two-stage approach was employed to represent the higher-order reflective-reflective constructs in this study [38]. In this approach, lower-order constructs were first assessed in relation to their respective indicators within the measurement model, a process already completed. Latent variable scores of the lower-order constructs were obtained. Subsequently, these scores were then used as indicators for the higher-order construct within the path model. Constructs not involved in this hierarchical aggregation remained unaltered. Due to *playfulness* been a third-order construct, the process has been repeated twice. Same tests were performed to evaluate the reliability and validity of the higher-order constructs. The test results are shown in Table 6 which demonstrate good reliability and validity.

Table 6. Reliability and validity of higher order constructs (HOC).

HOC	LOCs	Outer Loadings	CA	CR	AVE	VIF
Playfulness	Fun-seeking	0.878	0.760	0.856	0.665	1.454
	Uni	0.799				1.659
	Spo	0.765				1.545
Fun-seeking	Fun	0.847	0.828	0.897	0.744	1.814
	Ini	0.855				1.853
	Rea	0.885				2.037

The aforementioned assessments confirm the reliability and validity of the measurement model. Thus, the model is deemed suitable for the subsequent path analysis.

Path Analysis. A structural model was developed based on the proposed relationships, with the model and its path coefficients displayed in Fig. 3. Utilizing the bootstrapping method, a hypothesis was considered validated if its associated path coefficient was significant. The outcomes of these tests are consolidated in Table 7.

All the hypothesized relationships have been supported by the data, indicating strong links between *playfulness* trait, *attitude*, and *intention* towards gamified health behavior. In addition, indirect influence of *playfulness* on *intention* was also assessed. The indirect relationship appears to be significant with a path coefficient of 0.266 ($p < 0.001$).

Explanatory power (R-square) of the dependent variables, effect size (F-square) of the predictors, and predictive relevance (Q-square) of the model were assessed. The results are shown in Tables 8 and 9.

R-square value quantifies the proportion of the variance in the dependent variable that is predictable from the independent variables, indicates explanatory power of the predictor. For Attitude, an R-square value of 0.39 indicates that approximately 39% of the variance in the variable is accounted for by *playfulness*. For behavior *intention*, *playfulness* explains about 41% of its variance. According Chin's standard, playfulness trait exhibit a moderate explanatory power on these endogenous variables [36].

Effect size, represented by F-square values, offers insights into the magnitude of the relationships between the constructs. The effect size of Playfulness on Attitude is

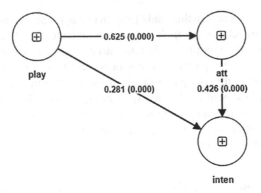

Fig. 3. Structural model with path coefficients (*p*).

Table 7. Hypothesis testing results.

Hypotheses	Path	t-value	p-values	Decision
H0: play - > att	0.625	17.859	0.000	Supported
H1: play - > inten	0.281	4.628	0.000	Supported
H2: att - > inten	0.426	6.133	0.000	Supported
play - > att - > inten	0.266	4.886	0.000	

Table 8. Explanatory power (R-square) and predictive relevance (Q-square).

	R-square	Q-square
Attitude	0.390	0.381
Intention	0.410	0.293

Table 9. Effect size (F-square) of the predictors.

	Attitude	Intention
Attitude		0.187
Playfulness	0.640	0.081

considerably large at 0.640, indicating a substantial impact. Conversely, the effect size of Playfulness on Intention is relatively small, with a value of 0.081. Effect size of Attitude on Intention is observed to be moderate at 0.187.

Q-square evaluates the model's ability to predict the observed values for a particular construct. The Q-square value for Attitude is measured at 0.381, and for Intention, it is found to be 0.293. Both values surpass zero, indicating that the model possesses satisfactory predictive relevance for both constructs.

5 Discussion

The primary objective of this research was to validate the hypothesized positive influence of the playfulness trait on individuals' attitude and intention towards engaging in gamified health behaviors. Through a survey approach, data pertaining to these three dimensions were collected and subsequently subjected to an in-depth structural equation modeling analysis.

Playfulness demonstrated a significant positive influence on both *attitude*, with a path coefficient of 0.625 ($p < 0.001$), and *intention*, marked by a coefficient of 0.281 ($p < 0.001$). Meanwhile, *attitude* also positively influenced *intention*, evident from a coefficient of 0.426 ($p < 0.001$). The R-square values indicated that *playfulness* accounted for 39% of the variance in *attitude* and 41% in *intention*, underlining its moderate explanatory power. Effect sizes highlighted *playfulness* trait's substantial impact on *attitude* (F-square of 0.640) and a lesser one on *intention* (F-square of 0.081). Additionally, the indirect relationship between *playfulness* and *intention* was marked at 0.266 ($p < 0.001$). Predictive relevance was affirmed with Q-square values of 0.381 for *attitude* and 0.293 for intention. The findings supported the proposed hypotheses, revealing a significant positive relationship between the playfulness trait and both attitude and intention towards gamified health practices. Additionally, given the significant indirect relationship tracing from the playfulness trait through attitude to intention, it can be concluded that attitude plays a role in partially mediating this relationship.

The study's findings highlight the clear role of playfulness trait in influencing one's attitude and intention towards gamifying health behaviors. The inherent playfulness trait can significantly impact an individual's attitude towards the concept of gamified health initiatives, which in turn impacts their willingness to engage with such interventions. This observation aligns with the theoretical frameworks surrounding the playfulness trait and has multiple implications. First, interpersonal difference in playfulness trait could explain the varied attitudes observed among participants in previous studies. Where these differences remained unaccounted for in the past, this research offers compelling evidence. Second, the result highlights the importance of considering the playfulness trait when suggesting gamification as a solution for specific demographics. For populations characterized by lower playfulness levels, one might anticipate a less favorable view of play-based initiatives, potentially leading to decreased engagement with gamified systems, gamification thus may not be the ideal solution for them. Conversely, highly playful groups could find gamification particularly attractive, consequently, promoting health behaviors with a play and game approach might be an effective strategy.

A notable limitation of this study pertains to the sample size. Of the initial 403 samples, nearly a quarter were not included in the analysis. The excluded data either had missing values or were deemed fraudulent, characterized by uniformly consistent answers. The debate surrounding the data quality of online surveys remains inconclusive. While some studies suggest there is no significant deterioration in quality [39], others highlight it as potential challenges [40]. This study did not incorporate measures to prevent invalid entries, potentially explaining the substantial number of such exclusions. Although the final sample size was less than the typical 385 respondents often considered ideal in health research for a 95% confidence interval with a 5% margin of error in expansive populations (>100,000) [41], a post hoc statistical power calculation in G*Power with the model parameters and the smallest archived effect size (0.081) showed that it has achieved a 97.19% statistical power.

6 Conclusion

The playfulness trait has not received adequate scholarly attention in healthcare gamification. Given the existing research gap in gamification and the synergy between playfulness and health behaviors, this study hypothesized and examined the potential role of playfulness in influencing an individual's attitude and intention towards gamified health behaviors. The findings, revealing positive relationships, underscore the importance of considering the playfulness trait when designing gamification solutions aimed at promoting health behaviors. Additionally, these results suggest the value of including playfulness as a tailoring factor in research on tailored gamification.

Acknowledgments. This research was supported by the Joint NTU-WeBank Research Centre on FinTech (Award No: NWJ-2021-007), Nanyang Technological University, Singapore.

Disclosure of Interests..   The authors have no competing interests to declare that are relevant to the content of this article.

Appendix

FUN1	I believe in having a good time
FUN2	I think fun is a very important part in life
INI1	I try to have fun no matter what I am doing
INI2	I am often the person who starts fun things in a situation
INI3	I can make almost any activity fun for me to do
INI4	I can find fun in most situations
REA1	I appreciate fun things started by others
REA2	When someone else starts something that is fun, I'm happy to follow along
REA3	I enjoy fun activities that other people initiate
UNI1	I understand social rules but most of the time I am not restricted by them
UNI2	I don't always follow rules
UNI3	Sometimes I can do things without worrying about consequences
UNI4	If I want to do something, I usually don't let what other people may think stop me

(continued)

(*continued*)

UNI5	I don't fear losing anything by being silly
SPO1	I often do things on the spur of the moment
SPO2	I often do unplanned things
SPO3	I often act upon my impulses
SPO4	I often pursue my spur-of-the-moment THOUGHTS
SPO5	I often follow my spur-of-the-moment FEELINGS
ATT1	I think play is compatible with diet control and regular exercises
ATT2	I think diet control and regular exercises in a playful way is a good idea
ATT3	I can have fun while managing my diet or doing regular exercising
INT1	If there's an application that helps me manage my diet and exercise in a game-like way, I intent to use it
INT2	If there's an application that helps me manage my diet and exercise in a game-like way, I can see myself using it frequently

References

1. Steffen, P.W., Sebastian, D.: "The Ambiguity of Games: Histories and Discourses of a Gameful World," in The Gameful World: Approaches, Issues, Applications. MIT Press, pp. 23–64 (2014)
2. Koivisto, J., Hamari, J.: The rise of motivational information systems: a review of gamification research. Int. J. Inf. Manage. **45**, 191–210 (2019). https://doi.org/10.1016/j.ijinfomgt.2018.10.013
3. Klock, A.C.T., Gasparini, I., Pimenta, M.S., Hamari, J.: Tailored gamification: A review of literature. Int. J. Hum.-Comput. Stud. **144** (2020). https://doi.org/10.1016/j.ijhcs.2020.102495
4. Barnett, L.A.: The nature of playfulness in young adults. Personality Individ. Differ. **43**(4), 949–958 (2007). https://doi.org/10.1016/j.paid.2007.02.018
5. Glynn, M.A., Webster, J.: The adult playfulness scale: an initial assessment. Psychol. Rep. **71**(1), 83–103 (1992)
6. Schaefer, C.E.: The Therapeutic Powers of Play. Jason Aronson (1993)
7. Trevlas, E., Grammatikopoulos, V., Tsigilis, N., Zachopoulou, E.: Evaluating playfulness: construct validity of the children's playfulness scale. Early Childhood Educ. J. **31**(1), 33–39 (2003)
8. Deterding, S., Dixon, D., Khaled, R., Nacke, L.: "From game design elements to gamefulness: defining "gamification"," In: presented at the Proceedings of the 15th International Academic MindTrek Conference: Envisioning Future Media Environments, Tampere, Finland, (2011). https://doi.org/10.1145/2181037.2181040
9. Cugelman, B.: Gamification: what it is and why it matters to digital health behavior change developers. JMIR Serious Games, **1**(1), e3 (2013). https://doi.org/10.2196/games.3139
10. Högberg, J., Hamari, J., Wästlund, E.: Gameful experience questionnaire (GAME-FULQUEST): an instrument for measuring the perceived gamefulness of system use. User Model. User-Adap. Inter. **29**(3), 619–660 (2019). https://doi.org/10.1007/s11257-019-09223-w

11. Nicholson, S.: A recipe for meaningful gamification, Gamification in education and business, pp. 1–20 (2015)
12. Nicholson, S.: A User-Centered Theoretical Framework for Meaningful Gamification. in Games+Learning+Society, Conference 8.0, Madison, WI, C. Martin, A. Ochsner, and K. Squire, Eds. (2012). https://doi.org/10.1184/R1/6686786.v1. https://kilthub.cmu.edu/articles/journal_contribution/Games_Learning_Society_GLS_Conference_8_0/6686786
13. Stenros, J.: Playfulness, Play, and Games: A Constructionist Ludology Approach (2015)
14. Landers, R.N., Tondello, G.F., Kappen, D.L., Collmus, A.B., Mekler, E.D., Nacke, L.E.: Defining gameful experience as a psychological state caused by gameplay: Replacing the term 'Gamefulness' with three distinct constructs. Int. J. Hum. Comput. Stud. 127, 81–94 (2019). https://doi.org/10.1016/j.ijhcs.2018.08.003
15. Barnett, L.A.: Playful people: fun is in the mind of the beholder. Imagin. Cogn. Pers. 31(3), 169–197 (2012). https://doi.org/10.2190/IC.31.3.c
16. Proyer, R.T., Gander, F., Bertenshaw, E.J., Brauer, K.: The positive relationships of playfulness with indicators of health, activity, and physical fitness. Front. Psychol. 9, 1440 (2018). https://doi.org/10.3389/fpsyg.2018.01440
17. Mannell, R.C.: Personality in leisure theory: the self-as-entertainment construct. Loisir Et Societe/society and Leisure 7(1), 229–240 (1984)
18. Proyer, R.T., Jehle, N.: The basic components of adult playfulness and their relation with personality: the hierarchical factor structure of seventeen instruments. Personality Individ. Differ. 55(7), 811–816 (2013). https://doi.org/10.1016/j.paid.2013.07.010
19. Staempfli, M.B.: Adolescent playfulness, stress perception, coping and well being. J. Leis. Res. 39(3), 393–412 (2007)
20. Proyer, R.T.: The well-being of playful adults. European J. Humour Res. 1(1), 84–98 (2013)
21. Proyer, R.T.: Playfulness over the lifespan and its relation to happiness: results from an online survey. Z. Gerontol. Geriatr. 47(6), 508–512 (2014)
22. Shen, X.S., Chick, G., Zinn, H.: Playfulness in adulthood as a personality trait: a reconceptualization and a new measurement. J. Leis. Res. 46(1), 58–83 (2014a)
23. Gimpel, H., Manner-Romberg, T., Schmied, F., Winkler, T.J.: Understanding the evaluation of mHealth app features based on a cross-country Kano analysis. Electron. Markets 31(4), 765–794 (2021). https://doi.org/10.1007/s12525-020-00455-y
24. Krittanawong, C., Aydar, M., Kitai, T.: Pokémon Go: digital health interventions to reduce cardiovascular risk. Cardiol. Young 27(8), 1625–1626 (2017)
25. Kim, Y., Bhattacharya, A., Kientz, J.A., Lee, J.H.: It should be a game for fun, not exercise: tensions in designing health-related features for Pokémon go. In: presented at the Proceedings of the 2020 CHI Conference on Human Factors in Computing Systems, (2020)
26. Fleming, T.M., et al.: Serious games and gamification for mental health: current status and promising directions. Front. Psych. 7, 215 (2017)
27. Ajzen, I.: The theory of planned behaviour. Organizational Behavior and Human Decision Processes, vol. 50, no. 2, pp. 179–211, 1991/12/01/ 1991, doi: https://doi.org/10.1016/0749-5978(91)90020-T
28. Shen, X.S., Chick, G., Zinn, H.: Validating the Adult Playfulness Trait Scale (APTS): an examination of personality, behavior, attitude, and perception in the nomological network of playfulness. Am. J. Play 6(3), 345–369 (2014b)
29. Ruch, W., Bakker, A.B., Tay, L., Gander, F.: Handbook of Positive Psychology Assessment. Hogrefe Publishing GmbH (2022)
30. Schwarz, N.: Attitude measurement. Attitudes Attitude Change 3, 41–60 (2008)
31. Browne, M.W., Cudeck, R.: Alternative ways of assessing model fit. Sociol. Methods Res. 21(2), 230–258 (1992)

32. Hu, L., Bentler, P. M.: Cutoff criteria for fit indexes in covariance structure analysis: Conventional criteria versus new alternatives. Struct. Equation Model. Multidiscip. J. **6**(1), 1–55 (1999)
33. Anderson, J.C., Gerbing, D.W.: Structural equation modeling in practice: a review and recommended two-step approach. Psychol. Bull. **103**(3), 411 (1988)
34. Hair, J.F.J., Hult, G.T.M., Ringle, C.M., Sarstedt, M.: A Primer on Partial Least Squares Structural Equation Modeling (PLS-SEM). Sage publications (2021)
35. Shi, J., Mo, X., Sun, Z.: "Content validity index in scale development," Zhong nan da xue xue bao. Yi xue ban= J. Central South Univ. Med. Sci. **37**(2) 152–155 (2012)
36. Chin, W.W.: The partial least squares approach to structural equation modeling. Mod. Methods Bus. Res. **295**(2), 295–336 (1998)
37. Cohen, J.: Statistical Power Analysis for the Behavioral Sciences. Academic press (2013)
38. Sarstedt, M., Hair, J.F., Jr., Cheah, J.-H., Becker, J.-M., Ringle, C.M.: How to specify, estimate, and validate higher-order constructs in PLS-SEM. Australas. Mark. J. **27**(3), 197–211 (2019)
39. Tuten, T.L., Urban, D.J., Bosnjak, M.: Internet surveys and data quality: a review. Online Soc. Sci. **1**, 7–26 (2002)
40. Bauermeister, J.A., Pingel, E., Zimmerman, M., Couper, M., Carballo-Dieguez, A., Strecher, V.J.: Data quality in HIV/AIDS web-based surveys: handling invalid and suspicious data. Field Methods **24**(3), 272–291 (2012)
41. Lemeshow, S., Hosmer, D.W., Klar, J., Lwanga, S.K., Organization, W.H.: Adequacy of Sample Size in Health Studies. Wiley, Chichester (1990)

Exploring the Variables of Empathy in Gamers: A Comprehensive Survey

Tânia Ribeiro[1]([✉]) [iD], Ana Isabel Veloso[1] [iD], and Peter Brinson[2] [iD]

[1] DigiMedia, University of Aveiro, Aveiro, Portugal
ribeirotania@ua.pt
[2] USC Games, University of Southern California, Los Angeles, USA

Abstract. The aim of this paper is to present the design, validation, and dissemination strategy of an inductively structured survey aimed at comprehending the factors influencing the development of empathetic relationships between gamers and playable characters in digital games. The survey encompasses six distinct sections, including gamers' personal characterization, socio-economic reality, digital playing habits, preferred gaming activities, empathy assessment utilizing the Interpersonal Reactivity Index (IRI), and personality assessment through the Big Five Inventory (BFI-2-S). Additionally, it evaluates empathy in specific digital games for identifiable playable characters, adapting the IRI structure for the digital gaming context.

Twenty participants were involved in the survey's structure validation, selected through convenience sampling, in three focus group sessions, namely, two with field experts in Human-Computer Interaction and one with gamers.

The number of sessions was determined inductively, addressing identified complexities until a comprehensive resolution was achieved. The iterative sessions dynamically approached relevant issues, with a focus on Gender and Religious Beliefs being the most discussed topics. As a result, three questions in the final survey were reformulated to address Gender Identity, Ethnic Groups, and the preferred gaming platform.

Following validation, the survey was disseminated within private gamer online Discord, Reddit, and Facebook communities. These social platforms were chosen to capture the diverse gamer population comprehensively. The dissemination aimed to gather insights from a broad spectrum of gamers and identify the key elements to understanding empathy in digital games.

Keywords: Survey · Focus Group · Digital Games · Empathy

1 Introduction

Empathy, within the context of pathos, according to Aristotle [1], refers to a speaker's ability to connect with the audience's emotions. Aristotle recognized that emotions play a crucial role in decision-making and that a persuasive speaker should be able to evoke specific emotional responses from their listeners. A speaker aiming to elicit empathy might use vivid language, storytelling, or examples that resonate emotionally with the audience. This emotional connection can create a stronger bond between the speaker and the audience, making the message more compelling and persuasive. Contemporary, understanding and tapping into the audience's emotions, this speaker can enhance the persuasive impact of the message. Empathy involves recognizing the audience's emotional state and sharing in or mirroring those emotions.

Empathy is a complex phenomenon to define and categorize scientifically [2]. The lack of conceptual clarity around empathy may affect the broad range of empathy-related phenomena with different outcomes for the individual, society, and science [2–5].

According to Batson [2], the different authors who have been dedicated to studying the concept of empathy and its applications use the term to define how someone can know what the other is thinking or feeling and what that leads the subject to respond with sensitivity to the feelings of another, often automatically. Empathic states can involve feelings of sympathy, compassion, or tenderness, which may lead to emotional contagion and empathy when communicated through verbal or non-verbal language [6].

A comprehensive review by Cuff, Brown, Taylor, and Howat [7], considering 43 definitions of empathy from various fields like psychology and neuroscience, establishes empathy as an emotional response influenced by both trait capacities and state influences in a communication process. This emotional response, akin to the perceived or imagined emotions of others, involves recognizing that the source is external. Empathy in communication involves two participants: the one transmitting emotional information and the one experiencing empathy.

This paper aims to present the design, validation, and dissemination strategy of an inductively structured survey aimed at comprehending the factors influencing the development of empathetic relationships between gamers and playable characters in digital games. A structured survey is reported, and its variables, or codes, are a starting point for understanding this phenomenon and trying to answer, in the future, the question, "How can a playable character communicate empathy?" is proposed.

1.1 The Survey Inductive Approach

The selection of an inductive approach in research methodology provides a nuanced and flexible framework for exploring complex phenomena, facilitating the emergence of patterns and insights [8]. In the context of digital game engagement, a multifaceted experience is shaped by diverse factors, such as personal characteristics, personality traits, socio-economic context, and individual gaming habits or preferences [9–12]. This option is also justified once the phenomenon of digital games becomes known; the factors influencing or illicit the Emphatic response in digital games are unknown [13–16]. This approach enables the comprehensive collection of diverse information, fostering a more holistic understanding of the intricate dynamics characterizing the empathetic communication between the two principal entities involved – the digital game and the gamer.

Inductive methods, characterized by their openness and adaptability, serve as a valuable tool for generating hypotheses and grounded theories [17–19]. The iterative nature of inductive inquiry allows for the refinement of conclusions over time, aligning with the inherent complexity of the digital game-gamer relationship.

By opting for an inductive survey design [20], this research embraces the inherent complexity of the subject matter and recognizes the need for a flexible exploration that accommodates the diverse and evolving aspects of digital game engagement [17, 21].

This paper reports the design, validation, and dissemination strategy of an inductively structured survey aimed at comprehending the factors influencing the development of empathetic relationships between gamers and playable characters in digital games, and it is divided into five sections. The next section describes the first approach (induction) survey design, including all the variables that may be important for emphatic communication between the gamer and the playable character. The third section delineates the survey's validation, narrating the three focus approach methodologies used for the survey validation, and it also encompasses the survey dissemination strategy. In section number four, the research results are discussed. This paper concludes by outlining the final survey structure, reporting the research limitations, and recommending further study directions.

2 Survey Design

This section delineates the survey's validation, encompassing its design and dissemination. The subsequent segment details the design process, followed by the validation strategy, which involves three focus group sessions, namely, two with field experts and one with gamers, employing a convenience sampling method. The section concludes by elucidating the survey dissemination strategy.

The survey's initial architecture is compartmentalized into seven distinct sections:

1. Sample personal characterization: gamer's personal characterization.
2. Context and Beliefs: gamer's socio-economic reality characterization.
3. Gaming Habits Characterization: gamer's digital playing habits characterization.
4. Type of Player: the typology of gamers' most preferred gaming activities based on [22].
5. Sample Empathy Assessment: implementing the IRI Empathy assessment scale.
6. Sample Personality Assessment: Implementing a Personality Assessment BFI-2-S [23].
7. Assessing Empathy in Digital Games: Access empathy in a specific digital game for a specific playable character (named by gamers' respondents), adapting IRI structure for the digital game context.

2.1 The Variables of the Subject

The survey's first six parts aim to collect data about gamers, focusing on their personal characteristics, socio-economic backgrounds, gaming habits, preferred gaming activities, empathic responsiveness, and personality.

In the initial survey section "1. Sample Personal Characterization", the main objective is to outline the sample's demographics, which involves characterizing respondents based on age group, gender, education level, and country of residence (Table 1).

The subsequent section, "2. Context and Beliefs", seeks information regarding respondents' ethnic background, social class, political affiliation, and religious beliefs (Table 2).

Table 1. Survey's section personal characterization section to test in Focus Group sessions:

Survey section	Variables	Question Type	Answer options
1. Sample personal characterization	Age group	multiple choice	[10–15] [16–20] [21–25] [26–30] [31–35] [36–40] [41–45] [46–50] [51–55] [56–60] [61–65] [66–70] [71–75] [76–80] [80+]
	Sex Assigned at Birth	multiple choice	[Female] [Male]
	Gender Identity	multiple choice	[Same as biological sex] [other: _]
	Education level	multiple choice	[Elementary School] [Middle School] [Bachelor's Degree] [Master's Degree] [Doctoral Degree] [other: _]
	Country of residence	Open-ended question	[_]

Table 2. Survey's Context and Beliefs section to test in Focus Group sessions:

Survey section	Codes to test	Question Type	Answer options
2. Context and beliefs	Ethnic Group	multiple choice	[I am white / Caucasian] [I am Hispanic /Latino] [I am Asian] [I am Indian] [I am Indian] [I am Afro-descendent] [other: _]
	Income	multiple choice	[Lower class] [working class] [middle class] [Upper class] [other: _]
	Political spectrum	multiple choice	[Left-wing] [Center] [Right-wing] [I don't care about politics]
	Religious beliefs	multiple choice	[Yes, I have a religion] [I believe in some kind of God, but I don't have any religion] [I don't believe in God]

In "3. Gaming Habits Characterization", the focus shifts to distinguishing between Players and Gamers [9, 11, 12, 24] while comprehending their gaming habits and consumption patterns [25]. Additionally, respondents are asked whether they have played a minimum of three video games in their lives to gauge their familiarity with the medium, drawing from Morrison and Ziemke's work [14] (Table 3).

Regarding the section "4. Type of Player", respondents are prompted to describe their gaming behavior by rating the options "Socialize with in-game", "Fight and kill others in-game", "Explore the game world," and "Conquer objectives or achievements". These response options are systematically coded to categorize participants into distinct

Table 3. Survey's Gaming Habits Characterization section to test in Focus Group sessions:

Survey section	Codes to test	Question Type	Answer options
3. Gaming Habits characterization	Hours played for the week	multiple choice	[I don't spend any time playing video games right now] [up to 1h per week.] [1 up to 4 h per week.] [5 up to 14 h per week.] [15 up to 24 h per week.] [25 up to 40 h per week.] [40 up to 50 h per week.] [More than 50 h per week.]
	Play Platform	multiple choice	[Personal Computer (Pc or Mac)] [Mobile Device (Smartphone/tablet)] [PlayStation Console] [Xbox Console] [Nintendo Switch] [other: _]
	Life period more active in the gaming	multiple choice	[Infant/Toddler (0–3)] [Pre-schooler (4–6)] [Kid (7–9)] [Preteen (10–13)] [Teen (14–17)] [Young Adult (18–24)] [Twenties & Thirties (25–35)] [Thirties & Forties (35–50)] [Fifties & up (50 +)]

gaming profiles, specifically Socializers, Killers, Explorers, and Achievers, as defined by Bartle [22].

In section "5. Sample Empathy Assessment", the Interpersonal Reactivity Index (IRI) self-report empathy scale is implemented. The option of this assessment compared to the other self-report empathy questionnaires. IRI covers the scale identified measuring empathy through four different constructs in 28 five-point Likert scale questions. It comprehends that humans can empathize with fictional Characters from movies and plays [26, 27].

IRI scale consists of four subscales that quantify cognitive and affective empathy: perspective-taking, fantasy, empathic concern, and personal distress. Perspective-taking measures an individual's tendency to adopt other (human) points of view spontaneously. The fantasy subscale measures an individual's tendency to imagine themselves in fictional situations, such as a character in a book or a play. The empathic concern subscale measures an individual's tendency to feel sympathy and compassion for those in need. The personal distress subscale measures an individual's tendency to experience discomfort when in the presence of those in need [26].

The sixth section, "6. Sample Personality Assessment," aims to gather information about the gamer and contemplates the implementation of a Five-Factor Model (FFM) assessment, specifically a short version of the construct of the BFI-2-S validated by [23], assesses human personality in five factors: openness to experimentation, conscientiousness, extraversion, emotional stability, and agreeableness in 30 five-point Likert scale items.

2.2 The Variables of the Emphatic Communicator: The Playable Character

The last survey section, "7. Assessing empathy in digital games", intends to find the most meaningful characters in digital games and implement a hypothesis to assess empathy in digital games based on IRI factorial structure and its empathy definition [26, 27]. This section hypothesizes the IRI structure adapted to the reality of digital games – Fictional Character Empathic Communication Assessment (FCECA) – aiming to measure empathy felt for a fictional character. FCECA is based on the IRI structure and is an attempt to assess empathy in digital games in 28 items (5-point Likert scale) and hinges on four proposed constructs (or subscales): Character Perspective Perception (CPP), Role Fantasy (RF), Character Concern (CC), and Personal Character Distress (PCD). Each construct comprises seven items, making the scale of 28 items.

Table 4. Assessing Empathy in Digital Games: Fictional Character Empathic Communication Assessment (FCECA), the last survey section:

	7. Assessing Empathy in Digital Games: FCECA
	Character Perspective Perception (CPP)
CPP1	When I am playing, I sometimes find it difficult to see things from [Character name] point of view as if I were in her/his skin. (-)
CPP2	As I play [Game title], I try to look at everybody's side of a disagreement before I make a decision
CPP3	I sometimes try to understand [Character name] better by imagining how things look from her/his perspective
CPP4	Before criticizing [Character name], I try to imagine how I would feel if I were her/him
CPP5	When I am right about something, I just do it, and I don't care about the [Character name] and the health damage I may induce to her/him. (-)
CPP6	When I'm upset in the game, I usually try to "put myself in the [Character name]'s shoes" for a while
CPP7	There are two sides to every question in the [Game title] game world, and try to look at them both
	Role Fantasy (RF)
RF1	I daydream and fantasize, with some regularity, about things that might happen to me as if I were [Character name]
RF2	I really get involved with [Character name]'s feelings
RF3	I am usually objective when I play [Game title], and I don't often get completely caught up in it. (-)
RF4	Becoming extremely involved in [Game title] world is somewhat rare for me. (-)
RF5	After playing [Game title], I have felt as though I were [Character name]
RF6	As I play, I imagine how I would feel if the game events were happening to me
RF7	When I play the game, I can very easily put myself in [Character name]'s place
	Character Concern (CC)
CEC1	I often have tender, concerned feelings for [Character name] in a less fortunate situation

(continued)

Table 4. (*continued*)

	7. Assessing Empathy in Digital Games: FCECA
CEC2	Sometimes I do not feel very sorry for [Character name] when she/he is having problems. (-)
CEC3	When I see someone taken advantage of [Character name], I feel kind of protective towards her/him
CEC4	If [Character name] experiences misfortunes, do not usually disturb me a great deal. (-)
CEC5	When I see [Character name] treated unfairly, I sometimes don't feel very much pity for her/him. (-)
CEC6	I am often quite touched by things that I see happen to [Character name] during the game
CEC7	I would describe myself as a pretty soft-hearted person in this [Game title]
	Personal Character Distress (PCD)
PCD1	In emergency game situations, I feel apprehensive and ill at ease
PCD2	As I play [Game title], sometimes I feel helpless when I am in the middle of a very emotional situation
PCD3	In the game [[Game title], when I see [Character name] getting hurt because of my actions, I tend to remain calm (-)
PCD4	When I see [Character name] almost dying in an emergency, I go to pieces. (-)
PCD5	Being in a tense, emotional in-game situation scares me
PCD6	I tend to lose control during emergencies in [Game title] game
PCD7	In the [Game title], I am usually pretty effective in dealing with emergencies. (-)

3   Survey Validation: Focus Group Sessions

The inductively designed survey was validated before dissemination to avoid unseen issues [28]. For this reason, a series of focus groups were conducted to capture diverse perspectives on the survey's structure and questions.

The survey structure was validated through three focus group sessions: two with field experts (Human-Computer Interaction field experts) and one with Gamers, comprehending 20 participants divided into the three sessions selected by a convenience sampling method [9, 24]. The choice to conduct three distinct sessions was not preordained but rather stemmed from a pragmatic response to the complexities of problem identification. The number of sessions was intricately linked to the evolving nature of the problem-finding process, persisting until a comprehensive resolution was achieved, leading to the survey's final version.

Due to the restrictions imposed by the lockdown in Portugal as a response to the global COVID-19 pandemic [29], legal constraints were placed on the civil rights related to travel and gatherings [30]. Consequently, with in-person meetings restricted, the focus group sessions were adapted to online meetings, conducted in two separate moments. The two-moment option was chosen to prevent participant fatigue [31–33].

Within this adapted focus group methodology, the lead researcher assumed the role of moderator to facilitate the dynamic of the focus groups. The sessions were organized into two distinct moments (Fig. 1):

- The overview session: in the initial session, the moderator exposed, within 15 min, the task's objectives and the intended purpose of the focus group. During this session, participants were instructed to review the survey and provide non-mandatory notes for each section. This approach was adopted to leverage participants' short-term memory and minimize fatigue while optimizing the efficiency of the subsequent focus group discussion session. Additionally, it allowed the moderator to prepare for the ensuing focus group guide without consuming valuable time during the second moment of the focus group discussion.
- The focus group discussion: following a one-week interval, the discussion session unfolded and extended to a maximum of one hour. The moderator drew upon the previously compiled notes in this phase to stimulate the discussion. These notes guided the researcher moderator in formulating pilot interview questions, setting the stage for the subsequent focus group session scheduled one week after the initial overview.

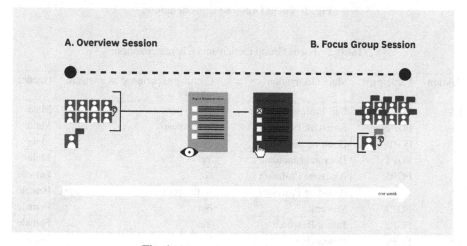

Fig. 1. Focus Group sessions method

With this method, three focus group sessions were conducted: Experts Session Number One (ES1), Experts Session Number Two (ES2), and Gamers Session (GS3), Fig. 2.

The initial two sessions, ES1 and ES2, were designed to engage subject matter experts in their respective fields. The criteria to participate in these sessions were possessing empirical and theoretical expertise in survey design and its practical implementation for data collection. The GS3 session involved gamers. Participants for this session were also recruited through convenience sampling, with invitations extended via private channels on the Discord platform. These invitations were primarily directed toward individuals actively engaged in gaming-related forums, ensuring their relevance and expertise in the subject matter (Tables 4 and 5).

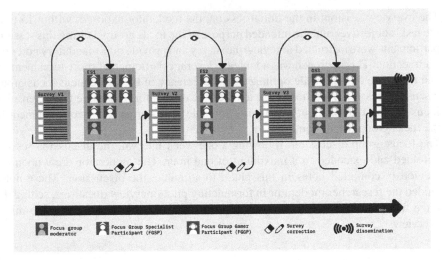

Fig. 2. Focus Group sessions iterations

Table 5. Focus Group Participants Characterization:

Session	Participant	Main Occupation	Gaming experience as a leisure activity	Gender
ES1	FGP1	Full Professor	In the past	Male
	FGP2	Assistant Professor	In the past	Male
	FGP3	Doctoral candidate	Yes	Male
	FGP4	Doctoral candidate	Yes	Male
	FGP5	Assistant Professor	No	Female
	FGP6	Assistant Professor	In the past	Female
	FGP7	Student	No	Female
	FGP8	Junior Research	Yes	Female
ES2	FGP9	Researcher	Yes	Male
	FGP10	Higher technician	In the past	Female
	FGP11	Researcher	Yes	Female
	FGP12	Doctoral Student. Student	Yes	Female
	FGP13	Doctoral Student. Student	No	Female
	FGP14	Assistant Professor	No	Female
GS3	FGP15	Unemployed	Yes	Male
	FGP16	Technician	Yes	Male
	FGP17	Student (Bachelor)	Yes	Male
	FGP18	Technician	Yes	Male
	FGP19	Unemployed	Yes	Male
	FGP20	Student (Bachelor)	Yes	Male

3.1   ES1 Outcomes:

The first focus group session (ES1) counted on eight participants, all academics proficient in survey design, validation, and implementation. Conducted online via a private Zoom meeting, the overview session on March 22, followed by the focus group discussion on March 29, 2021 (one week later).

During the discussion, specific questions within the questionnaire were scrutinized for redundancy or perceived lack of necessity. The main issue pointed out by participants was related to the section "1. Sample personal characterization", specifically the questions asked for the "Sex Assigned at Birth" and "Gender Identity" (Table 1): Participants (FGP5, FGP6, FGP7, and FGP8) raised apprehensions about political spectrum, religious beliefs, social class, and physical appearance questions. FGP4 additionally flagged redundancy in physical appearance queries.

FGP4 expressed deep reservations about paired questions, deeming "Sex Assigned at Birth" (Table 1) potentially offensive and the Gender Identity option "Same as biological sex" as "out of touch". Divergent perspectives emerged, with FGP1 emphasizing the intricate interplay of gender, sex, and cultural perspectives, while FGP2 and FGP5 highlighted the limited scientific basis for diverse genders in popular culture. FGP6 suggested reevaluating scientific categorization within the questionnaire, considering its potential impact on individuals' gender perceptions.

FGP1 proposed removing the "Biological Sex" (Table 1) question, a viewpoint supported by FGP4 and FGP6. This led to a discussion on alternative response options for the "Gender Identity" question, with FGP1 advocating for an open-answer format. FGP5 disagreed, citing challenges in analyzing open-ended responses and the risk of reduced participation. FGP8 suggested predefined options "Male", "Female", and "Other", prompting concerns from FGP4 about classifying "non-binary" individuals. The group reached a consensus on rearranging options to "Female", "Male", and "non-binary", with the latter as an optional open question.

The discussions, spanning approximately 45 min, were marked by protracted and polarized debates conveyed through non-verbal cues when a participant prompted an opposite opinion. With 15 min remaining, participants assessed the questionnaire's structure across seven sections: the designation of group section titles, the clarity of questions, the comprehensibility of the wording, and the overall structure of the questionnaire.

Concerning the questionnaire's length, FGP3, FGP4, FGP6, and FGP7 perceived it as too extensive. FGP3, FGP4, FGP6, and FGP7 deemed the questionnaire excessively long, with FGP7 suggesting retaining only the last set of questions, Sect. 7 (Table 4). FGP5 proposed adding titles or instructional sentences for Likert scale questions, while FGP2 criticized distracting illustrative images. FGP6 defended the images, asserting their appeal to the target audience: gamers. FGP5 proposed a reverse sequence for the questionnaire sections to prioritize critical questions, contrasting FGP1's view on maintaining the standard design. FGP2 suggested making the questionnaire web-responsive for improved mobile navigation. Subsequent to discussions, modifications were implemented, primarily in the gender section of Sample Personal Characterization, involving the deletion of the "Sex Assigned at Birth" (Table 1) question and alteration of the Gender Identity question.

3.2 ES2 Outcomes:

After addressing the concerns raised by ES1, the subsequent research phase involved the engagement of the second focus group (Fig. 2), (Table 4). This phase comprised the two key moments previously pointed (Fig. 1): 1) The preliminary overview session held on May 5, 2021, and 2) The focus group discussion convened on May 12 of the same year.

During this phase, the primary focus of discussion centered on the survey's questions, with specific attention to potential participant discomfort and their responses. Overall, participants expressed satisfaction with the question's clarity and appropriateness. However, discussions revealed a notable concern within the section "2. Context and Beliefs", more specifically regarding ethnic identity (Table 2), as it was suggested that the questions in this section adopt a more open-ended approach. In support of this notion, participant FGP9 invoked the writings of author Yuval Harari, though without recalling the specific title of the work. FGP9 argued that ethnic background holds greater significance than mere aesthetic considerations about skin color, as it can reflect one's cultural heritage, values, and way of life. Consequently, FGP9 advocated for a broader inclusion of comprehensive ethnic groups in the survey (Table 2).

This perspective gained unanimous agreement, leading to further suggestions. FGP11 proposed prefacing the question group with explanatory background information, a consensus supported by the participants. The decision to retain all questions, seen as valuable sources of information, was unanimous. Still, regarding section "2. Context and Beliefs", FGP14 suggested explicit coding for the income-related question, highlighting difficulties in identifying with predefined social classes (Table 2). Subsequent participants concurred, leading to recommendations for coding adjustments.

Regarding the section "3. Gaming Habits" (Table 3), FGP10 advocated for including the "Linux" option in the Play Platform question. FGP9 expressed concerns about the comprehensiveness and analytical complexity of game genre categorization in "5. Sample Empathy Assessment" section, pointing out a repeated question.

Participants collectively acknowledged the survey's comprehensive nature and considerable length but did not view its length as a hindrance to engagement.

3.3 GS3 Outcomes:

The introductory session, "1. The overview session" (Fig. 1), did not occur with this group due to the unavailability of a shared schedule to arrange the meeting. In lieu of the overview session, the researcher conducted individualized meetings with each participant to elucidate the objectives and explain the focus group discussion aims (Fig. 2). The conclusive focus group session, ES3, occurred on May 22, 2021, serving as a survey validation session with gamers previously identified in the Discord platform. The selection of these participants was predicated on their gaming practices and their distinct absence of academic background, in contrast to the characteristics of the antecedent participant sessions (Table 4).

In this 45-min session, the participants were asked to ascertain the clarity of the questions and the adequacy of the speech for the target audience.

The participants found the survey suitable and explanatory when asked about this. None of them pointed to any issue. They were curious about the results, mainly regarding section "7. Assessing Empathy in Digital Games" (Table 4), which they generally point to as "fun to answer" and "interesting to think about". They also suggested implementing this section as a small game on a proper website and giving people a score for how much they care about their favorite playable character.

3.4 Survey Implementation Strategy

After the survey's final implementation on the Lime Survey open-source survey platform [34], the survey was spread in private gamer networks dedicated to gaming on digital social platforms: Discord [35], Reddit [36], and Facebook [37]. The social media platforms were selected to reflect and capture the range of the scale's target population, gamers.

To target specific gamer groups on these social media platforms, the researcher selected what seemed to be the friendliest communities and took part in them, participating in some discussions and answering some questions to gain some status around the members. The researcher always identified herself as a female Ph.D. candidate who played some games, showing knowledge about the gaming culture and being agreeable to community members.

The survey was launched on June 8, 2021; a total of 13 posts were made on Reddit, followed by six posts on Facebook and four on Discord by the main researcher during the following four months, answering questions prompted by community participants.

The researcher encountered negative reactions within specific Facebook and Discord groups, with participants commenting about the researcher's gender, leading to expulsion from several groups. Following three months of collecting only 51 responses, the researcher enlisted three male colleagues to disseminate the survey using the same methodology, targeting online gamer groups with the pretext that it was conducted "for a friend". This approach yielded a significantly increased response rate, concluding with the last recorded response on November 29 of the same year, collecting a total of 303 responses.

4 Discussion

This paper reports the design, validation, and dissemination strategy of an inductively structured survey aimed at comprehending the factors influencing the development of empathetic relationships between gamers and playable characters in digital games.

The survey structure was validated through three focus group sessions: two with field experts (Human-Computer Interaction field experts) and one with Gamers, comprehending 20 participants divided into the three sessions selected by a convenience sampling method [12, 24, 38]. In each focus group session, the participants were asked to ascertain the questions' clarity and the speech's adequacy for the target audience (gamers) and to provide objective and constructive feedback about its structure and flow. The decision to conduct three distinct sessions was not preordained but rather stemmed from a pragmatic response to the complexities of the identified problem. The number of sessions (Fig. 2) was intricately linked to the evolving nature of the problem-solving process, persisting until a comprehensive resolution was achieved. This method proved to be a good method for attaining clarity without overloading the focus group participants (Fig. 1). The most discussed questions were related to the inquiry on Gender and Religious Beliefs. In the final survey, three questions were reformulated: Gender Identity (1. Sample personal characterization), Ethnic Group (2. Context and beliefs), and the preferred gaming platform Play Platform (3. Gaming Habits characterization) (Tables 1, 2 and 3). These variables, related to deeply personal questions, caused discomfort in ES1 and possibly in future survey respondents.

After the validation, the survey was shared in private gamer online communities dedicated to gaming on digital social platforms: Discord, Reddit, and Facebook. The social media platforms were selected to reflect and capture the range of the scale's target population, gamers [9, 38]. Besides selecting friendly communities with a previous effort to gain sympathy around the members and being agreeable, the researcher found an incredible amount of hate speech around academic methods, research, and feminity.

5 Conclusion, Limitations, and Further Research Directions

The research reports an inductive structured survey split into seven sections. The first section, personal characterization, aims to describe the gamer in terms of demographics, asking questions regarding their age, gender, education level, and country of residence. With the focus group session, it was possible to conclude that asking "the sex" to someone is rude, and the answer options should contemplate the non-binary option in order to be inclusive and complement genderqueer respondents (Table 1).

The second section of the survey – Context and Beliefs – aims to frame gamer's socio-economic reality. In this section, also regarding the focus group outputs, the answer options associated with income were changed: The *"lower class"* option was coded to *"I don't have any income; sometimes, I struggle to have money for my basic needs"*; the *"working class"* option was coded to *"My income is more or less on the average of the minimum wage of my country"*; *"middle class"* was coded to *"My income is more than the average of my country; I need to work for a living, but I can save some money and have some financial comfort"*; and finally, the *"upper-class"* option was coded to *"have way more money than I need to live; in fact, I didn't need to work"* (c.f. Tabe 2).

Regarding the changes of the section – Gaming Habits Characterization –just a change was made, adding the option Linux to the Play Platform question. Minor changes were made in the following sections –Type of Player; Sample Empathy Assessment; Sample Personality Assessment; and Assessing Empathy in Digital Games. This could be mainly because these sections rely on scales that are already widespread and accepted [22, 23, 26].

The diversity of questions will enable us to check if there is any pattern related to the relationship between the subject, the gamer, and the Empathic communicator, the playable character of a digital game. This is possible by checking the correlations between the variables corresponding to the first six sections of the proposed survey (Tables 1, 2, and 3) with the FCECA (Table 4). This proposed instrument to access empathy in digital games must also be tested further to check if it can access empathy in digital games by testing the proposed latent variables CPP, RF, CC, and PCD (Table 4) [39].

Regarding the limitations, inductive reasoning does not guarantee certainty; it only provides probable conclusions based on observed patterns [8]. The variables of Empathy in Gamers could be less or more depending on the analysis of the survey outcomes.

Although it is beyond the scope of this paper, the analysis based on the 301 collected answers will make it possible to explore the following research questions related to the future research directions: What are the psycho-social characteristics that define a Gamer? How can we measure and evaluate empathy in digital games? Is it possible for a Gamer to have an empathic connection with a Fictional/Playable Character? Who are the most empathetic characters in digital games? Additionally, it is useful to identify patterns of empathetic communication for playable characters in digital games. This can help game designers better understand how to create playable characters that elicit empathy and emotional resonance with their audience. This has been proven useful since Aristotle's time [1].

For the survey implementation strategy, we recommend using multiple distinct people to distribute the survey. This ensures that this distributor is people from different genres and gaming habits with enough familiarity with gamer networks and gamer communities.

All data produced, including the survey's initial and final structure, focus group observations, and outcomes, can be consulted (open access) at [40].

Acknowledgments. The study reported in this publication was supported by FCT – Foundation for Science and Technology (Fundação para a Ciência e Tecnologia), I.P. nr. SFRH/BD/143863/2019, DigiMedia Research Center, under the project UIDB/05460/2020, and FLAD, Luso-American Development Foundation, through the Papers@USA 2024 scholarship.

References

1. Aristotle, R.B.C.: Aristotle's Art of Rhetoric. The University of Chicago Press, Oxford (2019)
2. Batson, C.D.: These Things Called Empathy: Eight Related but Distinct Phenomena. In: The Social Neuroscience of Empathy. The MIT Press, pp. 3–16 (2009)
3. Mehrabian, A., Epstein, N.: A measure of emotional empathy. J. Pers. **40**, 525–543 (1972). https://doi.org/10.1111/j.1467-6494.1972.tb00078.x
4. Stein, E.: On the Problem of Empathy. Springer, Dordrecht (1964). https://doi.org/10.1007/978-94-017-5546-7
5. VandenBos, G.R.: APA dictionary of psychology. American Psychological Association (2016)
6. Planalp, S.: Communicating emotion: Social, moral, and cultural processes. Cambridge University Press (2015)
7. Cuff, B.M.P., Brown, S.J., Taylor, L., Howat, D.J.: Empathy: a review of the concept. Emot. Rev. **8**, 144–153 (2016). https://doi.org/10.1177/1754073914558466
8. Gray, D.E.: Doing research in the Real World, 2nd edn. SAGE Publications, Chennai (2012)
9. De Grove, F., Courtois, C., Van Looy, J.: How to be a gamer! Exploring personal and social indicators of gamer identity. J. Comput.-Mediat. Commun. **20**, 346–361 (2015). https://doi.org/10.1111/jcc4.12114

10. White, J.: Retro Gamer Book of Arcade Classics, 3rd edn. Future Publishing Limited (2017)
11. Ribeiro, T., Veloso, A.I., Brinson, P.: Be a Gamer: A Psycho-Social Characterization of the Player, pp. 301–314 (2023)
12. Shaw, A.: On not becoming gamers: moving beyond the constructed audience. Ada: J. Gender New Media Technol. **1**, 1–25 (2013). https://doi.org/10.7264/N33N21B3
13. Wulansari, O.D.E., Pirker, J., Kopf, J., Guetl, C.: Video games and their correlation to empathy: how to teach and experience empathic emotion. In: Advances in Intelligent Systems and Computing 1134 AISC, pp. 151–163 (2020). https://doi.org/10.1007/978-3-030-40274-7_16/ COVER
14. Morrison, I., Ziemke, T.: Empathy with computer game characters : a cognitive neuroscience perspective. In: AISB 2005 Convention Social Intelligence and Interaction in Animals, Robots and Agents: 12–15 April 2005 University of Hertfordshire, Hatfield, UK : Proceedings of the Joint Symposium on Virtual Social Agents: Social Presence Cues for Virtual Humanoids Empa. The Society for the Study of Artificial, United Kingdom (2005)
15. Van Looy, J., Courtois, C., De Vocht, M.: Player identification in online games. In: Proceedings of the 3rd International Conference on Fun and Games - Fun and Games 2010. ACM Press, New York, USA, pp. 126–134 (2010)
16. Farber, M., Schrier, K.: The Limits and Strengths of Using Digital Games as "Empathy Machines" (2017)
17. Charmaz, K., Thornberg, R.: The pursuit of quality in grounded theory. **18**, 305–327 (2020). https://doi.org/10.1080/14780887.2020.1780357
18. Walker, D., Myrick, F.: Grounded theory: an exploration of process and procedure. Qual. Health Res. **16**, 547–559 (2006). https://doi.org/10.1177/1049732305285972
19. Corbin, J.M., Strauss, A.: Grounded theory research: procedures, canons, and evaluative criteria. Qual. Sociol. **13**, 3–21 (1990). https://doi.org/10.1007/BF00988593
20. Angluin, D., Smith, C.H.: Inductive Inference: theory and methods. ACM Comput. Surv. **15**, 237–269 (1983). https://doi.org/10.1145/356914.356918
21. Woo, S.E., O'Boyle, E.H., Spector, P.E.: Best practices in developing, conducting, and evaluating inductive research. Hum. Resour. Manag. Rev. **27**, 255–264 (2017). https://doi.org/10.1016/j.hrmr.2016.08.004
22. Bartle, R., Muse, L.: Hearts, clubs, diamonds, spades: players who suit MUDs. J. MUD Res. **6**, 39 (1996). https://doi.org/10.1007/s00256-004-0875-6
23. Soto, C.J., John, O.P.: Short and extra-short forms of the Big Five Inventory–2: The BFI-2-S and BFI-2-XS. J. Res. Pers. **68**, 69–81 (2017). https://doi.org/10.1016/J.JRP.2017.02.004
24. Shaw, A.: Do you identify as a gamer? Gender, race, sexuality, and gamer identity. New Media Soc. **14**, 28–44 (2012). https://doi.org/10.1177/1461444811410394
25. ESA (2021) 2020 Essential facts about the video game industry
26. Davis, M.H.: Measuring individual differences in empathy: evidence for a multidimensional approach. J. Pers. Soc. Psychol. **44**, 113–126 (1983). https://doi.org/10.1037/0022-3514.44.1.113
27. Pulos, S., Elison, J., Lennon, R.: The hierarchical structure of the interpersonal reactivity Index. Soc. Behav. Pers. **32**, 355–360 (2004). https://doi.org/10.2224/SBP.2004.32.4.355
28. Freeman, T.: "Best practice" in focus group research: making sense of different views. J. Adv. Nurs. **56**, 491–497 (2006). https://doi.org/10.1111/j.1365-2648.2006.04043.x
29. WHO (2021) Coronavirus disease (COVID-19). In: Coronavirus disease (COVID-19) pandemic. https://bit.ly/3mdrxxK. Accessed 3 April 2021
30. Presidência do Conselho de Ministros; Diário da República Electrónico n.º9/2021, 1º Suplemento, Série I de 2021-01-14. Decreto n.º3-A/2021 13--(5)--13--(29) (2021)
31. Döring, N., De Moor, K., Fiedler, M., et al.: Videoconference fatigue: a conceptual analysis. Int. J. Environ. Res. Public Health **19**, 2061 (2022). https://doi.org/10.3390/IJERPH19042061

32. Jiang, M.: The reason Zoom calls drain your energy. In: BBC Worklife. https://www.bbc.com/worklife/article/20200421-why-zoom-video-chats-are-so-exhausting. Accessed 7 November 2022 (2020)
33. Wolf CR (2020) Virtual platforms are helpful tools but can add to our stress. Psychol. Today. https://www.psychologytoday.com/intl/blog/the-desk-the-mental-health-lawyer/202005/virtual-platforms-are-helpful-tools-can-add-our-stress. Accessed November 7 2022
34. LimeSurvey (2023) Forms UA
35. Discord (2022) Discord | Your place to talk and hang out. https://discord.com/. Accessed 14 April 2022
36. Reddit - Dive Into Anything. (2022). https://www.reddit.com/. Accessed 14 April 2022
37. Facebook. (2022). https://www.facebook.com/. Accessed 14 April 2022
38. De Grove, F., Cauberghe, V., Van Looy, J.: In pursuit of play: toward a social cognitive understanding of determinants of digital play. Commun. Theory **24**, 205–223 (2014). https://doi.org/10.1111/comt.12030
39. Hair, J.F., Babin, B.J., Anderson, R.E., Black, C.W.: Multivariate Data Analysis, 8th edn. Cengage Learning (2018)
40. Ribeiro, T., Veloso, A.I., Brinson, P.: Exploring the variables of empathy in gamers: a survey validation (2024)

Portfolio Management and Stock Request Behavior: Implications for Developer- and Economy-Oriented Game Design

Martin Stachoň[1,2]($\boxtimes$) (iD), Jakub Binter[1] (iD), Violetta Prossinger-Beck[3], Daniel Říha[4] (iD), and Hermann Prossinger[5] (iD)

[1] Faculty of Social and Economic Studies, University of Jan Evangelista Purkyně, Usti Nad Labem, Czech Republic
martin.stachon@ujep.cz
[2] Faculty of Business and Economics, Mendel University, Brno, Czech Republic
[3] Technical University Dresden, Dresden, Germany
[4] Faculty of Humanities, Charles University, Prague, Czech Republic
[5] Department of Evolutionary Biology, University of Vienna, Vienna, Austria

Abstract. The realm of retail investment encompasses a spectrum of decisions made by individuals seeking to allocate resources in anticipation of future returns. This study examines the implications of portfolio management and stock request behavior for developer- and economy-oriented game design. The research methodology uses a simulated investment game to bridge the gap between simulated environments and real-life investment scenarios. A total of 888 participants, aged 20–24 years, engaged in the game, which featured 66 companies and 49 rounds, simulating a 49-day tenure of companies in the market. We employed Bayesian statistical methodology to estimate the likelihood of participants being female based on the sex ratio in the sample. Additionally, we used SVD (singular value decomposition) to smooth the data matrix representing the investment choices made by participants across the companies and rounds. Furthermore, we employed the DBSCAN algorithm to detect clustering in the 66 rows of SVD-smoothed mean share prices. By incorporating elements of realism, complexity, and strong participant motivation, we provided a robust and immersive investment experience compared to existing investment games. The findings contribute to a better understanding of individual investment decision-making processes within the game theory framework.

Keywords: Investment Decision-making · Behavioral Finance · Singular Value Decomposition · Bayesian Statistics · Beta Distribution · DBSCAN algorithm

1 Introduction: The Stock Acquisition Game

1.1 Overview

Investing in the stock market is often viewed as a standard path to building wealth. Yet, despite its accessibility, only a portion of the population participates. This seeming paradox is due to two key factors: opportunity and risk. While investing offers the

X. Fang (Ed.): HCII 2024, LNCS 14730, pp. 114–126, 2024.
https://doi.org/10.1007/978-3-031-60692-2_9

potential for significant gains, it also carries inherent risks of losses, leading many individuals, particularly those with limited financial resources or risk tolerance, to shy away. Ultimately, the decision to invest becomes a personal calculation, weighing the potential rewards against the inherent risks and navigating the financial literacy gap that can further complicate the equation.

The current retail investment reflects the dynamic nature of today's financial landscape, characterized by almost innumerable factors that include economic shifts, technological advancements, and global interconnectedness. Within this context, investors face an increasingly complex terrain while seeking opportunities for wealth accumulation and at the same time managing risks inherent in volatile markets (Célérier and Vallée, 2017). Currently, personal investment serves as a cornerstone for securing individuals' and families' livelihoods, ensuring a certain standard of living, and preparing for retirement (Campbell, 2016; Frydman & Camerer, 2016). The evolution of investment strategies is shaped by ongoing adaptation to market dynamics, as well as the integration of emerging trends such as sustainable investing and emerging products within the market (e.g., crypto assets, and digital assets). In this era of rapid information dissemination and heightened market transparency, investment principles emphasize the importance of diversification and a long-term perspective to optimize returns and mitigate associated risks (Adam and Branda, 2021).

1.2 Specifics of Investing

The specifics of investing include challenges that investors confront in their pursuit of financial growth and stability. A major obstacle arises from the inherent complexity of learning from investment experiences, as financial markets exhibit unpredictable behavior. Unlike conventional learning environments in which feedback mechanisms facilitate knowledge acquisition and skill refinement, the feedback loop in investing is often opaque and ambiguous. Investors may receive delayed, erroneous, or inadequate feedback on their decisions, hindering their ability to discern effective strategies from erroneous ones (Lurie and Swaminathan, 2009). Therefore, neither knowledge nor expertise might protect investors against market volatility, let alone the influence of external factors beyond their control (Malmendier et al., 2020). Recognizing nuances is imperative for investors so that they adopt a prudent and adaptive approach to investing while at the same time acknowledging the limitations of 'conventional' wisdom and historical precedents. Finally, as postulated by Prospect Theory, people are generally risk-averse in the domain of gains (Ruggeri et al., 2020). Therefore, they rather prefer safe profits, for example in savings accounts, compared to the uncertain results of investments, even though the net value of the investment might greatly exceed the returns of savings accounts. This assumption could elucidate the phenomenon of underinvestment or complete abstention from market participation among retail investors.

1.3 Heuristics and Biases Influencing Individual Investment Decision-Making

Furthermore, individual investment decision-making is intrinsically influenced by personal characteristics and individual behavioral aspects, including cognitive heuristics and biases, which serve as cognitive shortcuts, but may also lead to systematic errors and suboptimal outcomes. Women are significantly more averse to investment undertakings than men are, whereas men have significantly stronger self-attribution, illusion of control, and confirmation biases than women do (Hsu et al., 2021). Stock allocations are higher for married investors, for younger investors, and for investors with higher savings in 401(k) retirement accounts (Agnew et al., 2000). Furthermore, many behavioral aspects influence individual investment decision-making. For example, investors tend to spread their assets uniformly across the selected investment opportunities, imitating diversification (Bardolet et al., 2011). Investors might also exhibit conservatism either in the form of the primacy effect or status quo preference (Harbi and Toumia, 2020). Some investors are reluctant to admit that their investment is not behaving according to plan and hold on to losses for too long (explained via the Disposition Effect), as is indicated by low numbers of underperforming assets sold within their portfolios (Haryanto et al., 2020). The above-named specifics of investing, coupled with cognitive limitations, contribute to the formulation of inadequate investment choices, resulting in a considerable number of retail investors failing to even match the performance of benchmark market indices.

1.4 Stock Market Games and Simulations

Various investment games address these issues. In serious as well as entertainment gaming, there is the potential to develop investment skills, risk management skills, and wealth accruement skills. Some well-known and ubiquitous board games are Monopoly, Cashflow101, Game of Life, and Puerto Rico. Some computer game examples are Wall Street Survivor, How the Market Works, and Stock Market Game. The professed idea behind these games is to improve one's ability to choose suitable and sustainable strategies. Investment games constitute simulated environments designed to emulate real-world market dynamics and test participants' investment insights. However, the efficacy of such games is marred by inherent imperfections, including their departure from reality, insufficient participant motivation, oversimplified market mechanisms, and the absence of real-life consequences. Despite their pedagogical value in fostering basic financial literacy and strategic thinking, most investment games fail to replicate the intricacies and nuances of actual investment scenarios, limiting their utility as comprehensive learning tools.

1.5 The Current Study

In response to the limitations of existing investment games, our methodology seeks to bridge the gap between simulated environments and real-life investment scenarios. By incorporating elements of realism, complexity, and strong participant motivation, our approach aims to provide a more robust and immersive investment experience. Additionally, our methodology allows for ex-post analysis of individual investment decisions, enabling us to track and evaluate performance on an individual level—without the influence of external factors. By addressing these shortcomings, our approach aims to enhance the understanding of individual investments and attendant decision-making processes, especially in the context of the game theory framework.

2   Materials and Methods

2.1   Participants

The 888 participants (456 females and 432 males) were aged 20–24 years; further attributes are listed in Table 1.

Table 1. The distributions of properties of the 888 game participants

Property	Distributions		
Nationality	Czech (72%)	Slovak (26%)	Others (2%)
Marital Status	Single (40.5%)	In Relationship (57.0%)	Married (2.5%)
Level of Education	High School (87.4%)	Bachelor (11.2%)	Master (1.3%)
Employment Status	Unemployed (40.7%)	Working student (53.5%)	Other (5.8%)
Investment Experience	Regular (25.2%)	Occasional (50.7%)	None (24.2%)

2.2   Rules of the Game

The game featured 66 companies and 888 participants. It encompassed 49 rounds, simulating a 49-day tenure of companies in the market. At the onset of the game, all participants possessed identical information and were faced with the same situation—namely, to initially guess what shares to acquire. The aggregate remuneration accrued by the participants comprised both wages received after each seven-round cycle and returns derived from their preceding investments.

During the 49 rounds, participants had the opportunity to invest their wages in this market by acquiring available shares or leaving the money in a current interest-free account. The investment was free of charge. Each of the participants could invest in any of the companies listed. The market conditions have been adjusted to reflect several years of actual trading. Every participant understood that at the end of the final round of investment, their accounts would be liquidated without any fees. All participants were motivated to participate, as they stand to earn a recommended grade for an 8 ETCS university course based on their accumulated capital. Each participant had the freedom to select their investment strategy.

The game generates research opportunities by enabling comparisons of share developments among companies in the market, thereby providing comparable data and minimizing the impact of external variables undermining research in real-world settings (such as company size, historical background, initial circumstances, marketing and innovation strategies, and other information).

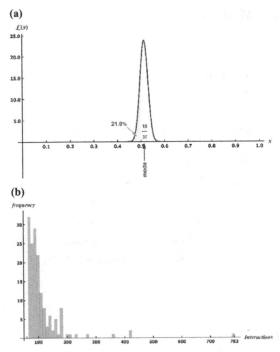

Fig. 1. Graphs displaying **(a)** the likelihood function (the *pdf* of the Beta distribution) of the probabilities of males $(1 - s)$ and females s participating in this investment game, and **(b)** the histogram of the participants most active in the game (61 or more requests, sales, or purchases) during the 49 rounds. In (a), we observe that the ratio ($\frac{19}{37} \approx 51\%$) is slightly skewed to a majority of females. However, the significance level (shaded area; 21%) is far too high. We conclude that the presented subsequent statistical analyses are (biological) sex-independent. (b) Of the 888 participants, very few (less than ten in each bin) participated more than 120 times (therefore, on average, more than twice a day). The most active participant had 783 activities.

2.3 Rigorous Statistical Analyses of Share Acquisition

1. Estimating the (biological) sex ratio: If there are n females (with probability s) in the sample, and m males (with probability $(1 - s)$, then the likelihood function is

$$\mathcal{L}(s) = c \times s^{n+1} \times (1 - s)^{m+1}$$

(Bishop, 2006; Lambert, 2018). The maximum of this function is the mode (*mode* = $\frac{n}{n+m}$), which is the most likely probability that a participant is female. The likelihood function, along with the mode's position, is shown in Fig. 1a. In Bayesian statistics, we estimate the significance by calculating the probability of the result not being $\frac{1}{2}$ (note that, in Bayesian statistics, the probability has a probability, namely the integral of the likelihood function (Kruschke, 2015; Lambert, 2018)).

2. Smoothing via SVD (singular value decomposition): The number of companies × the number of rounds is a 66 × 49 matrix. The entries in this matrix M are the scaled

means of share prices for each company at each round (scaled by dividing by the mean of each column and subtracting 1).

3. Clustering: We use the DBSCAN algorithm (Density-Based Spatial Clustering of Applications with Noise; Ester et al., 1996) to detect any clustering in the 66 rows (SVD-smoothed time series) of the mean share prices.

4. Heat map analysis: A comparison of one company's time series (a row in the heat map) with another one's requires constructing their 49-parametric Dirichlet distributions (Lambert, 2018) and using Monte Carlo methods; this method necessitates the computation of several billion random numbers for each comparison (a total of

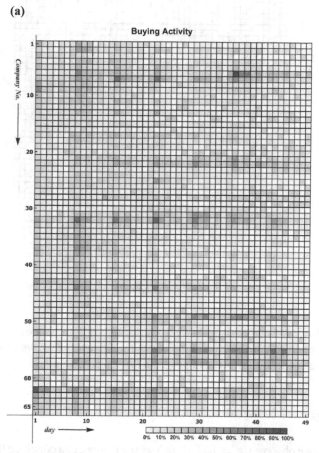

(a)

Fig. 2. The heat maps showing (a) buying activity, and (b) selling activity. (a) All frequencies of buying (share acquisition) are scaled versus the largest number of acquisitions for all days and all company shares. We observe that the acquisition numbers peak every 7th day and there are nine companies whose shares are preferentially bought. These preferences are not, however, significant (Fig. 3). (b) The scaling for the heat map of sales is the same as in Fig. 2a. We observe that hardly any selling of shares occurred during the 49 rounds. There are only four peak selling days, for three different companies (two for Company No. 25, one each for Company No. 37 and Company No. 58). On most days, no shares for any company were sold.

(b)

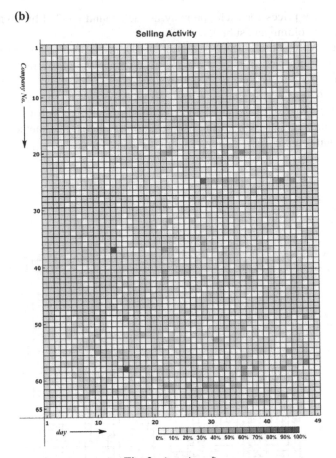

Fig. 2. (*continued*)

$\frac{1}{2} \times 66 \times 65 = 2145$ comparisons). We overcome this difficulty of excessive demands on computer performance with an approximation. For every row, we look at the totals of buys for all others, subtract, and generate the scaled heat map

3 Findings

In this sample, we observe $sig = \int_0^{1/2} \mathcal{L}(s)ds = 0.21$, so we can conclude that the difference between the number of females and the number of males is insignificant (Fig. 1a). We therefore can proceed in our analysis without regard to sex differences in game participation. Buying activity was not widely spread. We find, using DBSCAN, that only participants in the second cluster (168 of them; 19%) had more than 60 buying/selling activities during the 49 rounds (Fig. 1b).

All buying activities showed a periodicity—across all companies (Fig. 2a), and the peak buying activity was within 2 rounds after the wages had been paid. Furthermore,

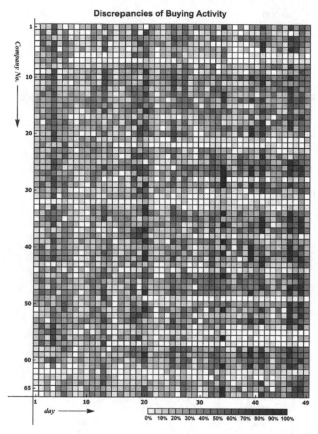

Fig. 3. The heat map showing the discrepancies in the buying activity of a company's shares versus all buying activities of the other companies combined. This heat map shows the result of testing whether there exists preferential buying of shares of a company versus other companies (see text for the algorithmic details of the test). The results are *scaled* (The maximum deviation is $\frac{16}{65} \approx 0.246$). We observe a 7-day periodicity (albeit not very pronounced), and only one company deviating markedly (Company No. 32).

there was no significant difference between the buying patterns of specific companies (Fig. 3).

Selling activities were very few (Fig. 2b). We observed no clustering (not shown).

The scree plot (not shown) of the squares of the singular values showed that the use of the first two singular values extracted 97% of the square of the Frobenius norm of the matrix of buying activities (Leon, 1999). The smoothed time series of the share price means occurred in four clusters (with 46, 3, 5, and 12 members—the last being isolates which we label 'stragglers'). We observed a trend of average share price increase for 46 (Cluster No. 1) of the 66 companies (Fig. 4a). This trend was overlaid with a 7-day periodicity (Fig. 4a), coinciding with the periodicity observed in the heat map (Fig. 2a). The smoothed share price time series clustered of Clutters No. 2 (three companies) and No. 3 (five companies) showed an increasing trend, but no perceptible pattern beyond

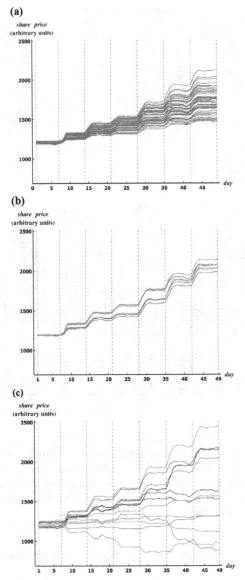

Fig. 4. The smoothed time series of the mean share prices paid by participants during the 49-day game, separated by clusters. The time series of **(a)** the 46 companies in Cluster #1, **(b)** the 3 companies in Cluster #2 (magenta) and the 5 companies in Cluster #3 (olive), and **(c)** the 12 'singletons' (various colors). In Clusters #1 and #2, we observe the anticipated periodicity. The 12 'singletons' ($\frac{12}{66} \approx 18.5\%$) have erratic behavior (some of the mean share prices fall). The smoothing was achieved using SVD (singular value decomposition); details are described in the text.

periodicity (Fig. 2b). The times series of the 12 'stragglers' (those not in Cluster No.1 nor Cluster No. 2) were those with no statistically significant pattern (Fig. 4c).

4 Discussion

The investment game aimed to bridge the gap between simulated environments and real-life investment scenarios by incorporating elements of realism, complexity, and participant motivation. Drawing upon the principles of game theory, this article delves into the strategic interactions among market participants and their investment decision-making processes and investment strategies. The findings indicate a remarkable lack of selling previously acquired shares within personal investment portfolios. This finding is consistent with the assumption of Prospect Theory, suggesting that investors are likely to focus on gains rather than the perceived risk of loss when the outcome of the investment is uncertain. The significance of this assumption is heightened in instances characterized by positive nominal values of investments, which align with the price dynamics of companies in the environment under examination. (Barberis, 2013; Zhuo et al., 2021).

Participants showed no strong preferences for individual companies nor were there any recurring patterns in selecting the stocks of firms they wanted to purchase. The only exception was the buying and selling behavior 1–2 days after receiving the wage. What we observed is typical consumer behavior in which individual demand increases after receiving a wage. Especially cash-strapped people are more likely to increase their spending after receiving income, with the response mainly due to the convenience of linking regular payments to regular income (Gelman et al., 2014). However, the information about spending indicates that the perceived heightened responsiveness of spending primarily stems from the simultaneous occurrence of regular income and regular spending. Increased sensitivity is predominantly found among individuals who possess lower liquidity. However, none of the above-described reasons are confirmed in the observations concerning our data. Within a managerial simulation game, most of the participants kept a large amount of money in their current accounts and made most of their investment decisions only in the 1–2 trading days of the cycle after receiving wages.

The problems of inappropriate and insufficient investment can be addressed within a cautiously defined psychological framework. Within long-term investment decision-making, in the realm of game design, the concept of "Save More Tomorrow" (SMarT; Thaler and Benartzi, 2004; Reiff et al., 2023) offers valuable insights into fostering suitable investment behaviors among players. Inspired by behavioral economics principles, SMarT and analogous strategies encourage people to save more over time based on an advanced commitment to their current savings and accompanying investment increases in the future. As with other deferred remuneration experiments (Cheng et al., 2019), within the context of game design, players may be prompted and remunerated to allocate a percentage of their wealth towards long-term investments. Moreover, game designers might incorporate features that facilitate the automatic escalation of investment commitments over time.

The insights gained from this management simulation game serve as a presentation of both the strengths and the limitations inherent in this paper. While the findings obtained from a student sample exhibited some reasonable internal validity, the external validity is constrained. The game environment mimics and simplifies the financial markets in comparison to real investment scenarios, with participants regularly receiving updated information on companies' historical and current stock performances. Despite this gaming constraint, the simulation game's characteristics suggest that the knowledge gained might be cautiously applied by the participants in future, actual investment environments. The simulation was complex enough, as it spanned several months (49 rounds) with participants presumably highly motivated. Participants were particularly interested in their outcomes due to the connection between game results and course credits. A key advantage of the simulation game was its ability to analyze an inhomogeneous group of investors (Fig. 1b) operating under identical initial conditions. Furthermore, the financial market comprised companies that were shaped solely by investors' supply and demand without external interference.

5   Conclusion: Inferences for Future Game Designs

While the current retail investment landscape mirrors the dynamic nature of our financial world, with complex factors such as economic shifts and global interconnectedness demanding strategic navigation, many young individuals remain hesitant to enter the field. This hesitancy might stem from the daunting complexity, inherent risks, and individual psychological aspects associated with traditional investing. Enter gamified finance—a potential solution that leverages young adults' digital fluency and engagement with games to introduce them to investment principles in a safe, engaging environment.

A computer game is where young individuals can experiment with different investment strategies, track virtual market fluctuations, and learn from both successes and failures without risking real money.

This gamified approach could address the following three key challenges confronting young investors:

1. Unpredictable Feedback: Unlike real-world markets, games can provide immediate and clear feedback on investment decisions, allowing players to refine their skills and strategies iteratively.
2. Knowledge Gap: Many games can be designed to incorporate educational elements, teaching players about different asset classes, market dynamics, and risk management.
3. Risk Aversion: By removing the threat of real-world financial stakes, a game like this one can create a safe space for experimentation, thereby fostering confidence and encouraging informed risk-taking.

While traditional expertise and knowledge are always valuable, the rapid pace of financial innovation demands alternative avenues for learning and encouraging engagement. Gamified finance has the potential to bridge the gap for young investors, equipping them with the skills and confidence needed to navigate the complexities of the modern financial landscape. This, in turn, could lead to a more informed and active investor base, shaping the future of the financial ecosystem.

Gamified finance shouldn't be perceived as a replacement for financial education or encouraging responsible investment practices in the real world. Rather, it should be a cornerstone providing a foundation for further learning and engagement with the real market.

Ethics Statement. As a student project, this data collection did not necessitate an IRB approval; the Helsinki Declaration and GDPR rules were adhered to at all times. All data provided were fully anonymized. Participants signed an informed consent prior to participation.

Acknowledgments. We thank Jan Zak for sharing the data obtained from the management simulation game.

Conflict of Interest. The authors declare they have no conflicts of interest.

References

Agnew, J., Balduzzi, P., Sunden, A.: Portfolio choice, trading, and returns in a large 401(k) plan. In: Center for Retirement Research Working Papers, 40 (2000)

Barberis, N.C.: Thirty years of prospect theory in economics: a review and assessment. J. Econ. Perspect. **27**(1), 173–196 (2013)

Bardolet, D., Fox, C.R., Lovallo, D.: Corporate capital allocation: a behavioral perspective. Strateg. Manag. J. **32**(13), 1465–1483 (2011)

Bishop, C.M.: Pattern Recognition and Machine Learning. Springer, New York, NY, USA (2006)

Campbell, J.Y.: Restoring rational choice: the challenge of consumer financial regulation. Am. Econ. Rev. **106**(5), 1–30 (2016)

Cheng, M.M., Dinh, T., Schultze, W., Assel, M.: The effect of bonus deferral on managers' managers' investment decisions. Behav. Res. Account. **31**(2), 31–49 (2019)

Ester, M., Kriegel, H.-P., Sander, J., Xu, X.: A density-based algorithm for discovering clusters in large spatial databases with noise. In: Simoudis, E., Han, J., Fayyad, U.M. (eds.) Proceedings of the Second International Conference on Knowledge Discovery and Data Mining (KDD-1996), pp. 226–231. AAAI Press (1996)

Frydman, C., Camerer, C.F.: The psychology and neuroscience of financial decision making. Trends Cogn. Sci. **20**(9), 661–675 (2016). https://doi.org/10.1016/j.tics.2016.07.00

El Harbi, S., Toumia, O.: The status quo and the investment decisions. Manag. Financ. **46**(9), 1183–1197 (2020)

Gelman, M., Kariv, S., Shapiro, M.D., Silverman, D., Tadelis, S.: Harnessing naturally occurring data to measure the response of spending to income. Science **345**(6193), 212–215 (2014)

Haryanto, S., Subroto, A., Ulpah, M.: Disposition effect and herding behavior in the cryptocurrency market. J. Indus. Bus. Econ. **47**, 115–132 (2020)

Hsu, Y.L., Chen, H.L., Huang, P.K., Lin, W.Y.: Does financial literacy mitigate gender differences in investment behavioral bias? Financ. Res. Lett. **41**, 101789 (2021)

Kruschke, J.K.: Doing Bayesian Data Analysis: A Tutorial with R, JAGS, and Stan, 2nd edn. Elsevier/Academic Press, London, UK (2015)

Lambert, B.: A Student Guide to Bayesian Statistics. Sage Publications, London, UK (2018)

Leon, S.J.: Linear Algebra with Applications, 5th edn. Prentice Hall, NJ, USA (1999)

Malmendier, U., Pouzo, D., Vanasco, V.: Investor experiences and international capital flows. J. Int. Econ. **124**, 103–302 (2020)

Lurie, N.H., Swaminathan, J.M.: Is timely information always better? The effect of feedback frequency on decision making. Organ. Behav. Hum. Decis. Process. **108**(2), 315–329 (2009)

Reiff, J., Dai, H., Beshears, J., Milkman, K.L., Benartzi, S.: Save more today or tomorrow: the role of urgency in precommitment design. J. Mark. Res. **60**(6), 1095–1113 (2023)

Ruggeri, K., et al.: Replicating patterns of prospect theory for decision under risk. Nat. Hum. Behav. **4**(6), 622–633 (2020)

Strang, G.: Linear Algebra and Learning from Data. Wellesley-Cambridge Press, Wellesley (2019)

Thaler, R.H., Benartzi, S.: Save more tomorrow: Using behavioral economics to increase employee saving. J. Polit. Econ. **112**(S1), 164–187 (2004)

Zhuo, J., Li, X., Yu, C.: Parameter behavioral finance model of investor groups based on statistical approaches. Q. Rev. Econ. Finance **80**, 74–79 (2021)

Digital Gamification Design of Chinese Landscape Painting Based on Gesture Interaction

Jiaqi Xie⬤, Hao Zheng⬤, Junxian Lin⬤, and Xiaoying Tang^(✉)⬤

Guangdong University of Technology, Guangzhou, China
1009415641@qq.com

Abstract. Gamification design, as a mean of interactive design which is capable of increasing the sense of entertainment and enhancing user experience in non-gaming environments, has become an important avenue for the dissemination of traditional culture. This article is based on Leap Motion interaction technology and has designed an enframed scenery gamification system which allows viewer to experience the implicit beauty of Chinese landscape painting by appreciating one painting's performance under the layer of visual in different styles to improve the experience of painting experience. The design draws inspiration from the art of enframed scenery of Chinese classical garden, extracting 4 common frames as interactive windows between the participants and Chinese landscape painting. Viewers can use three simple hand gestures, "index extended", "index pinching and releasing with thumb", with the Leap Motion devices to achieve real-time switching between 2D and 3D styles of Chinese landscape painting, explore the landscapes, collage, and generate personalized Chinese landscape painting. 16 volunteers were recruited for interface usability testing, and the experimental results indicated that most volunteers preferred immersive visual appreciation in highly engaging non-contact interactive systems rather than rapid selection of images. They all agreed that this gamification system provides a reference for the digital design combing Chinese landscape painting and the art of enframed scenery of Chinese classical garden.

Keywords: Chinese Landscape Painting · The Art of Enframed Scenery · Gamification Design · Gesture Interaction

1 Introduction

Chinese landscape painting, as an essential component of traditional Chinese art, possesses significant aesthetic value and unique artistic concepts [1]. However, with the rapid advancement of science and technology and the impact of modern life, people's awareness of the preservation and inheritance of traditional Chinese art has dwindled. Most individuals are only familiar with the colorful Chinese green landscape painting, with limited knowledge of other styles of Chinese landscape painting. To stimulate people's interest in traditional art, the digital preservation of traditional culture has become

X. Fang (Ed.): HCII 2024, LNCS 14730, pp. 127–142, 2024.
https://doi.org/10.1007/978-3-031-60692-2_10

a focal point in both academic and artistic fields. Exploring how to deeply convey the classical and implicit beauty of Chinese landscape painting has become a trending topics in creativity. Chinese new media artist Cao, using Touch Designer programming technology, combined the renowned Chinese green landscape painting "Thousand Miles of Rivers and Mountains" with environmental pollution issues. He employed an open interactive narrative system to bridge the gap between traditional culture and the audience, allowing viewers to appreciate Chinese landscape painting while recognizing the urgency of environmental protection [2]. Tang et al. [3] analyzed interactive installations in ink art from the perspective of narrative context construction, conducting in-depth research on immersive digital design in Chinese ink art using interactive projection technology. Based on the theory of landscape spatial painting, Ding [4] created an immersive landscape experience that combined poetry and painting for participants using Kinect gesture interaction technology, enriching their understanding of traditional Chinese landscape painting. In 2018, the British Museum combined the light red landscape painting "Pictures of Reading in Autumn Woods" with 3D technology, creating an immersive space for viewers to explore. Based on the aforementioned case studies and literature, it is evident that existing research and creative works primarily focus on the visual representation of a single two-dimensional or three-dimensional style of the same one, lacking diverse interpretations of other types of Chinese landscape painting styles. Additionally, few artists have connected the art of Chinese classical garden, closely related to the artistic expression and content of Chinese landscape painting, with their artwork [5]. In the initial design phase, we interviewed 6 young volunteers who had visited The Suzhou Garden and collected their most memorable images. We discovered that people's routes while observing Chinese classical garden were highly random, and visual focal points were scattered, similar to the scattered perspective in Chinese landscape painting. We also found that the most frequently occurring element in the 87 collected photos was the enframed scenery. Therefore, this paper uses the Chinese Green landscape painting "Peach Blossom Wonderland" as a case study and combines it with the art of enframed scenery of Chinese classical garden. We employed Leap Motion gesture interaction technology to create an exhibition experience gaming system for real-time switching between various styles of Chinese landscape painting. Unlike other works, we cleverly combined Chinese line drawn landscape painting, Chinese ink landscape painting, and Chinese Green landscape painting styles through real-time 2D and 3D visual effects and sound effects. We defined three simple interaction gestures to switch between enframed mode and panoramic mode, allowing participants to control the scenery frame with simple gestures, achieve multiple style changes of Chinese landscape painting, and create personalized enframed artworks. This deepened participants' impressions and feelings of different artistic styles of the same Chinese landscape paintings, enriching their understanding of the diversity of Chinese landscape painting styles (Fig. 1).

This paper makes three contributions:

- It explores the design of switching between different styles of Chinese landscape painting in 2D and 3D, broadening participants' understanding of the various types of Chinese landscape painting and providing design ideas for similar traditional culture digital designs.

- It investigates the possibility of combining Chinese landscape painting with the enframed scenery in Chinese classical garden. During the design process, it provides interview content from volunteers regarding their experiences in viewing Chinese classical garden, serving as material for the digital art of enframed scenery.
- It explores the potential of non-contact interaction based on Leap Motion device in the digital design of Chinese landscape painting and conducts experiments on interface layout for enframed mode and panoramic mode based on the randomness of participants' movement paths and dispersed viewpoints in real-life garden viewing, providing material for highly engaging public non-contact interactive interface design.

Fig. 1. Three visual style renderings

2 Background

Chinese landscape painting and Chinese classical garden both embody the philosophical concept of "advocating nature, learning from nature, and integrating with nature" in traditional Chinese culture. They are the material carriers for Chinese art creators to express their personal emotions [26,36-37, 6] and Chinese classical garden and Chinese landscape painting also have similarities in their appreciation methods and visual aesthetic characteristics [61,7]. The garden designer arranged the natural landscape and man-made objects according to specific compositions, and set up different types of scenery frames in various directions in the garden to increase the enjoyment of appreciation: viewers see the scenery through the scenery frames, and the scenery frames serve as picture frames, the placed scenery and pedestrians act as still life and animals. Therefore, the scenery frame and the combination of dynamic and static scenery constitute a miniature dynamic landscape painting. The viewers standing in front of the scenery frame is admiring the scenery as well as the picture; while the pedestrians standing behind the scenery frame form a whole with other scenery. During the process of appreciation, people are not only a viewer but also a part of the garden scenery, and the frames like windows integrate the viewer and the garden scenery to form a unique visual experience, which is the art of emframed scenery (see Fig. 2) [38,6]. And when the viewer stands in front of the frame, he can see different scenery in the frame by changing his position and viewing angle. The scenery in the frame also changes due to changes in time and space. This appreciation effect is reflected in traditional Chinese art expressions. Which is called "Changing Scenery with Each Step" (see Fig. 3). Changing scenery with each step is an artistic expression technique based on scattered point perspective. It is widely used by

Chinese art creators in the drawing of Chinese landscape painting. Compared with the Western focus perspective method, its advantage is that it can present multiple time and space pictures at the same time in a limited canva, allowing the viewers to see dynamic narrative stories on a static picture [41,6].

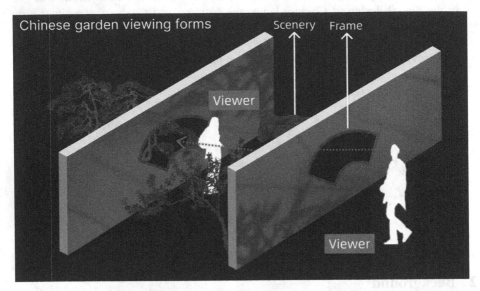

Fig. 2. Principles of the enframed of art appreciation

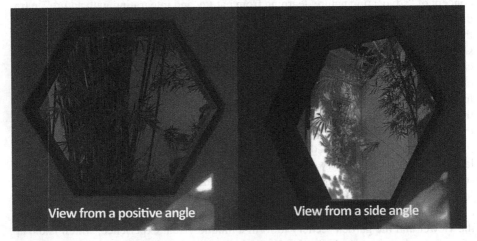

Fig. 3. The viewing effect of changing steps and scenery

With the rapid development of digital technology today, the technique of Changing Scenery with Each Step has also been widely used in the creation of games and gamification systems [8]. "Flappy Bird", which was launched on May 24, 2013, became popular due to its simple gameplay. The players only need to click on the screen to control the bird to pass through the pipe gap. The game background will switch to day and night according to the advancement of game time to enrich the visual performance of the game; In the "Cup Head" 2D side-scrolling adventure game launched on September 29, 2017, the player's behavior will affect the game progress, and the game scene will be converted in real time as the game progress changes to affect the player's operations, allowing the player to experience a variety of experiences in the limited 2D horizontal board space. The fun of space transformation increases the immersion and entertainment of the game; In order to attract more young people to pay attention to China's tea-ordering culture, Li et al. [9] designed a remote VR tea-ordering game based on the "Dian cha" teaching model and "Dian cha" process. In terms of visual expression, dispersed perspective and multi-layer ink effects are used to represent China's unique ink painting style. Players can appreciate the scene through different angles and viewing media in the VR scene, thereby achieving different visual effects. Based on the above background and cases, we can find the possibility of using the of changing scenery with each step in gamification design, and viewers can only passively accept a given scenery and picture whether they are appreciating Chinese classical garden or Chinese landscape painting, lack of multi-style conversion and independent exploration and creation. Therefore, our design goal is to integrate the way of appreciating the scenery of Chinese classical garden through the landscape frame into the appreciation of Chinese landscape painting, viewing and creating different landscape paintings through the "window".

3   Design and Implementation

Understanding the behavioral logic of the viewers is the prerequisite for more effective interaction design [10]. Therefore, to clarify the gamification system's interaction model before starting the design, it became our research goal to understand the behavioral preferences of viewers when appreciating Chinese classical garden' landscapes. We used semi-structured interviews and interviewed 6 volunteers who had visited the Suzhou Garden in the past three months. Their ages ranged from 19 to 25 years old. The interview questions mainly revolved around route selection, focus and aesthetic feelings. In terms of route selection, all 6 volunteers pointed that there were no clear routes and signs in the park. Tourists generally choose viewing spots freely, and the walking routes were very random. The main factor that affected their decision-making on walking routes was the flow of people. They will alienate those places tourists are massively gathering and choose to enjoy the scenery in a far distance with bird view; in terms of focus, 1 volunteer said that the color matching of the frame in the architectural elements attracted him, and 3 volunteers paid attention to the type of frame in the architectural elements. This indicates that the shapes of the frames in the garden are different. 2 volunteers paid more attention to the natural visual elements and believed that the natural visual elements would be more artistic when it was combined to the garden's design. At the same time, we required volunteers to provide photos of the scenic spots that they thought were most impressive, and used the rocks, water, flowers, trees, and buildings contained in the photos as the basis for counting the number of scenic elements [4, 7]. We collected a total of 87 photos, of which 19 involved mountain and rock elements, 16 involved water elements, 42 involved flowers and trees, and 53 involved architectural elements. During the photo classification process, it was found that 68 enframed scenery elements appeared in 87 photos. Combined with Jiang's [66,7] eye movement experiment, it was concluded that people are more likely to be attracted by the implicit space created by the frame during the viewing process. It was attractive and plays an important role in creating the visual effect of changing scenery with each step. Therefore, we confirmed that the art of enframed scenery will be used to the design of the interactive system design, and Chinese landscape painting of various styles will be used as the gamification system's interactive content.

3.1 Design Purpose

Based on the above analysis of the relationship among the art of emframed scenery and Chinese landscape painting and user research, we clarified three design goals.

Appreciate. Viewers can use Leap Motion gestures to interactively draw, move, and zoom the scene frame to appreciate Chinese landscape painting in three styles: 2D Chinese line drawn landscape painting, 3D Chinese ink landscape painting, and Chinese green landscape painting, thus approaching the real effect of changing scenery with each step, allowing viewers to fully understanding the types and layers of Chinese landscape painting is also the core of this gamification system.

Creation. Viewers can add new scene frame at any time to enrich the picture during the viewing experience, allowing viewers to use different types and shapes of frames to form new pictures, and scan the QR code to save the picture as a souvenir. It allows viewers to truly participate in the creation of Chinese landscape painting while appreciating Chinese landscape painting, making Chinese landscape painting more diverse and specific.

Experience. Viewers can feel the changes in natural sound effects while switching between Chinese landscape painting styles. The application of sound implies the "Borrowed Scenery" artistic expression technique that combines audio and video that often appears in Chinese classical garden [34,6]. Natural sound effect plays a role in imaginative extension in a limited interactive space, thus improving the experience of the viewers.

3.2 Gamification System Design

The gamification system that revolves around the art of emframed scenery of Chinese classical garden and the switching of Chinese landscape painting styles, using Leap Motion devices as the gesture interaction media. The gameplay for viewer is that viewer use different hand gesture under the guidance of the prompt proving by the user interface and applied their imagination to assemble their 3D Chinese ink landscape painting as the game reward (see the section on interactive gesture design). It allows viewers to have a deeper perception of one specific Chinese ink landscape painting with its performance under various painting styles, and a more unique insight of the emframed scenery. Since the ultimate goal of gamification design is to allow viewers to appreciate Chinese landscape painting, there is no time limit on the entire gamification interaction process.

Interactive Gesture Design. To embrace more people, appreciate and understand different types of Chinese landscape painting, we set the usage scene of the game device in a public exhibition hall and use it with a large monitor. In public exhibition halls where the purpose of interaction is to appreciate Chinese landscape painting, non-contact interaction has become the preferred interaction method [11]: 1. The adjustment of the interaction distance between the audience and the display is relatively flexible, and under a certain interaction distance, the viewer is allowed to Observe the entire screen layout to facilitate interaction with the audience. 2. Public interactive devices are increasingly popular in daily life, and non-contact interaction provides a more hygienic experience, which can effectively reduce the viewer's concerns about hygiene issues. For example, in special environments such as children's hospitals, Lim et al. [12] designed a non-contact interactive information kiosk for family members to use to reduce the tension of children's family members while ensuring hygiene and safety. 3. The layout of the display is more flexible without the constraint of the touch interaction method. 4. Reduce the probability of equipment damage due to touch on the.

After choosing non-contact interaction as the basic techniques for the gamification system, we learned that Leap Motion gesture interaction was a higher-precision non-contact interaction method, which could give the viewer high-resolution visual feedback and could generally be used to preview screen effects, displayed operation prompts, and selected objects, and other interactive behaviors, so we set the interaction distance between the screen and the viewer as 0.5m. In order to fit the viewer's behavioral habits during interaction using Leap Motion gestures as much as possible [13] and reduce the cognitive cost of interaction [14], we defined four Leap Motion gestures: (1) keep the index extended (see Fig. 4-a), (2) the thumb and index pinch together (see Fig. 4-b), (3) the thumb and index open (see Fig. 4-c) [15], (4) the thumb and index maintain relative positions and rotate (see Fig. 4-d) four gestures action completed the following game process (see Fig. 5):

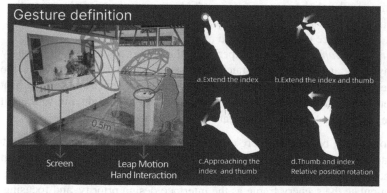

Fig. 4. Interaction scenario simulation diagram and gesture definition

Firstly, the viewers could activate the rectangular menu bar at the bottom of the interface by sliding left and right with (a) gesture: on the left side of the rectangle menu four types of scenery frames, and on the right side is a menu bar used to select shape of a certain scenery frame. When the viewer slid the rectangle menu left and right to select a shape according to the text prompts, the selected shape will be moved to the middle of the screen, and the corresponding dotted line graphic will automatically appear on the blank screen above, and the selected graphic will be emphasized and enlarged to avoid unnecessary Interaction blind spots caused by unclear interaction design [16]. Then, the viewer can use the (a) gesture to follow the auxiliary lines to complete the drawing of the scenery frame. If the viewer fails to complete the drawing of the frame, he will be required to redraw. Once the scenery frame is successfully drawn, a Chinese line drawn landscape picture will automatically appear in the scenery frame, and the viewer will be reminded in text that the scenery frame type cannot be modified; the "Peach Garden Wonderland Picture" will appear in the top left corner of the interface. The Picture Scroll Navigation is used as a game map to remind the viewer of the location of the content in the scenery frame; the viewer can also move the scenery frame to observe the entire painting; there are three button located at the top screen: "Switch Chinese Landscape Painting Style", "Save the Scenery Frame" and "Start Again" appear" buttons, viewer can use the (a) gesture to click the corresponding button at any time to switch styles for viewing or saving the satisfied picture as a game reward, and finally end the game; if viewer want to change the shape or type of the scenery frame during the interaction process, then viewer need to click the "Restart" button.

When the viewer interacts, this gamification system provides the following three functions to enrich the interactive experience.

1. *Change the Content.* Viewers can use the (a) gesture to click anywhere on the left scroll navigation to change the content in the scenery frame, allowing the viewers to freely explore the Scroll Map, strengthening the viewers' autonomy in viewing path selection and viewpoint dispersion, and trying to cater viewers' habits on the sight-seeing the gardens. The mentioned viewers' behavior habits when actually viewing the Chinese classical garden.
2. *Reduce the Scene Frame.* During the experience, the viewer can use gesture (c) at any time to shrink the scenery frame, which is convenient for observing the overall appearance of the scene frame and locating the position of the scenery frame. At this time, the interface is in the enframed mode.
3. *Enlarge the Frame.* During the experience, the viewer can enlarge the scenery frame at any time, and zoom in as much as possible to enter the panoramic mode for immersive viewing. The viewer can also add new scenery frames in the panoramic screen to enrich the picture, Once the scenery frame is reducing to the enframed mode, the internal scenery frame cannot be modified.

Among them, because the core of the game system is to allow the viewer to fully appreciate the changes in the visual effects style of Chinese landscape painting, two ideas had emerged in the interface design: taking the range of movement that the viewer can manipulate the scenery frame as the interface design priority, and focusing on the scenery. The interactive space of the scenery frame; or the interface design priority was to allow the viewer to jump to the position of the scenery frame at any time to observe the picture scroll, focusing on the quick selection of the content of the scenery frame. Both of them served the goal of viewing Chinese landscape painting, but the service side The user experience will be different if the focus is different. According to the

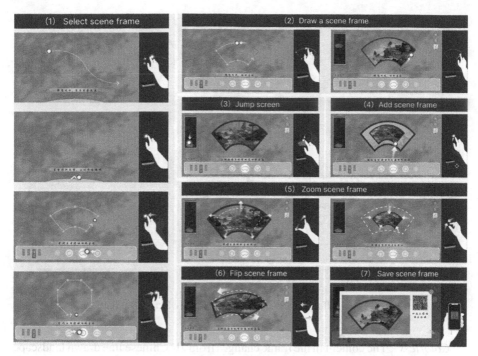

Fig. 5. Flow of interaction

content of early interviews, we had learned that the route selection of viewers when viewing Chinese classical garden is highly random; and the visual movement lines of viewing are scattered and there is no fixed viewpoint [60,7]. Therefore, we designed two sizes of the picture scroll navigation interfaces for the *Change the Content* function, enframed mode and panoramic mode interface: 1. The picture scroll navigation accounts for 1/14 of the entire interface, and the rectangle menu is placed right at the button of the interface (see Fig. 6-a, c). 2. The picture scroll navigation only occupies 1/5 of the entire interface, and the rectangular navigation bar is placed on the lower-right of the interface (see Fig. 6-b, d). Subsequently, we conducted experiments to evaluate the usability and the user experience of these two ratios.

Interaction Hierarchy Design. In terms of the audio-visual language expression, this design used the famous Chinese green landscape painting "Peach Blossom Wonderland" as the basic visual style, and extended the Chinese ink landscape painting and Chinese line drawn landscape painting versions of "Peach Blossom Wonderland" as the auxiliary visual styles, and based on this painting, three different visual style were designed for mutual conversion among them (see Fig. 7):

1. *"Intangible"*. The content in the frame changes from white wall (a) to 2D Chinese line drawn landscape painting (b) picture. The viewer uses gestures to draw a frame on the blank interface to capture the content of the Chinese line drawn painting picture, which is the process of Chinese landscape painting from intangible to tangible.

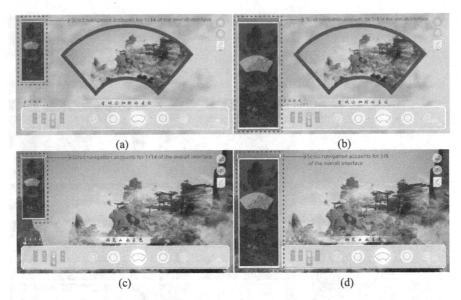

Fig. 6. Two different ratio design of the Picture Scroll Navigation

2. *"Colorless"*. The content in the frame changes from 2D Chinese line drawn landscape painting (b) to 3D Chinese ink landscape painting(c) picture. The viewer clicks the button to switch styles to switch the picture to Chinese ink landscape painting picture, realizing real-time conversion between 2D and 3D, which is the process of Chinese landscape painting from colorless to colored.

3. *"Silent"*. The content in the frame changes from 3D Chinese ink landscape painting(c) picture to 3D Chinese green landscape painting(d) picture. The viewer clicks the switch style button to switch the screen to a 3D Chinese green landscape painting(d) screen. As the screen changes, natural sound effects such as water flow and bird calls will appear. Auditory-assisted vision plays the role of "Borrowing Scenery" in the Chinese classical garden landscaping techniques during the viewing process [34,5]. The intervention of auditory senses enriches the viewing experience, expanding the content of observation from a single painting to a three-dimensional and realistic landscape.

The three visual styles can be switched at any time according to the preferences of the viewer, and the corresponding three levels will also transform into each other, allowing the viewer to understand the concept of advocating nature and being close to nature in classical Chinese philosophy, and experience the elegant spirit of Chinese art creators pursuit [17].

In terms of scenery frame selection, we selected four types of scenery frames, including Kong Chuang, Lou Chuang, Jing Chuang and Dong Men that are commonly types of the scenery frames in Chinese classical garden (see Fig. 8) [18], as "windows" for the interaction between viewer and multi-style Chinese landscape painting. 3D models were then constructed based on the authentic scenery frames.

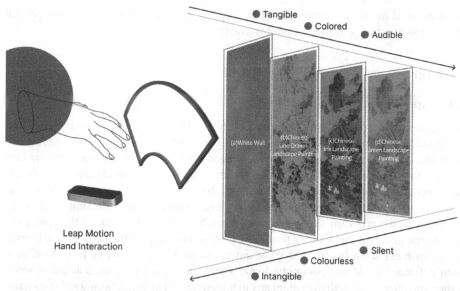

Fig. 7. Three audio-visual levels corresponding to three visual styles

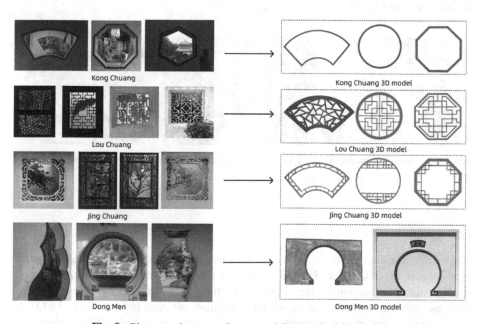

Fig. 8. Pictures of scenery frames and the matched 3D model

Implementation of Interactive Technology. In order to restore the original painting effect as much as possible, we used Blender software to build a model with reference to "Peach Blossom Wonderland" and the scenery frames of the real Suzhou Garden, and create stylized material, and then imported all the materials into Unreal Engine 5 to build the scene and use it the Unreal Engine 5 blueprint developed the Leap Motion gesture interaction program to realize gesture interaction.

4   User Experience and Assessment

4.1   Experimental Design

To explore the impact of two picture scroll navigation ratios on user experience, we designed two interface ratios specifically for the function of *Change the Content*. 10 volunteers, including 5 males and 5 females aged between 19 and 25, were recruited for the interface usability experiment. Among them, three had previous experience with gesture interaction devices, while seven had no such experience. To assess their behavioral tendencies when fully understanding the interaction processes and functions, before the experiment, we provided the volunteers with a brief description of all the functions, interaction processes, and interaction goals involved in the gamification system. During the experiment, we instructed the 10 volunteers to interact freely using Leap Motion in both enframed mode and panorama mode. After the experiment, we conducted semi-structured interviews with the volunteers to understand their concerns towards this gamification system, preferences for the two picture scroll navigation designs, and overall evaluations (see Fig. 9).

Fig. 9. Researcher introduced the system to volunteers and guided them to interact with the system.

4.2   Result

Meanwhile, we also invited 6 volunteers who had undergone interviews regarding the viewing patterns of Chinese classical garden to participate in the experiment, examining whether the gamification system aligns with their actual garden viewing movement patterns and visual effects. The main interview questions included (see Table 1): Q1: In enframed mode and panorama mode, what is your first step, and why? Q2: In these two modes, what do you think the impact of the two picture scroll navigation ratios, 1/14 and 1/5, respectively, will have on your interactions? Q3: In these two modes, which picture scroll navigation ratio do you prefer, and why? Q4: Do you think this gamification system enhances your impression of Chinese landscape painting styles? Q5: What suggestions and comments do you have for this gamification system? We summarized the noteworthy Q&A highlights and suggestions.

Table 1. Interview questions.

Dimensions	Question
Interactive behavior	Q1: In enframed mode and panorama mode, what is your first step, and why?
	Q2: In these two modes, what do you think the impact of the two picture scroll navigation ratios, 1/14 and 1/5, respectively, will have on your interactions?
Interactive preference	Q3: In these two modes, which picture scroll navigation ratio do you prefer, and why?
Interactive experience	Q4: Do you think this gamification system enhances your impression of Chinese landscape painting styles?
	Q5: What suggestions and comments do you have for this gamification system?

Regarding the Focus. More than 80% of volunteers were more concerned about interactive logic and immersive experiences. Among them, four volunteers raised questions during the interaction process regarding the movement of the scenery frame and 3D scenes. They pointed out that there is a lack of clear prompts for the target of operation in enframed mode, making it difficult for volunteers to determine whether the frame or the 3D scene is moving. This may lead to misunderstandings during the interaction process. Additionally, three volunteers were more focused on the interactive effects in panorama mode and attempts to interact with 3D objects in this mode. They hoped the gamification system could provide more interaction trigger points, such as prompting users to interact at a certain forest location, guiding viewers to click on the forest to trigger animations like birds flying out of the trees.

Regarding the Choice Between the Two Scroll Navigation Ratios. More than 85% of volunteers preferred the 1/14 interface ratio for picture scroll navigation. They believed that in a gamification system primarily focused on immersive appreciation of artworks, *Changing the Content* rapidly was not the main function. Therefore, the problem of insufficient autonomous interaction space caused by excessive picture scroll navigation should be reduced. Eight volunteers suggested that the picture scroll navigation ratios for both modes should be 1/14, as they felt a 1/5 picture scroll navigation area was too large, potentially hindering the immersive experience in panorama mode and diminishing the overall experience. They further pointed out that directly removing the picture scroll navigation in panorama mode could maximize the immersive experience. Additionally, four volunteers suggested providing a button in the interface, allowing viewers to switch between the two picture scroll navigation ratios at any time: when viewers want to observe the original painting details and quickly jump between screens, they can switch to the 1/5 picture scroll navigation ratio. When they want to autonomously manipulate the scenery frame to preview the overall scene, they can switch to the 1/14 picture scroll navigation ratio, increasing viewers' autonomy in choosing between the two picture scroll navigation ratios. Two volunteers proposed using a 1/5 picture scroll navigation ratio in enframed mode to better emphasize the viewer's autonomous selection of images, while using a 1/14 picture scroll navigation ratio in panorama mode to better emphasize the immersive exploration of images. This differentiated design highlights the interaction focus in the two modes.

Regarding the Overall Evaluation of the System. Volunteers who participated in interviews during the early design phase all stated that the interactive methods of this gamification system align with their actual habits of touring gardens. Their views were consistent with those of the volunteers recruited during the experimental phase, believing that the 3D scenes and UI visual designs, referencing the original paintings, have the stylistic characteristics of Chinese classical garden and Chinese landscape painting. Volunteers also found the interaction method of exploring various styles of Chinese landscape painting through the art of enframed scenery to be novel and interesting, deepening their impressions of various styles of Chinese landscape painting. In terms of optimizing the gamification system, volunteers suggested adding more explicit function reminders in the interactive interface. For example, in enframed mode, they proposed that the gamification system should remind volunteers that they can switch to panorama mode by enlarging the scenery frame, achieving the goal of having an immersive view experience. Additionally, volunteers hoped for a more immersive interactive experience, suggesting adding more interactive content in panorama mode, guiding volunteers to trigger object animations, allowing volunteers not only to appreciate but also to interact and communicate with objects within the scenery frame.

5   Conclusion

Chinese landscape painting is one of the traditional arts in China that significantly represents classical Chinese philosophy and Eastern aesthetics. It shares a close connection with classical Chinese gardens in terms of principles of appreciation and cultural expression. However, existing interactive Chinese landscape painting artworks and research predominantly focus on the digital interpretation of a single style of Chinese landscape painting, lacking in-depth exploration of multiple styles. Therefore, based on the artistic technique of "Changing Scenery with Each Step", we designed a gamification system utilizing Leap Motion gesture interaction technology to create a visual experience that allows the seamless transition between various styles of Chinese landscape painting. The purpose of this gamification system is to enable viewers to freely appreciate and explore different styles of Chinese landscape painting through gesture-based transitions and to create their own landscape painting using different scenery frames. To assess the interface usability of the gamification system, we recruited 16 volunteers for testing and conducted in-depth interviews with them. The experimental results indicate that the majority of volunteers prefer the alignment of random visual path selection and dispersed viewpoints during the appreciation of digital Chinese landscape painting, consistent with their habits in appreciating Chinese classical garden. All volunteers stated that the gamification system had a positive effect in helping them understand the style of Chinese landscape painting. This gamification system serves as a reference for the digitized integration of Chinese landscape painting and the art of enframed scenery of Chinese classical garden.

Acknowledgments. This study was funded by 2023 National College Student Innovation Training Project (202311845071); 2023 National Social Science Fund Art General Project "Research on the Narrative Aesthetics of Virtual Reality Art from the Perspective of Technical Aesthetics" (23BC048).

Disclosure of Interests. The authors have no competing interests to declare that are relevant to the content of this article.

References

1. Li, X., Yue, Y.: Research on the landscape thought of traditional Chinese landscape painting. Sichuan Build. Sci. Res. **41**(1), 286–288 (2015)
2. Feng, Q., Huang, T.: Digital design innovation of Cantonese opera based on touch designer visual programming technology. Packag. Eng. **44**(6), Front insert 1-Front insert 2, 1–11 (2023)
3. Tang, X., Deng, Y., Luo, L.: Research on digital innovation and design of ink art. Packag. Eng. **42**(18), 308–315 (2021)
4. Ding, X.: Research on immersive landscape painting design and aesthetic experience based on Kinect. Harbin Institute of Technology (2014)
5. Liu, X., Li, Y., Liu, K.: Quantitative analysis of "image blankness" in the humble administrator's garden. J. Southwest Forestry Univ. **6**(6), 55–62 (2022)
6. Qiu, Z.: Research on the relationship between landscape painting and Chinese classical gardens. Central South University of Forestry and Technology (2006)
7. Jiang, S.: Research on traditional garden aesthetic perception based on visual cognition—taking the art garden as an example. Huazhong Agricultural University (2022)
8. Chen, X., Geng, Y.: Analysis of scene changes in video games based on traditional composition "changing scenes with each step." Art Grand View **9**, 128–129 (2016)
9. Li, J., Zheng, Z., Chai, Y., Xu, S., Wei, X., Shi, H., et al.: DianTea: designing and evaluating an immersive virtual reality game to enhance youth tea culture learning. In: Proceedings of the 25th International Conference on Mobile Human-Computer Interaction (Mobile HCI 2023 Companion), pp. 1–8. Association for Computing Machinery, New York (2023)
10. Xin, X.: Interaction design: from physical logic to behavioral logic. Decoration **1**, 58–62 (2015)
11. Sorce, S., Gentile, V., Enea, C., Gentile, A., Malizia, A., Milazzo, F.: A touchless gestural system for extended information access within a campus. In: Proceedings of the 2017 ACM SIGUCCS Annual Conference (SIGUCCS 2017), pp. 37–43. Association for Computing Machinery, New York (2017)
12. Lim, B., Rogers, Y., Sebire, N.: Designing to distract: can interactive technologies reduce visitor anxiety in a children's hospital setting?. ACM Trans. Comput.-Hum. Interact. **26**(2), 9 (2019)
13. Dingler, T., Funk, M., Alt, F.: Interaction proxemics: combining physical spaces for seamless gesture interaction. In: Proceedings of the 4th International Symposium on Pervasive Displays (PerDis 2015), pp.107–114. Association for Computing Machinery, New York (2015)
14. He, C., Lv, C.: Embodied cognition: cognitive exploration of unconscious behavior. J. Nanjing Univ. Arts (Art Des. Ed.) **3**, 69–73 (2020)
15. Waugh, K., McGill, M., Freeman, E.: Push or pinch? Exploring slider control gestures for touchless user interfaces. In: Nordic Human-Computer Interaction Conference (Nordi CHI 2022), pp. 1–10. Association for Computing Machinery, New York (2022)

16. Hardy, J., Rukzio, E., Davies, N.: Real world responses to interactive gesture based public displays. In: Proceedings of the 10th International Conference on Mobile and Ubiquitous Multimedia (MUM 2011), pp. 33–39. Association for Computing Machinery, New York (2011)
17. Xu, Z.: The essence of "hidden" cultural thinking in the artistic conception of traditional Chinese art. J. SE Univ. (Philos. Soc. Sci. Ed.) 24(5), 121–128 (2022)
18. Chen, Y.: The expression of "elephant" in the frame of Chinese classical gardens - taking the humble administrator's garden in Suzhou as an example. Mod. Hortic. 4, 135–136 (2019)

Game-Based Learning

Enhancing Emergency Decision-Making Skills Through Game-Based Learning: A Forest Fire Simulation Exercise Game

Xingchen Ji, Fei Wang, Haitao Zheng, and Xiaomei Nie[✉]

Tsinghua Shenzhen International Graduate School, Shenzhen 518055, China
nie.xiaomei@sz.tsinghua.edu.cn

Abstract. Natural disasters create a demand for emergency exercises, but traditional drill methods present many inconveniences. This study began with online and field research on similar products, proposing a simulation game design framework for emergency decision-making in natural disasters based on the actual needs of emergency drills. Then the research developed a simulation game themed around forest fires. The game design is based on emergency decision-making theories for forest fires and integrates a forest fire spread model. This game provides players with a safe virtual environment to practice and refine their strategies for handling fires, aiming to enhance the emergency decision-making abilities of rescue personnel. This game is expected to offer robust empirical support for the gamified design of emergency exercises.

Keywords: Game-based learning · Emergency decision-making · Forest fire simulation · Disaster management training

1 Introduction

Natural disasters, characterized by their unpredictability and high destructive potential, exert a profound influence on human societies worldwide. These calamities range from typhoons and earthquakes to floods and forest fires. Their inherent unpredictability and capacity for widespread destruction often lead to significant human casualties and substantial property damage, thereby posing major challenges to communities and nations [10].

Specifically, forest fires, with their rapid spread and unpredictable behavior patterns, become one of the most destructive natural disasters. These disasters can destroy vast forest resources in a short time, causing long-term damage to ecosystems, and pose a serious threat to human settlements [13].

In an effort to reduce the devastating effects of these natural disasters, governments and various international organizations are relentlessly pursuing more effective strategies for prevention, preparedness, and response. Key among these strategies are emergency drills, which are crucial in preparing relevant governmental departments, rescue organizations, and individuals. These drills provide essential opportunities to gain practical experience in managing disaster scenarios and to develop and refine effective methods for dealing with various types of emergencies.

However, traditional emergency drills frequently face limitations in terms of financial and time costs, as well as their ability to accurately simulate real-life disaster conditions. Recognizing these constraints, this study focuses on utilizing gamified learning approaches to enhance emergency decision-making skills. Specifically, it involves the design and implementation of a forest fire emergency simulation drill game. This innovative approach aims not only to offer a cost-effective and realistic training alternative but also to provide a framework for other natural disasters.

2 Related Work

2.1 Emergency Exercises

Emergency drills prepare for crises and are divided into three types: tabletop [6], live, and simulation [8] exercises.

Tabletop exercises involve discussions and problem-solving in a controlled setting, ideal for theoretical learning and team communication without field deployment. Their main limitation is the lack of real-world experience.

Live exercises provide immersive, real-world scenarios with actual resource deployment, enhancing practical skills and team readiness. However, they can be costly and complex to organize, with potential safety risks.

Simulation exercises use technology to create realistic virtual scenarios, allowing safe and repeatable practice of diverse situations. They offer the benefits of realism and safety but require technological support.

Each drill type is essential for crisis preparedness, chosen based on goals, resources, and the emergency context (Table 1).

Table 1. Different Forms of Emergency Exercises

Exercise Type	Organizational Form	Advantages	Limitations
Tabletop Exercise [6]	Simulation of disaster scenarios through discussion and analysis	Low cost, easy to organize, facilitates strategic discussion and theoretical learning	Lack of practical operation, insufficient realism and urgency
Live Exercise	Actual operations at a simulated disaster site	Provides practical experience, enhances emergency response and teamwork	High cost, requires extensive resources, potential safety risks
Simulation Exercise [8]	Utilizing computer technology to simulate disaster scenarios	High realism and interactivity, cost-effective, no real-world safety risks	Requires advanced technological support, may lack the complexity of real-world scenarios

2.2   Simulation Exercises

Computer and virtual reality advancements have introduced simulation exercises as an innovative emergency training method. These exercises use technology to simulate natural disasters, offering realistic and interactive scenarios that surpass traditional drills in realism and cost-effectiveness [8].

Users can virtually experience and learn how to respond to various disasters [11] without the real-world risks or costs [15]. These simulations integrate technologies like 3D rendering and real-time computation to teach natural disaster dynamics and response strategies effectively. Scenarios range from forest fires to floods, providing valuable response training and insights.

Additionally, gamification [7] elements in these exercises increase engagement and learning. By incorporating game design elements, such as goals and feedback, simulations become more interactive and educational, enhancing the learning experience in disaster response training.

2.3   Simulation for Environment - Geographical Modeling

Environmental simulation mainly relies on geographical modeling techniques. Geographical modeling techniques in simulation environments are mainly divided into two categories: raster models and vector models. The core difference lies in how to build appropriate data structures and computing frameworks to store and further calculate geographical information of different local positions on the simulated environment map.

In raster models, simulations are often based on cellular automata [3]. Each cell in a cellular automaton contains only a finite number of discrete states, and the cells follow a set of uniform local rules for system updates. By establishing simple rules, cells can interact with each other to form complex dynamic systems. Due to the high compatibility of cellular automaton data structures with GIS data structures, they can be well integrated with DEM (Digital Elevation Models), making them suitable for simulating complex dynamic systems in natural spaces [9].

In vector models, more precise vector data are used to define concepts such as position, direction, and length. Vector models generally combine Huygens' Principle for calculations: simulating the geographical environment as a continuously expanding polygon over time, with each vertex of the polygon considered an independent fire point. The spread of the fire is adjusted by calculating the spread from these points.

Since raster models have a more orderly structure, making it easier to store geographical information through a uniform data structure, and are also more suitable for large-scale parallel computing, they are more widely used in research on such problems (Fig. 1).

2.4   Simulation for Forestfire - Spread Model

In the simulation of forest fires, selecting an appropriate fire spread model is a critical step. Fire spread models predict fire behavior, such as spreading speed,

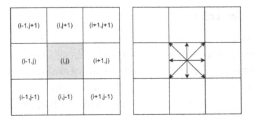

Fig. 1. Cellular automata

by using input parameters like fuel properties, terrain slope, and meteorological information. The commonly used fire spread models can be roughly divided into four types [2]:

- Physical Model: Based on the chemical combustion process and physical heat radiation conduction, simulated through complex fluid computation equations.
- Semi-Physical Model (e.g., Rothermel Model [14]): Combines energy conservation and heat conduction mechanisms with specific combustion parameters.
- Empirical Model (such as the Wang Zhengfei Model): Based on extensive experimental data and statistical analysis to fit the forest fire spreading process. This model mainly relies on experimental data and data fitting, with a simple and fast calculation process, but requires a large amount of fire experiments to collect data.
- Statistical Model (such as the Canadian National Forest Fire Spread Model [16]): Established based on past statistical data and formulas.

Among these, the Rothermel Model, due to its relative simplicity in calculation, is more widely used in computer simulations.

3   Methods

3.1   Survey

First, we analyzed the current state of research. On one hand, we conducted an online survey of games or software related to our field of study. On the other hand, we visited a city's safety monitoring center in person to investigate the application of existing products.

Product Survey. We investigated simulation software or games related to forest fires available on the market. The image shows four representative cases, including professional simulation software, web-based platforms, video games, and board games. We assessed these software or games based on four dimensions: Interactivity, Visualization, Application of Forest Fire Spread Models, and Suitability for Exercises. This evaluation provided reference and inspiration for our subsequent development (Fig. 2).

Survey cases	Interactivity	Visualization	Application of Forest Fire Spread Models	Suitability for Exercises
 Forest Fire Spread Simulation Software "Wildfire Analyst"	★★☆☆☆	★★☆☆☆	Yes	No
 Online Forest Fire Simulation Website https://wildfire.concord.org	★☆☆☆☆	★☆☆☆☆	Yes	No
 Adventure Game "Forest Fire: Animal Rescue"	★★★★★	★★★★☆	No	Yes
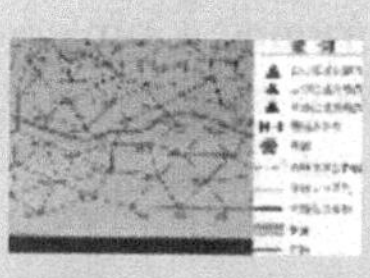 Forest Fire Disaster Relief Board Game "Wildfire Crisis"	★★★★☆	★★★☆☆	No	Yes

Fig. 2. Product Survey cases

Field Survey. For the purpose of field investigation, we visited the Foshan City Urban Safety Operation Monitoring Center. There, a comprehensive urban safety detection system is in place, of which forest fire detection and simulation is a subsystem. Initially, we examined the use and interaction interface of this system. Subsequently, we conducted brief interviews with relevant decision-makers. This provided guidance for our next steps in development (Fig. 3).

Fig. 3. Field investigation of the Foshan City Urban Safety Operation Monitoring Center

3.2   Current Research Gaps

Through our survey, we have summarized the shortcomings in the current research in the field of disaster simulation drill games.

Lack of a Versatile Design Framework. In the design of disaster simulation drill games, there is often a lack of a clear and structured framework. This deficiency complicates the systematic development of such games, as it becomes challenging to align specific requirements with the actual game development process.

Imbalance Between Gamification and Professionalism. In the field of forest fire simulation software or games, the significant gap between gamified interaction design and professional knowledge presents a challenge in integrating the two. Simulation software tends to overemphasize realism, sacrificing interactivity, which results in an informative yet less engaging user experience. Conversely, games that primarily focus on entertainment often lack the necessary depth and accuracy of professional knowledge required for disaster response.

3.3   Framework Design

Prior to the specific development of a forest fire simulation game, this study articulates a comprehensive methodology for the design and development of disaster simulation drill games. The framework encapsulates a synthesis of specialized knowledge in disaster emergency decision-making and integrates it with the widely-utilized MDA (Mechanics, Dynamics, Aesthetics) framework [5] in game design.

This design framework positions the theoretical underpinnings of emergency response methods for natural disasters as the foundation. It delineates the interplay between the core aspects of disaster simulation: environmental visualization, which provides a realistic backdrop; simulation methods that underpin the dynamic behavior of the game elements; and interaction design, which facilitates user engagement with the simulation.

This structured, layered approach not only facilitates a systematic development process but also ensures that each component of the game is purposefully aligned with educational objectives. The versatility of the framework makes it a valuable reference for the design of other emergency decision-making games, enabling developers to adapt and apply its principles to a wide range of scenarios beyond forest fire management, such as floods, earthquakes, or other natural or man-made disasters (Fig. 4).

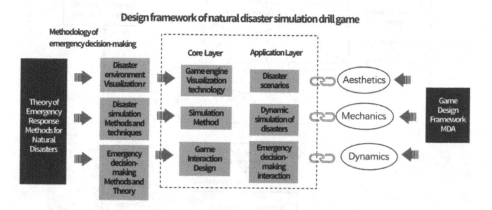

Fig. 4. Design framework of natural disaster simulation drill game

3.4   Gamification

Gameplay Design. This game is a strategy game themed around forest fire suppression, with a core gameplay focus on resource management and rapid response to emergencies. The core gameplay can be summarized into the following key parts:

Resource Management: Players need to make rational use of the resources provided, including various firefighting units, water sources, and firefighting tools, etc. Effectively allocating and using these resources is crucial for controlling the fire and minimizing losses.

Unit Command: Controlling the fire is the main goal of the game. Players must continuously monitor changes in the fire situation and make quick decisions based on the specifics of the fire and terrain. This includes choosing the appropriate firefighting units and flexibly utilizing their special abilities, such as using cutting tools to reduce combustible materials in advance or using fire hoses to quickly diminish the intensity of the fire.

Strategy Planning: Successfully extinguishing forest fires requires not only quick reactions but also foresighted strategy. Players must take into account natural factors such as terrain and rivers, observe the trends of fire development, think about how to optimize resource allocation, and formulate corresponding response plans.

Game Objective: The ultimate goal of the game is to control the fire as much as possible within a set timeframe. The game records the total loss caused by

the fire, and the player's objective is to minimize losses under this constraint
(Fig. 5).

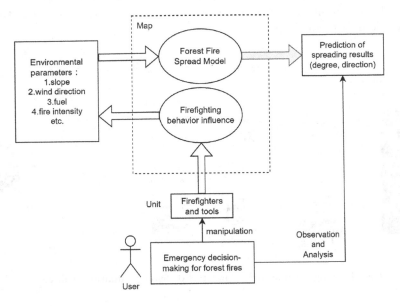

Fig. 5. Gameplay Design

Firefighting Unit Design. In this study, we designed a series of firefighting
units within the game based on real-world methods [4] and tactics for combat-
ing forest fires. The design of these units reflects the diversity and complexity of
real-world strategies for responding to forest fires, as well as considering the flexibility and emergency response capabilities required in actual operations. Each
firefighting unit possesses unique abilities, movement speeds, and operational
capacities, with these characteristics being grounded in a thorough analysis of
real-world firefighting equipment and personnel capabilities.

- Unit Name: The unit name is the basic identifier of the unit.
- Unit Ability: Unit abilities refer to the strength of a unit's special abilities. Different units have different abilities and corresponding attribute values
  based on their type.
- Movement Speed: Movement speed indicates the speed at which a unit moves
  across the map.
- Water Capacity: Water capacity is an attribute specific to certain types of
  units, usually related to units dealing with water storage, such as helicopters.

The game provides six main types of firefighting units, each with different
functionalities and limitations. Players need to flexibly use various skills based
on the fire situation and terrain characteristics (Fig. 6 and Table 2).

Table 2. Firefighting Units

Type	Ability	Limitation
Beater Tools	Extinguish fire by beating	Limited range
Wind Fire Extinguisher	Extinguish fire with wind power	Slower movement speed
Fire Hose	Extinguish fire with water	Requires proximity to water source
Cutting Tools	Reduce fuel by cutting	Requires trees
Helicopter	Terrain-independent movement	Limited water storage capacity
Ignition Tools	Can ignite fires actively	Requires coordination

Fig. 6. Firefighting Units Art Design

4   Process and Result

4.1   Forestfire Simulator - Game Development

Geographic Modeling Pipeline - Terrain, River and Forest. Terrain generation is a core component of environmental simulation in this study [12], and it utilizes noise-related algorithms to generate natural terrain features. Noise algorithms have the capability to produce random patterns that closely resemble those found in nature. These algorithms mathematically simulate terrain features such as mountain ranges, valleys, and plains. The inherent randomness of these algorithms ensures that the generated terrain exhibits a high degree of variability and realism. By adjusting parameters of the noise function, such as frequency and amplitude, it is possible to control the terrain's roughness and level of detail.

It should be noted that, for the purpose of simulating real-world terrain, providing a heightmap of the actual terrain can be used, thus skipping this step.

River generation is based on terrain data and is achieved through a computational method used in the GIS field. This method calculates the accumulation and flow path of water as it passes over terrain, thereby forming river channels. The river paths are smoothed using a mathematical method based on Catmull-

Rom splines to produce more natural river bends. Finally, a river mesh model is generated based on the river curves and rendered.

Forests are represented as visualizations of fuel density, used to enhance the realism and detail richness of the virtual environment (Fig. 7).

Forestfire Simulation. In this algorithm, the process specifically includes the following key steps:

Grid Representation of Terrain. The terrain is abstracted as grid data at the algorithm's core. This means that the entire terrain is divided into small grid cells, each containing information about the slope, fuel type, and quantity of that area. This grid-based representation provides a detailed and manageable terrain framework for simulation.

Parallel Computing Using ComputeShader. To handle large-scale data and achieve efficient simulation, we use ComputeShader for parallel computing. This allows the algorithm to process multiple grid cells simultaneously, significantly improving computational efficiency. ComputeShader is particularly suitable for handling complex physical simulations and extensive data operations.

Each Grid Cell as a Cell. In the algorithm, each grid cell is considered a cell, similar to a cellular automaton model. The state of each cell, including fuel quantity and burning status, is updated over time. The internal state changes of the cell are primarily calculated based on the Rothermel model [14], specifically designed to calculate physical characteristics of forest fire spread, such as combustion rate and flame propagation speed.

Simulating Flame Spread Between Adjacent Cells. The spread of flames from one cell to adjacent cells is calculated based on the combustibility of the fuel, wind direction and speed, and the distance between cells. This propagation mechanism reflects the flame diffusion behavior in actual forest fires, making the simulation results more realistic and reliable. The quantity of fuel and the extent of burning in the grid are calculated based on the principles of cellular automata [1].

In summary, our simulation process accurately simulates the behavior of forest fire spread by combining the comprehensive effects of terrain, fuel, and meteorological conditions with efficient computational methods. This approach is not only theoretically sound but also has shown high feasibility and effectiveness in practical applications.

A simplified Rothermel model is utilized within the game to calculate the forest fire spread process [14]. The Rothermel fire spread model is a mathematical model for predicting the rate of spread of a wildfire in a uniform fuel bed. The model is expressed by the following fundamental equation:

$$R = \frac{I_x}{\rho_b Q_{ig}} \cdot \epsilon \cdot \xi \tag{1}$$

where:

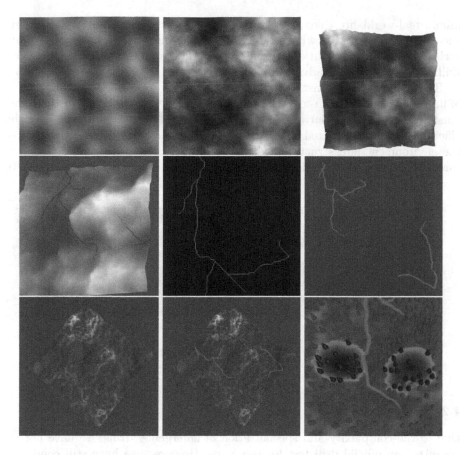

Fig. 7. The Process of Forestfire Environmental Modeling

- R: Fire spread rate (length/time).
- I_x: Reaction intensity (energy/area/time).
- ρ_b: Oven-dry fuel bed density (mass/area).
- Q_{ig}: Pre-ignition heat (energy/mass).
- ϵ: Effective heating number (dimensionless).
- ξ: Propagating flux ratio (dimensionless).

Gameplay and Interface. Following a comprehensive development phase, we have successfully produced a playable prototype of our forest fire simulation game. This iteration features an array of straightforward tutorials aimed at acquainting players with the game mechanics, as well as a selection of scenario-based levels that challenge the player's ability to manage and mitigate wildfire spread effectively.

As gameplay commences, players witness the initiation and subsequent propagation of fire from a designated ignition source. The simulation is designed to mimic real-world fire dynamics, presenting a realistic and challenging experience. Players are tasked with strategically deploying various firefighting units, each with unique capabilities and limitations. These units must be maneuvered skillfully to combat the advancing flames.

The game is set against a backdrop of a ticking countdown, adding a layer of urgency to the decision-making process. The players' actions are critical: they must work swiftly to control the blaze, using the resources and time available efficiently. If the calculated loss, a quantitative measure of the fire's impact on the environment and structures within the game, crosses a predefined critical threshold before the countdown concludes, the scenario ends in failure (Fig. 8).

Fig. 8. Game Interface

4.2 Preliminary Evaluation

Due to the complexity and specialization of emergency drills, we have not yet organized an official drill test for the game. However, we have still conducted some preliminary evaluations of the developed content of the game for reference in the next phase of development. Through video websites, we contacted 5 individuals with knowledge and experience in forest fire fighting for a brief trial play. Each player engaged in the game for 25 min and filled out a questionnaire afterward.

The questionnaire includes a series of questions related to emergency drills. Responses to each question are categorized into five levels: Strongly Agree, Agree, Neutral, Disagree, and Strongly Disagree.

The questions cover two main aspects, totaling 8 questions:

Aspects of Game Interactivity

- Is the game's user interface intuitive and easy to understand?
- Are the game's command feedbacks timely and accurate?
- Can players easily switch and control different firefighting units?
- Does the game effectively enhance player immersion through its design?

Aspects of Drill Practicality

- Does the game effectively simulate the spread of forest fires?
- Do the fire response strategies in the game correspond with actual firefighting operations?
- Can the game help players understand the complexity of emergency fire handling?
- Does practicing with the game help improve players' emergency decision-making skills?

From the questionnaire feedback and interviews, we obtained the following results: In terms of game interaction, the immersion is good due to the ability to interact through a 3D perspective. However, the game is not smooth enough in switching and controlling units. In terms of drill practicality, the evaluation that fire response strategies correspond with actual firefighting operations is high. However, the rating is lower in "helping players understand the complexity of emergency fire handling," mainly because the current variety of units is limited, and the interaction methods are too simple. For the same reasons, the evaluation on whether it "helps to improve players' emergency decision-making skills" is also moderate. Despite this, all players participating in the test believe that this system has potential for conducting drills.

5   Discussion

5.1   Contributions

During the research process, a comprehensive design framework for disaster drill games was summarized, and a simulation game themed around forest fires was developed.

Emergency Drill Game Framework. A universal framework suitable for various types of disaster emergency drill games was summarized during the research process. This framework guided the development of a game themed around forest fires. The practical application of this framework provides a reference for future similar projects, paving the way for further exploration and development in the gamified learning field for disaster preparedness.

Interactive Game Design for Forest Fire Simulation. The research involved a gamified design approach to forest fire simulation, combining theoretical knowledge with interactive gameplay to enhance learning and decision-making skills in emergency situations. It showcases the specific development process and principles, offering valuable insights for further iterations.

5.2   Limitations and Future Work

Due to the complexity of game development and the difficulty in organizing personnel, the gameplay is currently relatively simple, and larger-scale comparative experiments have not yet been organized, making the persuasiveness of the drill's effectiveness insufficient. In the next phase, we will enrich the game's interactivity and improve the operational feedback. At the same time, more professional tests will be organized to more specifically evaluate the role of gamified design in enhancing decision-making skills.

5.3   Conclusion

This research has successfully demonstrated the potential of gamified learning in enhancing emergency decision-making skills through the development of a forest fire simulation game. By integrating theoretical knowledge with practical, interactive gameplay, we have laid a foundation for further advancements in disaster preparedness training. While recognizing the limitations in current game complexity and the need for more extensive testing, this study provides a solid framework for future exploration. The insights gained from preliminary evaluations and expert feedback highlight the game's potential as a valuable tool in emergency management education.

Acknowledgments. This work was supported by a research grant from Shenzhen Key Laboratory of next generation interactive media innovative technology (Funding No: ZDSYS20210623092001004), and the Center for Social Governance and Innovation at Tsinghua University, a major research center for Shenzhen Humanities & Social Sciences Key Research Bases.

References

1. Alexandridis, A., Vakalis, D., Siettos, C.I., Bafas, G.V.: A cellular automata model for forest fire spread prediction: the case of the wildfire that swept through Spetses island in 1990. Appl. Math. Comput. **204**(1), 191–201 (2008)
2. Bukhori, S.: Forest fire model. In: Forest Fire, p. 73 (2018)
3. Codd, E.F.: Cellular Automata. Academic Press (2014)
4. Drapalyuk, M., Stupnikov, D., Druchinin, D., Pozdnyakov, E.: Forest fires: methods and means for their suppression. IOP Conf. Ser. Earth Environ. Sci. **226**, 012061 (2019)
5. Hunicke, R., LeBlanc, M., Zubek, R., et al.: MDA: a formal approach to game design and game research. In: Proceedings of the AAAI Workshop on Challenges in Game AI, San Jose, CA, vol. 4, p. 1722 (2004)
6. Husna, C., Kamil, H., Yahya, M., Tahlil, T., Darmawati, D.: Does tabletop exercise enhance knowledge and attitude in preparing disaster drills? Nurse Media J. Nurs. (2020)
7. Kapp, K.M.: The Gamification of Learning and Instruction: Game-Based Methods and Strategies for Training and Education. Wiley (2012)

8. Li, N., Sun, N., Cao, C., Hou, S., Gong, Y.: Review on visualization technology in simulation training system for major natural disasters. Nat. Hazards **112**(3), 1851–1882 (2022)
9. Nelson, A., Reuter, H., Gessler, P.: Dem production methods and sources. Dev. Soil Sci. **33**, 65–85 (2009)
10. Neumayer, E., Barthel, F.: Normalizing economic loss from natural disasters: a global analysis. Glob. Environ. Chang. **21**(1), 13–24 (2011)
11. Ning, H., Pi, Z., Wang, W., Farha, F., Yang, S.: A review on serious games for disaster relief. In: 2022 4th International Conference on Data Intelligence and Security (ICDIS), pp. 408–414. IEEE (2022)
12. Olsen, J.: Realtime procedural terrain generation (2004)
13. Robinne, F.N., Secretariat, F.: Impacts of disasters on forests, in particular forest fires. In: UNFFS Background Paper (2021)
14. Rothermel, R.C.: A Mathematical Model for Predicting Fire Spread in Wildland Fuels, vol. 115. Intermountain Forest & Range Experiment Station, Forest Service, US (1972)
15. Schmidt, E., Goldhaber-Fiebert, S.N., Ho, L.A., McDonald, K.M.: Simulation exercises as a patient safety strategy: a systematic review. Ann. Internal Med. **158**(5_Part_2), 426–432 (2013)
16. Stocks, B.J., et al.: The Canadian forest fire danger rating system: an overview. For. Chron. **65**(6), 450–457 (1989)

Making Learning Engaging and Productive: **SimLab**, a VR Lab to Bridge Between Classroom Theory and Industrial Practice in Chemical Engineering Education

Juhyung Son[1] , Ahmad Alhilal[2] , Reza Hadi Mogavi[3] , Tristan Braud[2] , and Pan Hui[1,2(✉)]

[1] Hong Kong University of Science and Technology (Guangzhou), Guangzhou, China
json120@connect.hkust-gz.edu.cn
[2] Hong Kong University of Science and Technology, Hong Kong, China
aalhilal@connect.ust.hk
{panhui,braudt}@ust.hk
[3] University of Waterloo, Waterloo, Ontario, Canada
rhadimog@uwaterloo.ca

Abstract. Engineering education faces a gap between theory and industrial practice due to the expense, space requirements, and limited utility of industry-specific equipment. Universities thus hesitate to invest in such machinery. Metaverse provides virtually limitless digital space at minimal operational costs, facilitating avatar-based interaction and collaboration. This paper explores the potential of the Metaverse in connecting engineering education and industrial practice. We introduce SimLab, a simulated chemical plant in the Metaverse designed to complement chemical engineering courses. By incorporating gamification elements, SimLab emulates the hands-on experience of a physical lab, facilitating embodied operation and fostering enjoyable collaborative learning. We evaluate SimLab through a user study and observe a significant improvement in learning outcomes compared to physical and 2D game-based labs (11% and 15% respectively). SimLab also enhances perceived engagement, interaction, and learning efficiency. Collaboration among students and with the tutor greatly accelerates task completion. In the multi-user mode, task completion time and the number of attempts decrease by 65% and 55% respectively, compared to the single-user mode.

Keywords: Virtual Reality · Simulation · Virtual Lab

1 Introduction

The Metaverse is a shared virtual space accessible across various devices and platforms. It expands our environment beyond the constraints of the physical

---

J. Son and A. Alhilal—Contributed equally to this work.

X. Fang (Ed.): HCII 2024, LNCS 14730, pp. 160–179, 2024.
https://doi.org/10.1007/978-3-031-60692-2_12

world through the use of mixed reality (XR), encompassing virtual reality (VR), augmented reality (AR), and mixed reality (MR). These technologies create immersive and interactive 3D environments for users. By integrating technology, peer collaboration, and prompt feedback [4,7,11], interactive learning enhances student engagement and learning motivation through hands-on and captivating activities. This approach facilitates the transition to a student-centered learning environment [6]. XR technologies are contemporary tools that provide entry points to the Metaverse, allowing users to interact and experience different digital worlds. Recently, the Metaverse has come under the spotlight to empower future education. For instance, the MetaHKUST project[1] aims to establish the world's first physical-digital twin to enhance teaching and learning. Novartis [2] is a VR lab simulator to practice life-saving procedures. HoloLab Champions [1] and VR Chemistry Lab [3] are VR-based chemistry labs that allow students to perform actual measurements correctly and safely, allowing them to complete tasks (e.g., chemical reaction and molecule creation) and learn real lab procedures without having to worry about breaking materials and running out of resources. ColabAR [26] is a toolset for manipulating virtual objects in Tangible Augmented Reality (TAR) labs via physical proxies. ColabAR introduces haptic-based configurable interaction to enable collaboration among students.

On the one hand, chemical and mechanical engineering (CENG) labs are more complicated than chemistry labs. VR and AR-based chemistry lab settings fall short of fulfilling the CENG lab experience. On the other hand, many industrial operations rely on expensive and bulky equipment that universities cannot prioritize due to their often highly specialized nature, despite potential widespread usage in the industry. For instance, distillation is the workhorse of the chemical process industry, accounting for 40% of the energy utilization of a plant [19]. However, industrial distillation columns are rarely available at universities. As a result, students cannot experience equipment operation as well as related safety procedures, leading to significant training costs. Experiential learning is a critical aspect of laboratory work in academia. It allows students to solidify the theory learned in class and go beyond the course material by addressing specific phenomena and enabling cooperative learning where students work non-competitively in groups to complete a task in a structured environment, assisted by a lab tutor [23].

This paper presents SimLab, a VR-based simulation that provides CENG students with a synthetic hands-on lab experience. SimLab focuses on the operation of the distillation column (DC) in a manufacturing plant due to its widespread usage in the petrochemical industry. SimLab can be used as a standalone application where students operate the equipment autonomously. However, it is primarily meant as supplementary material for CENG courses, replicating the advantages of physical laboratory practice. SimLab enables cooperative learning in CENG lab settings through multi-user capabilities. SimLab enables audio communication, gestures, and real-time motion between class members (students

---

[1] https://hkust.edu.hk/news/research-and-innovation/hkust-launch-worlds-first-twin-campuses-Metaverse.

and instructors). It allows students to follow lectures supplemented with presentation sharing. More importantly, SimLab lets students form small groups that develop a laboratory protocol (procedure) in consultation with the lab specialist or course tutor. SimLab incorporates gamification elements, such as interactive valve operations, a competition challenge, and teamwork, to enhance student involvement, motivation, and enjoyment in chemical engineering learning. By providing visual and auditory effects, including precise 3D representations and realistic chemical plant sounds, SimLab creates an immersive and playful experience that fosters enthusiasm and deeper engagement within the virtual CENG lab environment. In this paper, our objectives are threefold: (i) to evaluate if SimLab offers a superior learning experience compared to 2D game-based and real physical labs; (ii) to examine whether the multi-user interaction in SimLab enhances learning efficiency compared to single-user interaction; and (iii) to assess the level of motion sickness experienced in VR, both in single-user and multi-user modes. The contribution can be summarized as follows:

- **Design** SimLab as a virtual chemical plant facility based on real-world layout and specifications of chemical plants.
- **Enable** interaction and communication between instructors, tutors, and students to playfully complete lab tasks in the virtual environment.
- **Implication** SimLab presents guidelines for educators, students, HCI researchers, and designers of all forms of instruction that include risky or heavy equipment.
- **Evaluate** SimLab against benchmarks. SimLabenhances learning outcomes compared to physical and 2D game-based labs by 11% and 15% respectively, and improves perceived engagement, interaction, and learning efficiency. Besides, SimLab multi-user mode accelerates task completion and improves the interaction by 28%, while decreasing frustration by 23%, compared to single-user mode, thanks to two-way interactions among students and with the tutor.

2   Related Works

Virtual labs provide a new form of hands-on experience and exposure to sophisticated technologies. Many works developed virtual labs to integrate them into chemistry, chemical, and mechanical engineering courses. These works can be classified into AR and VR-based labs or web simulation-based labs.

AR/VR-Based Virtual Labs. Many lab simulators were developed to provide immersive and interactive virtual chemistry labs. Novartis [2] is a VR lab simulator that allows students to step into a hyper-realistic virtual manufacturing facility to practice life-saving procedures in a lab environment. HoloLAB Champions [1] engages students playfully with chemistry lab equipment in VR to perform actual measurements correctly and learn real lab procedures. The VR Chemistry Lab [3] is a research tool where studies of VR learning environments could be explored. It contains experiences where players can explore molecule creation in an immersive environment as well as play a game of catalyzing a chemical reaction. ColabAR [26] is a toolset for manipulating virtual objects in Tangible Augmented Reality (TAR) labs via physical proxies. It incorporates haptic configurable interaction techniques, facilitating collaboration between students.

Web Simulation-Based Virtual Labs. Web-based simulators allow students to visualize unobservable phenomena such as chemical reactions, heat transfer, or internal tensions. Kapilan et al. [16] develop web-based simulators for fluid mechanics chemical engineering labs to cope with the difficulty of completing laboratory experiments. Jamshidi and Milanovic [15] integrate a new module comprising simulation assignments into the mechanical engineering materials course. They aim to improve students' critical skills and decision-making in design problems by predicting the results of material testing. Lu et al. [20] introduce VR2E2C, Virtual Reality Remote Education for Experimental Chemistry. VR2E2C provides safe and highly fault-tolerant experimental topics, demonstrating the benefits of VR and robotics technology in traditional chemical education. Singh et al. [24] design a VR-based learning environment (VLE) aimed at providing engineering students with an early opportunity to learn the operation of oscilloscopes and function generators in the electronics lab.

Lecture and Business MR Platforms. Apart from lab-focused education, other systems facilitate meetings and cooperation in virtual environments. Perlin et al. [14,22] explore face-to-face interactions and their impact on improving learning and engagement during lectures. To this end, they developed an MR platform based on Chalktalk[2]. CollaboVR [13] is a collaboration system for business meetings that leverages cloud architecture to support multi-user sketch, audio communication, and collaboration. Through real-time techniques, it shares freehand sketches in 3D space and allows interaction with animations in collaborative virtual reality. A review study [25] reveals cognitive and pedagogical advantages of using VR in engineering education. It improves learnability, learning efficiency and cognition, and the overall education experience. Virtual labs allow students to interact safely and learn real lab procedures without having to worry about breaking materials, equipment failure, or running out of resources. This boosts the students' confidence and lessens their cognitive load.

Most of the above-mentioned works provide virtual labs for chemistry (i.e., [15,20], ColabAR, and HoloLAB Champions), while a few enable peer collaboration. Among the available options, only Kapilan et al. [16] provide support for chemical engineering labs through a simplified, non-immersive, and web-based simulation, recognizing the inherent complexity of such labs.

In our work, we design a virtual CENG lab to complete distillation tasks in complex virtual environments (i.e., a virtual chemical plant). We enable interaction with virtual equipment and units and collaboration among students and

---

[2] https://chalktalk.com/.

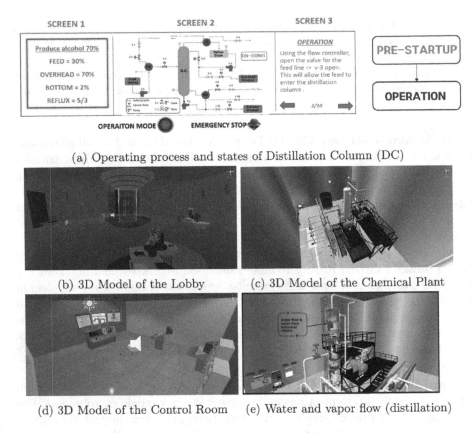

(a) Operating process and states of Distillation Column (DC)

(b) 3D Model of the Lobby   (c) 3D Model of the Chemical Plant

(d) 3D Model of the Control Room   (e) Water and vapor flow (distillation)

Fig. 1. Three virtual spaces to launch the distillation.

instructors. Being an MR platform, our system ensures an immersive and interactive user experience. This pioneering VR lab supplements chemical engineering courses with hands-on labs in a chemical plant. The system allows students to virtually operate a distillation column based on a distillation task. This research is easily generalizable to all forms of instruction that include risky or heavy equipment. For instance, running a power plant or managing a factory line, significant applications in mechanical engineering, civil engineering, industrial engineering, and skill development.

3   System Design and Interaction Framework

SimLab aims to introduce students to the operation of a distillation column in a virtual chemical plant, on their own or cooperatively. We focus on a gamified scenario where the students concentrate alcohol from a 30% feed to a 70% distillate and watch the animation of liquid flow in the distillation column and the vapor flow in the upper pipe. We design SimLab as an interactive experience over

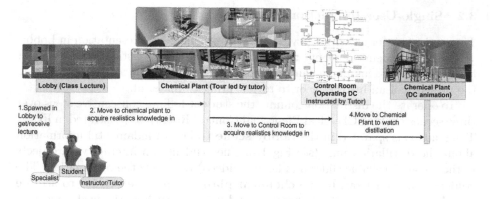

Fig. 2. Task flow diagram of user interaction over time.

a succession of scenes allowing students to take instructions, operate the distillation column, and observe the results of their actions. To ensure the adequacy of SimLab with current CENG curricula, we collaborate with domain experts. To establish the requirements of the power plant, we interviewed a professor from the Department of Chemical Engineering at our home university. Throughout the development process, two CENG postgraduate students assisted in ensuring adherence to the requirements outlined during the interview. After detailing the design of the virtual chemical plant, we present SimLab's functions under its single and multi-user interaction modes.

3.1   Design of the 3D Virtual Chemical Plant

SimLab's objective is to simulate real-world chemical plants. Therefore, we base the design of the chemical plant's units and equipment on existing plant layouts and equipment specifications[3]. We use *Fusion* and *Blender* to construct the 3D models of the simulated facility. Figure 1 represents the resulting virtual chemical plant. We decompose the facility into three scenes as follows: a lobby where students can get instructions and explanations for the lab (Fig. 1b); a control room where students operate the distillation column (Fig. 1c); and a chemical plant reflecting the students' actions in real-time (Fig. 1d). The chemical plant includes all traditional elements commonly found in such facilities, such as a distillation unit, preheater, reboiler, condenser, reflux drum, pumps, pipes, and valves. We also adjust the spacing and layout to comply with the heuristics commonly used in actual chemical plants. Finally, we rely on images and visual representation from Explain Media's 3D Refinery [6] for the texture. We import the resulting scenes and assets into Unity to implement the gamification and interaction mechanics through Unity's scripting language, C#. This allows the students to playfully manipulate the virtual facility individually or in groups.

---

[3] http://www.3d-refinery.com/units.html.

3.2 Single-User Interaction Mode

The students interact with the virtual environment (e.g., presentation in Lobby, valves in the chemical plant) to practice operating the distillation column at their own pace. This mode can be used as a preparation for actual practice in the presence of an instructor or to review practice material.

To operate the distillation column, the student follows consecutive steps over three scenes (Lobby, Chemical Plant, and Control Room), as illustrated in Fig. 2. The student is spawned in the **Lobby scene** to learn fundamental information about the distillation unit (see Fig. 1b). The student can interact with objects in the scene (scrollable slides and lecture videos) to review the information. The student can then move to the **chemical plant scene** (see Fig. 1c) to acquire knowledge of chemical plant operation and its units such as the feed tank, pre-heater, distillation column, and steam pipes. Afterward, the student can learn the production objectives, the overall process flow diagram, and the operational procedures of the plant in **the control room scene**. This scene contains three screens with interactable buttons for isolating and controlling valves and pumps on the displayed screen. The DC operation undergoes three consecutive states: non-active (initial), pre-startup, and operation. The student ought to conduct on-site checks and follow guidelines to prepare for operating the plant units in the **chemical plant scene**. Such activities correspond to real-life safety checks to ensure safe operation. This scene provides the student with a list of protocols for inspection (e.g., turning valves or checking the pump system). Afterward, the student answers questions to assess oneself understanding after which the DC becomes operable (Pre-startup state).

To gamify the learning experience, the **Control Room scene** in SimLab features three interactive virtual widescreen (see Fig. 1a). Students can observe the liquid flows in the distillation column while working towards the objective of concentrating alcohol from a 30% feed to a 70% distillate. The screens present the distillation objective, distillation instructions, and the graphical representation during the transition between the DC states. Upon completing the operational tasks, a see-through feature enables students to observe the distillation of the mixture through an animated representation of fluid and vapor flow within the distillation column.

3.3 Multi-user Interaction Mode

We incorporate multi-user interaction and multimedia communication modules into SimLab. This helps to bring instructors, students, and chemical specialists together. SimLab allows the course instructor to prepare the students with theory in the **Lobby**. The lab tutor can then provide hands-on experience to the students on operating the chemical plant in the **control room** and the **chemical plant** scenes. We enable multi-user interaction through Photon[4] and use Photon cloud to enable two-way audio communication between the users and relay

---

[4] https://www.photonengine.com/.

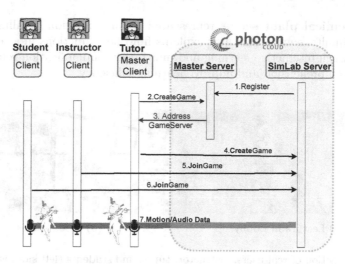

Fig. 3. Establishment of multi-user interaction through Photon.

motion (interaction) data (see Fig. 3). The master client establishes a connection with other remote clients through Photon's game server. The system spawns a new avatar from a prefab for each newly connected user. SimLab supports audio communication between instructors and students for presentations and Q&A sessions, as well as between students and tutors for collaborative practice in operating the distillation column. Figure 4a depicts an interaction and communication scenario in the virtual Lobby between an instructor and two students. SimLab enables the use of supporting material such as slides in shared PDF documents. The students can browse and interact with lecture documents using Ray Interactors from the XR Interaction Toolkit[5]. The students can also individually play lecture videos to improve their understanding.

After the lecture, the instructor divides the class into groups, with a tutor in charge of each group. The group tutor begins in the **chemical plant**, providing students with unit information and interaction instructions. A specialist can also join to explain each unit's function in a real chemical plant. Such two-way communication and cooperation boost the students' engagement and thus improve their understanding of real-world chemical plants. Figure 4b illustrates an interaction and communication scenario between a tutor, a specialist, and a student (obtained during our user study). The student can check the task to accomplish and the units' functions through interactable UIs. Afterward, one can proceed to open three valves to operate the distillation column. Then the students follow the tutor to **control room** to learn the DC protocols and operating procedures. The specialist reinforces this knowledge by commenting on the connection with real-world protocols. At this stage, the student has accomplished all the operation tasks. The students can see water flow and vapor in the distillation column

---

[5] https://docs.unity3d.com/Packages/com.unity.xr.interaction.toolkit@2.0.

in the **Chemical plant scene**, represented as an animation (as illustrated in Fig. 1e). Simultaneously, the tutor explains fluid flow functions in a real chemical plant. Such interactive learning and multi-user communication reinforce the students' comprehension and improve learning efficiency.

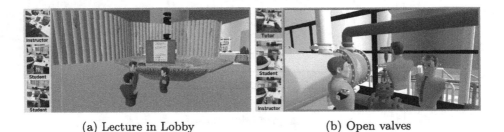

(a) Lecture in Lobby   (b) Open valves

Fig. 4. Interaction of real users, instructor, tutor, and students (left side) with virtual Lobby and Chemical Plant (right side).

4   Experimental Setup

This section details our experimental method to evaluate SimLab. We conduct a thorough user study to collect data on participants' performance (learning outcomes, task completion, and motion sickness) and system performance.

4.1   Study Participants

We recruited 43 participants, UG students (referred to as P1-P43) from the local university, along with two CENG postgraduate students who served as an instructor and a tutor. We sought consultation from a CENG professor and a Ph.D. student to ensure the organization of the lecture and lab content aligned with the domain knowledge. The participants ranged in age from 22 to 28, with 24 males and 9 females. All participants come from the same cohort and they all attend the same course, to make sure that background knowledge and study progress is somewhat synchronized. Half of them have never used VR, while 8 participants use VR a few times a year, and 6 use VR frequently. The participants range from not familiar with VR (7 participants), to slightly and moderately familiar (8 in each category), and very familiar (9).

4.2   Protocol

We aim to assess three primary factors: (*i*) whether SimLab provides a better learning experience than the traditional 2D game-based and video-based labs, (*ii*) whether SimLab's multi-user interaction improves the learning efficiency compared to the single-user interaction, and (*iii*) What is the level of severity experienced in terms of motion sickness in VR, both in single-user and multi-user modes?. As such, we conduct two user experiments on two separate groups of users. In the first experiment, we assign 30 participants to three groups in a round-robin fashion: (A) 10 participants perform in the physical lab environment, (B) 10 participants use SimLab and (C) 10 participants use tablet-compatible 2D lab environment. In the second experiment, we assign each of the 13 participants to both conditions: (I) SimLab single-user interaction, and (II) SimLab multi-user interaction.

Experiment 1: SimLab versus 2D Lab and Physical Lab. The participants receive a lecture (pre-lab session) and a lab session depending on the condition they have been assigned to. In the real physical study environment, they are delivered to the participant via PowerPoint slides and video. In the 2D game-based environment, they are delivered to the participant via PowerPoint slides and 2D simulation. Otherwise, the lecture (pre-lab session) and the lab are delivered in the Lobby scene using SimLab. In SimLab condition, the participants wear Oculus Quest 2 to complete the sequential steps of the virtual training across the virtual lab (see Fig. 2).

In each condition, we give the participants two surveys to complete, one brief survey before the lab session and the second comprehensive survey after the lab session. Both surveys encompass two test questions to measure their improvement as a result of the labs. Likewise, the two surveys encompass questions to assess the participant's mastery of the concepts learned.

Experiment 2: Single versus Multi-user Interaction. In the single-user mode, each participant follows the tasks to operate the distillation column, detailed in Sect. 3.2. In the multi-user mode, one instructor (acting as a tutor), another instructor (acting as a specialist), and the participant join the virtual lab simultaneously. The tutor guides the participant in the navigation and operation of the distillation column (see Fig. 2). After each run, we ask the participants to complete a survey to assess their understanding of the learned knowledge, perception of the performance, and feelings of motion sickness.

Task Performance. As part of the operation of DC, the participant must open three valves (valve1, valve2, valve3) in the Chemical Plant. The participant can not open any successive valve without completing the opening tasks of the prior valve. To determine the participant's task performance, we collect (i) the completion time on each of the three tasks (open valve 1, open valve 2, and open valve 3); and (ii) the number of gestures performed to complete each task.

Motion Sickness. VR users usually encounter feelings of discomfort, nausea, dizziness, vomiting, and cold sweats. this side effect of using VR known as motion sickness limits the interaction of VR systems [21]. Motion sickness creates a barrier in the full adaptation of this fascinating technology [17]. Motion sickness can be dangerous in some situations, such as disorientation and vertigo [5]. We quantify it using Simulator Sickness Questionnaire (SSQ) [18] which is widely adopted to quantify sickness elicited by VR systems.

4.3 User Survey (Questionnaire)

We design three surveys, two of them serve the first experiment (SimLab versus 2D game-based and Physical labs), and the third serves the second experiment (single versus multi-user interaction).

For **experiment 1**, we design two surveys, before-lab and after-lab survey. Both include two test questions to assess the participant's comprehension of the knowledge learned before and after the lab. They also include a question to asses the mastery of the concepts of the distillation column which ranges from 1: recalling facts and basic concepts to 6: producing new or original work.

In **experiments 1 and 2**, we select Frustration, Mental Demand, and Success from the NASA TLX [12] survey to assess their perceived task load. We supplement this with questions to asses the Interaction, Immersion, and Learning Efficiency on a [1–5] Likert scale. Participants rate each criterion on a [0–20] scale. *Frustration scale ranges from 0: being not frustrated at all, to 20: being extremely frustrated, Mental demand scale ranges from 0: being easy and simple, to 20: being demanding and complex, whereas Success ranges from 0: being not successful at all, to 20 is extremely successful. Interaction scale ranges from 1 to 5, with 1: being extremely difficult and 5: being extremely easy. Engagement ranges from 1 to 5, with 1: being not engaging and 5: being extremely engaging. Learning Efficiency ranges from much worse (value:1) to much better (value:5), compared to normal class.*

In **experiment 2**, we quantify motion sickness using Simulator Sickness Questionnaire (SSQ). The survey encompasses four questions to rate the motion sickness severity on a [1–7] scale, *from 1: feeling no symptoms to 7: experiencing vomiting, with 2: feeling discomfort, 3: feeling dizzy, 4 feeling moderate nausea, 5: feeling severe nausea, and 6: feeling retching.*

4.4 Ethics

In this study, we diligently adhered to stringent ethical standards to ensure the protection of participants' rights and well-being [9]. We obtained approval for the research from our university's Institutional Review Board (IRB). Prior to participating, all individuals were required to sign an informed consent form. This document thoroughly detailed their legal and ethical rights, as well as the benefits and potential risks (e.g., motion sickness) associated with their participation in the study. We informed participants of their right to withdraw from the experiment at any time without incurring any negative consequences, thereby guaranteeing that their involvement was entirely voluntary.

5 Results

We first present the findings on SimLab's performance relative to traditional physical CENG laboratories. We then present its effectiveness in both single-user and multi-user interaction modes.

5.1 SimLab, 2D Lab and Physical Lab

Figure 5 compares the performance of SimLab with the real physical CENG lab and 2D simulation-based CENG lab. Figure 5a illustrates the learning outcomes of SimLab in terms of correctly answered pre and post-lab test questions and the mastery over concepts of the operation of the distillation column. SimLab improves the learning efficiency, enabling more students to answer the questions correctly in both pre-lab (mean 8.5/20) and post-lab conditions (mean 15/20), compared to real physical lecture (mean 6.5/20) and lab conditions (mean 13.5/20) and PowerPoint-based lecture (mean 6/20) and 2D lab condition (mean 13/20). Besides, SimLab improves the perceived mastery over concepts of the chemical plant operation (mean 2.9/6), compared to the real physical lab (mean 1.3/6) and 2D lab (mean 1.6/6). We attribute this improvement to SimLab's immersive setting and its higher level of engagement as compared to other learning environments. To verify this, we record the participants' perceived learning efficiency and engagement, as well as the interaction. Figure 5b illustrates the perceived learning efficiency and immersion of SimLab compared to the real physical CENG lab. SimLab increase the perceived learning efficiency, engagement, and interaction by an average of approximately 2.5/7, compared to Real Physical lab, and by an average of approximately 3/7, compared to 2D simulation-based lab. We used Student's paired two-tailed t-test to assess the difference between the two study conditions. We find a statistically significant difference ($p < 0.005$ for all measures). The improvements observed in the pre-lab and post-lab test scores, as well as the perceived mastery over concepts of the chemical plant operation, indicate that SimLab facilitates a deeper understanding and application of the subject matter. The immersive setting and higher level of engagement that SimLab offers appear to promote the development of more advanced cognitive skills, such as analyzing and evaluating, which comply with the higher levels of Bloom's Taxonomy [8]. For unversed readers, it should be mentioned here that Bloom's Taxonomy is a framework that outlines six hierarchical cognitive levels: remembering, understanding, applying, analyzing, evaluating, and creating.

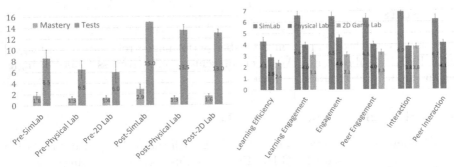

(a) Pre- and post-lab learning efficiency   (b) Learning efficiency and immersion

Fig. 5. Comparison of performance with 2D game-based lab and physical lab.

5.2 SimLab Single-User and Multi-user Interaction

We then compare the performance of SimLab single-user with multi-user interaction. The comparison covers four aspects, perceived efficiency, perceived load, task performance, and motion sickness.

Perceived Immersion, Interaction, and Learning Efficiency: Figure 6a summarizes the perceived interaction, learning efficiency, and engagement of SimLab single-user interaction compared to SimLab multi-user interaction. Multi-user mode presents relatively higher scores with averages of 4.23 ± 0.6, 4.38 ± 0.65, and 4.46 ± 0.52, respectively, compared to single-user mode with averages of 3.3 ± 0.75, 4.15 ± 0.75, and 3.92 ± 0.55. Our t-test indicates a statistically significant difference between single-user and multi-user modes in terms of interaction ($p < 0.05$), while we cannot reject the null hypothesis in immersion and learning efficiency. However, group work is at the core of experiential learning, and multiple studies have shown its effectiveness for achieving learning outcomes [10].

Overall, SimLab's multi-user mode demonstrates a superior improvement in all the above-mentioned aspects, making it highly effective in significantly enhancing students' understanding of operating the distillation column (DC), and the associated technical concepts.

Perceived Load and Success: Figure 6b depicts the perceived frustration, mental demand, and success of SimLab single-user interaction compared to SimLab multi-user interaction. The participants rated multi-user mode to exhibit relatively lower scores for frustration and cognitive load with averages of 7.08 ± 3.4 and 4.54 ± 3, respectively, compared to single-user mode with averages of 9 ± 3.6 and 5.7 ± 3.1. The participants also rated the multi-user mode to have a higher perceived success in accomplishing the tasks with an average of 18.5 ± 2.3, compared to the single-user mode with an average of 16.6 ± 2.43.

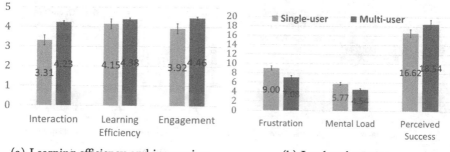

(a) Learning efficiency and immersion.   (b) Load and success

Fig. 6. Perceived performance of SimLab single-user vs multi-user interaction.

We note a statistically significant decrease in frustration in multi-user mode ($p < 0.005$), while there is no statistically significant difference in terms of mental demand and perceived success ($p ¿ 0.01$). The decrease in frustration comes together with the increase in interaction in multi-user mode, where participants cooperate with the tutor to complete the task, increasing the interaction, and avoiding making mistakes. Perceived success is very high for both single-user and multi-user, while the cognitive load is very low, so it is expected to have no statistically significant difference between both modes.

Task Performance: Figure 7 illustrates the participants' task performance to complete the three tasks. In single-user interaction, participants completed the three tasks, open valve1, open valve2, and open valve3, in an average of 7, 7, and 6 gestures and 60, 59, and 57 s, respectively. We note that participants perform better in the multi-user mode, with an average number of gestures of 3,3,3 and a completion time of 22.7, 18.2, and 21.3 s, respectively. We perform a two-tailed t-test and find a statistically significant difference for both the number of gestures and completion times in all three tasks ($p < 0.005$ for all measures). This difference between single-user and multi-user modes can be explained by the cooperation between students. In single-user mode, students struggle to interact with the virtual object to operate the distillation column, requiring more attempts (more gestures) and more time. Comparatively, students parallelize tasks and collaborate towards completion in multi-user mode, allowing for a significant decrease in the time to complete these tasks.

Motion Sickness: Table 1 illustrates the mean motion sickness score in the two interaction modes. The Participants experience almost similar motion sickness in single-player and multi-user interaction, and Student paired two-tailed t-test shows no statistical significance. In the single-user mode, the participants reported feelings ranging from no symptoms to discomfort (mean 1.6/7) in the Lobby scene and (mean 1.69/7) in the Control Room scene. However, their feelings of sickness increased to range from discomfort to moderate nausea (mean

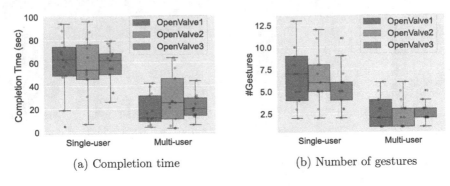

(a) Completion time   (b) Number of gestures

Fig. 7. Task completion performance in single/multi-user modes.

Table 1. Reported motion sickness severity

	Single-user Interaction		Multi-user Interaction	
	Mean	STD	Mean	STD
Lobby	1.62	0.77	1.85	0.80
Chemical Plant	2.62	1.04	2.54	1.20
Control Room	1.69	0.95	1.54	0.88
Overall	2.08	1.04	2.08	0.95

2.6/7) in the chemical plan scene, while they reported an overall feeling of sickness ranging from discomfort to dizziness (mean 2/7) in all the scenes during the single-user interaction. In the multi-user mode, the participants reported feelings ranging from discomfort to dizziness (mean 1.84/7) in the Lobby scene. This feeling decreases slightly in the Control Room scene (mean 1.5/7). However, their feelings of sickness increase significantly to range from discomfort to moderate nausea (mean 2.53/7) in the chemical plan scene. The participants reported a sickness feeling of discomfort to dizziness as an overall experience (mean 2/7).

6 Findings and Discussion

This section presents the main findings, discusses the implications of these findings, and highlights the limitations with potential directions to address them.

6.1 Main Findings

SimLab exhibits improved learning outcomes in comparison to physical and 2D game-based labs. A higher number of students answered test questions correctly and rated SimLab as enhancing their mastery of the learned concepts. Consequently, SimLab enhances learning efficiency. Additionally, the perceived learning efficiency, interaction, and engagement significantly increase when SimLab is utilized as a platform for conducting CENG labs.

Both the single-user and multi-user modes of SimLab contribute to improved student interaction, engagement, and cognitive efficiency. However, SimLab's multi-user mode surpasses in enhancing these aspects, proving highly effective in significantly improving students' understanding of practical concepts learned during the lab. Additionally, the multi-user mode shows lower frustration and cognitive load, along with higher perceived success in accomplishing lab tasks, compared to single-user interaction.

In terms of task performance, participants exhibit faster completion of essential operation tasks in the multi-user mode, attributed to the cooperation among students. In the single-user mode, students face challenges in interacting with the virtual object to operate the distillation column, resulting in increased attempts and time required. Conversely, in the multi-user mode, students parallelize tasks and collaborate to achieve task completion more efficiently. Furthermore, participants experience a similar level of motion sickness severity in both single-user and multi-user interactions.

6.2   Contributions and Practical Implications

VR labs have demonstrated cognitive, engagement, and pedagogical advantages in education. They provide an immersive, risk-free environment for students to engage with real lab procedures, alleviating concerns about safety and resource limitations. Thus, they boost students' confidence and reduce cognitive load. However, the current state of the art falls short in providing comprehensive simulated chemical engineering (CENG) labs. They primarily focus on chemistry labs, with limited options for peer collaboration. Besides, existing simulated CENG labs are predominantly 2D game-based and lack immersion and realism.

Contributions and Implications: SimLab is a VR-based CENG lab that assists in manipulating a virtual chemical plant facility, thus offering an immersive and interactive environment and complementing traditional coursework. It is faithfully designed based on the design of the chemical plant's units and equipment on existing plant layouts and equipment specifications. We compare SimLab with two different lab platforms: a 2D game-based CENG lab and a physical CENG lab. SimLab enhances the learning outcomes, enhanced interaction, engagement, and cognitive efficiency, compared to the benchmarks. The enhanced learning efficiency is evident by the improvements observed before and after using SimLab, as well as the perceived mastery over concepts of the chemical plant operation. The immersive setting and higher level of engagement that SimLab offers appear to promote the development of more advanced cognitive skills, such as analyzing and evaluating, which comply with the higher levels of Bloom's Taxonomy [8]. Both single-user and multi-user modes of SimLab contribute to these benefits, with the multi-user mode exhibiting superior performance in task completion, reduced frustration, and cognitive load. SimLab fills the research gap by providing a playful and semi-realistic VR-based CENG lab experience. In the single-user interaction mode, SimLab allows students to engage with the virtual chemical plant safely and enjoyably. They can watch presentations, and practice operating the distillation column at their own pace. Additionally, SimLab incorporates multi-user interaction and two-way audio communication modules. The multi-user mode facilitates collaboration among instructors, students, and chemical specialists. It fosters teamwork in a gamified setting, where course instructors can provide theoretical knowledge, and lab tutors can offer hands-on experience in operating the chemical plant. Moreover, SimLab enables instructors and tutors to incorporate short quizzes on distillation column operation practices, adding another element of gamification to the learning experience.

Learning Styles and Abilities: SimLab is designed to accommodate the diverse learning styles and abilities of students. While also supporting reading from interactable slides, SimLab caters to students with visual and auditory learning preferences. In the single-user interaction, students can playfully interact with the virtual chemical plant at their preferred pace. Students have the chance to review presentations, explore graphical representations of chemical plant elements, and practice distillation at their own pace. This helps to solidify students' understanding of concepts and technical terms by connecting them with visual representations of units and equipment. This flexibility caters to students' specific needs when it comes to preparing for real-life practical sessions or reviewing their practice materials. By accommodating individual learning preferences and providing self-paced learning opportunities, SimLab offers a tailored learning experience that supports students in their CENG education.

In the multi-user mode, SimLab empowers students to form teams, enabling them to collaborate effectively. This caters to students' preferences for practicing and learning in groups. This mode accelerates task completion as students can parallelize, cooperate, and collaborate on tasks. It also enhances cognition and fosters high levels of knowledge retention, aligning with the preferences of the majority of students. This fosters a gamified experience that promotes increased engagement, enthusiasm, and learning efficiency. SimLab is recognized by the participants as an effective platform in complementing CENG courses. Whether single or multi-user mode, SimLab accommodates the students' preferences which is particularly important for tailored learning experiences. Additionally, SimLab facilitates slide sharing that supports instructors and tutors in updating the review materials.

Graphical Quality and Realism: The 3D model of the virtual chemical plant and its units faithfully replicate the layouts and specifications of real-world chemical plant units and equipment. This meticulous design yields a substantial increase in student engagement, resulting in enhanced comprehension and knowledge retention, and thus enhanced learning outcomes. This is evident by SimLab's evaluation with non-immersive benchmark labs. Enhancements in SimLab, including visually stunning and realistic environments with high-quality graphics and meticulous attention to detail in rendering, significantly improve student engagement, comprehension, knowledge retention, and overall learning outcomes, thereby increasing its educational value.

6.3 Limitation and Future Improvement

The realistic design of the virtual chemical plant, intended to replicate real-world experiences and immerse students, results in slow movement within scenes. Participants experienced a higher level of motion sickness (i.e., dizziness) due to the sluggish rendering of scenes during movement. We plan to implement a teleport function with waypoints and reduce the 3D model's size to minimize motion. This would speed up the rendering, assist in moving faster in the scenes, and decrease the feeling of motion sickness. We also plan to minimize unnecessary polygons and optimize textures and shaders to address slow motion and rendering issues. Blender's decimate modifier[6] function will aid in implementing these strategies. Consequently, SimLab can achieve enhanced scalability, overcome slow rendering problems, and offer users a seamless experience. The participants also find difficulty in locating the virtual objects (i.e., valves in the Chemical Plant) and interacting with them on their own. To simplify locating the intractable objects and following the operation protocol, we plan to implement an eye-gaze tracking function. This function would pop up intractable and informative UIs that interactively guide them to the objects, and provide operation hints.

SimLab is designed to replicate the real-world experience in a chemical plant facility. However, SimLab Unity assets can be modified to include relevant 3D models and environments specific to other engineering labs. Besides, SimLab game mechanics, such as C# scripts, can be customized to simulate industry-specific interactions and processes, such as aircraft simulations or ship dynamics, ensuring a tailored and immersive experience for students in fields like Aerospace or Marine Engineering. We open-source the game mechanics code, provide access to SimLab Unity assets, and make the simulation available on GitHub[7]. This enables the research community to replicate the system, customize it, or guide them to develop simulations that complement other engineering courses.

7 Conclusion

This paper presents SimLab, a VR chemical engineering (CENG) lab that provides students the opportunity to virtually and safely manipulate chemical plants. We designed the 3D model of the chemical plant to accurately replicate the layouts of the real-world facility. We sized the virtual equipment and units to match the real ones, ensuring a high level of realism. After importing the models as assets, we implemented the gamification elements and interaction mechanics using Unity. We enabled both single-user and multi-user interaction modes. We conducted a user study to evaluate SimLab against benchmarks. Our findings

---

[6] https://docs.blender.org/manual/en/latest/modeling/modifiers/generate/decimate.html.

[7] Available at:https://github.com/JuhyungSon/SimLab.

revealed SimLab improves the learning efficiency and mastery over learning topics, and increases student engagement and interaction, compared to learning the practice using real and 2D game-based labs. SimLab multi-user mode accelerates the task completion while improving the immersion, interaction, and learning efficiency, compared to single-user mode.

Acknowledgement. This research was supported in part by a grant from the Guangzhou Municipal Nansha District Science and Technology Bureau under Contract No.2022ZD01 and the MetaHKUST project from the Hong Kong University of Science and Technology (Guangzhou).

Disclosure of Interests. The authors have no competing interests to declare that are relevant to the content of this article.

References

1. HoloLAB Champions (2018). https://schellgames.com/portfolio/hololab-champions/
2. Novartis (2018). https://www.gronstedtgroup.com/novartis-1
3. The VR Chemistry Lab (2021). https://www.oculus.com/experiences/quest/3919613214752680/
4. Abouhashem, A., Abdou, R.M., Bhadra, J., Santhosh, M., Ahmad, Z., Al-Thani, N.J.: A distinctive method of online interactive learning in stem education. Sustainability **13**(24), 13909 (2021)
5. Chattha, U.A., Janjua, U.I., Anwar, F., Madni, T.M., Cheema, M.F., Janjua, S.I.: Motion sickness in virtual reality: an empirical evaluation. IEEE Access **8**, 130486–130499 (2020). https://doi.org/10.1109/ACCESS.2020.3007076
6. Chen, C.C., Chen, C.M.: The application of interactive media display technology in environmental science learning. In: Stephanidis, C. (ed.) HCI International 2011 - Posters' Extended Abstracts, pp. 484–488. Springer, Berlin Heidelberg, Berlin, Heidelberg (2011)
7. Eos Trinidad, J., Radley Ngo, G.: Technology's roles in student-centred learning in higher education. IJAR-Int. J. Action Res. **15**(1), 13–14 (2019)
8. Forehand, M.: Bloom's taxonomy. Emerg. Perspect. Learn., Teach. Technol. **41**(4), 47–56 (2010)
9. GDPR. 2018: The european union's general data protection regulation. https://gdpr-info.eu/ (2018). Accessed 16 Dec 2022
10. Gosen, J., Washbush, J.: A review of scholarship on assessing experiential learning effectiveness. Simul. Gaming **35**(2), 270–293 (2004)
11. Hadi Mogavi, R., Zhao, Y., Ul Haq, E., Hui, P., Ma, X.: Student barriers to active learning in synchronous online classes: Characterization, reflections, and suggestions. In: Proceedings of the Eighth ACM Conference on Learning @ Scale, pp. 101–115. L@S '21, Association for Computing Machinery, New York, NY, USA (2021). https://doi.org/10.1145/3430895.3460126, https://doi.org/10.1145/3430895.3460126
12. Hart, S.G.: Nasa-task load index (nasa-tlx); 20 years later. In: Proceedings of the Human Factors and Ergonomics Society Annual Meeting, vol. 50, pp. 904–908. Sage publications Sage CA: Los Angeles, CA (2006)

13. He, Z., Du, R., Perlin, K.: Collabovr: A reconfigurable framework for creative collaboration in virtual reality. In: 2020 IEEE International Symposium on Mixed and Augmented Reality (ISMAR), pp. 542–554 (2020) .https://doi.org/10.1109/ISMAR50242.2020.00082
14. He, Z., Perlin, K.: Exploring the effectiveness of face-to-face mixed reality for teaching with chalktalk. arXiv preprint arXiv:1912.03863 (2019)
15. Jamshidi, R., Milanovic, I.: Building virtual laboratory with simulations. Comput. Appl. Eng. Educ. **30**(2), 483–489 (2022)
16. Kapilan, N., Vidhya, P., Gao, X.Z.: Virtual laboratory: a boon to the mechanical engineering education during Covid-19 pandemic. High. Educ. Future **8**(1), 31–46 (2021)
17. Katsigiannis, S., Willis, R., Ramzan, N.: A Goe and simulator sickness evaluation of a smart-exercise-bike virtual reality system via user feedback and physiological signals. IEEE Trans. Consum. Electron. **65**(1), 119–127 (2019). https://doi.org/10.1109/TCE.2018.2879065
18. Kennedy, R.S., Lane, N.E., Berbaum, K.S., Lilienthal, M.G.: Simulator sickness questionnaire: an enhanced method for quantifying simulator sickness. Int. J. Aviat. Psychol. **3**(3), 203–220 (1993)
19. Kiss, A.A.: Advanced distillation technologies: design, control and applications. John Wiley & Sons (2013)
20. Lu, Y., Xu, Y., Zhu, X.: Designing and implementing vr2e2c, a virtual reality remote education for experimental chemistry system (2021)
21. Mazloumi Gavgani, A., Walker, F.R., Hodgson, D.M., Nalivaiko, E.: A comparative study of cybersickness during exposure to virtual reality and classic motion sickness: are they different? J. Appl. Physiol. **125**(6), 1670–1680 (2018)
22. Perlin, K., He, Z., Rosenberg, K.: Chalktalk: A visualization and communication language–as a tool in the domain of computer science education. arXiv preprint arXiv:1809.07166 (2018)
23. Serafin, J.M., Chabra, J.: Using a cooperative hands-on general chemistry laboratory framework for a virtual general chemistry laboratory. J. Chem. Educ. **97**(9), 3007–3010 (2020)
24. Singh, G., Mantri, A., Sharma, O., Kaur, R.: Virtual reality learning environment for enhancing electronics engineering laboratory experience. Comput. Appl. Eng. Educ. **29**(1), 229–243 (2021)
25. Soliman, M., Pesyridis, A., Dalaymani-Zad, D., Gronfula, M., Kourmpetis, M.: The application of virtual reality in engineering education. Appl. Sci. **11**(6), 2879 (2021)
26. Villanueva, A., Zhu, Z., Liu, Z., Wang, F., Chidambaram, S., Ramani, K.: Colabar: A toolkit for remote collaboration in tangible augmented reality laboratories. Proc. ACM Hum.-Comput. Interact. **6**(CSCW1) (Apr 2022). https://doi.org/10.1145/3512928, https://doi.org/10.1145/3512928

Immersive Interactive Game Design for Cultural Relics and Monuments Based on Situated Cognition Theory

Yuchen Wang[1], Xiran Huang[2], Yushan Mo[3], Jun Huang[4], Tianxin Feng[5], Wei Huang[1], and Xiaomei Nie[1(✉)]

[1] Tsinghua University Shenzhen International Graduate School, Shenzhen, China
`nie.xiaomei@sz.tsinghua.edu.cn`
[2] University of the Arts London, London, UK
[3] Tsinghua University Academy of Arts and Design, Beijing, China
[4] Hunan Normal University, Changsha, China
[5] Tongji University, Shanghai, China

Abstract. Cultural relics and monuments are the tangible embodiments and carriers of humanity's core wisdom and culture, possessing significant educational and dissemination value. However, existing research on their digitization often lacks comprehensive guiding theories to enhance on-site tour experiences, leading to a shortfall in meeting the cultural learning needs of visitors in terms of narrative, immersion, and interaction. Addressing this gap, this paper presents an immersive interactive game design framework, specifically crafted for cultural relics and monuments. This framework integrates the principles of situated cognition theory with the features of immersive technology.

We applied this framework in the development of "Voices of Yungang," an immersive interactive game using the Yungang Grottoes as its thematic learning environment. The game's effectiveness was evaluated using a mix of research methodologies, including questionnaires, knowledge tests, and semi-structured interviews. Our findings indicate that "Voices of Yungang" has a positive influence on enhancing learning effectiveness, enriching the educational experience, and fostering learner initiative. This study not only contributes to the theory and practice of digital education for cultural relics and monuments but also offers empirical insights for future research in this field.

Keywords: Cultural Relics Digitization · Immersive Interactive Game · Gamification of learning · Mixed Reality · Situated Cognition Theory

1 Introduction

Cultural relics and monuments, embodying the tangible legacy of human history, are pivotal in the educational dissemination of core human wisdom and culture. Despite their significant value, the current methodologies in cultural heritage education and engagement encounter several challenges. These include (1) Complex Backgrounds: The intricate histories behind cultural heritage often pose a high educational barrier, leading to

X. Fang (Ed.): HCII 2024, LNCS 14730, pp. 180–198, 2024.
https://doi.org/10.1007/978-3-031-60692-2_13

passive viewing experiences for visitors. (2) Limitations of Traditional Media: Conventional media formats often fall short in capturing the extensive scope of cultural heritage, lacking in dynamic engagement methods. (3) Unidirectional Interaction: Predominantly one-way interactive methods contribute to visitor disinterest and fatigue.

In response to these challenges, and building upon existing research in the digitization of cultural relics and monuments, this paper proposes an innovative approach to invigorate traditional cultural heritage tours. We utilize situated cognition theory as a foundation to develop an immersive interactive game designed for heritage site visitors. This game, resembling a journey through time, enables visitors to actively participate in the construction and exploration of historical sites, thereby deepening their understanding of the site's historical context, construction process, and artistic significance. Our approach aims to enhance the effectiveness and experience of cultural learning and heritage dissemination.

The primary contributions of this paper are threefold:

1. Design Methodology: We have formulated a design framework for immersive interactive games at heritage sites, incorporating situated cognition theory and mixed reality technology. This framework facilitates the reconstruction of cultural heritage's historical context, using simulation activities to ignite interest and comprehension.
2. Practical Implementation: We have developed "Voices of Yungang," an immersive interactive game for the Yungang Grottoes. Through MR headsets, visitors embark on a 10-min journey, engaging with the site's historical background, construction process, artistic value, and multicultural aspects, thus enriching their cultural learning experience.
3. Effectiveness Evaluation: A small-scale user study, employing mixed research methods such as surveys, knowledge tests, and semi-structured interviews, was conducted. The results indicate the game has a positive influence on enhancing learning effectiveness, enriching the educational experience, and fostering learner initiative, but requires improvements in operational guidance and learning pace control.

This paper commences with an overview of the relevant theoretical and technical background. It then elucidates the proposed design framework for immersive interactive games in cultural relics and monuments, followed by a detailed account of the design and development process for the Yungang Grottoes game. Subsequently, the evaluation methodology and results of the user experiment are presented, ending in a discussion of the findings and potential directions for future research.

2 Theoretical Background and Related Work

This section first provides an investigation on the digitalization of cultural relics and monuments, identifying limitations in existing research. It then introduces our proposed solutions, including situated cognition theory, mixed reality technology, and simulation game design, laying a theoretical and technical foundation for developing an immersive interactive game framework for cultural relics and monuments.

2.1 Digitalization of Cultural Relics

Maria (2022) highlights the foremost technologies in cultural heritage digitalization, such as 3D visualization, 3D modeling, Augmented Reality (AR), Virtual Reality (VR), and motion capture systems [1], this paper conducts an investigation of existing applications research in the digitization of cultural relics and monuments [2–10]. Based on the types of digital technologies employed, current research is categorized into three directions: digital museums based on 3D reconstruction technology, digitization of relics using game technology, and digitization based on immersive technologies.

Table 1. Investigation of Digitalization Cases of Cultural Relics and Monuments

Type	Application	Experience Scenario	Narrativity	Immersion	Interactivity
Digital Museums Based on 3D Reconstruction	Forbidden City Museum: Panoramic Forbidden City & Digital Artifact Repository	Online	✗	★	★
	British Museum, Metropolitan Museum of Art, Louvre, etc.: Digital Exhibition Halls	Online	✗	★	★
Heritage Digitization Based on Gaming Technology	Bellotti: Educational Mission-Embedded Sandbox Function Game [4]	Online	✗	★	★
	NetEase and Forbidden City Museum: "True to Life Brushstrokes in a Thousand Hills"	Online	★★	★★	★★
	Tencent: Virtual Tour of Dunhuang, Great Wall	Online	★	★★	★★
Heritage Digitization Using Immersive Technology	Macau's Ruins of St. Paul: Immersive Digital Experience Exhibition	On-site	★	★★★	★★★
	PICO VR Interactive Documentary: "Ancient Book Quest"	Online	★★	★★★	★★★
	Huawei and Mogao Caves, Dunhuang: AR Cave Exploration	On-site	✗	★★	★★

To evaluate these applications, we analyze them across four dimensions: experience scenarios, narrativity, immersion, and interactivity, as detailed in Table 1. Experiential Scenarios evaluate whether applications necessitate on-site experiences at cultural sites, impacting the understanding and experience of cultural heritage. Narrativity enhances cultural heritage education through storytelling, fostering emotional engagement. Immersion leverages technology to create authentic historical and cultural experiences, while Interactivity focuses on engaging users with digital content, thereby deepening learning and educational effectiveness.

Our investigation reveals certain limitations in current digitization research on cultural relics and monuments. A significant gap is the lack of digital applications designed for on-site touring and comprehensive guiding design theories. Consequently, these applications often fail to meet visitors' expectations in terms of narrativity, immersion, and interactivity. We present a detailed analysis of the three primary application categories:

Digital Museums Based on 3D Reconstruction: These primarily display artifact details and historical information, with digital content offering limited presentation and interaction forms.

Heritage Digitization Based on Gaming Technology: While this area is expanding, it often lacks the support of educational theories, and the industry's approach does not fully cater to the educational dissemination needs of cultural heritage.

Heritage Digitization Using Immersive Technologies: VR technologies tend to disconnect users from the physical world, AR requires high user presence but offers limited interaction, and MR is underutilized in cultural heritage. Additionally, there is a deficiency of educational theories guiding scientifically in this domain.

2.2 Situated Cognition Theory

The concept of Situated Cognition was prominently introduced by Brown, Collins, and Duguid in their 1989 article, "Situated Cognition and the Culture of Learning" [11]. Challenging the traditional separation of knowledge and practice in public schooling, this seminal work posited that knowledge is inherently intertwined with the social and physical context of its application. Subsequent research expanded this theory, underscoring its importance in educational psychology. Situated learning, drawing on insights from psychology, education, sociology, and more, plays a crucial role in enriching traditional education methods, skill training, and teaching methodologies [12].

2.3 Mixed Reality Technology

Mixed Reality (MR) represents a fusion of real and virtual worlds, facilitating interactions between real-world and virtual objects within a shared environment. The term "Mixed Reality" was first coined by Milgram and Kishino in their 1994 paper, "A Taxonomy of Mixed Reality Visual Displays" [13]. MR is situated on a "Virtuality Continuum", as depicted in Fig. 1, spanning from completely real to fully virtual environments, and includes Augmented Reality (AR) and Augmented Virtuality (AV).

MR is known for enhancing user perception and interaction, offering flexibility, immersion, and interactivity. Core technologies in MR encompass 3D registration for accurate alignment of virtual and real objects, along with advanced features like gesture and voice recognition, haptic feedback, and eye-tracking. As an emerging field, MR holds substantial promise for a wide range of applications.

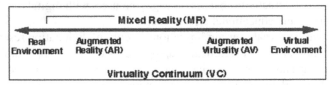

Fig. 1. The concept of the "Virtuality Continuum" proposed by Milgram and Kishino [13].

2.4 Simulation Game Design

Simulation games, a subset of electronic games, emulate real-life activities and environments. They create interactive virtual settings that mirror real-world scenarios, serving purposes such as training or entertainment. Increasingly utilized in educational contexts, simulation games offer hands-on experiences and problem-solving opportunities, rendering learning more engaging and dynamic compared to conventional methods [14]. Ke (2016) highlighted that educationally oriented game design often involves conceptual representation and contextualized simulation of scientific problems [15]. This methodology significantly boosts student motivation and interest in learning.

3   Game Design Model

This section introduces the Immersive Situated Cognition Interaction Design Model, which synergizes Situated Cognition Theory with the 3I features of immersive technology: Imagination, Immersion, and Interaction. This model is tailored for on-site cultural heritage tours, forming the basis of our framework for immersive interactive games grounded in situated cognition.

3.1   Construction of the Immersive Situated Cognition Interaction Design Model

Situated Cognition Theory illustrates the interplay among knowledge, context, and behavior, underscoring the significance of context in the learning process. In this model, we consider three key aspects: the integration of knowledge within the learner's context, the influence of context on activities, and the construction of knowledge through interactive experiences. These aspects are aligned with the 3I features of immersive technology as identified by Grigore and Philippe: (1) Imagination: conceptualizing a three-dimensional virtual space, (2) Immersion: experiencing a sense of reality within a virtual environment, and (3) Interaction: engaging with and receiving natural feedback from the environment [16].

Figure 2 illustrates our model, integrating these elements: (1) Knowledge Layer: Focused on transforming learning elements into narratives, this layer corresponds with Imagination. (2) Contextual Layer: This layer uses mixed reality technology to craft interactive scenes, facilitating Immersion. (3) Behavioral Layer: Through simulation games, we develop interactive mechanisms, thus achieving Interaction.

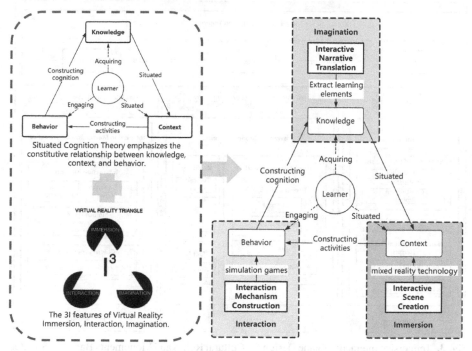

Fig. 2. Construction Process of the Immersive Situated Cognition Interaction Design Model.

3.2 Immersive Interactive Game Design Framework for Cultural Heritage and Monuments

Addressing the specific requirements of exploring cultural heritage sites, our proposed design framework, as depicted in Fig. 3, comprises:

1. Knowledge Layer: Concentrating on transforming elements of cultural heritage into interactive storytelling, this layer enhances the imaginative experience. It involves reinterpreting heritage characters, events, and structures into captivating narratives for interactive game scripts.

2. Contextual Layer: Utilizing mixed reality technology, this layer creates interactive scenes that provide immersive experiences. By blending real and virtual elements, visitors are able to experience historical contexts through rich visual, auditory, and tactile dimensions.

3. Behavioral Layer: Focusing on simulated gamified interactions, this layer introduces mechanisms to improve user interactivity, inviting visitors to engage in virtual reconstructions and other interactive activities, thereby deepening their engagement and connection with historical narratives.

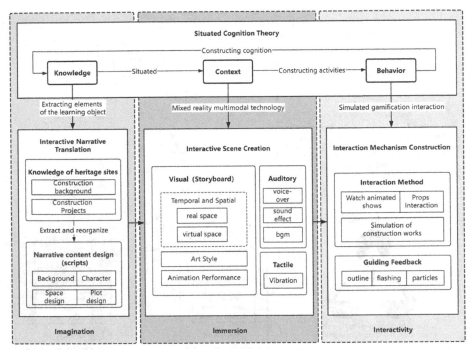

Fig. 3. Immersive Interactive Game Design for Cultural Relics and Monuments Based on Situated Cognition Theory.

4 "Voices of Yungang": an Immersive Interactive Game at the Yungang Grottoes

Leveraging the immersive interactive game design framework previously discussed, this paper focuses on the Yungang Grottoes, a significant cultural heritage site, to design and implement an immersive interactive game titled "Voices of Yungang."

4.1 Overview of "Voices of Yungang" Immersive Interactive Game

Situated in Datong City, Shanxi Province, the Yungang Grottoes stand as one of China's four grand ancient Buddhist temple grottoes, imbued with substantial research and educational significance. Despite their importance, existing digitalization efforts, primarily focused on 3D reconstruction-based digital museums, have shown limitations in educational efficacy. A notable gap exists in the application of gaming and immersive technologies for educational purposes.

As depicted in Fig. 4, "Voices of Yungang" is an MR headset-based immersive narrative game. Themed "When years fall silent, the stones speak," the game invites visitors on a 10-min temporal journey, targeting an audience aged 10 to 50, especially those present at Cave 20 of the Yungang Grottoes. During the game, participants are virtually transported back in time, immersing themselves in the construction of the grottoes. They experience the history etched into the cliffside, gaining insights into the historical context, construction techniques, artistic significance, and the cultural melding of the Northern Wei Dynasty's Chinese and nomadic cultures. This immersive experience aims to enhance the cultural learning experience of visitors at the Yungang Grottoes.

Fig. 4. Overview of "Voices of Yungang" Immersive Interactive Game.

4.2 Design Concept of "Voices of Yungang"

The following section provides a detailed account of the construction process for "Voices of Yungang" based on the aforementioned design framework.

Knowledge Layer: Interactive Narrative Translation. The heart of the game is the transformation of historical insights into an interactive narrative. We have meticulously compiled historical and cultural information from scholarly works and documentaries about the Yungang Grottoes to create a storyline enriched with heritage elements. These elements are categorized into construction background, historical figures, artistic value, and building projects, forming the foundation for the narrative content of the interactive game. To ensure the accuracy and credibility of this knowledge, experts from the Yungang Grottoes Research Institute were invited for guidance on plot storylines, character costumes, and historical and cultural contexts.

Worldview Construction. The immersive setting of the game is anchored in the 1930s journey of the renowned Chinese architectural historian Liang Sicheng and his team, as they set out to document China's architectural heritage. Their quest leads them to the Yungang Grottoes, where an unexpected temporal shift transports them back to the era of the Northern Wei dynasty. Here, under the guidance of the eminent monk Tan Yao, they participate in the creation of the grottoes.

(1) Character and Spatiotemporal Design. Set in front of Cave 20 of the Yungang Grottoes, the game weaves characters from three different epochs—Tan Yao in the 460s, Liang Sicheng in the 1930s, and the contemporary player—into its narrative. Tan Yao and Liang Sicheng, as the main Non-Player Characters (NPCs) in "Voices of Yungang," lead the player through the history of the grottoes, fostering a deeper connection with the site's past. The players, as contemporary visitors, engage in first-person exploration and learning about the grottoes alongside these NPCs. Table 2 outlines the key roles, their spatiotemporal settings, and the design objectives.

Table 2. Character and Spatiotemporal Design of "Voices of Yungang"

Role	Era & Location	Description	Design Purpose
Tan Yao	460s, Wuzhou Mountain	Builder of the Yungang Grottoes, a high monk in Northern Wei, well-versed in Buddhism	To guide players through the historical and cultural context of the grottoes and explain the construction process
Liang Sicheng	1930s, Yungang Grottoes	Protector of the Yungang Grottoes, a renowned Chinese architect, on a survey mission	To lead players to appreciate the artistic value of the grottoes and emphasize the importance of preserving cultural relics
Player	2020s, Yungang Grottoes	Admirer of the Yungang Grottoes, a visitor exploring the site	To experience and feel the culture and history on-site at the grottoes

Plot Design. Following the "Three-Act Structure" by Syd Field for screenplay writing, and integrating the narrative design with the collected literature, "Voices of Yungang" unfolds in three stages: Dream Entry, In-Dream, and Dream Awakening, as detailed in Table 3. The script, consisting of over 4,000 words, meticulously lays out the specific plot points.

Contextual Layer: Interactive Scene Creation. In "Voices of Yungang," the Contextual Layer extensively employs mixed reality multimodal technology to craft an immersive interactive scene, engaging users visually, auditorily, and tactilely.

(2) Visual Aspect: This includes storyboard and scene design, artistic style design, and temporal and spatial scene design.

Storyboard and Scene Design: The narrative is transformed into a dynamic 3D interactive game through detailed storyboard and scene designs. Unlike the static perspectives of 2D films, MR technology enables dynamic exploration in 3D space. "Voices of Yungang" employs dual storyboarding: one detailing the player's viewpoint for guiding animated sequences and another illustrating the 360° layout surrounding the player. This

Table 3. "Voices of Yungang" Plot Design Based on the "Three-Act Structure"

Stage	Plot Event	Narrative Summary	Educational Content
Act One: Dream Entry	Beginning	Liang Sicheng and the Society for the Study of Chinese Architecture arrive at Yungang Grottoes for surveying and mapping	1. Introduction of Liang Sicheng and historical context of their visit 2. Architectural knowledge of Northern Wei Dynasty displayed in the Grottoes
	Inciting incident	Player takes a photo of Cave 20	None
	Climax of Act One	Player travels back to the Northern Wei Dynasty	None
Act Two: In-Dream	Ascending action	Dialogue between Tan Yao and Liang Sicheng, showcasing the interaction between the builder and protector of the grottoes	1. Reasons and historical background for carving the Yungang Grottoes 2. Tan Yao's background 3. Buddhist art and culture
	Midpoint	Tan Yao guides the construction of Cave 20	1. Construction process of Yungang Grottoes 2. Artistic characteristics of Cave 20
	Climax of Act Two	Player completes the construction process	None
Act Three: Dream Awakening	Climax of Act Three	The newly built facade of Cave 20 disappears, and the player returns to the present	Collapse event of the front wall of Cave 20 and its side Buddhas and Bodhisattvas
	Warp-up	Liang Sicheng reflects on the wisdom of ancient artisans and the importance of preserving ancient architecture	Survey results and research value of the Society for the Study of Chinese Architecture
	End	Exhibition of old photos of Yungang Grottoes	1. Growth history of the grottoes: Characteristics of three phases 2. Conservation achievements over generations

includes detailed model animations and character pathways, which are crucial for visual development (refer to Fig. 5).

Artistic Style: The game adopts an ink painting artistic style, characterized by bold outlines and shaded with gradient transitions, creating a historically immersive environment (illustrated in Fig. 6).

Temporal and Spatial Scene Design: The game differentiates historical eras using MR's video perspective capability. For the 1930s scenes, virtual characters are integrated with real-world settings, while the 460s scenes are portrayed in a fully virtual environment, depicting the Northern Wei era's construction activities (see Fig. 6).

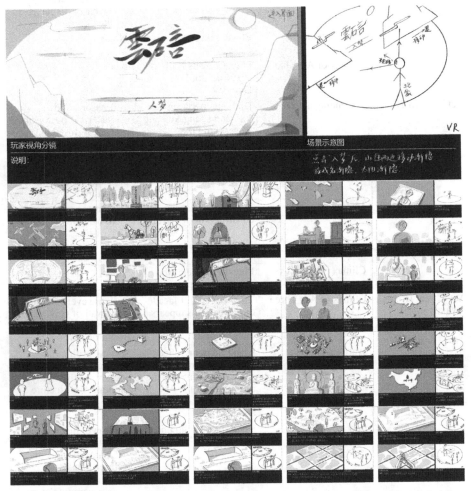

Fig. 5. Storyboard and Scene design of "Voices of Yungang": Illustrates the transformation from narrative to interactive 3D space, highlighting player viewpoints and a 360° environmental layout essential for immersive visual development.

Auditory Aspect: "Voices of Yungang" enhances the immersive experience through the use of sound elements such as background music, sound effects, and voiceovers. The

(a) Artistic Style

(b) Dream Entry and Dream Awakening Phase: MR   (c) In-Dream Phase: VR

Fig. 6. Visual design of "Voices of Yungang": (a) Artistic Style: Depicts the ink painting style that contributes to the historical immersion. (b) and (c) Temporal and Spatial Scene Design: In the Dream Entry and Dream Awakening phases (1930s), Mixed Reality (MR) connects visitors to the environment by overlaying virtual characters onto real-world views. During the In-Dream phase (460s), Virtual Reality (VR) immerses players in the Northern Wei Dynasty's grotto construction within a fully virtual setting.

background music, professionally composed, aligns with the historical theme. Professional voice actors lend authenticity to the narrative and character dialogues. Sound effects, meticulously sourced and edited, add a layer of realism to the user's interactions.

(1) Tactile Aspect: The game leverages haptic feedback from mixed reality headset controllers to further enrich immersion and interactivity. These controllers deliver precise vibration feedback in response to user interactions, creating a nuanced tactile experience.

Behavioral Layer: Interaction Mechanism Construction In "Voices of Yungang," the Behavioral Layer is dedicated to enhancing user engagement through simulated gamified interactions and intuitive guidance feedback.

(2) Interaction Methods: The primary mode of interaction in "Voices of Yungang" is engaging with animated performances. Users, equipped with MR headsets, can navigate

(a) Old Photo Interaction: Grab
and flip to view.

(b) Photo-taking: Complete the photography
interaction, examine old photos.

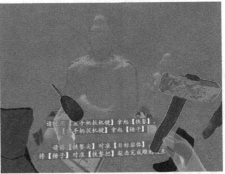

(c) Simulating Grotto Construction: Rock
cutting interactive task.

(d) Simulating Grotto Construction:
Buddha statue carving task.

Fig. 7. Behavioral Layer design of "Voices of Yungang".

a 360° immersive scene by moving their bodies and heads. As the story unfolds through character animations and dialogues, users are drawn deeply into the narrative. The game also incorporates natural gamified interactions, such as manipulating virtual props like old photographs, which reveal more details and advance the storyline.

A key interactive element is the simulation of grotto construction, broken down into essential steps like site selection, mountain exterior shaping, internal layering, and statue carving. These are depicted through 2D animations on a construction sand table, offering a macro view of the process. More intimate interactions involve tasks like stone splitting and Buddha statue carving, providing a tactile experience of the intricate construction details (refer to Fig. 7).

Guidance and Feedback: "Voices of Yungang" employs various visual and auditory-tactile cues for natural guidance and immediate feedback. For example, interactive objects are indicated through highlighted outlines when a user's hand approaches them, and blinking effects on camera buttons signal interactive prompts. These visual guides, combined with sound effects and vibrations, significantly enhance the interactive experience, making it more engaging and immersive (illustrated in Fig. 7).

4.3 Development and Operational Environment for "Voices of Yungang"

Game Development Environment. For the Development of "Voices of Yungang," We Chose the Unity Engine, Celebrated for Its User-Friendliness and Flexibility Across Various Platforms. Unity Offers Comprehensive Functionalities Such as Advanced Rendering, Physics Engines, Audio Systems, and Cross-Platform Compatibility. These Features Make It an Ideal Choice for VR Game Development, Given Its Ability to Support Intricate and Dynamic Game Environments.

Game Operational Environment. The PICO 4 Pro headset was selected as the operational device due to its cost-effectiveness and advanced features. This VR headset is equipped with color passthrough, eye and facial tracking capabilities, and utilizes video see-through technology. This technology enables the overlay of virtual elements onto real-world settings, thereby facilitating an immersive mixed reality experience (Fig. 8).

Fig. 8. This figure illustrates the Unity game development engine and the PICO 4 PRO mixed reality headset, highlighting the key tools utilized in bringing the immersive experience of "Voices of Yungang" to life.

5 User Test

To validate the effectiveness of our design framework and assess the quality of "Voices of Yungang," we conducted an experimental evaluation using a combination of social and data science methodologies. The evaluation tools included a Likert scale questionnaire, objective knowledge tests, and semi-structured interviews. A blend of qualitative and quantitative methods was employed to analyze the data, aiming to measure learning effectiveness, learning experience, learning initiative, and assess the overall quality of the game.

5.1 Experimental Tools

Questionnaire. A comprehensive 16-item survey was developed focusing on four indicators: learning effectiveness, learning experience, learning initiative, and system usability [17]. Responses were recorded using a 5-point Likert scale (Table 4).

Knowledge Test. To quantitatively measure participants' understanding, a test comprising 7 multiple-choice and 4 fill-in-the-blank questions was administered. These questions were based on the content presented in the game and were completed independently by participants via smartphone.

Table 4. Questionnaire design of "Voices of Yungang"

Learning Effectiveness	Learning Experience	Learning Initiative	System Usability
Q1: The game enhanced my understanding of the construction background of the Yungang Grottoes Q2: The game deepened my knowledge of historical figures related to the Yungang Grottoes Q3: The game enriched my appreciation of the artistic value of the Yungang Grottoes Q4: The game improved my understanding of the construction process of the Yungang Grottoes	Q5: I was able to immerse myself in the game Q6: I found the game to be interesting Q7: During the game, I was able to control my own learning pace Q8: During the game, I could sense my environment and physical sensations Q9: I was able to understand and learn the cultural content presented in the game	Q10: I am willing to continue similar learning experiences Q11: I enjoy this mode of learning Q12: This game made me want to learn more about the Yungang Grottoes	Q13: The operational guidance in the game was clear and precise Q14: The audio-visual experience was attractive Q15: The way knowledge was presented in the experience was easy to understand Q16: The interaction difficulty of the game was appropriate

Semi-structured Interviews. Participants were encouraged to share their feedback on aspects such as satisfaction, immersion, playability, and usability of the game. The interviews were recorded and transcribed for thorough analysis, with participants' consent.

5.2 Experimental Process

Due to time constraints, a small-scale user test was conducted. The sample selection criteria were as follows: (1) non-experts in history and culture; (2) no prior knowledge or understanding of the Yungang Grottoes; (3) a high level of acceptance and understanding of emerging immersive technologies. A group of 7 student volunteers from Tsinghua University's Shenzhen International Graduate School, comprising 3 males and 4 females, participated in the user test.

A before-and-after comparison method was employed for the experiment. Initially, a background survey confirmed that all participants met the selection criteria. None had previously visited the Yungang Grottoes, and their average self-assessment score for knowledge of the site's history and culture was 1.29 (on a scale up to 5), indicating limited prior understanding. However, they demonstrated high interest in immersive technologies. During the test, participants experienced the game using the PICO 4 PRO headset for approximately 10 minutes (Fig. 9). Post-experience, they completed the evaluation questionnaire, a learning effectiveness test, and participated in semi-structured interviews, each lasting between 10–25 min.

Fig. 9. Users are experiencing "Voices of Yungang."

5.3 Results Analysis

Questionnaire. The reliability of the questionnaire was confirmed with a Cronbach's alpha value of 0.805, indicating good internal consistency. This suggests that the questionnaire is a reliable tool for further analysis.

(1) Learning Effectiveness: Participants reported significantly enhanced understanding of the Yungang Grottoes' construction, historical figures, and artistic values. Scores were particularly high in understanding construction background (average 4.71) and historical figures (average 4.57).

(2) Learning Experience: High ratings in immersion and interest (average 4.71) indicate that participants were thoroughly engaged and enjoyed the game.

(3) Learning Initiative: The high willingness to engage in similar experiences (average 4.86) demonstrates the game's effectiveness in stimulating learning interest.

(4) System Usability: Participants praised the game's audiovisual appeal and the clarity of knowledge presentation. However, areas for improvement were identified in operational clarity (average 4.00) and control over learning pace (average 3.29).

Knowledge Test. Participants showed a high accuracy rate of 83.11% in the knowledge test, indicating effective learning about the Yungang Grottoes' history and culture through the game. Nonetheless, to improve knowledge transfer and reinforce understanding, adjustments in the game's knowledge presentation are suggested, particularly to address commonly incorrect responses.

Semi-structured Interviews. Participants generally rated their gaming experience positively, noting its enhancement of the interaction between visitors and attractions and deepening impressions of the sites. This highlights the game's effectiveness in improving learning outcomes and engagement. However, users identified areas for improvement, including object sizing and interaction fluidity, which could impact the overall experience. User feedback was categorized and analyzed in the following aspects:

(1) Narrative: Users found the story clear and engaging, effectively enriching their knowledge about the Yungang Grottoes (P4). However, some perceived a lack of narrative tension and climax, leading to didacticism (P6).

(2) Interaction: Users particularly enjoyed the hands-on sculpting activity, emphasizing the value of tactile interaction. Suggestions included refining interaction details and offering more diverse interactive options, especially in dialogue interactions (P3, P5, P7).

(3) Visual Artistry: Most users commended the visual and historical richness, with the starting interface making a strong impact. However, the need for more dynamic scenes and cultural elements was highlighted to address visual monotony (P6). VR device limitations, such as model quality and performance, were also mentioned (P7).

(4) Mixed Reality: The innovative use of mixed reality, such as viewing the Great Buddha in a formal experimental environment, was praised for its surprise factor and potential (P1, P2, P4).

6 Conclusion and Future Work

This paper addresses the gaps in current research on the digitization of cultural relics and monuments by introducing an immersive interactive game design framework grounded in situated cognition theory. Focusing on the Yungang Grottoes, we developed "Voices of Yungang," an immersive interactive game. User experiments indicate that the game has a positive influence on learning effectiveness, experience, and initiative.

Despite these promising results, our research has certain limitations. Moving forward, we plan to refine the system's usability before conducting a more comprehensive user test at the Yungang Grottoes site. Based on the feedback received, our goal is to diversify interactive forms and improve the interaction experience's guidance and detail. In terms of art design, we aim to incorporate additional artistic elements pertinent to the Yungang Grottoes to deepen users' immersion.

Owing to the limited scope of our initial user test sample, we aim to augment the precision of our experimental outcomes. Our subsequent steps encompass a larger-scale user test on-site at the Yungang Grottoes, utilizing a comparative experimental approach. Considering the popularity of videos and images as multimedia formats in cultural relic and monument tours, we intend to compare the immersive interactive game with traditional video and image formats. This comparison will aid in further verifying the game's effectiveness in facilitating cultural learning.

Our research bridges educational psychology, information technology, and game design. It demonstrates the application of mixed reality in digitizing cultural sites to enhance on-site cultural learning experiences. This study contributes to the field of digital heritage research, offering valuable insights for future design methodologies and technological innovations.

Acknowledgments. This work was supported by a research grant from Shenzhen Key Laboratory of next generation interactive media innovative technology (Funding No: ZDSYS20210623092001004), and the Center for Social Governance and Innovation at Tsinghua

University, a major research center for Shenzhen Humanities & Social Sciences Key Research Bases.

References

1. Skublewska-Paszkowska, M., Milosz, M., Powroznik, P., Lukasik, E.: 3D technologies for intangible cultural heritage preservation-literature review for selected databases. Herit. Sci. **10**(1), 3 (2022). https://doi.org/10.1186/s40494-021-00633-x
2. Andreoli, R., et al.: A framework to design, develop and evaluate immersive and collaborative serious games in cultural heritage. J. Comput. Cult. Herit. **11**(1), 4:1–4:22 (2017). https://doi.org/10.1145/3064644
3. Bekele, M.K., Champion, E.: A comparison of immersive realities and interaction methods: cultural learning in virtual heritage. Front. Robot. AI **6**, 91 (2019). https://doi.org/10.3389/frobt.2019.00091
4. Bellotti, F., Berta, R., De Gloria, A., D'ursi, A., Fiore, V.: A serious game model for cultural heritage. J. Comput. Cult. Herit. **5**(4), 17:1–17:27 (2013). https://doi.org/10.1145/2399180.2399185
5. Antoniou, A., Lepouras, G., Bampatzia, S., Almpanoudi, H.: An approach for serious game development for cultural heritage: case study for an archaeological site and museum. J. Comput. Cult. Herit. **6**(4), 1–19 (2013). https://doi.org/10.1145/2532630.2532633
6. Boboc, R.G., Bautu, E., Girbacia, F., Popovici, N., Popovici, D.-M.: Augmented reality in cultural heritage: an overview of the last decade of applications. Appl. Sci.-Basel. **12**(19), 9859 (2022). https://doi.org/10.3390/app12199859
7. Chong, H.T., Lim, C.K., Rafi, A., Tan, K.L., Mokhtar, M.: Comprehensive systematic review on virtual reality for cultural heritage practices: coherent taxonomy and motivations. Multimed. Syst. **28**(3), 711–726 (2022). https://doi.org/10.1007/s00530-021-00869-4
8. Anderson, E.F., McLoughlin, L., Liarokapis, F., Peters, C., Petridis, P., de Freitas, S.: Developing serious games for cultural heritage: a state-of-the-art review. Virtual Real. **14**(4), 255–275 (2010). https://doi.org/10.1007/s10055-010-0177-3
9. Sylaiou, S., Liarokapis, F., Kotsakis, K., Patias, P.: Virtual museums, a survey and some issues for consideration. J. Cult. Herit. **10**(4), 520–528 (2009). https://doi.org/10.1016/j.culher.2009.03.003
10. Theodoropoulos, A., Antoniou, A.: VR games in cultural heritage: a systematic review of the emerging fields of virtual reality and culture games. Appl. Sci.-Basel. **12**(17), 8476 (2022). https://doi.org/10.3390/app12178476
11. Brown, J.S., Collins, A., Duguid, P.: Situated cognition and the culture of learning. Educ. Res. **18**(1), 32–42 (1989). https://doi.org/10.3102/0013189X018001032
12. Lave, J., Wenger, E.: Situated Learning: Legitimate Peripheral Participation. Higher Education from Cambridge University Press. https://www.cambridge.org/highereducation/books/situated-learning/6915ABD21C8E4619F750A4D4ACA616CD. Accessed 25 Oct 2022
13. Milgram, P., Takemura, H., Utsumi, A., Kishino, F.: Augmented reality: a class of displays on the reality-virtuality continuum. In: Telemanipulator and Telepresence Technologies, SPIE, December 1995, pp. 282–292 (1995). https://doi.org/10.1117/12.197321
14. Dorn, D.S.: Simulation games: one more tool on the pedagogical shelf. Teach. Sociol. **17**(1), 1–18 (1989). https://doi.org/10.2307/1317920
15. Ke, F.: Designing and integrating purposeful learning in game play: a systematic review. Etrd-Educ. Technol. Res. Dev. **64**(2), 219–244 (2016). https://doi.org/10.1007/s11423-015-9418-1

198   Y. Wang et al.

16. Burdea, G.C., Coiffet, P.: Virtual Reality Technology. John Wiley & Sons, London (2003)
17. Makransky, G., Petersen, G.B.: The cognitive affective model of immersive learning (CAMIL): a theoretical research-based model of learning in immersive virtual reality. Educ. Psychol. Rev. **33**(3), 937–958 (2021). https://doi.org/10.1007/s10648-020-09586-2

Computer Game Design for Eye Contact Exercise for Children with Autism

Jizhao Xie[1,2], Qian Ji[1(✉)], and Zicheng Lin[3]

[1] Department of Industrial Design, School of Mechanical Science and Engineering, Huazhong University of Science and Technology, Wuhan, China
jiqian@mail.hust.edu.cn
[2] School of Design, Shanghai Jiao Tong University, Shanghai, China
[3] Shenzhen International Graduate School, Tsinghua University, Shenzhen, China

Abstract. Lack of concentration and eye contact are common characteristics of many children with autism spectrum disorder (ASD). If not intervened early, it will accompany the children as they grow up and cause more problems. To help ASD children improve their attention and sensitivity to eye contact, this study designed computer game products for high-functioning ASD children between ages of 3–10 years. This study used game science and implicit learning theory, combined with eye-tracking technology, to design the entire gameplay experience using eye gaze as a means of interaction. Players needed to maintain focus and interact with game characters using their eye gaze, thereby progressing through the game. It established a story about becoming a carrot garden protector, and players were told that they must protect the rabbit and his carrot garden. After the completion of the game prototype, it was used by children at the ASD Rehabilitation Center in the Huazhong University of Science and Technology. The design was evaluated for feasibility, safety, and intervention effectiveness. The test results and user feedback revealed that the game received high ratings in novelty, practicality, interactivity, ease of use, and safety. Moderate-to-high functioning children with autism performed well while using the game, with nearly half of them able to participate. Rehabilitation specialists and doctors regard the game as having the potential to become an effective rehabilitation tool. Furthermore, active guidance from parents during gameplay played a crucial role in improving the children's technical skills. Through two weeks of follow-up tests for a total of four times, it was found that the game could help improve some symptoms of autistic children to a certain extent, including eye contact, gaze attitude, and concentration. In general, the game provided positive gaming experiences for moderate -to-high functioning children with autism, demonstrating value and significance for its usage and promotion.

Keywords: Autism Spectrum Disorder · Computer Game Design · Concentration · Eye Contact

X. Fang (Ed.): HCII 2024, LNCS 14730, pp. 199–217, 2024.
https://doi.org/10.1007/978-3-031-60692-2_14

1 Introduction

As the incidence of diagnosed autism in China steadily increases, the need for early intervention training for autistic children is growing. Game-based intervention training is gaining prominence due to its flexibility in terms of space and time constraints. Moreover, eye contact plays a pivotal role in children's early learning abilities. This study employs games to offer supplementary exercises aimed at improving eye contact and related skills in children. The objective is to furnish children with autism an accessible and engaging tool for daily exercises, while also serving as a source of inspiration for the autistic games in future studies.

Eye contact is a phenomenon where the perception of eye contact is established with another person's face. Studies on adults indicate that eye contact can modulate the activity of the social brain network. It shows that from early in life, individuals tend to directly gaze at faces and process them [1]. Eye contact, or gaze communication, is a crucial and fundamental form of communication in everyday human social interactions, widely present in various social scenarios. In the standards set by the American Psychiatric Association in the Diagnostic and Statistical Manual of Mental Disorders, "lack of eye contact" is identified as a typical early symptom of autism spectrum disorder and is often included in early diagnosis, and assessment programs.

Recent studies indicate that difficulties in extracting relevant information from the eye region can hinder the recognition of facial identity, facial emotions, or the inference of others' attention and intentions [2]. The absence of eye contact and gaze communication is a common symptom in children on the autism spectrum. Research suggests that children with autism lack interest in human faces [3], while eye-tracking studies reveal that they are not disinterested in faces but tend to focus more on areas such as ears, chin, and hairline [4]. By training to enhance eye contact skills, individuals with ASD can better understand others' behavior and emotions, thereby improving their social skills and engagement.

Shared attention refers to the coordinated ability of children to share interest and understand others' intentions by using gestures or eye contact to focus attention on a common object or event [5]. In the process of children's growth and learning, shared attention plays a crucial role in areas such as language imitation and social interactive activities. For example, if a person looks at a cat and says "kitty", a child hearing this word will direct attention to the person's gaze direction and associate the word with the cat in front of them. This learning strategy based on the use of someone's gaze direction emerges in children between 12 to 19 months old [6]. Shared attention is not only a foundation for early social interaction but also a fundamental aspect of language learning and development [7].

The ability for shared attention and eye contact is connected to eye movements, which, in turn, are closely linked to brain activity. Cases in neuropsychology involving patients with brain injuries and extensive studies utilizing neuroimaging and magnetoencephalography suggest the existence of specialized neural circuits dedicated to the processing of eyes and gaze [2]. In a gaze test, there are observable differences in brain activity between children with autism and normal children. The results indicate that the ventrolateral prefrontal cortex of normal children exhibits reliably increased activity during both direct and avoidant gaze, unlike in children with autism [8]. Another study recruited autistic people with normal intelligence for an experiment involving eye movement stimuli. The findings reveal that different gaze durations elicit distinct brain region activities, including the orbitofrontal and pregenual anterior cingulate regions [9]. Moreover, mutual gaze activates new cortical areas [10]. These experimental results emphasize that eye contact stimulates brain activity.

In addition, eye contact and gaze are closely associated with shared attention and cognitive functions. By practicing these skills, children with autism may enhance their ability to focus, comprehend, and memorize information more quickly, better coping with challenges in learning and daily life. A study from 2005 indicated a positive correlation between vocabulary development in 18-month-old children and eye gaze at 10–11 months, highlighting the interconnectedness of language acquisition, eye gaze, and shared attention. Subsequent research suggests that eye gaze can influence a child's vocabulary development until the age of 2 [11, 12]. A study focusing on eye contact in neurotypical individuals revealed that prolonged eye contact fosters positive emotions and a sense of social connection [13]. Additionally, guiding autistic children to pay attention to eye contact and gaze direction can be helpful for their cognitive understanding of surroundings and awareness of whether someone is paying attention to them [14, 15].

In conclusion, practicing eye contact and gaze in children with autism may lead to improvements in both their social and cognitive abilities, facilitating better adaptation to societal norms and the demands of learning. The relationship between eye movement functions and shared attention in this context is summarized (see Fig. 1).

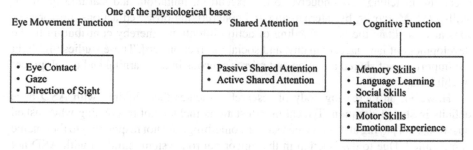

Fig. 1. Relationship between eye movement function and shared attention

2 Relative Research

2.1 Game Interventions

Presently, behavioral therapy for autism is effective but expensive and challenging to access [16]. However, computer-assisted therapeutic solutions can increase training frequency while parents await intervention courses, easing the growing demand for interventions. Game-based intervention training demonstrates increasing potential due to its less constrained spatial and temporal features. Research has already indicated the feasibility of digital technology platforms for treating children with autism [17, 18]. Such products offer the advantage of on-the-spot utilization, allowing users to engage anytime, anywhere, without the need to visit specific locations such as rehabilitation centers or clinics. Furthermore, these products are cost-effective, reducing the demand for special education teachers and alleviating financial pressure on families with autistic children.

Additionally, children with autism share similar age-appropriate interests and hobbies with normal children. According to statistics, 70% of children with autism do not have intellectual disabilities [19], enabling them to comprehend and adhere to game rules. The autism community also exhibits a particular interest in screen-based media and computer games [20]. Given that playing games is a natural inclination for many children, game-based rehabilitation programs not only address training objectives but also captivate children's attention with lively visuals and interactive formats. Combining eye movement training with game may further engage children actively in the training, potentially leading to enhanced rehabilitation outcomes.

2.2   Research on Eye Contact and Shared Attention

In the 2007 study, Posner and others proposed an explanation for the neural mechanisms underlying shared attention. Experimental analysis identified brain regions associated with shared attention, including the frontal eye field, prefrontal cortex, anterior cingulate gyrus, orbitofrontal cortex, and cortical networks in the insula [21–23]. These networks involve core areas of mirror neurons. Mirror neurons exhibit the characteristic of "observation-action matching" [24]. Neural activity involving "observing actions - executing matching" is conducive to the execution, imitation, and learning of motor skills [25]. Moreover, by internalizing and concretizing observed actions, mirror neurons also facilitate the understanding of action intentions, thereby contributing to the development of language, empathy, and social interaction [26]. These studies highlight the importance of shared attention and mirror neurons in the learning and development of children.

However, an increasing body of research indicates that children with ASD have deficits in shared attention. Typical manifestations include not responding when asked questions, not paying attention when shown something, and not responding to their name being called. Due to dysfunction in the mirror neuron system, children with ASD not only exhibit deficits in shared attention but also experience difficulties in understanding actions, emotional expression, and social interaction [27, 28]. Deficits in shared attention serve as a potential link to the social interaction difficulties, narrow interests, and repetitive behaviors observed in children with ASD, playing a crucial role in their overall development [29]. Studies suggest that interventions targeting shared attention in children with ASD can promote and drive development in other areas, emphasizing the prioritization of shared attention as a key intervention skill [30].

Regarding eye contact, during interactions with others, children with ASD rarely engage in eye contact. A 2005 study revealed that, at 6 to 8 months of age, children with ASD show less inclination towards others' gaze and social stimuli (eye contact, facial expressions, sounds, movements) compared to typically developing infants or even developmentally delayed infants. Additionally, parents of children with ASD often report that their children tend to avoid eye contact with others [31]. Furthermore, the lack of observation with others' eyes makes it challenging for children with ASD to understand and interpret facial expressions and social cues. The signals coming from the eyes of others, especially, are often avoided by these children. Such situations make it even more difficult for children with ASD to integrate into social life.

3 User Research and Design Developing

We aim to preserve the natural characteristics of children with autism. The goal is to leverage their innate tendencies rather than impose mandatory training, thereby implementing an intervention program as a supportive measure.

3.1 Interviews

We conducted interviews with parents of children with ASD (aged between 4 and 16). The choice of interviewing parents was based on their intimate familiarity with their children's situations and their typically comprehensive knowledge of various intervention and training programs available in the market. Due to the pandemic restriction, the interviews were taken online. The questionnaires introduced the team's information, the research purpose, the current game design (ask for feasibility and improvement), and after receiving feedback from four parents, the results of the interviews were compiled and organized (see Table 1).

Table 1. User interview feedback

	Mom Gao 37 years old son 8 years old	Mama Ma 34 years old son 5 years old
Can a 3 ~ 10-year-old tell the difference between a white rabbit and a thief?	Yes	Some of the 3 ~ 10-year-olds recognize it and some don't, depending on their level
Can a child explore ways to chase away a thief on his own? (eye contact)	Not really, still need a reminder	First, my kids need tips. Or a demonstration of how to play once. If let him figure out that on his own that it would take longer
Do you think children will enjoy playing this game? Are there any sections that need to focus or improve?	He seems to have played a similar game before. However, his interest waned after just two or three sessions because the actions were quite simple and couldn't hold his attention for long. It would be better if the game is more entertaining, with stronger appeal, and preferably featuring challenging levels	First, my children will be curious. For a while, will not particularly like to play, and if the parents play together will be better. They have a low sense of initiative and little interest in any toy

Summary of the interview content: a. It is possible to differentiate the game roles. b. It is necessary to remind the game play appropriately. c. There are more levels set to increase the interestingness.

3.2 Field Research and Feedback

Throughout this on-site research in the Autism Rehabilitation Training Center at Huazhong University of Science and Technology University and a local autism welfare institution in Wuhan (see Fig. 2), we conducted thorough and detailed investigations, observing and engaging in discussions with the professionals at the rehabilitation center. The Rehabilitation Center has nurses with certificates who teach rehabilitation classes to autistic children in the community. The Public Welfare Center provides daycare for parents of autistic children. Children live in the center during the day, most of them are taken home by their parents. Also, for the game program, the rehabilitator and the doctor gave advice. We showed the static prototypes to the children and let them choose their favorite characters and scenes. Since they rarely use words, we used a large portable screen to allow the children to interact with the pictures and observe their concentration and body language on the different colors, characters, and play scenes to infer the most popular set for the children.

Fig. 2. Field Research

Through on-site interviews, comprehensive data was collected. After analysis, all feedback and suggestions were summarized (see Table 2), and relevant theories were adopted to provide design guidance for the program (see Table 3).

Applying Behavior Analysis Theory. Applying Behavior Analysis Theory. Behavior analysis is a branch of behavioral science [33] that employs the Antecedent-Behavior-Consequence (ABC) principles for behavioral intervention. In practical terms, 'A' refers to antecedents, such as instructions or commands given by the teacher. 'B' denotes behavior, covering both externally observable actions and internal thought processes. 'C' stands for consequences, involving feedback through reinforcement or punishment.

This study draws on this theory to guide the enhancement of the complete gaming experience process, involving issuing instructions - behavior - feedback.

Implicit Learning and Memory Implicit learning and memory involve forms of learning and memory that occur without the individual's awareness [34]. These processes rely on distinct brain systems, unlike the conscious control associated with explicit learning and memory. Implicit learning is a subconscious behavior, and research by Ammons et al. (1958) suggests that skills acquired through implicit strategies can endure for a

Table 2. Feedback Summary

Issues	Suggestions	Improvement points
Game sessions are simple	Make it like a picture drawing book	• The game unfolds according to the story. Difficulty increases slowly
Some of the behaviors in the game can be risky when generalized to life	It is important to avoid, for example, staring at thieves and generalizing to life by staring at thieves when they come across them	• Add characters other than the thief, such as the lamb, and set up friendly, sharing-themed game sessions; increase interaction
Overly difficult and may be hard to play for low to medium features children	Reduced Difficulty	• Enhance the visual and auditory feedback of the interface, playing timely video reminders of gameplay;
Role-playing can be difficult for children to understand	A parent or teacher needs to be present and tell the child the rules of the game; start with fewer characters	pay attention to the design of the background sound
Inattention	Might get caught up in the background music and not concentrate; make the game the expression more exaggerated	

relatively longer duration compared to those acquired through explicit strategies [35]. The theory of implicit learning guides the "instruction" phase designed in this study.

Emotional Design Theory Emotional design theory is widely used in game design, highlighting the importance of users' emotional experiences. Studies focus on how certain visual elements of game characters, like color, shape, expression, or dimensions, impact learners' emotions [36]. In this program's design, we pay attention to the emotional experiences of children with autism. The theory guides the design of elements such as game interface colors, shapes, spatial dimensions, and game characters.

Neurofeedback Training Theory and Practice Neurofeedback training is used in treating various neurological conditions, including Attention Deficit Hyperactivity Disorder (ADHD). For effective therapy in ADHD, it's crucial to balance rewards and inhibition thresholds, with an average reward threshold set at 70% [37]. Since children with autism often have attention-related issues, the game's "feedback" design can benefit from insights in neurofeedback training theories to provide effective support.

Table 3. Game Theoretic Framework

Processes	Key Point	Design Points	Theoretical Support
Instruction	Send	No mandatory directives	Implicit Learning and Memory: Psychological and Neural Aspects: Implicit learning and implicit memory refer to forms of learning and memory that occur without the individual's conscious awareness. They rely on distinct brain systems, unlike the conscious control associated with explicit learning and memory
	Receive	Creating interaction scenarios (game character voices, text)	Interactive Intervening Design of Autistic Children with Buggy as Carrie: Enhancing social skills in children with autism is a key objective of various intervention therapies. This involves encouraging the child's initiative to engage with others. Through instructions, opportunities are created for children with autism to actively participate in interactions and gradually embrace playful engagement, one step at a time
Action	Eye contact	Gameplay Passing feedback	/
	Gaze		
	Complete		

(continued)

Table 3. (*continued*)

Processes	Key Point	Design Points	Theoretical Support
Feedback	Overall visual feedback	Cool colors and graphic aids	The Impact of Interior Spaces' Color on Autistic and Psychiatric Patients' Well-Being: In addition, they preferred cold and secondary colors over primary colors. It was found that avoiding excessive colors is important in indoor environments because of their negative impact on children with autism, causing anxiety and distress. Suggest choosing neutral and calm colors. [32]
	Reward feedback	The training program set an average incentive threshold of 70 per cent	Neuromodulation technologies: An attempt at classification: The Othmer training program sets an average reward threshold of 70%

4   Gameplay Design

4.1   Game Introduction

Bonnie Manor is made for 3 to 10-year-old kids with high-functioning autism, helping them improve focus and practice eye contact. The game combines eye-tracking tech with memory learning. Players become defenders of a carrot garden, entrusted with protecting the rabbit and its carrots.

Bonnie Manor introduces a narrative where players take on the role of protectors of the manor, tasked with safeguarding a bunny and his carrot garden in various story scenarios. Players must stay focused, engage in dialogue, and direct their gaze to specified areas to progress through levels (see Fig. 3). To create tension, the game incorporates sounds and animations of the rabbit and bird, with feedback provided through their cues (Quick, Chase away the thieves!). Players must quickly make eye contact with the thief. The typical duration for eye contact aligns with regular gaze times, ranging from approximately 0.4 s to 3 s, progressively challenging.

Participants are not initially informed of the game rules (e.g., expelling the thief). Instead, through exploration within the game interface, players discover that specific eye contact triggers other behaviors in the game characters. This approach aims at achieving implicit learning, helping children generalize the skills mastered in game training to real-life situations. The overall game script underwent four iterations, incorporating feedback from doctors, parents, and caregivers. The detailed game script is outlined below.

Entering - Self-introduction As the sun rises, a little bunny comes out from the house, greets you, and introduces itself. You respond with your own introduction, kicking off a day of activities.

Helping the Little Bunny - Harvesting Carrots With a bountiful carrot harvest, the little bunny is ready to pick carrots. Your task is to help the bunny pull out carrots (you need to focus on the carrot to see the pulling effect). Once pulled, the carrots go into the basket at the bottom right.

Chasing Away the Thief The thief appears next to the carrots and is stealing it. You need to look at the thief and last for a little while to get rid of the thief.

Little Lamb want a carrot A hungry little lamb shows up, attempting to sneak a bite of carrots. Use the same method as with the thief to thwart the lamb. It stops, expressing hunger and a desire for carrots. Players decide whether to share carrots with the lamb. Keep staring at "no" for no sharing and "yes" for sharing.

Sunset – Farewell Encourage players to talk and say goodbye to the bunny.

Comforting the Bunny If a carrot is stolen, the bunny cries. Comfort her by looking at her eyes, uttering soothing words. The bunny stops crying, expressing gratitude.

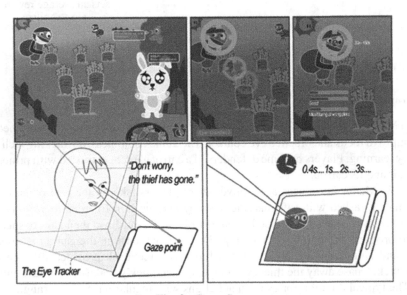

Fig. 3. Game Scene

The game role is shown in the table below (see Table 4):

Table 4. Game Characters

Characters	Descriptions	Presentation
Bunny	Bonnie Manor's protagonist is Bunny, a little white rabbit. Residing year-round in a treehouse on the farm, Bunny has a passion for planting and harvesting carrots. Diligent and kind-hearted, Bunny fears mischief-makers. As the central character in the game, many levels revolve around the adventures of this industrious bunny.	
Birdy	The bird is brave, and frequently aids Bunny in shooing away carrot-stealing villains. It serves as the player's helpful companion in the game.	
Lamb	The lamb is one of the animals in the manor, residing in the grasslands and occasionally dropping by to ask carrots from Bunny. It's one of the surprise characters that appear in certain levels of the game.	
Thief	The thief is a common character in the manor, lurking around various areas and specializing in carrot theft. A key character in the game, players must thwart the thief to protect Bunny and the carrots.	

4.2 Game Prototyping

Each level of the game is seamlessly connected through video segments. To achieve this, we crafted detailed video scripts and oversaw the animation design and production process.

After editing the videos in PS, AI, and AE, we established an interactive flowchart to serve the programming. The game program, written in Python, integrates the data from the eye tracker – specific user gaze positions on the screen – and links it with the transitions between game levels. The interactive logic is illustrated through a process example of successfully and unsuccessfully driving away the thief (see Fig. 4).

The eye tracker is positioned below the computer screen and displays, in real-time, the location where the player is looking in the form of a circle on the screen. The program takes screenshots at a rate of every 0.02 s. When the circle falls within the specified coordinates (a point set at the positions of the thief and the rabbit's eyes), it triggers a game mechanism.

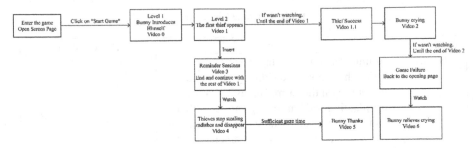

Fig. 4. Game Flowchart

5 Experiment

5.1 Recruitment and Preparation

The participants in this experiment are children aged 3 to 10 diagnosed with autism. These children are from the Rehabilitation Training Center at the East Campus of Huazhong University of Science and Technology, and their involvement is entirely voluntary. After setting up the necessary equipment, the rehabilitation therapist extends an invitation near the end of a game class. Throughout the experiment, teachers provide encouragement and guidance to the children, and parents offer support and assistance.

The experimental setup includes a gaming laptop powered by an Intel i7 core processor, equipped with embedded speakers for sound output, the Bonnie Manor game system, and the Tobii 5 eye tracker along with its accompanying system (see Figs. 5 and 6).

Fig. 5. The left image is an overview of the experimental setup, while the two photos on the right showcase the experimental setups arranged by the author in Game Room 1 and Game Room 2 at the rehabilitation center.

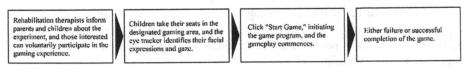

Fig. 6. Experimental Procedure

5.2 Result

In two rounds of user testing (see Fig. 7), a total of six autistic children voluntarily participated in the game. Accompanied by their parents, they sat at the game table to engage in the activity. Among them, three children successfully completed the game, while three experienced game failure. Two encountered mid-game setbacks, and one faced difficulty as the eye tracker couldn't recognize facial expressions and gaze (see Table 5).

Table 5. Gameplay Testing Result

Name	Age	Ability Levels	Outcome	Reasons/Notes
Lei Lei (Male)	6	Moderate to Low	Completed	Likes to play with electronic products; Requires minimal reminders. Easily follows game instructions
Dou Dou (Male)	3	Moderate	Failed	Small stature and facial features Eye tracker failed to recognize gaze
Xuan Xuan (Male)	6	Low	Failed	Unable to concentrate; Looks around without focus on the game interface; Eye tracker unable to recognize gaze
Xiao Bei (Male)	7	High	Completed	Uses hands to click on the screen and objects being viewed
Dian Dian (Male)	6	Moderate	Mid-game failure	Unstable emotions midway; Suddenly nervous, looks around, parent takes them away from the gaming area. Required frequent reminders
Dao Dao (Male)	6	Moderate	Completed	Initially resistant to playing; Observed and played under parental guidance

Fig. 7. Experimental Procedure

After each phase of the experiment, the author interviewed doctors, rehabilitation therapists, parents, and caregivers at the rehabilitation center, collecting their suggestions and feedback (see Table 6). The responses were documented and evaluated, covering users' overall engagement, feedback on the novelty, utility, interactivity, usability, safety of the games.

Table 6. User Feedback

	Novelty	Utility	Interactivity	Usability	Safety
Z Doctor	Very innovative. Has the potential to develop into an interesting and well-rounded gaming product	Relatively practical; Can add more elements to help children exercise cognitive abilities	Good interactivity; Can add more interactive elements	Requires some assistance and guidance for children to use	Prolonged use may strain the eyes; Can adjust the duration of each gaming session
J Therapist	Very novel	/	Weak interaction with the outside world; Requires children to stay focused	Challenging for younger children	Relatively safe
L Therapist	Very innovative	Eye tracker circle may attract children's attention; Better to remove	/	Requires parental assistance	/
A Parent	Seen similar games; the way of playing is quite innovative	/	Noticed parents helping and guiding, strong interactivity	Some difficulty; Most children may struggle to maintain continuous focus alone	Prolonged use may be harmful to the eyes
L Caregiver	Very innovative; Helps with logical thinking for children	Playable for medium to high-ability, instruction-following children	Good interactivity; Some children show clear emotional responses	Suitable for slightly older children	Relatively safe

5.3 Tracking Experiment

Experiment Overview. To Better Assess the Impact of This Game on Eye Contact and Attention in Children with Autism, We Conducted a Tracking Test on a 6-Year-Old Child with Moderate-Low Functioning Autism (Referred to as the Participant). The Participant Engaged in the Game Four Times Over a Span of 2 weeks, with Specific Participant Information Detailed in Table 7. Following Each Regular Game Class Session, a Dedicated Time for Playing the Game Was Added for the Participant. Before selecting the participant, we introduced the game design to the therapist, experienced the entire game, and received assistance from the therapist in recruiting autistic children participating in daily exercise courses at the rehabilitation center. Prior to the testing, communication occurred between the therapist, the author, and the parents to ensure mutual trust. After recruitment, this suitable participant was ultimately chosen. (Participant criteria met: age-appropriate, high attendance in daily classes, parental consent, child's voluntary interest in and curiosity about the game).

Table 7. Participant Information

Name	Age	Ability Levels	Symptoms
Leilei (Male)	6	Moderate to Low Functioning	1. Lack of eye contact 2. Lack of concentration 3. Unnatural eye movements

Experimental Procedures and Indicators. Before Each Test, the Researcher Activates the Timer to Record the Time Taken by the Participants to Complete the Game. Throughout the Testing Period, Researcher, Along with the Participants' Parents, Remains Present to Provide Assistance and Guidance if the Participants Face Challenges Such as Lack of Concentration or Unexpected Disruptions in the Testing Environment. The Aim is to Assist the Participants in Seamlessly Experiencing the Game. The Level of Engagement and Immersion in the Game is also Considered a Crucial Reference Metric for Later Assessments. After each test, the researcher stops the timer, documenting the time taken by the participants to complete the game. Based on the researcher's observations (and, if conditions allow, recorded footage of the participants playing the game), the researcher notes the participants' level of engagement in the game. This includes factors such as successful completion, frequency of interruptions, instances of effective verbal interactions, and instances of ineffective verbal interactions.

The testing also includes an assessment where the therapist intuitively evaluates the participant's classroom performance, focusing on eye contact behavior. The therapist observes the participant's behavior in various settings, assessing whether the game has contributed to improvements in eye contact. In initial discussions, the therapist noted that, aside from potential challenges with eye contact, the participant displays unnatural eye postures in classroom and everyday situations, such as unintentional squinting, tilting the head back while staring at the teacher, and prolonged gaze at people.

The therapist suggests the participant's behavior might be linked to nervousness or anger. After trying the game, the therapist observed it requires a specific range of eye postures for the eye tracker to work effectively. The game prompts shift in gaze and attention with character transitions, rather than prolonged fixation. The therapist believes that children enjoying the game and playing in a relaxed manner could lead to natural eye behavior, potentially improving certain stereotyped behaviors in the participant.

Experimental Results. The Participant's Game Completion Time Gradually Decreased. Game Interruptions Reduced, Leading to a Smoother Overall Experience. In Terms of Interaction, There Was a Progression from no Interaction to One Proactive Interaction with the Bunny by the Fourth Attempt. Gaze Shifts from Screen to Surroundings Decreased from Four Times to One. In Classroom Performance, Therapists Observed a Slight Improvement in Unnatural Eye Contact Behavior, with More Natural Head Movements and a Minor Frequency Decrease. The Participant Demonstrated Quicker Attention Focus on Teacher-Presented Tools and Instructions, Indicating Improved Passive Shared Attention (Tables 8, 9).

Table 8. Experimental Results

	First Attempt	Second Attempt	Third Attempt	Fourth Attempt
Game Completion Time	2 min 58 s	2 min 34 s	2 min 35 s	2 min 6 s
Completion Status	Yes	Yes	Yes	Yes
Interruption Count	5 times	3 times	3 times	1 time
Effective Verbal Interaction	0 times	Completed self-introduction once with parental reminder	Completed self-introduction once with parental reminder; Looked at bunny, greeted, and said goodbye once	Proactively self-introduced once
Ineffective Verbal Interaction	Looked around 4 times; Spoke once	Looked around 3 times;	Looked around 2 times; Spoke once	Looked around 1 time

Table 9. Observation notes from the rehabilitation therapist in class

Before	A class after the fourth use
Before game instructions, the participant appeared tense. When I seated at the endpoint, directed to look at the floor mat and run, the participant's attention wavered. Upon seeing the participant staring at my chin, I was pretending to be stern, advised against it. Surprisingly, the participant intensified the gaze, widening the eyes and pulling the chin further back	The participant responded faster to instructions in this class. When I pointed at grandma and said, Look at grandma, he looked correctly. Passive joint attention improved, possibly due to the game's prompts. The occurrences of looking in the wrong direction during the game class reduced. Unnatural eye postures in class slightly improved but still occur. Tension and anger moments should gradually improve with more training and guidance

6 Conclusion

The participant has improved skills needed for game completion (maintaining eye contact and focus), with reduced completion time indicating increasing proficiency.

The participant is better able to maintain focus and actively engage in the game. There is an increase in effective interactions during the game, suggesting improved focus and active participation. The reduction in ineffective interactions indicates a better ability to immerse in the gaming experience.

The participant's eye posture appears more natural. In classroom performance, as observed by two therapists, there is a slight alleviation of unnatural eye contact behavior. Additionally, the participant can quickly shift attention to teaching aids and items mentioned by the therapists in class, indicating improved passive shared attention through game training.

In summary, the game has shown promising results in performance and usability, with nearly half of the 3–10-year-old children with autism actively participating. Therapists and doctors view it as a potential rehabilitation tool, and parental involvement has been key to children mastering game skills. Over time, tracking tests indicate that the game can help improve some symptoms in children with autism, including eye contact, eye posture, and attention.

However, due to limited samples and no control group, generalization is uncertain. For sustained and frequent use, the author suggests a game series with additional elements to enhance the overall gaming experience for children.

We aim to offer valuable insights and methods in designing games for children with autism through this research. Sharing observations of ASD children's behavior and emotions during the design process is intended to inform the development of game solutions. The goal is to contribute to the improvement of design and development for games tailored to children with autism, ultimately providing them with more comfortable, convenient, and effective services and support.

Acknowledgments. This research was supported by Teaching and Research Project of Huazhong University of Science and Technology (2023042).

References

1. Senju, A., Johnson, M.H.: The eye contact effect: mechanisms and development. Trends Cogn. Sci. **13**(3), 127–134 (2009). https://doi.org/10.1016/j.tics.2008.11.009
2. Itier, R.J., Batty, M.: Neural bases of eye and gaze processing: the core of social cognition. Neurosci. Biobehav. Rev. **33**(6), 843–863 (2009). https://doi.org/10.1016/j.neubiorev.2009.02.004
3. Jemel, B., Mottron, L., Dawson, M.: Impaired face processing in autism: fact or artifact? Autism Dev. Disord **36**(1), 91–106 (2006). https://doi.org/10.1007/s10803-005-0050-5
4. Dalton, K.M., Nacewicz, B., et al.: Gaze fixation and the neural circuitry of face processing in autism. Nat. Neurosci. **8**(4), 519–526 (2005). https://doi.org/10.1038/nn1421
5. Jones, E.A., Carr, E.G.: Joint attention in children with autism: theory and intervention. Focus on Autism & Other Developmental Disabilities **19**(1), 13–26 (2004). https://doi.org/10.1177/10883576040190010301
6. Baron-Cohen, S., Baldwin, D.A., Crowson, M.: Do children with autism use the speaker's direction of gaze strategy to crack the code of language? Child Dev. **68**(1), 48–57 (1997)
7. Schietecatte, I., Roeyers, H., Warreyn, P.: Exploring the nature of joint attention impairments in young children with autism spectrum disorder: associated social and cognitive skills. J. Autism Dev. Disord. **42**(1), 1–12 (2012)
8. Davies, M.S., Dapretto, M., Sigman, M., et al.: Neural bases of gaze and emotion processing in children with autism spectrum disorders. Brain Behav. **1**(1), 1–11 (2011)
9. Hasegawa, N., Kitamura, H., Murakami, H., et al.: Neural activity in the posterior superior temporal region during eye contact perception correlates with autistic traits. Neurosci. Lett. **549**, 45–50 (2013)
10. Cavallo, A., Lungu, O., Becchio, C., et al.: When gaze opens the channel for communication: integrative role of IFG and MPFC. Neuroimage **119**, 63–69 (2015). https://doi.org/10.1016/j.neuroimage.2015.06.025
11. Brooks, R., Meltzoff, A.N.: The development of gaze following and its relation to language. Dev. Sci. **8**(6), 535–543 (2005). https://doi.org/10.1111/j.1467-7687.2005.00445.x
12. Brooks, R., Meltzoff, A.N.: Infant gaze following and pointing predict accelerated vocabulary growth through two years of age: a longitudinal, growth curve modeling study. Child Lang. **35**(1), 207–220 (2008). https://doi.org/10.1017/s030500090700829x
13. Wever, M.C.M., et al.: Neural and affective responses to prolonged eye contact with one's own adolescent child and unfamiliar others. Neuroimage **260**, 119463 (2022)
14. Ristic, J., Mottron, L., Friesen, C.K., et al.: Eyes are special but not for everyone: the case of autism. Brain Res. Cogn. Brain Res. **24**(3), 715–718 (2005). https://doi.org/10.1016/j.cogbrainres.2005.02.007
15. Wallace, S., Coleman, M., et al.: A study of impaired judgment of eye-gaze direction and related face-processing deficits in autism spectrum disorders. Perception **35**(12), 1651–1664 (2006)
16. Voss, C., Schwartz, J., et al.: Effect of wearable digital intervention for improving socialization in children with autism spectrum disorder: a randomized clinical trial. JAMA Pediatr. **173**(5), 446–454 (2019)
17. Grynszpan, O., Weiss, P.L., et al.: Innovative technology-based interventions for autism spectrum disorders: a meta-analysis. Autism **18**(4), 346–361 (2014)

18. Wong C., Odom, S., L., et al.: Evidence-based practices for children, youth, and young adults with autism spectrum disorder: a comprehensive review. J. Autism Dev. Disorders **45**(7), 1951–1966 (2015). https://doi.org/10.1007/s10803-014-2351-z

19. Xiao, W., Li, M., et al.: Deep interaction: Wearable robot-assisted emotion communication for enhancing perception and expression ability of children with autism spectrum disorders. Futur. Gener. Comput. Syst. **108**, 709–716 (2020)

20. Sundberg, M.: Online gaming, loneliness and friendships among adolescents and adults with ASD. Comput. Hum. Behav. **79**, 105–110 (2018)

21. Mundy, P., Sullivan, L., et al.: A parallel and distributed-processing model of joint attention, social cognition and autism. Autism Res. **2**(1), 2–21 (2009)

22. Posner, M.I., Rothbart, M.K.: Research on attention networks as a model for the integration of psychological science. Annu. Rev. Psychol. **58**(1), 1–23 (2007)

23. Redcay, E., Kleiner, M., et al.: Look at this: the neural correlates of initiating and responding to bids for joint attention. Front. Hum. Neurosci. **6**(6), 169 (2012)

24. Rizzolatti, G., Fogassi, L., et al.: Mirrors of the mind. Sci. Am. **295**(5), 54–61 (2006)

25. Buccino, G., Vogt, S., et al.: Neural circuits underlying imitation learning of hand actions: an event-related fMRI study. Neuron **42**(2), 323–334 (2004)

26. Chen, W., Yuan, T.F.: Mirror neuron system as the joint from action to language. Neurosci. Bull. **24**(4), 259–264 (2008)

27. Gallese, V., Rochat, M.J., et al.: The mirror mechanism and its potential role in autism spectrum disorder. Dev. Med. Child Neurol. **55**(1), 15–22 (2013)

28. Iacoboni, M., Dapretto, M.: The mirror neuron system and the consequences of its dysfunction. Nat. Rev. Neurosci. **7**(12), 942–951 (2006)

29. Chen, Y., Chen, Z., Lin, Z., et al.: Analysis of shared attention characteristics in children with autism spectrum disorders. Chinese J. Clin. Pediat. **35**(02), 102–105 (2017). https://doi.org/10.3969/j.issn.1000-3606.2017.02.006

30. Mundy, P., Sigman, M., et al.: Defining the social deficits of autism: the contribution of non-verbal communication measures. J. Child Psychol. Psychiatry **27**, 657–669 (1986). https://doi.org/10.1111/j.1469-7610.1986.tb00190.x

31. Volkmar, F., Chawarska, K., Klin. A.: Autism in infancy and early childhood. Ann. Rev. Psychol. **56**(1), 315–336 (2005). https://doi.org/10.1146/annurev.psych.56.091103.070159

32. Al-Badrani, A.I., Sanad, R.A.: The impact of interior spaces' color on autistic and psychiatric patients' well-being. J. Eng. **10**(2), 17–23 (2022). https://doi.org/10.15640/jea.v10n2a3

33. Virués-Ortega, J.: Applied behavior analytic intervention for autism in early childhood: meta-analysis, meta-regression and dose–response meta-analysis of multiple outcomes. Clin. Psychol. Rev. **30**(4), 387–399 (2010). https://doi.org/10.1016/j.cpr.2010.01.008

34. Curran, T., Schacter, D. L.: Implicit learning and memory: psychological and neural aspects, international encyclopedia of the social & behavioral. Sciences, Pergamon 7237–7241 (2001)

35. Ammons, R.B., Farr, R.G., et al.: Long-term retention of perceptual-motor skills. J. Exp. Psychol. **55**(4), 318 (1958)

36. Plass, J.L., Kaplan, U.: Emotional Design in Digital Media for Learning. Emotions, Technology, Design, and Learning, pp. 131–161. Academic Press (2016) https://doi.org/10.1016/B978-0-12-801856-9.00007-4

37. Othmer, S.: Neuromodulation technologies: an attempt at classification. Introduction to quantitative EEG and neurofeedback: Advanced theory and applications, 3–26 (2009). https://doi.org/10.1016/B978-0-12-374534-7.00001-01

Cloth Tiger Hunt: An Embodied Experiential Educational Game for the Intangible Cultural Heritage of Artistic Handicraft

Junjie Zhu, Yanan Li, Haitao Zheng, and Xing Sun(⌧)

Shenzhen International Graduate School, Tsinghua University, Shenzhen, China
liyanan22@mails.tsinghua.edu.cn, {zheng.haitao,
sunxking}@sz.tsinghua.edu.cn

Abstract. Digital gaming has become an innovative avenue for showcasing and disseminating intangible cultural heritage (ICH). Presently, there's a challenge in educational games centered on handicraft ICH: balancing enjoyment and engagement with effective heritage learning. Addressing this, the article introduces an Embodied Experience Educational Game Model. This model integrates a digitization framework for handicraft ICH, aligning it with the structural elements of the game model. Utilizing this approach, the study develops "Cloth Tiger Hunt," an educational game themed on a traditional Chinese handicraft ICH, the Cloth Tiger. The research then undertakes a comprehensive evaluation through controlled experiments, both qualitative and quantitative, to assess the game's impact on learning outcomes, user experience, and motivational aspects related to the Cloth Tiger ICH. This research contributes innovatively to the theory and practice within the field of ICH education, offering valuable insights and a reference point for future studies in this area.

Keywords: Intangible cultural heritage education · Education games · Embodied cognition · Experiential learning · Gesture interaction · Handicraft intangible cultural heritage

1 Introduction

In the past few years, digital technology has emerged as an innovative tool for preserving and sharing intangible cultural heritage (ICH). This heritage manifests in diverse forms, notably in handicrafts, which combine artisanal techniques with tangible artifacts. These crafts often reflect the cultural essence of specific times, customs, and regions [1].

Digital games, known for their strong interactivity, high-fidelity simulations, and engaging nature, have opened new avenues in ICH education. Educational games, particularly those centered on ICH, create immersive and proactive learning environments. This approach effectively showcases the artifacts, skills, and cultural narratives associated with handicraft ICH.

Nevertheless, the use of educational games in teaching about handicraft ICH faces several hurdles. The limited research and applications in this area, along with a lack

© The Author(s), under exclusive license to Springer Nature Switzerland AG 2024
X. Fang (Ed.): HCII 2024, LNCS 14730, pp. 218–232, 2024.
https://doi.org/10.1007/978-3-031-60692-2_15

of balance between educational and entertainment values and weak interactivity and immersion, curtail the potential of games as effective learning tools for this heritage. Identifying strategies to effectively teach intangible heritage through games, fostering a connection with the heritage, and improving the engaging and immersive aspects of game-based learning are areas needing further investigation.

Considering the hands-on nature of learning handicrafts, game designs should integrate interactive, experiential elements. This study proposes an educational game model that combines embodied cognition with experiential learning principles. The aim is to enhance the effectiveness and appeal of learning about handicraft intangible heritage through gaming, thereby aiding its wider dissemination. This model also serves as a theoretical and practical guide for developing educational games focused on handicraft heritage.

To validate this model, an educational game featuring gesture interaction technology was developed, centered on a traditional Chinese handicraft ICH, the Cloth Tiger. This embodied learning approach allows users to deeply engage with the artistry and culture of handicraft heritage, significantly enhancing both the learning experience and interest in intangible heritage.

2 Related Work

2.1 Theoretical Basis of the Embodied Experience Game Model

Designing educational games for handicraft ICH aims to enable learners to acquire a comprehensive understanding of handicraft skills and their cultural significance through interactive game experiences. Embodied Cognition, a theory stating that cognition develops through physical interactions with the environment, provides a framework for this learning approach. Additionally, Experiential Learning Theory, which highlights learning through active engagement and reflection on experiences, supports the integration of both the tangible aspects (such as physical artifacts of the heritage) and intangible elements (like artisan skills and traditions) into the learning process. This integration is essential for effectively applying game-based learning to handicraft ICH.

Embodied Cognition Theory. Embodied Cognition Suggests that Cognition Arises from the Body's Sensory Perceptions and Interactions with Its Surroundings. This Theory Emphasizes that Cognitive Information, Vivid and Tangible, is Closely Linked to the Body's Sensory Channels. In the Context of Educational Games for Handicraft Heritage, This Entails Creating a Virtual Environment Where Learners Can Interactively Explore and Understand the Skills and Cultural Aspects of the Heritage. By Engaging Both Sensory and Kinesthetic Experiences, Learners Can Develop a Deeper Understanding and Appreciation of the Heritage.

Experiential Learning Theory. Experiential Learning involves acquiring knowledge and skills through direct participation in activities, followed by observation, reflection, and mental involvement. The Experiential Learning Game Model by Killi categorizes this process into four cyclic stages: encountering challenges, engaging in active experimentation, reflecting on observations, and conceptualizing the learned material. Building on these theories, the proposed Embodied Experience Game Model, implemented in a game setting, encompasses these four stages of experiential learning through interactive, embodied activities. This model engages learners in challenges within the game, prompting them to experiment and interact physically. Feedback from these interactions leads to sensory and kinesthetic experiences, fostering a cycle of reflection, understanding, and skill enhancement. This cyclical process guides learners to apply their new knowledge and skills to upcoming challenges, thus facilitating continuous learning and engagement with the heritage (Fig. 1).

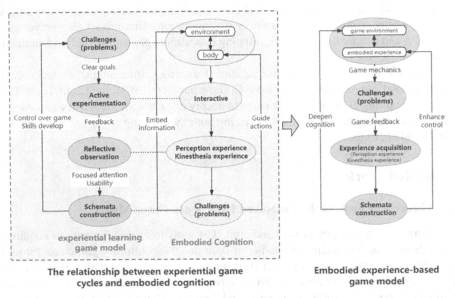

The relationship between experiential game cycles and embodied cognition

Embodied experience-based game model

Fig. 1 Illustrates the construction of the embodied experience-based game model

2.2 The Architecture of the Embodied Experience Game Model and Its Application in Digitizing Handicraft ICH

Architecture of the Embodied Experience Game Model. The Embodied Experience Game Model Emphasizes Essential Components Such as the Gaming Environment, Challenges Created by Game Mechanics, and the Physical Interaction of Learners Within the Game. Implementing These Elements Effectively Requires a Carefully Designed Game System and the Right Interactive Technologies. Drawing from the Educational Game Structure DPE (Design, Player, Experience) by Winn and Colleagues [5], This Model Integrates Learning Content, Narrative, Gameplay Mechanics, and User Experience into Its Design. The Game System's Elements Are Categorized into Two Types: Those Forming the Core Mechanism and Those Creating an Immersive Emotional Experience [6].

Digitization of Handicraft ICH. When Digitizing Traditional Handicraft ICH, It's Crucial to Capture the Essence of the Physical Artifacts, Encompassing Their Core

Skills, Thematic Motifs, and Stylistic Expressions [7]. The Digitization Process Should not Only Replicate the Physical and Intangible Aspects but also Convey the Interplay Between Traditional Skills and Everyday Life. This Includes Preserving and Displaying the Heritage's Physical Form, Its Craftsmanship Features, and the Processes Involved. It also Involves Encapsulating the Heritage's Underlying Knowledge and Values [8]. The Selection of Digital Technologies, Ranging from Multimedia Capture to Virtual Reality, Should Align with the Unique Interactive Needs of Handicraft ICH, Ensuring an Authentic Representation of Its Environmental and Physical Interactivity [9].

3 Methods

3.1 Architecture of the Embodied Experience Game Model

This study structures the educational game system into three distinct modules, integrating various elements of the embodied experience game model:

Contextual Perception Module. This Module Develops the Game's Setting Based on the Learning Content, Forming an Initial Understanding of the Game's Educational Context. It Incorporates Audiovisual Elements, Storytelling, Character Development, and Plot Design to Enhance the Learning Experience.

Gameplay Module. Here, the Educational Content is Translated into Game Mechanics, Involving Objectives, Processes, Rules, and Resources. These Components Are Tailored to the Specific Needs of the Learning Material, Creating Varied Learning Cycles Within the Game's Framework.

Kinesthetic Interaction Module. Focused on the Learner's Physical Interaction with the Game, This Module Involves Three Key Aspects Include the Input of the Learner's Motions, Transformation of These Actions Within the Game, and Responsive Feedback from the Game System. This Module is Pivotal in Realizing an Embodied and Interactive Gaming Experience.

3.2 Digitization of Handicraft Intangible Cultural Heritage

In this study, the digitization of handicraft intangible cultural heritage is grouped into three categories:

Creative Motifs. This Aspect Deals with the Physical Representations of Intangible Heritage and Their Associated Cultural Meanings. It Involves Visualizing Heritage Knowledge and Crafting Game Scenarios Based on Digitized Content.

Expression Procedures. This Refers to the Cultural Context of the Handicraft Objects. The Integration of the Context Awareness and Mechanism Structure Modules Serves to Convey the Cultural Background of the Heritage.

Core Skills. This Focuses on the Craft Techniques and Processes. By Utilizing Motion Capture Technology, Players' Physical Movements Are Integrated into the Game. The Game Engine then Generates Audiovisual Feedback. This Process, Supported by Both the Mechanism Structure and Kinesthetic Interaction Modules, Aligns the Game Mechanics with the Specifics of the Craft Techniques, Facilitating an Immersive Learning Experience Where Players Actively Engage with the Skills of the Handicraft ICH (Fig. 2).

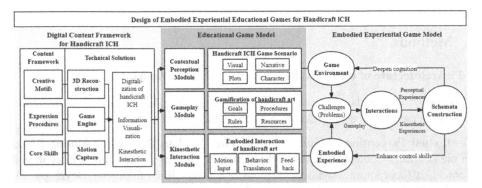

Fig. 2 Design of Embodied Experiential Educational Games for Handicraft ICH

4   Game Design

In this study, an educational game titled "Cloth Tiger Hunt" was developed, leveraging the Embodied Experience Game Model and Unity for its creation. The game centers around the Cloth Tiger, a folk handicraft emblematic of northern China's rural culture, embodying rich aesthetic values and folklore. With the cultural relevance of the Cloth Tiger diminishing [10], this game aims to pioneer new digital methods for its preservation and transmission.

The game sets out with several key objectives: To impart an understanding of the Cloth Tiger's cultural essence, highlighting its historical background, aesthetic attributes, and folklore; To offer an interactive experience of the Cloth Tiger's crafting process; To convey the heritage's evolving nature and spark a passion for learning about it. The game encompasses three primary components: Contextual Perception Module; Gameplay Module and Kinesthetic Interaction Module.

4.1   Contextual Perception Module

This module immerses players in the world of the Cloth Tiger, acquainting them with its stylistic features, cultural symbolism, and heritage context. The game narrative unfolds across four thematic challenges include Dispelling Disasters, Life Worship, Welcoming

Prosperity and Harmony with Nature, each reflecting aspects of the Cloth Tiger's cultural significance [11]. Visually, the game utilizes 2D and 3D graphics and sound-rich interactive animations to depict the Cloth Tiger's intricate patterns and forms, alongside associated folklore. Character-wise, the game features a triad of roles: the player's avatar, supportive characters resembling Cloth Tigers, and antagonistic characters challenging the player. These roles are designed to foster emotional connection and deepen understanding of the Cloth Tiger's cultural narrative. The game's storyline progresses through an amalgamation of color schemes, environmental settings, sound effects, and music, all meticulously crafted to enhance the player's emotional journey.

Fig. 3 Scene interface for the game's visual elements

4.2 Gameplay Module

This module enables players to immerse themselves in the craftsmanship of the Cloth Tiger through a variety of game mechanics. At its core is an embodied experience that combines gesture interaction with visual recognition. Challenges within the game involve managing resources like health and time, focusing on developing players' gesture skills and visual memory. The game gradually increases in difficulty, offering rewards for mastering various craft gestures and understanding the aesthetic features of the Cloth Tiger. Additionally, knowledge cards about Cloth Tiger artifacts are used as rewards outside of gameplay, encouraging players to complete challenges while aiding in the recall and reflection on the heritage, thereby enriching their overall understanding of the Cloth Tiger tradition (Fig. 4).

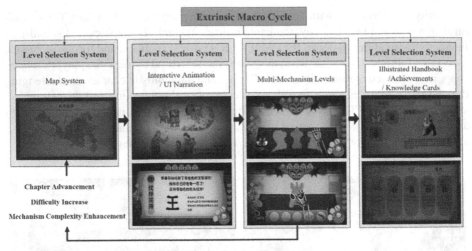

Fig. 4 The macro architecture of the game

4.3 Kinesthetic Interaction Module

This module captures the complete sequence of gestures involved in Cloth Tiger craftsmanship. It simplifies these into four player-friendly actions: holding a pen, using scissors, sewing, and picking up objects. Players replicate these gestures to interact with the game, using tools corresponding to each action. The game enhances this interaction with UI visual guides, 2D particle effects, and animations, alongside sound effects, offering real-time feedback to the players. Figure 3 illustrates the mapping of the skill flow to the interaction of the game (Fig. 5).

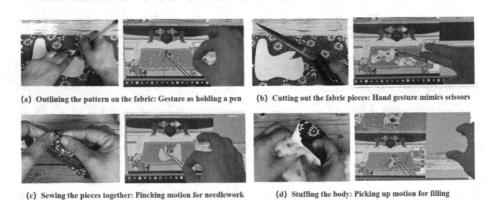

(a) Outlining the pattern on the fabric: Gesture as holding a pen   (b) Cutting out the fabric pieces: Hand gesture mimics scissors

(c) Sewing the pieces together: Pinching motion for needlework   (d) Stuffing the body: Picking up motion for filling

Fig. 5 Demonstrates the correlation between the craftsmanship process and the game interaction effects.

The game also uses the Leap Motion Controller to accurately capture player gestures. The Cloth Tiger crafting process is divided into four stages: pattern drawing, fabric cutting, shape sewing, and stuffing. Gestures for each stage are mapped into the game, with specific interaction points defined. A combination of gesture programming and logic judgment modules drives the game's visual and mechanical responses, making the learning experience both interactive and engaging (Fig. 6).

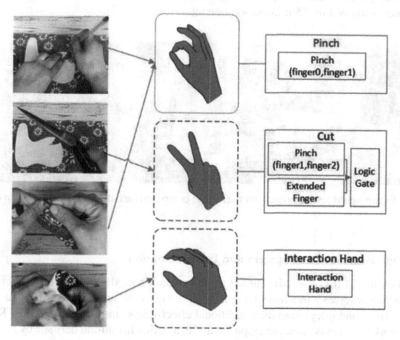

Fig. 6 Gesture gamification mapping and system definition.

5 Experimental Research

This study employed a mixed-methods approach, including surveys, objective tests of learning outcomes, and semi-structured interviews, to assess the impact of the game application on learners' outcomes, experiences, and motivation. It also aimed to validate the effectiveness and feasibility of an embodied experiential educational game model.

A total of 62 volunteers participated in the experiment, comprising 57 university students and 5 non-student individuals, with ages ranging from 18 to 30 years. The group included 29 males and 31 females. Pre-experiment surveys indicated that none of the volunteers had specialized knowledge or understanding of the intangible cultural heritage of cloth tiger-making. Additionally, there was no significant difference in the level of familiarity with this heritage between the two groups (p > 0.05).

The volunteers were randomly assigned to a control group or an experimental group:

- The control group, consisting of 30 valid samples, learned about the cloth tiger-making heritage through videos, graphic materials, and hands-on craft kits;
- The experimental group, also with 30 valid samples, engaged in learning through the "Fabric Tiger Hunt" educational game.

Considering time costs, both groups were provided with equivalent amounts of information on the culture and skills of Li Hou Tiger, a specific type of cloth tiger, and had a 20-min learning experience. After completing the learning experience, participants from both groups filled out questionnaires and underwent objective tests of learning outcomes, followed by 15-min one-on-one interviews (Fig. 7).

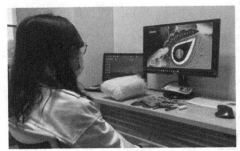

Fig. 7 Experimental testing process for the control group (left) and the experimental group (right)

5.1 Questionnaire Development and Implementation

Based on the MEEGA + educational game evaluation model proposed by Petri et al. [12], which assesses game learning quality across three dimensions: Knowledge, Skill, and Attitude, and integrating the educational effectiveness indicators from the FRACH framework for serious game development and evaluation in cultural heritage by Andreoli et al. [13], this study evaluated the learning quality of the "Cloth Tiger Hunt" educational game in three dimensions: learning outcomes, learning experience, and learning motivation. A 12-item survey questionnaire was designed (as shown in Table 1):

Learning outcomes included five items, based on the intangible cultural heritage (ICH) digital content framework proposed in this study. It covered three categories of knowledge on ICH: aesthetic features Q1, craft techniques Q2-Q3 (process and method), and cultural context Q4-Q5 (cultural settings, background, and associated meanings). The survey also incorporated recall and drawing activities of patterns and motifs to assist learners in assessing their learning outcomes.

Learning experience, comprising four items, included engagement Q6 (sense of immersion in the experience), enjoyment Q7 (fun and playability of the experience), and control Q8-Q9 (sense of mastery and comprehensibility during knowledge acquisition).

Learning motivation included three items: willingness to participate in the learning process Q10, cultural identification and willingness towards the learned knowledge Q12, and overall interest in learning about intangible cultural heritage Q11.

The questionnaire utilized a Likert five-point scale, ranging from 1 (strongly disagree) to 5 (strongly agree). The study first tested the reliability and validity of the survey: The reliability tests for the three indices showed Cronbach's alpha values greater than 0.8 (Learning Outcomes 0.847, Learning Experience 0.901, Learning Motivation 0.899), and the Corrected Item-Total Correlation (CITC) values were all above 0.5. Validity tests revealed Kaiser-Meyer-Olkin (KMO) values above 0.7 (Learning Outcomes

Table 1. Design of questionnaire items.

Learning Outcomes	Learning Experience	Learning Motivation
This experience deepened me: Q1: Understanding of the aesthetic characteristics of cloth tiger shapes, colors, and patterns (combined with recalling and drawing patterns and prints) Q2: Understanding of the technique of making cloth tigers Q3: Knowledge of the basic craft methods of the cloth tiger making process Q4: Knowledge of the context of the use of cloth tigers in folklore Q5: Knowledge of the cultural connotation and background of the non-heritage of cloth tigers	Q6: I was able to im-merse myself in the experience Q7: I felt that the experi-ence was fun Q8: I was able to pace my learning during the experience Q9: I was able to under-stand the knowledge related to Buhu's non-heritage through this experience	Q10: I would like to continue this form of intangible cultural herit-age learning experience Q11: This experience has made me want to learn more about Chi-na's intangible cultural heritage Q12: This experience has stimulated my inter-est in the intangible cultural heritage of Buhu

0.893, Learning Experience 0.751, Learning Motivation 0.759), and the Bartlett's Test of Sphericity approached zero, indicating a good overall level of reliability and validity for the questionnaire.

5.2 Evaluation of Learning Outcomes Through Objective Testing

The learners' mastery of the handicraft ICH knowledge was quantitatively analyzed through a closed-answer test. The test comprised 19 questions, including 16 multiple-choice questions, 1 sequencing question, and 2 keyword response questions, covering topics related to the physical styles of cloth tigers (questions 1–15, 18), craft techniques (question 16), and cultural contexts (questions 17, 19). The total possible score was 30 points.

5.3 Conducting Semi-Structured Interviews

Through semi-structured interviews, we gained a deeper understanding of learners' perceptions of game-based learning. This approach provided comprehensive insights, supplementing and enriching other experimental data with nuanced explanations and confirmatory details. The interviews focused on gathering participants' feedback on several aspects: satisfaction, experiential quality, enjoyment, practicality, and preference for acquiring knowledge through the game. These responses were meticulously recorded and transcribed using Tencent Meeting software for thorough analysis.

6 Results

6.1 Analysis of Questionnaire Responses

The non-parametric test results for different groups, as shown in Table 2, reveal significant findings: there were highly significant differences between the experimental group and the control group in Q1, Q3-Q7, and Q9-Q12 ($p < 0.001$), and significant differences in Q2 and Q8 ($p < 0.01$). Additionally, the median values in the experimental group were higher than those in the control group.

Table 2. Non-parametric Test Results for Different Groups

Indicator	Item	Median M(P25 ~ P75)		Mann Whitney		P
		Control Group (n = 30)	Experimental Group (n = 30)	U Value	Z Value	
Learning Outcomes	Q1	4.000(4.000 ~ 5.000)	5.000(5.000 ~ 5.000)	195	−4.237	0.000**
	Q2	4.000(4.000 ~ 5.000)	5.000(4.000 ~ 5.000)	240	−3.435	0.001**
	Q3	4.000(4.000 ~ 4.000)	5.000(4.750 ~ 5.000)	185.5	−4.312	0.000**
	Q4	4.000(2.750 ~ 4.000)	5.000(5.000 ~ 5.000)	124	−5.209	0.000**
	Q5	4.000(4.000 ~ 5.000)	5.000(4.000 ~ 5.000)	220	−3.796	0.000**
Learning Experience	Q6	3.000(3.000 ~ 4.000)	5.000(4.000 ~ 5.000)	66	−5.98	0.000**
	Q7	3.000(3.000 ~ 4.000)	5.000(4.750 ~ 5.000)	80	−5.788	0.000**
	Q8	4.000(3.000 ~ 4.000)	4.000(4.000 ~ 5.000)	270	−2.856	0.004**
	Q9	4.000(3.000 ~ 5.000)	5.000(4.000 ~ 5.000)	225	−3.641	0.000**
Learning Motivation	Q10	3.000(2.750 ~ 4.000)	5.000(5.000 ~ 5.000)	87.5	−5.747	0.000**
	Q11	3.000(3.000 ~ 4.250)	5.000(4.000 ~ 5.000)	176.5	−4.321	0.000**
	Q12	3.000(2.000 ~ 4.000)	5.000(4.750 ~ 5.000)	135.5	−4.988	0.000**

Note: * p<0.05 indicates highly significant difference; ** p<0.01 indicates extremely significant difference, the same below.*

6.2 Analysis of Objective Test Outcomes

The results of the objective test for learning outcomes showed that the experimental group had an average total score of 26.33, significantly higher than the control group's average of 21.53. This indicates that the educational game positively impacted learning outcomes related to cloth tiger ICH. The non-parametric test results for scores in the three knowledge categories are shown in Table 3. It is evident that there were significant differences between the experimental and control groups in scores related to physical styles and craft techniques ($p < 0.01$), and considerable differences in cultural context ($p < 0.05$). Furthermore, the median scores of the experimental group were higher than those of the control group in all three categories.

Table 3. Non-parametric Test of Learning Outcomes by Knowledge Category Items for Different Groups

Dimension	Item	Median M(P25 ~ P75)		Mann Whitney		P
		Control Group (n = 30)	Experimental Group (n = 30)	U Value	Z Value	
Physical Styles	Q1-Q15	11.00(10.75 ~ 13.25)	15.00(13.75 ~ 15.00)	104.5	– 5.211	0.000**
Craft Techniques	Q16	3.00(3.00 ~ 5.00)	5.00(5.00 ~ 5.00)	200	– 4.261	0.000**
Cultural Context	Q17-Q19	6.50(4.75 ~ 8.00)	8.00(6.75 ~ 9.00)	282.5	– 2.514	0.012*

6.3 Thematic Analysis of Semi-Structured Interview Transcripts

Analysis of the interview transcripts from the experimental group revealed that most participants found embodied learning particularly effective for remembering craft techniques and enhancing hands-on experience. Participant A26 remarked, "Drawing the pattern left a profound impression on me as I considered which part of the cloth tiger it represented, making the shape more memorable." In terms of learning outcomes, approximately 70% of the experimental group reported a significant retention of knowledge about cloth tiger ICH techniques, styles, and cultural content, as compared to traditional learning methods such as online articles, documentaries, and TV shows. The embodied game-based learning approach offered a more authentic and comprehensive understanding of cloth tiger ICH, proving to be more engaging and appealing. About 90% of participants expressed a desire to continue with this type of game-based learning to explore various cloth tiger crafts and their cultural backgrounds. Over half the participants also noted a deepened understanding of the cultural context, as illustrated in the game's narrative CG animations and achievement system cards. Participant A18 shared, "The opening CG animation and final knowledge cards expanded my understanding of the ICH's background and history, going beyond just its appearance."

Most learners in the experimental group found the embodied learning method more challenging yet enjoyable and effective, sparking a heightened interest in cloth tiger ICH. Participant A27 stated, "The challenge of remembering the order of sewing points and the gesture-based threading of the needle left a deep impression, unlike in video tutorials." Around 80% of participants felt that the game allowed them to learn and reflect on various aspects of cloth tiger ICH. 56.7% (17 participants) found the gesture interaction and the levels of game challenge appropriate, enhancing their sense of control and engagement. Participant A5 commented, "The first level involving drawing was more challenging, while the second level with scissor gestures felt easier, creating a sense of achievement. The varying levels of difficulty contributed to an immersive game experience." Over half of the volunteers reported that interacting with the virtual 3D cloth tiger model they created in the game, upon completing all levels, deepened their connection with cloth tiger ICH.

In contrast, over 70% of the control group indicated that while videos and graphic materials provided a general understanding of the Cloth Tiger ICH, they often experienced attention drift or loss of interest, resulting in less impactful learning. They also had limited autonomy in learning specific knowledge, being confined to the sequence provided in the materials. Over 80% showed interest in game-based learning, opting to watch screen recordings of the game learning experience or use the game application post-experiment.

Regarding interactive behavior, all participants in the experimental group found that gesture-based embodied interaction enhanced the challenge and memorability of the levels. For instance, participant A27 remarked, "Remembering the order of sewing points and then using gestures to thread the needle was more challenging but also more memorable; it differed significantly from using a mouse." More than 90% (28 participants) with no prior experience in gesture interaction initially found it challenging to locate and adapt to the gesture capture area, experiencing fatigue with continuous use. Participant A7 noted, "In the initial drawing levels, adjusting my wrist angle and height to stabilize the drawing tool was tiring due to the unclear movement range."

Regarding learning motivation, over 90% of volunteers stated that the embodied game-based learning approach stimulated their interest in exploring more about other types of ICH. Participant A17 expressed, "Playing this game not only educated me about the Cloth Tiger ICH but also fostered a sense of identification with it, aiding in its dissemination and raising awareness for its preservation." Over 70% (23 participants) reported increased attention to the Cloth Tiger ICH in everyday life following the game learning experience. Participant A13 mentioned, "As someone interested in handicrafts, I'd like to try making a cloth tiger using the kit, but I wouldn't have been attracted to it without this game experience."

7 Conclusion and Discussion

This study developed an embodied experiential educational game design model and created a game based on this model to validate its effectiveness in enhancing the public's learning, experience, motivation, and interest in handicraft ICH. The experimental data and interview results indicated significant differences in learning outcomes, motivation, and interest between the experimental group, which used our game for learning, and the control group, which employed traditional methods like videos and text.

Specifically, at the level of learning outcomes, survey results showed that learning about the Cloth Tiger ICH through an embodied experiential educational game was overall more effective than traditional methods using videos, images, and craft kits. The scores from objective learning outcome tests also indicated that the game application significantly improved learning in physical styles and craft techniques, as well as understanding of the ICH cultural context. Most participants in semi-structured interviews stated that embodied learning had a superior effect on memory and hands-on experience of craft techniques. This may be due to the game's inclusion of multiple learning modalities, such as visual, auditory, and kinesthetic stimuli. Narrative CG animations and achievement system knowledge cards in the game also provided participants with cultural context knowledge, enriching their understanding of the Cloth Tiger ICH.

In the experimental group, gesture-based interactions were highlighted as enhancing challenge and memorability of the learning experience. For example, participant A27 noted the memorability of using gestures over a mouse. Most participants, unfamiliar with gesture control, initially faced difficulties but found the experience impactful. Participant A7 commented on the physical demands of adjusting to gesture controls during the drawing task.

In terms of learning motivation, survey data showed that learning the Cloth Tiger ICH through an embodied serious game significantly enhanced learners' motivational aspects, including emotional, behavioral willingness, and cultural identification with ICH. This was overall more effective than traditional methods. Interview feedback suggested that this embodied learning approach not only encouraged players to learn more about the Cloth Tiger knowledge but also stimulated a majority to learn about other types of intangible cultural heritage. This could be due to players being attracted by the game's engaging nature and rich cultural content, thereby increasing their identification with traditional ICH.

In conclusion, the embodied experiential educational game model provides effective design ideas for the education and dissemination of handicraft ICH from a game learning perspective. The game's situational content enhances the immersion of learning both tangible and intangible aspects of handicraft ICH. The game's mechanism structure strengthens the enjoyment of learning experiences, thereby stimulating learners' willingness and motivation. The incorporation of kinesthetic interactions in the game leaves a deeper impression of ICH craftsmanship, facilitating the integration of skills with cultural connotations.

The study has limitations; it hasn't covered all types of handicraft ICH. Future research should explore motion capture tech and new gaming devices to refine the educational game design model. Game difficulty settings should optimize the difficulty gradient of levels and improve overall usability. The current narrative lacks depth and needs to align with level challenges to enhance immersion.

References

1. Zhang, L., Shi, J.: Research on inheritance and innovation of Shandong intangible cultural heritage from the perspective of traditional handicrafts. J. Guangdong Indus. Polytechn. **21**(04), 77–80 (2022). https://doi.org/10.13285/j.cnki.gdqgxb.2022.0059
2. Wang, J., Chen, W.: Embodied Cognition Theory and Enlightenment to Instructional Design and Technology. J. Dist. Educ. **30**(03), 88–93 (2012). https://doi.org/10.15881/j.cnki.cn33-1304/g4.2012.03.016
3. Morris, T.H.: Experiential learning–a systematic review and revision of Kolb's model. Interact. Learn. Environ. **28**(8), 1064–1077 (2020)
4. Kiili, K.: Digital game-based learning: towards an experiential gaming model. Internet Higher Educ. **8**(1), 13–24 (2005)
5. Winn, B.M.: The design, play, and experience framework. In: Handbook of Research on Effective Electronic Gaming in Education, pp. 1010–1024. IGI Global, Heidelberg (2009)
6. Fullerton, T.: Game Design Workshop: A Playcentric Approach to Creating Innovative Games. CRC Press, Boca Raton (2014)
7. Wu, F.: Modern transformation of the ontology language of folk art in a cross-media context. Media **17**, 82–85 (2018). https://doi.org/10.3969/j.issn.1009-9263.2018.17.035

8. Ma, X.N., Tu, L., Xu, Y.Q.: Development status of the digitization of intangible cultural heritages (in Chinese). Sci Sin Inform **49**, 121–142 (2019). https://doi.org/10.1360/N112018-00201

9. Lyu, Y.R., Zhang, L.: Innovative applications of multimedia technologies in digital display for intangible cultural heritage. Pack. Eng. **37**(10), 26–30+10 (2016). https://doi.org/10.19554/j.cnki.1001-3563.2016.10.008

10. Ma, Z.Y.: Field reflections on the protection of intangible cultural heritage: a reconsideration of the current status of folk cloth tiger in Northern China. Folk. Stud. **04**, 23–29 (2012). https://doi.org/10.3969/j.issn.1002-4360.2012.04.004

11. Zhou, J.: Study on the Artistic Characteristics and Innovative Application of Folk Cloth Tiger in the Middle and Lower Reaches of the Yellow River. Jiangnan University (2021)

12. Petri, G., von Wangenheim, C.G., Borgatto, A.F.: MEEGA+: an evolution of a model for the evaluation of educational games. INCoD/GQS **3**, 1–40 (2016)

13. Andreoli, R., Corolla, A., Faggiano, A., et al.: A framework to design, develop, and evaluate immersive and collaborative serious games in cultural heritage. J. Comput. Cult. Herit. (JOCCH) **11**(1), 1–22 (2017)

Games and Artificial Intelligence

Navigating Between Human and Machine-Based Evaluation: Judgment and Objectivity in Economic Games Exemplified in the Analysis of MMA Fights

Jakub Binter[1]([✉]) [iD], Daniel Říha[2] [iD], Silvia Boschetti[1] [iD], Violetta Prossinger-Beck[3], Martin Stachoň[1,4] [iD], and Hermann Prossinger[1,5] [iD]

[1] Faculty of Social and Economic Studies, University of Jan Evangelista Purkyne, Usti Nad Labem, Czech Republic
jakub.binter@ujep.cz
[2] Faculty of Humanities, Charles University, Prague, Czech Republic
[3] Technical University Dresden, Dresden, Germany
[4] Faculty of Business and Economics, Mendel University in Brno, Brno, Czech Republic
[5] Department of Evolutionary Biology, University of Vienna, Vienna, Austria

Abstract. UFC (Ultimate Fighting Championship) video games aim to provide a realistic virtual experience of MMA (Mixed Martial Arts) fights. However, despite the seeming simplicity of the point-based scoring system used during these fights, judges' holistic verdicts of identifying the winner often fail to accurately reflect the performances because, we find, they do not rely on the point-awarding system used during the fights. We investigate the extent to which judges employ holistic approaches in their scoring decisions, even though they are consistent in applying them. To overcome the shortcomings of the holistic approach, we propose a merit-based set of rules (based on the Bayesian statistical approach that is driven by the points accrued in each round of the fight) for identifying the winners of matches and tournaments. Merit-based sets of rules are commonplace in economic games, in which strategic decision-making and performance evaluation are common, and such rules infer that quantified measures do objectify the assessment of player/fighter performance in a far more satisfactory (and non-controversial) manner. We thereby emphasize the importance of significant strikes being a key component of scoring. Our analysis of data from 3039 UFC decision fights demonstrates that the potential of objective scoring methods will make tournaments more attractive for not only gamers but also spectators. Likewise, such objective evaluation methods are useful in economic games.

Keywords: UFC video games · Bayesian statistical approach · Significant Strikes · Objective Scoring · Holistic Evaluations · MMA Tournament Scoring

X. Fang (Ed.): HCII 2024, LNCS 14730, pp. 235–246, 2024.
https://doi.org/10.1007/978-3-031-60692-2_16

1   Introduction

MMA (Mixed Martial Arts) is a contact fighting sport in which opponents can be struck or subdued in various ways. The scoring method (a prerequisite for determining the victor) is complicated. In real-world matches, he/she is determined by a panel of three judges—more about this later. An MMA match consists of three five-minute rounds (five in a title match). MMA matches often occur in tournaments in which an overall champion is then to be determined. The best-known umbrella organization for MMA tournaments is the UFC (Ultimate Fighting Championship) organization.

Nowadays, UFC is also the go-to organization for MMA video games—games in which the players are allowed to control their favorite fighters and compete in virtually (no pun intended) realistic matches. However, replicating the complexity and nuances of scoring in MMA video games is as challenging as it is in real-world MMA, where judges score each round based on a variety of criteria (oftentimes subjectively; [1]). UFC video games usually implement a much simpler point-based system: the player with the most points at the end of the round is the winner of that round and the winner of the match is the fighter who has won two rounds (out of three) or three rounds (out of five). That is, of course, if the match does not end with a knock-out or a submission—i.e., whenever the victory is decided by incapacitating the opponent. In the analyses we present in this paper, we restrict ourselves to bouts decided by the judges' scores.

It has been observed that, in both real-world matches and video games, an uproar occasionally occurs because of a mismatch (pun intended) between the spectators' (oftentimes also the players') expectations of who is victorious. The root of the problem lies in the way the fighter gains points during the match and how the judges 'use' them when determining the victor.

In both a virtual game and a real-world fight, each round is rated separately. Verdicts about the victor of the fight should be arrived at by tallying the wins of the rounds, not the accumulated points. However, both psychologically and realistically, the performance in later rounds tends to sway the judges more (we suspect). Those fighters performing better (no matter how slightly) in the last round may be declared the winner by the judges, even if his/her performance had been (objectively, as determined by points awarded in rounds) far inferior in the earlier rounds. This causes seemingly endless discussions among the fans/spectators/gamers. Winners are determined (or should be determined) by counting the significant strikes during each round—these counts should have the highest weight (or: the only weight) in the final judgment call. Even though the mixed rulings allow for the applicability of all possible—within rules—techniques to incapacitate the opponent, it is the damage that is caused by the number of 'significant' punches that is the most obvious and (potentially undisputable) measurement technique, whereas other scores can—in principle—be nullified by the opponent. This also applies to attempts, location in the ring, and 'insignificant' strikes. In other words, the activity or the position in the ring should not be a reason for awarding higher evaluations.

Significant strikes (defined as 'clean') are powerful strikes that have a high likelihood of causing damage to the opponent; they are the crucial scoring elements. These strikes can be delivered to the head, the body (trunk), or the legs. The point-based system (in which only the tallying of the number of significant strikes counts) can lead to situations where the outcome of the fight may not accurately (let alone statistically robustly) reflect the fighters' performances during the fight. Below, we suggest a solution based on the Bayesian statistical approach similar to the one that has been developed for economic games and behavioral studies interpretation; needless to say, comparable implications follow [2].

Currently, the reliance on the holistic assessment of the performances of the fighters in a match is widespread; it is then used to decide who the winner is. We are interested in, and investigate in this paper, whether the holistic assessment by the judges is reliable in the sense of consistency. Judges may be consistent yet holistic. Consistency is not to be equated with accuracy. In the scenario of consistent holistic winner determination, however, the points awarded during each round must be considered superfluous (in the sense of using them to determine the winner, not in the sense of assessing performance). This system of using judges to determine the winner, rather than the tallied significant strikes in each round, is what we call holistic judgment.

Economic games are widely used in simulation economics in which phenomena such as bargaining, competition, and cooperation can be studied while at the same time constraining the number of confounding variables. Such games typically force players to make strategic decisions, and their performance is evaluated based on various metrics, such as the amount of money earned or the effectiveness of their strategies. Many of these decisions involve timing and the willingness to take risks. Analogously, each fighter in either a real MMA match or a video MMA match is making decisions about the effort to be invested, along with the risks to take, as well as the timings of attack or defense.

It is, of course, crucial to base the results on a standardized definition of the significance of these strikes and to tally their number. This is easy to implement in game design and one could include advanced technologies, such as motion capture combined with AI (artificial intelligence), to detect significant strikes.

Significant strikes are the key component of a non-holistic scoring system. Whenever holistic judgments are avoided, this will encourage players and fighters to focus on landing powerful strikes that determine the outcome. Our approach is, therefore, to analyze all data from 3039 UFC three-round fights in which a round-by-round decision was made (and made available). We not only compare these numerical outcomes with possible holistic methods of declaring the winner (these outcomes were also made available). We also developed a statistical approach that overcomes, we claim, the challenges associated with subjective evaluations. Our approach provides a more consistent and unbiased assessment of player/fighter performance, we argue. We also argue that, in the long run, objective scoring will make tournaments applying such methods more attractive to gamers and spectators alike.

We attempt to identify to what extent—and with what probability—judges are holistic. In other words, we investigate several straightforward numerical operations to identify the winner and compute the probability that the judges implemented these.

Based on our suspicions, and the outcomes of our in-depth analyses presented here, we propose a set of rules to identify the winner. This set can then be applied in future tournaments.

2 Materials

2.1 Matches

Our data set consists of 3039 matches with three rounds each. Published outcome decisions for all these fights were based on the judges' verdicts. In each fight, points were awarded for each (significant) strike and the marginal totals of the contingency tables were stored as entries in the data set. The marginal totals of the contingency tables for a randomly chosen match (Match No. 13) are displayed in Table 1.

Table 1. The points awarded for the match in Event No. 13. The values inside the contingency table are not available; the marginal totals are, however. The numbers in bold are the sums of the marginal totals. Observe that the sum of the marginal totals of rows and the sum of the marginal totals of columns are the same. In this event, Fighter 1 had achieved $10 + 7 + 5 = 22$ points, while Fighter 2 had achieved $4 + 2 + 4 = 10$ points. Fighter 1 achieved three wins (because $\{10 > 4, 7 > 2, 5 > 4\}$). Arguably, Fighter 1 should have been the winner of this fight on both counts, both when considering the wins in each round and when considering the total sum of the marginal totals ($22 > 10$). The judges, however, unanimously declared Fighter 2 as the winner. This discrepancy occurred not only in this event (Fig. 1). One topic of this paper is analyzing such discrepancies

	Fighter 1				Fighter 2			
Round 1								
Head				0				3
Body				10				0
Leg				0				1
	0	10	0	**10**	1	0	3	**4**
Round 2								
Head				4				1
Body				2				0
Leg				1				1
	2	1	4	**7**	1	0	1	**2**
Round 3								
Head				4				2
Body				0				1
Leg				1				1
	1	0	4	**5**	1	1	2	**4**
	Distance	Clinch	Ground		Distance	Clinch	Ground	

2.2 Winners

The verdicts of the three judges declare the winner; these verdicts are also available in the data set. However, in this paper, we analyze other methods of determining the winner:

(i) The winner of a round is the fighter with the greater sum of the marginal totals. (ii) The winner is the one with the larger number of higher marginal totals, round per round (in Table 1, Fighter 1 is the winner of Round 1, Round 2, and Round 3; thus this match outcome is 3:0). (iii) The winner is the one who has a higher probability mode of the Dirichlet distribution of the (three) marginal totals (Fig. 3).

3 Methods

3.1 Objective Winners

We compute, in each match, for each fighter the triples (a vector) of the sums of the marginal totals. We also compute the totals of these triples. In the first analysis, we determine the winner by comparing the wins per round, as defined by a comparison of components of the triples. In the second analysis, we find the sums of the vector components and compare these.

3.2 Judges' Verdicts

We quantify the underlying holistic approach used by the judges to arrive at a verdict as to who is the winner. We constructed the matrix with 3039 rows × 1 column. For each event, we classified the judges' verdicts by mapping the events into the win/lose component of the column (class), using a suite of classification algorithms (listed in Table 2). We added an extra layer of classifications by using not only the vector of all three verdicts (model A), but also the verdict based on the last two rounds (model B), and, finally, only on the last round (Model C). In model B, we avoided ties by choosing as winner the one with the greater sum of the marginal totals (remarkably, no ties were observed, despite such a large number of matches). The idea behind this test: perhaps the judges better remembered the fighters' performances solely in Round 3 (Model C) or only in Round 2 and 3 (Model B).

3.3 Confusion Matrices

The triples for each fighter in an event are Dirichlet-distributed. Specifically, if Fighter 1 is awarded the vector $n = \{10, 7, 5\}$ and Fighter 2 the vector $m = \{4, 2, 4\}$ (as in Table 1), then the likelihood functions of the Dirichlet distributions are $\mathcal{L}_1 = pdf(\mathcal{D}ir(11, 8, 6), s_1, s_2, s_3)$ and $\mathcal{L}_2 = pdf(\mathcal{D}ir(5, 3, 5), s_1, s_2, s_3)$, where the s_k with $k = 1 \ldots 3$ are the (Bayesian) probabilities for each of the rounds (the numerical values are from Table 1.). The modes are $mode_1 = \left\{ \frac{10}{10+7+5}, \frac{7}{10+7+5}, \frac{5}{10+7+5} \right\}$ and $mode_2 = \left\{ \frac{4}{4+2+4}, \frac{2}{4+2+4}, \frac{4}{4+2+4} \right\}$. The winner determined this way is the one with the majority of higher win components (in this case Fighter 1).

However, we need to determine whether the winner determined in this way is a winner due to chance. Here, we describe how to calculate this probability. We first generate two sets of random numbers (ran_1 distributed according to $\mathcal{L}_1$) and (ran_2 distributed according to $\mathcal{L}_2$), each of cardinality ran_n. We then compute, for each ran_{1i} $i = 1 \ldots ran_n$, the validity of $\mathcal{L}_1(ran_{1i}) > \mathcal{L}_2(ran_{1i})$; we then obtain a vector $v_1 = \{n_{1\text{true}}, n_{1\text{false}}\}$. We repeat for $\mathcal{L}_2(ran_{2i}) > \mathcal{L}_1(ran_{2i})$ to obtain $v_2 = \{n_{2\text{true}}, n_{2\text{false}}\}$. We compute the confusion matrix.

$$\text{confusion matrix} = \begin{pmatrix} \frac{n_{1\text{true}}}{ran_n} & \frac{n_{1\text{false}}}{ran_n} \\ \frac{n_{2\text{false}}}{ran_n} & \frac{n_{2\text{true}}}{ran_n} \end{pmatrix}.$$

The off-diagonal entries in this matrix determine the significance of the overlap of the two likelihood functions. In conventional significance testing, the significance level is assumed to be 5%; then each off-diagonal element must be $\frac{n_{1\text{false}}}{ran_n} < 0.1$ and $\frac{n_{2\text{false}}}{ran_n} < 0.1$. This method of computing the confusion matrix involving two Dirichlet distributions is the same for all other cases we investigate in this paper.

3.4 Tournament Rules

In the rules for a tournament, which we suggest below, we choose a numerical value (labeled *cut*) and compute $\frac{n_{1\text{false}}}{ran_n} < cut$ and $\frac{n_{2\text{false}}}{ran_n} < cut$. We use this modification of significance testing because—in most tournaments—fighters have such comparable performance reputations that there are no matches where the performance differences are statistically significant. The method of determining the probability of overlap of the two likelihood functions is the same.

4 Findings

Judges' Verdicts Probabilities. The use of the three sums of marginal totals is not what the judges used to arrive at their verdict as to who the winner is. In this analysis, we find the probability that the judges' verdicts are non-holistic—but based on this method—to be 3×10^{-227} (Fig. 1).

Classification Algorithm. The best classification algorithm that attempts to mimic the judges' holistic verdicts is the Gradient-Boosted Tree (Table 3). We find, however, no evidence that the judges' memories influenced their verdicts. Model C does not classify better than Model B, and Model A is the best. For all models, the Gradient-Boosted Tree best simulates the judges' holistic verdicts, but only with a probability of ~85%.

Judges' Verdicts Distributions. The judges' verdicts of winners and losers are both Dirichlet-distributed (Fig. 2). Whatever their (the judges') holistic approach may be, they apply it consistently: the Dirichlet distributions have no significant overlap, so the confusion matrix is $\begin{pmatrix} 1 & 0 \\ 0 & 1 \end{pmatrix}$ to better than 13 significant digits (computation not shown).

Players' Marginal Totals. The marginal totals of each player in each round are Dirichlet-distributed. We found that at a 5% significance level (i.e. both off-diagonal entries are < 0.1), roughly $\frac{1}{3}$ of the matches are tied (in the sense that the two distributions of the fighters in this round are not significantly different). This shows that matches are usually very close and that a clear winner (one who did not win due to chance) occurs in only $\sim\frac{2}{3}$ of all matches. We infer that this low probability of identifying a not-due-to-chance winner is why judges judge holistically.

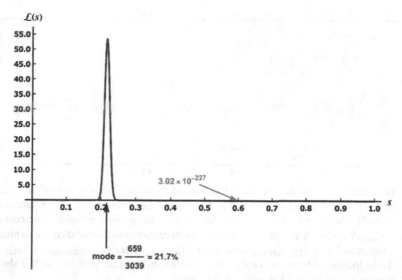

Fig. 1. The Beta distribution of misclassification by the judges determining the winner. The probability of correct classification is s, the likelihood function $\mathcal{L}(s) = pdf((n+1, m+1), s) = c \cdot s^n \cdot (1-s)^m$, where Be is the Beta distribution, c is a constant so that $\int_0^1 \mathcal{L}(s)ds = 1$, n are the valid cases, and m the invalid (contradictory) cases. The probability is the integral of the likelihood function. The probability that the result is due to chance is $\int_{\frac{1}{2}}^1 \mathcal{L}(s)ds = 3.02 \times 10^{-227}$ (Technical comment: the computations were carried out to 80 significant digits beyond the decimal point to find the probability.) Note that the likelihood function is extraordinarily sharp. The probability due to chance is so small that it cannot be explicitly rendered in this graph.

Table 2. The distribution of how the judges ruled to determine winners and losers in the 3039 events/matches/fights investigated in this data set. Unanimous: all three judges concurred; Majority: two judges awarded 'win' and one judge awarded 'draw'; Split: two judges awarded 'win' and one judge awarded 'loss'. In this system, which we criticize in this paper, ties are never the outcomes of the events.

Outcome	Unanimous	Majority	Split
Win	1500 (72.1%)	31 (4.0%)	343 (23.9%)
Loss	840 (80.0%)	47 (1.7%)	278 (18.3%)

Holistic Verdicts by Judges. We have evidence that judges judge holistically, but we have no evidence that the high due-to-chance probability is the reason for holistic judging.

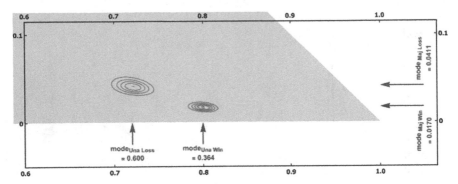

Fig. 2. The contour maps of the likelihood functions of the distributions of judges' verdicts as to the winners of the 3049 fights investigated in this paper. The verdicts were either "unanimous" (labeled "Una" in the graph), "majority" (labeled "Maj" in the graph), or "split". Contours are in steps of $\frac{1}{5}\mathcal{L}_{max}$. We observe that the distributions of win verdicts and loss verdicts are significantly different. Horizontal axis: $s_{Unanimous}$; vertical axis: $s_{Majority}$. Because $s_{Unanimous} + s_{Majority} + s_{Split} = 1$, the likelihood function is only defined within the triangle (part of which is shown in gray). Note that the origin {0, 0} is outside this graph.

Table 3. The prediction reliability (in %) of the various classifier algorithms for the three models. Model A is for all three rounds, Model B is for the last two rounds, and Model C is for the last round only. The dimensions of the feature vector decrease from Model A to Model C. We observe that the prediction reliability decreases (slightly) with decreasing feature vector dimension. We investigate whether this is due to the decrease in feature vector dimension or to less reliable judges' verdicts in the last rounds, which necessitates further investigations.

Classification Method	Model A	Model B	Model C
Decision Tree	84.3	82.2	77.2
Neural Network	82.8	79.6	74.3
Gradient Boosted Tree	85.3	81.2	77.5
Naïve Bayes	82.4	78.9	74.2
Nearest Neighbors	79.2	78.2	74.0
Logistic Regression	81.2	78.5	74.3

5   Our Suggestion for a Non-holistic Game Design

In the analyses of the 3039 real-life matches in the data set, we provided evidence that judges make their decisions holistically. In gaming tournaments, we neither need judges nor do we desire to have verdicts arrived at holistically (nor, presumably, do the tournament participants). We therefore propose the following method for determining a winner:

1. Determine the position of the modes of the Dirichlet distributions of the two fighters, as described in the Methods section and illustrated in Fig. 3.

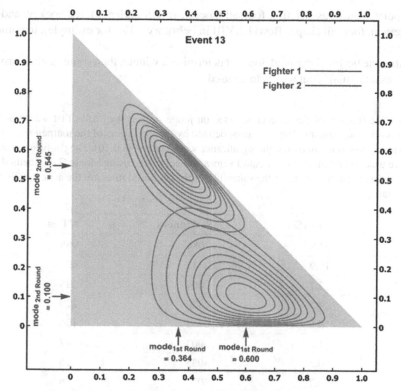

Fig. 3. The contour map of the likelihood functions of the probability of winning in each of the three rounds of Event No. 13. The criterion of 'win' is the marginal total of the contingency table, where the marginal totals here are those of the rows (see text for details). The likelihood functions overlap, but the Monte Carlo method of calculating the confusion matrix yields $\begin{pmatrix} 98.8 & 1.2 \\ 1.7 & 98.3 \end{pmatrix}\%$, so there is a high significance of one of the fighters being the winner. The computation method is described in the text. In this case, the analysis of the awarded scores in each round results in Fighter 1 being the winner of the match/event; the judges, however, awarded the win to Fighter 2. This discrepancy (not only for this event) is investigated in this paper.

2. If the modes are significantly different (as determined by the confusion matrix and the parameter *cut*— see Item No. 3 below), then the winner is the fighter with higher components of his/her mode vector. This "significantly different" is not the conventional one used in statistics, but one determined by a specification of the value of *cut*, as described in the Methods section. Before the first game, the organizers of the tournament can (or should) decide on which *cut* to prescribe. Alternatively, UFC can prescribe a value for *cut*. Table 4 lists, for the 3039 actual matches in the data set, how a choice of *cut* influences the fraction of ties.

3. Ties are the challenge. If the organizers decide on a value for *cut*, (preferably something like *cut* = 0.7 resulting in ~0.5% ties, as in Table 4), then an extra round ("tie-breaker") will determine the winner. A "tie-breaker" method is quite ubiquitous

in sports: tennis, association football (soccer, in US parlance), ice hockey, and US-American football (Super Bowl LXVIII in February 2024, for example), to name but a few.

4. If, after the tie-breaker round does not determine a winner, then some random process, such as a (virtual) coin toss is to be used.

Table 4. The fraction of ties in events, based on judge-independent rules that we propose for applications in tournaments. The *cut* can be defined by the organizers of the tournament before it begins (for conventional statistics, the significance would be *cut* = 0.10). The confusion matrices, which are used to find the results of cutoff values, are computed using Monte Carlo methods (see text). The data used to investigate the suitability of the proposed rules are the actual 3039 events in this dataset.

Cut	Ties (%)	*N*Winners	*N*Ties
10%	31.8	2084	965
20%	19.9	2443	606
30%	12.7	2664	385
40%	7.5	2820	229
50%	3.5	2943	106
60%	1.6	3002	47
70%	0.5	3033	16
80%	0.2	3043	6
90%	0.1	3046	3

6 Further Developments

A version of the tie-breaker, albeit somewhat less rigorous than the one we suggest here, has been advanced with the so-called Underground Rules by the Czech Oktagon organization [3]. The same organization also opted for another novelty: to announce to the combatants and the spectators the judgment call at the end of each round; it allows for strategy adjustments by the players and mitigation of some disputes (not that these disappeared; the disagreement with the judgment could now begin sooner—namely before the fight has been completed).

The Bayesian approach has been used in the context of MMA fights by Saabas (author of the data-oriented blog blog.datadive.net [4]) who applied the TrueSkill algorithm to MMA fights (online), enabling him to find the *objectively* best-performing fighter (as defined by this algorithm).

Ever since fighting games were developed, scientifically-minded players entertained the thought of two AIs fighting each other and quantifying the outcome of having caused the most damage to the opponent. Examples are games such as Street Fighter, Tekken, and Mortal Kombat. [5] Two years later, Mendonça et al. [6] demonstrated how to mimic human behavior in fighting games by using artificial neural networks. Just one year after that, Tang et al. [7] tested VR MMA training.

Statistical approaches are now often used: Elo (to evaluate high-performance chess players; a zero-sum game system), TrueSkill (a method developed by Microsoft® [8]), and TrueSkill2 (it can handle more than two players [9]). Some of these algorithms are patented (even though the code is publically available—algorithms are not patentable) and are used only by Microsoft® in their game applications. Recently, QuickSkill has been introduced; it aims to solve the cold start problem [10].

Today's technological advancements implement numerous versions of AI and are evolving extremely rapidly and, consequently, are further enhancing serious as well as entertainment uses. It should, therefore, be of the highest priority to maximize the joy of the interaction with machines (and other human beings) in any virtual game by making it fair and, arguably, rewarding. These rapid developments, and the possibility of making outcomes objectively decidable, also infer the educational and training value of their use in economics games.

7 Conclusions

We are surprised at how holistically yet consistently judges identify the winner. We provided statistical methods to overwhelmingly validate our claim of their holistic approach (which they have never denied). We consider this holistic aspect unfortunate. Granted, there are many other sports in which holistic aspects are included, sometimes manifestly so: figure skating, gymnastics, ski jumping, etc. Holistic approaches in economics are the realm of stock exchange speculators. It is not our intent to champion the elimination of the holistic aspect in MMA, but we did document it and use the outcomes of our analyses to propose a set of rules that can be applied, whereby judges (and their attendant holistic approach to identifying winners) are not involved.

We consider it fortunate that the probability of ties can be made very small by a suitable choice of the numerical value of the parameter *cut*. Tournaments can then be held fairly and non-controversially.

The implications of our research for the gaming world and the economic world are important. By introducing a more objective and statistically sound method for determining the winner in combat-related video games, we can enhance the fairness and accuracy of tournaments, undoubtedly making them more attractive to both gamers and spectators. Our approach eliminates the potential for bias and controversy about determining the winner of a round (but not about the significance of strikes). As numerous economic games also thrive on competition (think of market competitions for share acquisitions [11]), objective methods of identifying winners in such games also benefit from our approaches. Since currently available algorithms (such as TrueSkill) focus on the final result of the match but use a Bayesian approach to determine the players' best matches, we believe that our (also Bayesian) approach to handling the performance offers novel possibilities.

Additionally, our research opens up new possibilities for game developers to explore alternative scoring systems and game mechanics that promote strategic decision-making and reward players for their skills and performance, even if only one will be the winner.

By embracing data-driven approaches and leveraging statistical techniques, the gaming industries (both MMA and economic competition) can continue to evolve and provide players with innovative and immersive experiences.

Ethics Statement. Only publicly available historical data were used.

Conflict of Interest. The authors declare they have no conflicts of interest.

References

1. Berthet, V. Improving MMA judging with consensus scoring: A Statistical analysis of MMA bouts from 2003 to 2023. arXiv preprint arXiv:2401.03280 (2024)
2. Baley, I., Veldkamp, L.: Bayesian Learning. In: Handbook of Economic Expectations, pp. 717–748. Academic Press, USA (2023)
3. https://oktagonmma.com/cs/underground-rules/
4. https://blog.datadive.net/who-are-the-best-mma-fighters-of-all-time-a-bayesian-study/
5. Lu, F., Yamamoto, K., Nomura, L.H., Mizuno, S., Lee, Y., Thawonmas, R.: Fighting game artificial intelligence competition platform. In: 2013 IEEE 2nd Global Conference on Consumer Electronics (GCCE), pp. 320–323. IEEE (2013)
6. Mendonça, M.R., Bernardino, H.S., Neto, R.F.: Simulating human behavior in fighting games using reinforcement learning and artificial neural networks. In: 2015 14th Brazilian Symposium on Computer Games and Digital Entertainment (SBGames), pp. 152–159. IEEE (2015)
7. Tang, J.K., Leung, G.Y., Ng, B.K., Hui, J.H.K., Kong, A., Pang, W.M. VR-MMA: a virtual reality motion and muscle sensing action game for personal sport. In: Proceedings of the 13th International Conference on Advances in Computer Entertainment Technology, pp. 1–6 (2016)
8. Dangauthier, P., Herbrich, R., Minka, T., Graepel, T.: TrueSkill through time: Revisiting the history of chess. In: Advances in Neural Information Processing Systems, vol. 20 (2007)
9. Minka, T., Cleven, R., Zaykov, Y.: TrueSkill 2: An improved Bayesian skill rating system. Technical Report (2018)
10. Zhang, C., et al.: QuickSkill: novice skill estimation in online multiplayer games. In: Proceedings of the 31st ACM International Conference on Information & Knowledge Management, pp. 3644–3653. (2022)
11. Stachoň, M., Binter J., Prossinger-Beck V., Řiha D., Prossinger, H.: Portfolio management and stock request behavior: implications for developer- and economy-oriented game design. In: Fang, X. (Ed.) HCII 2024, LNCS, vol. 14730, pp. 114–126 (2024)

Managing the Personality of NPCs with Your Interactions: A Game Design System Based on Large Language Models

Muyun Dai, Chun Yuan, and Xiaomei Nie(✉)

Tsinghua University, Shenzhen, China
nie.xiaomei@sz.tsinghua.edu.cn

Abstract. How to create a Non-player character (NPC) that has its own personality and also consistent with the intention of game designers is a problem to be discussed. This study is aim to design a system for designers to create NPCs quickly and easily that can accept open input of player and make a variety of reasonable feedback adaptively in the game based on the dynamic interactions of player. The system comprises two essential components: an adaptive personality model manager and a drama mechanism manager based on retrieval augmented generation. In our experiment, a role-playing game is designed using this system, and corresponding user research is conducted to verify its effectiveness.

Keywords: Development methodology · Design tools/technologies · LLMs · NPC design · Interactive System

1 Introduction

Non-player characters (NPCs) are an essential component of the player's interactive experience in video games as interactive narrative develops because they are appropriate agents for delivering story content. They offer crucial information, direction, and interaction possibilities to players, and they even have an impact on gameplay and advancement. But coming up with realistic and interesting conversation and actions for these characters may be a labor-and time-intensive process that involves expensive scriptwriting and complex development. It can also lead to dialogue that is monotonous and repetitive, which would detract from the overall gaming experience. In order to produce game prototypes, a research topic has thus emerged, that is how to create NPCs with compelling traits and deep personalities quickly.

Procedural Narrative development (PNG) is another field that is involved in the automatic development of interaction scripts with NPC. [1] However, PNG has encountered significant obstacles thus far, including issues with pathfinding and story space, making it challenging to communicate sufficiently large stories. These two issues have been superseded by the Transformer model's quick development, which, using ChatGPT as an example, has resolved the issue at the text level.

X. Fang (Ed.): HCII 2024, LNCS 14730, pp. 247–259, 2024.
https://doi.org/10.1007/978-3-031-60692-2_17

Therefore, this research have developed an Interactive System with NPCs (ISNIN) based on large language models (LLMs), [2] which we have chosen GPT4 as a specific instance. ISNIN enables creators to quickly design intelligent NPCs that satisfy design specifications and facilitate richer interactions without requiring them to write individual dialogue behavior scripts.

Integrating LLMs into games has become a promising research direction, which make it possible for NPCs to produce contextualized, dynamic dialogue that reacts to player interactions more organically. By allowing NPCs to change and engage in meaningful dialogue in response to the player's decisions and actions, this not only makes the game environment more realistic but also gives gamers a more immersive experience. Instead of directly training the model, which takes a lot of time and resources, regular developers can adjust or manage the AI-generated content to fit the game's tone and aesthetic and make sure it flows naturally with the story as a whole.

Supporting open user interactions while maintaining a dramatic user experience and consistent character personality is a major design problem for non-player character interaction systems [3, 4]. The need that the behaviors of the story's characters be both responsive to the user and consistent with their own inherent goals is a significant research challenge for system designers. Furthermore, designers frequently want to place limitations on the way that content develops; for instance, they may stipulate that specific dramatic objectives must be met. By managing the generating process, this research seeks to strike a compromise between the freedom of NPCs and the limitations imposed by designer expectations.

In order to accommodate open user interactions and dynamically generate narrative content that not only satisfies designer constraints but also empowers players to increase their initiative and immersion during the experience, this research aims to design a interaction design system that strikes a balance between the autonomy of NPCs and constraints of the designer.

2 Related Work

Large language models (LLMs) are effectively used in various scenarios. Kasneci et al.'s work investigates the potential educational applications of LLMs like ChatGPT [5].

Natural language has been successfully employed in experimental playable experiences within academic study. With a keyboard and mouse, players can communicate and engage with NPCs in Façade. (Fig. 1) Discourse acts from natural language are recognized by a rule-based bottom-up island parser [6]. Prom Week has shown how to combine social simulation, drama management, and natural language to produce original player experiences [7].

A text-based game named "AI Dungeon" was released as early as 2019 with Gpt-2 in the game. Instead of using pre-written, limited alternatives from developers, players can individually insert text as they see fit, and the game As the system communicates with one another, the artificial intelligence creates storylines at random by interpreting the words that the player types. Traditional video games like "Mount and Blade 2" and "Backwater" will also be integrated with GPT technology in 2023. This would let players to communicate naturally with non-player characters (NPCs) in the game by giving them a sense of intelligence.

Fig. 1. Strong autonomy and a story are balanced in Façade.[6]

All drama management techniques, according to David Roberts and others, are built around four main elements: a set of story points; a set of possible drama management (DM) actions; a model of the player's reaction to the drama manager's actions; and a model of the author's intentions. Simultaneously, David Roberts distinguished three categories of drama management systems: those that rely on planning, those that depend on optimization, and those that neither [8].

Retrieval-Augmented Generation (RAG), which incorporates information from external databases, has emerged as a potential alternative. This improves the models' credibility and accuracy, especially for activities requiring a high level of knowledge [9]. It also makes it possible to integrate domain-specific data and update knowledge continuously. RAG combines the internal knowledge of LLMs with the large, dynamic databases from outside sources in a synergistic way.

3   Methodology

3.1   The Architecture of System

The concept of interactive narrative utilized in this research is based on a widely accepted practitioner theory that stems from McKee's narrative theory, which regards narrative as a sequence of connected events [10]. Whether the creator arranges these connected moments into scenes, beats, cinematic shots, or images, from the experiencer's point of view, we experience the narrative linearly in individual moments. The narrative framework for finishing a single interaction process is split into the following three layers in accordance with the three parts of interaction design, as illustrated in Fig. 2.

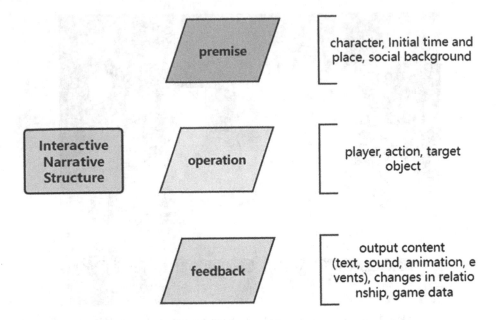

Fig. 2. Three layers of the interactive narrative structure, which imply how to design the interactive system.

Enabling NPC to think independently while yet representing the designer's goal is a major research topic in interactive system design [11]. As a result, the system consists of two essential parts: an adaptive personality model manager and a drama mechanism manager based on Retrieval Augmented Generation (RAG).

1. The adaptive personality model manager makes the NPC's dialogue logic more consistent with the personality and can make adaptive changes according to the player's operations.
2. The drama mechanism manager using RAG retrieves content that is permitted by the game by interpreting the content that designers have provided as the NPC's comprehension of the game environment. Then prompt engineering approaches are used to automatically produce organized narrative prompt leading gpt-4 to generate content that satisfies the designer's requirements, this also makes NPC's responses more relevant to the game and more credible.

After that, the generated material is fed into a discriminator for analysis, which modifies the game environment data and predicts the possible verbal or behavioral responses from the NPC. Dynamic real-time updates are made possible by these feedbacks, which have an impact on the current data in the drama mechanism manager and the personality model manager. The overall architecture is illustrated in Fig. 3. We will discuss the design of the personality model manager and drama mechanism manager in detail in the next two sections.

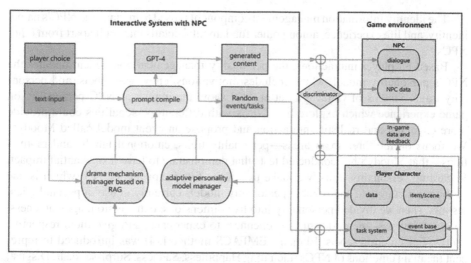

Fig. 3. Overall Architecture of system. The red part represents the player's operation, the yellow part represents the system's processing of the player's operation and the designer's expectations, and the green part represents the content generated by GPT4 and subsequent processing

3.2 Adaptive Personality Model Manager

The personality model manager can adjust the NPC dialogue logic based on the player's actions and makes it more compatible with the personality. The personality model manager will have three components in order to carry out this function: an embedded word management component, a personality characteristic management component, and an identity information management component (Fig. 4).

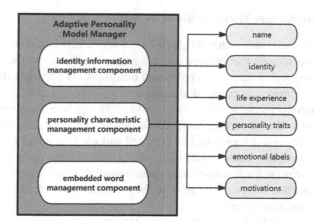

Fig. 4. The components of the adaptive personality model manager

The identity information management component is used to manage the NPC's name, identity, and life experience, among other fundamental details that set it apart from other NPCs.

Based on player interactions, the personality management component updates the NPC's personality model, which includes motivations, emotional labels, and personality traits. Studies of Garavaglia et al. [12] show the impact of NPC personality on game experience which explore how NPCs with different personalities could provide more engaging and realistic interaction and propose an agent model called Moody5. We focus on the three main areas—personality traits, emotional labels, and motivations—that Moody5 has conducted tests that demonstrate to have a substantial impact. Regarding personality traits, we make use of the five-factor model, [13] which is one of the most complete and reliable personality models currently in use in psychological testing. Then we divided personality into five dimensions: extraversion, agreeableness, conscientiousness, neuroticism, and openness to experience, and give them respective scores. For emotion labels, Ekman's EMFACS method [14] was introduced to represent the main emotions of NPCs, including Happiness, Sadness, Surprise, Fear, Disgust, Anger, and Contempt. In practical applications, the impact of the agent's emotions on the created discourse tone and the player's favorability are taken into consideration, as the agent itself is devoid of genuine emotions. Motivations is set by designers at the beginning and follow the mission of players, however could update as the game goes on and will exist in the form of a function.

To control the generating process and start further random events and task generation, NPC's preset expected reaction trigger words are managed using the inbuilt word management component. Expanding this attribute description will allow you to call any function that comes after it, such as character actions, animation status, audio, etc. For instance, If I say something that indicates the conversation is over, such as "Okay," end the conversation and add the phrase "END_CONVERSATION" to your reply.

3.3 Drama Mechanism Manager Based on RAG

We hope that the information that NPCs discuss with players is directly related to the game or may recommend that players take certain actions based on the current status, since the in-game world may be complex and designers may provide the game some experiences that players are expected to achieve.

We have introduced the setup of the world knowledge base because there will be a lot of content in the game that needs to be established separately and understood by NPCs, including which scenes can be explored and what resources can be collected. Here, the world knowledge base mostly consists of text, which the game creator included as a written description for in-game data. These contents, which are essentially private data, can be generated and retrieved prior to the personality model and will be updated dynamically as the game goes on.

The world knowledge base of the drama mechanism manager consists of the following components to make it easier for designers to manage and alter it: information management component, event management component and mechanism management component. (Fig. 5).

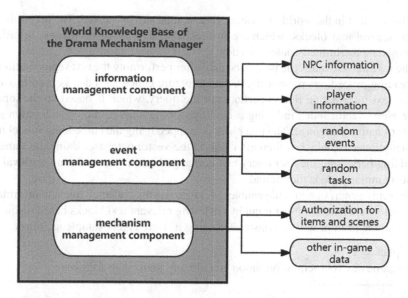

Fig. 5. The components of the world knowledge base

The "general level" knowledge of gpt-4 does not know what is contained in the World Knowledge Base. To influence what gpt-4 creates, we need to take more steps to include the most pertinent portions of player input into the prompt build. Here, a retrieval enhancement generation method is shown. RAG blends a text generating model with an information retrieval component. Without requiring a complete model retraining, RAG can be adjusted and its internal knowledge changed in an effective way.

Given an input and a source, RAG retrieves a group of pertinent and supportive documents. In our study, the text generator generates the final result by concatenating the global knowledge base with the initial input prompt. Because of this, RAG may adapt to circumstances in which the facts may change over time. Given that the parametric information of LLMs is static, this is quite helpful. With retrieval-based generation (RAG), language models can avoid retraining and have access to the most recent data, resulting in dependable outputs. The precise procedure is as follows (Fig. 6).

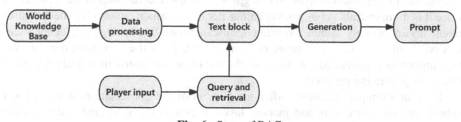

Fig. 6. Steps of RAG.

First, the text in the world knowledge base is read and processed. The text is divided up into several text blocks, which are further separated based on tokens, in order to accommodate the limited context window.

Then we need to index the processed data after performing the text segmentation and data reading procedures previously. A data structure called an index is used to swiftly retrieve text information that is pertinent to the query, which is based on the input of player. Here, vector index indexing is employed, which takes into consideration some aspects of natural language. The text block is mapped using the embedding model into a fixed-length vector, which is thereafter kept in the vector database. Using the same text embedding paradigm, the user query text is mapped into a vector during retrieval, and the most similar node is then found.

The reply generation module enables LLMs to use the collected relevant information to generate responses to player input by retrieving relevant text blocks based on queries. After that, the prompt will be constructed using it. Here is an example as follow.

- template = f"'
- The game environment information you already know is as follows:
- ------------------------
- {context_str}
- ------------------------
- Please answer my question based on your information: {query_str}
- If the information is not valuable, base your response on your own personality model.
- "'

3.4 Pipeline and Game Design

In our research, a role-playing game (RPG) named "Codename: Ming" (Fig. 7) that takes place in the Ming Dynasty of China was built based on our system using Unreal Engine 5.

In the game, the player will play as a role in the Ming Dynasty. Player is free to express themselves using natural language. Other than the number of words, there are no constraints on input here. NPCs can respond to players in their native tongue or even speech pattern.

The NPCs will provide the player with language feedback and certain modifications to the game data based on the actions of the two managers mentioned before and the assessment of the discriminator. While gpt-4 is adopted at the step of the generation since it is more operable compared to earlier iterations, which enables it to deduce user intent more accurately without requiring significant model fine-tuning [15]. It guarantees that NPCs in discussions are aware of their context, gives the user more control over the output that is generated, and supports the use of certain instructions and prompts to direct the generating process.

In certain unique situations, when the NPC ends the conversation, it will trigger subsequent random events and random tasks to add to the story and make it more entertaining.

Fig. 7. Game screen where players communicate with NPCs.

4 Results and Discussion

To verify the effectiveness of our designed system and to evaluate whether the players' participation experience meets the design objectives, we designed a controlled experiment. Refer to the control experiment method adopted by Google researchers, [16] three game designers who were at least eighteen years old and had some writing experience were chosen for the experimental phase, and they were asked to create a brief description of an NPC in response to a prompt. The baseline is the NPCs produced on this method directly. To validate the efficiency of the system design, we carried out comparative experiments using the interactive system pipeline described in this paper, which includes two managers and a feedback loop. Evaluation method we adopted refer to the evaluation indicators of narrative generation [17] (Table 1) and a measurement tool based on user-based empirical research proposed by Ivar Vermeulen et al. [18].

Table 1. Indicators of evaluation

Indicator	Description
Speed	Players should not suffer from immersion due to delays in spawning
Believability	Whether NPCs' feedback can be understood by players
Controllability	Whether it is allowed to use special methods to obtain the desired results
Expressivity and diversity	Whether the generated content is versatile and engaging

In order to validate our system's design goals, we conducted a small exploratory pilot study. We invited twenty participants at least 18 years old who were familiar with video games. Pre-interview and post-interview questions focused on engagement, interest (especially in backstories), NPC agency, and interaction techniques were part of the process. In order to assess the players' prior experience and take into account any biases before gameplay, the introductory questionnaires asked about the players' overall interest in NPC interactions and their past experiences with different video game genres.

After the preliminary questions, we introduced players to the scenario presented in the prototype as a role-playing game. We provided our players with control instructions and a brief context to account for the historical theme.

During the study, players are divided into two groups to interact with the NPCs, Fanjin's mother, Fanjin's wife, the merchant, etc. With a specific goal, players need to survive and finish their tasks, not merely chat with him. We would recommend making a statement to move or exit the game if we discovered a flaw and the player was trapped in a loop. Players were instructed to use the think-aloud method [19] usual in gaming research while they were playing. By using this technique, we were able to record spontaneous reactions and obtain more understanding of the system and player interactions.

Post gameplay, the interactive story experience was assessed through semi-structured interviews and a gaming experience questionnaire, in accordance with the user research experience framework Murray et al. [20] devised for interactive narrative products, which centers on agency, immersion, and transformation.

"Agency" refers to the satisfying power obtained when one takes meaningful actions and observes the outcomes of decisions and choices. It describes a user's active sense of intentionally influencing the game or narrative world. "Immersion" pertains to the ability of interactive narrative works to maintain our interest, where the user's attention is captivated by an entirely different reality, encompassing both perceptual and narrative dimensions. Perception is influenced by flow and presence, whereas the narrative aspect includes character identification (the player's empathy with the role played), curiosity (the player's desire to explore the uncertain and unknown), suspense (the player's emotional involvement in the overall narrative), and credibility (NPC behaviors and the emotional responses they evoke). "Transformation" refers to the impact of such works penetrating into the user's real life, such as generating positive or negative emotional states and yielding enjoyment. Here are some specific questions list as Table 2.

As a result, NPCs built on our system can produce realistic interactive narrative content, complete with natural language and behavioral feedback, in a dynamic and adaptive manner based on players' free-form interactions.

To verify the correlation between each variable within every research category, we employed the Kaiser-Meyer-Olkin (KMO) [21] test method, resulting in the calculation of the KMO coefficient (Table 3).

The Mann-Whitney U test [22] was utilized to analyze the statistical differences between the experimental and control groups (Table 3). The results indicated significant differences ($p < 0.05$) across all dimensions between the samples of the experimental group and the control group.

Compared to control group, test group indicate that participants' agency, immersion, and cognitive understanding of historical and cultural experiences of Ming Dynasty

Table 2. A list of key questions

Category	Specific questions
Agency	Does the application of interactive frameworks improve users' sense of
Agency	freedom and control?
Agency	Can users perceive the impact of interaction on the development of their own
Agency	attributes?
Immersion	Can users perceive the impact of interaction behaviors on NPC attitudes?
Immersion	Can users perceive the connection between conversation content and random
Immersion	events/tasks?
Transformation	Does the user feel that the NPC is trustworthy during the interaction?
Transformation	Is the user interested/curious about possible events?
Transformation	Can you identify with your character through interactions with NPCs?
Transformation	Have you generated positive or negative emotions?
	Did you feel bored or exhausted during the process?
	Has the game improved your knowledge of Ming Dynasty history, customs,
	and social mores?
	Is there an incentive to play again and again?

experienced significantly higher levels. Furthermore, the indices Roberts presented for a partial evaluation of drama manager [8] were used to assess the performance of the system's core managers.

Table 3. Results of the questionnaire

Category	X1	X2	KMO	p
Agency	4.32	3.91	0.901	0.021
Immersion	4.21	4.06	0.892	0.013
Transformation	4.58	3.41	0.903	0.022

Still, according to the interview, there are several issues with the system as it is right now. Open dialog systems frequently provide an authoring issue because of the open input, which necessitates a lot of composing. Limited authorship did present challenges for research participants. Although it was challenging to anticipate and create a player's input, open dialog systems had benefits. It was discovered that the player's capacity to assume roles and contribute to a feeling of freedom was improved by natural language input. Open dialog systems are therefore a two-edged sword.

5   Conclusion and Future Work

The following are this paper's primary contributions:

Design Methodology and Application Innovation: We provide an interactive framework between non-player characters and player that is based on industry-standard conventional interactive system with NPC architecture and McKee's Interactive Narrative

Theory [10]. The interactive system with NPC can be expanded to meet the design requirements of different interactive narrative works by breaking it down into premise, operation, and feedback components. This makes it easier for creators to create NPCs that encourage free-form interactions and improve player agency and immersion.

Innovation in Technical Integration: We have combined multiple technical approaches, including large language models, knowledge modeling, retrieval augmented generation, and prompt engineering. The drama mechanism manager based on RAG and the adaptive personality model manager's visualizable and editable performance might help designers work more effectively in their creative process.

However, the dialogue history between the agent and the player must be preserved in order to produce meaningful context; nevertheless, the player's perception of the current condition is what determines whether or not the dialogue content is more vivid and detailed. Because the discussion history is incorporated into the prompts, as the game goes on, more tokens will be needed, increasing the expenses. Future research should combine more sophisticated artificial intelligence technology to find a more efficient and responsive way to integrate creative tools with intelligence, as our system still needs some manual labor from the creator. This will enable interactive narrative creators to offer convenient creation conditions and give each player a more engaging narrative experience.

Acknowledgments. This work was supported by a research grant from Shenzhen Key Laboratory of next generation interactive media innovative technology (Funding No: ZDSYS20210623092001004) , and the Center for Social Governance and Innovation at Tsinghua University, a major research center for Shenzhen Humanities & Social Sciences Key Research Bases.

References

1. Martens, C., Cardona - Rivera, R.E.: Procedural narrative generation. In: Game Developers Conference (2017)
2. LLanzi, P. L., Loiacono, D.: Chatgpt and other large language models as evolutionary engines for online interactive collaborative game design. arXiv preprint (2023). arXiv:2303.02155
3. Si, M., Marsella, S.C., Pynadath, D.V.: Thespian: using multi - agent fitting to craft interactive drama. In: Proceedings of the Fourth International Joint Conference on Autonomous Agents and Multiagent Systems, pp. 21–28, July 2005
4. Warpefelt, H.: The Non - Player Character: Exploring the believability of NPC presentation and behavior (Doctoral dissertation, Department of Computer and Systems Sciences, Stockholm University) (2016)
5. Kasneci, E., et al.: ChatGPT for good? On opportunities and challenges of large language models for education. Learn. Individ. Differ. **103**, 102274 (2023)
6. Mateas, M., Stern, A.: Façade: An experiment in building a fully - realized interactive drama. In: Game Developers Conference, vol. 2, pp. 4–8, March 2003
7. McCoy, J., Treanor, M., Samuel, B., Reed, A. A., Wardrip - Fruin, N., Mateas, M.: Prom week. In: Proceedings of the International Conference on the Foundations of Digital Games, pp. 235–237, May 2012

8. Roberts, D.L., Isbell, C.L.: A survey and qualitative analysis of recent advances in drama management. Int. Trans. Syst. Sci. Appl. Special Issue Agent Based Syst. Human Learn. **4**(2), 61–75 (2008)

9. Gao, Y., et al.: Retrieval - augmented generation for large language models: a survey. arXiv preprint (2023). arXiv:2312.10997

10. McKee, R.: Dialogue: The Art of Verbal Action for Page, Stage, and Screen. Hachette, UK (2016)

11. de Lima, E.S., Feijó, B., Furtado, A.L.: Managing the plot structure of character - based interactive narratives in games. Entertain. Comput. **47**, 100590 (2023)

12. Garavaglia, F., Nobre, R.A., Ripamonti, L.A., Maggiorini, D., Gadia, D.: Moody5: personality - biased agents to enhance interactive storytelling in video games. In: 2022 IEEE Conference on Games (CoG), pp. 175–182. IEEE , August 2022

13. McCrae, R.R., John, O.P.: An introduction to the five-factor model and its applications. J. Pers. **60**(2), 175–215 (1992)

14. Russell, J.A.: Is there universal recognition of emotion from facial expression? A review of the cross-cultural studies. Psychol. Bull. **115**(1), 102 (1994)

15. Achiam, J., et al.: Gpt - 4 technical report. arXiv preprint (2023). arXiv:2303.08774

16. Park, J.S., O'Brien, J., Cai, C.J., Morris, M.R., Liang, P., Bernstein, M.S.: Generative agents: interactive simulacra of human behavior. In: Proceedings of the 36th Annual ACM Symposium on User Interface Software and Technology, pp. 1–22 , October 2023

17. Shaker, N., Togelius, J., Nelson, M.J.: Procedural Content Generation in Games, 1st edn. Springer, Cham (2016). https://doi.org/10.1007/978-3-319-42716-4

18. Vermeulen, I.E., Roth, C., Vorderer, P., Klimmt, C.: Measuring user responses to interactive stories: towards a standardized assessment tool. In: Aylett, R., Lim, M.Y., Louchart, S., Petta, P., Riedl, M. (eds.) Interactive Storytelling. ICIDS 2010. LNCS, vol. 6432, pp. 38–43. Springer, Heidelberg (2010). https://doi.org/10.1007/978-3-642-16638-9_7

19. Lankoski, P., Björk, S.: Game Research Methods: An Overview (2015)

20. Murray, J.H.: Hamlet on the Holodeck, Updated Edition: The Future of Narrative in Cyberspace. MIT Press, Cambridge (2017)

21. Shrestha, N.: Factor analysis as a tool for survey analysis. Am. J. Appl. Math. Stat. **9**(1), 4–11 (2021)

22. MacFarland, T.W., Yates, J.M.: Mann - Whitney u test. In: MacFarland, T.W., Yates, J.M. (eds.) Introduction to Nonparametric Statistics for the Biological Sciences using R, pp. 103–132. Springer, Cham (2016). https://doi.org/10.1007/978-3-319-30634-6_4

23. Corradini, A., Mehta, M., Ontañón, S.: Evaluation of a drama manager agent for an interactive story - based game. In: Iurgel, I.A., Zagalo, N., Petta, P. (eds.) Interactive Storytelling. ICIDS 2009. LNCS, vol. 5915, pp. 246–257. Springer, Heidelberg (2009). https://doi.org/10.1007/978-3-642-10643-9_29

Player-Oriented Procedural Generation: Producing Desired Game Content by Natural Language

Binlin Feng[1(✉)], MingYang Su[2], Keyi Zeng[2], and Xiu Li[2]

[1] Shenzhen University, Shenzhen, China
`fengbinlin2021@email.szu.edu.cn`
[2] Tsinghua Shenzhen International Graduate School, Shenzhen, China

Abstract. Procedural Content Generation (PCG) plays a vital role in digital games and interactive media, using algorithms and rules to automatically generate the core elements of a game, aiming to provide a rich and unique experience for the player. This study proposes an innovative player-oriented PCG approach to integrate PCG into the player's gaming experience to enhance game interactivity. We developed a Quick Custom Map Generation System (QMBS) using Large Language Modelling (LLM), allowing players to describe and create game content directly through natural language. This approach allows players to engage in game design intuitively and makes the gaming experience more personalized and diverse. In addition, this research highlights the great potential of LLM in facilitating human-computer interaction and creative tasks, opening up the possibility of new areas of game design.

Keywords: Procedural Content Generation · Large Language Model · Custom Map Editor · Player Experience · Video Game

1 Introduction

Procedural Content Generation (PCG) is crucial in digital games and interactive media. The automated generation of key game elements, such as maps, levels, and characters, through algorithms and rules has dramatically improved content creation efficiency and enriched games' variety and complexity. Procedural Content Generation (PCG) emerged from the need for more profound levels of creation in the digital world, especially in the gaming space, where traditional manual methods of creating content were becoming time-consuming and limiting creativity as the game's complexity grew. PCG has not only reduced the cost of content creation but also brought unique and personalized experiences to the players, thus driving the development of digital games and interactive media.

As the demand for game creation overgrows, the field of PCG has developed significantly. Early research focused on the application of traditional mathematical methods, such as evolutionary computation and structure generation [3]. With the emergence of deep learning techniques, data-driven methods are

X. Fang (Ed.): HCII 2024, LNCS 14730, pp. 260–274, 2024.
https://doi.org/10.1007/978-3-031-60692-2_18

increasingly being utilized to create high-quality game content [4]. While PCG algorithms are primarily designed for game developers, their fundamental purpose is to provide players with more prosperous and unique game experiences, which raises the question: Can we develop a PCG method oriented explicitly toward the player, allowing them to create unique game content that enhances their gaming experience without requiring extensive technical knowledge?

This study aims to explore a more user-friendly PCG approach that enables players to describe the game content they want to create through natural language. Our goal is to explore the possibilities of player-oriented procedural content generation to bring players a richer and more interesting experience and make PCG part of the game experience. Our research takes map editing in a PCG as an example. Based on the natural language description features of the Large Scale Language Model (ChatGPT), we developed Quick Custom Map Generation (QMBS) as a research example to verify the feasibility of player-oriented procedural content generation.

In many sandbox games and simulation games, players often need to spend a lot of time and effort to individually edit each block on the map in order to generate a game map that meets their expectations. The core of the generation system is to use text to represent the attributes of each tile in the map. In our developed game, available tile attributes include water, desert, grassland, mountain, stone, hamlet, and wood. By concatenating the text representing the tile attributes according to the tiles' spatial relationship, we can store the positions and attribute information of each tile in a two-dimensional text matrix. We input natural language rules and examples into a large language model, enabling the model to understand these rules and generate corresponding content. Next, the large model generates a text matrix for the map based on the player's text description, and our program visualizes it as a map in the game.

Our research not only provides strong support for the improvement of game experience but also brings more flexibility and possibilities to the field of game development and design. Our research is also expected to spark similar innovations in other fields, providing new paradigms for the use of large-scale language models to enhance human-computer interaction and creative tasks.

2   Related Work

2.1   PCG

Traditional PCG Algorithms and Applications. Traditional procedural content generation (PCG) methods are diverse, inspired by traditional mathematical methods, and fall into two main categories: rule-based and search-based [1,2]. In rule-based approaches, the generated content must satisfy predefined conditions. The level designer determines the specific characteristics the generated map should follow and inputs these characteristics into the constraint solver algorithm to generate content that meets the requirements. Search-based algorithms, on the other hand, focus on generating content through an iterative process of quality assessment until a satisfactory result is achieved. This assessment can be performed by humans or algorithms, but when executed by algorithms, it may require significant resources for computational optimization, especially to ensure the interpretability of the generated content.

Rule-based constraint approaches focus on ensuring that generated content conforms to the specific constraints of the game logic. For example, dungeon-based Roguelike games such as Rogue create block-based maps on each startup, demonstrating the ability for complex gameplay and rapid game world creation [3]. Erik et al. [8] use grammar-based PCG techniques to construct game narratives, resulting in smoother storytelling. Yuri et al. [9] improve meta cellular automata methods for generating game maps. Yahya et al. [10] combine meta cellular automata and Poisson disc sampling to generate levels for "Roguelike" games. "games more quickly". Another recent example is No Man's Sky [7], which uses pseudo-random numbers to generate details of the solar system and planets (including terrain, flora, and fauna) and even aspects of the game's soundtrack.

The search-based approach filters the most suitable solutions according to the criteria defined by the designer by using an evaluation function. This iterative approach builds on top of the best solution from the previous iteration in each iteration until the generated result meets high-quality standards. For example, TrackGen [6] uses evolutionary algorithms to generate tracks for the 3D racing games TORCS and Speed-Dreams and ensures that each track has the right length and number of corners. KartalKartal et al. [4] use the Monte Carlo Tree Search (MCTS) method to study the generation of levels for PCG pushbutton games. They defined the generation of such puzzles as a Monte Carlo tree search optimization problem and applied the corresponding search techniques. Sturtevant [5] explored the use of large-scale BFS to analyze and generate levels for Fling! His research focuses on developing a tool that uses a database of endgames to provide all solutions for Fling! Board sizes in the range of 1 to 10 through reverse search.

PCGML. With the advancement of deep learning, procedural content generation (PCG) is also integrating the learning abilities of neural networks to produce game content, known as Procedural Content Generation via Machine Learning (PCGML) [11]. Guzdial et al. [18] used a hierarchical clustering method to generate "Mario" levels, which is based on K-mean clustering and automatic K-estimation to train the model, and then OpenCV was used to parse the "Mario" levels in real-time. The method is based on K-mean clustering and automatic K-estimation to train the model, and then OpenCV is used to parse the "Mario" game video in real-time to generate new levels.

Kuang and Luo [13] developed an interactive map design system that uses different generative models to generate 2D maps, which can be extended to 3D scens. Volz et al. [12] proposed a latent space-inspired method (LVE), which uses quality maps, such as covariance matrix adaptive mapping (CMA-ME), to generate new levels. CMA-ME) Moreover, other mass diversity algorithms search the potential space of trained generators to increase the diversity of generated levels. Park et al. [14] trained a multi-step deep convolutional generative network modified from Volz, where the levels were initially represented as 2D arrays with top-down perspectives and then converted to 3D game levels. Jake et al. combined the same network model with the GraphGrammar method to generate maps for "The Legend of Zelda" [15]. Bontrager et al. [16] generated maps for "Zelda" using reinforcement learning. Irfan et al. [17] generated "Freeway," "Zelda," and "Celda" from deep convolutional generative adversarial networks.

2.2   Custom Map Editor

The Blizzard-developed map editors in Warcraft [19] and Starcraft [20] provide players with powerful tools for creating custom maps and modes. These tools advanced the game itself, spawned new game genres such as Tower Defence [21], and provided the basis for games such as Dota [22].

  With the explosive growth of the gaming industry, commercial game engines have emerged to provide quick map editing tools for game development. For example, Unity can use TileMap to define which sprite is suitable for a scene, allowing simple 2D scenes to be created quickly, just like using the stamp brush in Photoshop, directly covering the canvas with the corresponding texture [25,26]. These tools can generate pixel-style game scenes in batches, such as "Stardew Valley" and "Terraria", allowing players to create and edit custom environments in the game world, enhancing creativity and personalized experience of the game [23,24]. As it develops, Unity has also launched 3D TileMap.

  In player-facing game experiences, many games also offer custom map functionality, which has become critical in attracting and keeping players engaged. For example, the Civilisation series demonstrated the powerful use of map editors as a 4X strategy games, where players could create maps containing specific terrain and resources, thus greatly enriching the game experience [27]. Minecraft, on the other hand, as a survival-building game, offers players almost unlimited creative possibilities through its pixel block-based map editing mechanism [28]. Players can utilize a variety of blocks and resources to create anything from simple buildings to complex mechanical structures. Additionally, the Age of Empires series offers a feature-rich map editor that allows players to design maps with specific challenges and objectives, thus increasing the replayability and tactical depth of the game [29].

3   Player-Oriented Procedural Content Generation

3.1   LLM

Large Language Models (LLMs) represent a significant breakthrough in natural language processing; they are deep learning-based AI models with excellent natural language understanding and generation capabilities. LLMs are usually pre-trained models based on large-scale corpora, learned from large amounts of textual data and parameter-tuned to enable them to understand and generate human natural language.

LLM works based on neural networks and usually adopts the Transformer architecture, which has successfully succeeded in natural language processing. The core idea of LLM is to learn linguistic patterns and regularities from a large amount of textual data so that the model can predict the next word or sentence in the text and thus gain a deep understanding of the language. This pre-training approach enables LLM to handle various natural language tasks, including text generation, classification, and semantic understanding.

In this study, we have chosen a large-scale language model as the core component for player-oriented procedural content generation. This LLM has robust text comprehension and generation capabilities that enable players to interact with the system in a natural language manner. Players can use verbal or written descriptions of the game content they wish to generate, and the LLM will interpret these descriptions and translate them into rules for the generation of game content. The introduction of the LLM provides players with a more intuitive, interactive, and personalized way of authoring their game content, which enhances the enjoyment and depth of the game experience.

In conclusion, LLMs represent the latest advances in natural language processing technology, and their natural language understanding and generation capabilities provide a solid foundation for a player-oriented approach to procedural content generation, enabling players to participate more quickly in creating and customizing game content.

3.2   A Player-Oriented Approach to Procedural Content Generation

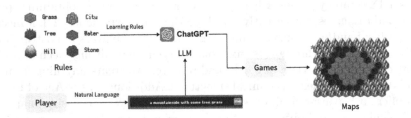

Fig. 1. the flow of the QMBS

The core idea of our approach is to translate players' natural language input into rules for generating game content, enabling them to engage in game content creation more intuitively and interactively, thespecific execution process of the QMBS is shown in Fig. 1.

First, we develop rules and examples for characterizing different elements and attributes in the game. These rules include the types of tiles in the map, characteristics of characters, quest settings, and so on. These rules and examples are fed into our LLM for learning and understanding. The LLM has powerful natural language processing and generation capabilities. Once the LLM understands the rules and examples, players can use natural language to describe what they want to see in the game. The LLM can interpret the players' natural language descriptions and translate them into game content rules, including tile types, locations, and attributes.

After successfully getting the LLM to learn the rules, we will access the LLM in our game, which will be developed in Unity, to provide the player with a Quick Map Building System (QMBS) as a core component of the game's content generation. This system is designed to provide users with an intuitive and rich authoring interface and real-time feedback output from LLM models. This means that the LLM can directly interact with the game environment and understand the player's creative intent provided through their natural language descriptions.

Next, we designed a user-friendly interface that allows players to use natural language to describe the game content they wish to create. For example, a player could tell the system, "An island in the middle of the map with lush forests" These descriptions are passed as input to the LLM model, which understands the player's description and generates the appropriate textual feedback. This feedback is generated by the LLM model, which has learned to understand the rules based on the player's ideas and descriptions, and it ensures that the game's content meets the player's expectations.

In order to enable players to understand better and visualize their ideas, we combine the LLM feedback text with pictures of specific map elements. This means that the generated map elements will be presented visually to the game players, who can see the results of their creations in real-time. For example, villages, forests, and rivers will be presented as in-game images and scenes so players can visualize how their creations have been translated into in-game elements.

This approach provides a rich creative experience and allows players to engage more deeply in creative design. They can observe in real-time how their ideas are rendered in the game, making adjustments and fine-tuning at any time to ensure that the content meets their expectations. This visual generation process enhances the player's sense of engagement and provides an intuitive feedback mechanism for them to explore and create unique game worlds.

4   Design and Implementation of the QMBS System

4.1   Rules

The QMBS is an innovative tilemap generation system designed to enhance the efficiency of map editing by allowing players to input text descriptions to create map layouts. After researching popular map editing games, the system introduces seven types of tiles for players to choose from according to their needs. In addition to the core text-based tilemap generation editing mode, the QMBS provides additional features such as brush editing and preset map settings, making it closer to a realistic game map editing experience. The system is not designed specifically for a specific game but is a universal and exploratory map editing solution. The design philosophy and principles of the QMBS system can be integrated into existing game map editing tools with simple adaptation, helping players customize their game maps more effectively.

4.2   Tile Map Elements

Grassland Mountain Hamlet Desert Stone Wood Water

Fig. 2. Seven kinds of basic tiles

A tilemap is constructed from a series of carefully arranged tiles, and the number of editable tile types is a critical factor in determining its content richness and visual diversity. Each tile has unique features and attributes that play a different role in different game environments. After thoroughly studying the characteristics of the basic map elements in the mainstream simulation management games currently on the market, we considered both the traditional characteristics and diversity requirements of the tiles. Ultimately, we identified seven types of tiles, each with its own unique features yet complementing each other. These serve as preset options in our system for players to choose from. These seven tile types include grassland, mountain, hamlet, desert, stone, wood, and water, as shown in Fig. 2, each embodying rich gameplay implications waiting to be explored and experienced by players. The specific connotations of each tile type are as follows:

1. *Grassland*: In both reality and games, grassland serves as a place for people to walk and engage in activities, and it is also a fundamental terrain element in games. For example, grass blocks in "Minecraft" are one of its distinctive features. Grassland typically represents areas where players can build or develop agriculture in games, and it can also be transformed into other terrains like sandy soil or rocks.
2. *Mountain*: Mountain tiles represent undulating terrains, adding complexity to navigation and exploration. In games, mountain tiles may be the location of resources or strategic points, providing advantages in terms of visibility, among other things. For example, mountain tiles in "Civilization VI" offer additional defensive advantages and resources for city development. Additionally, mountain tiles in the "Animal Crossing" series enhance the natural beauty of the game and diversify its layout.

3. *Hamlet*: Hamlet tiles represent residential areas for players or NPCs in games and serve as critical interactive nodes. They provide functions such as resting and trading for players and are the living areas for residents in simulation and management games. For example, in "The Sims" series, players can design and build various houses, representing homes for residents and reflecting the game's social and cultural environments.

4. *Desert*: In simulation management games, desert tile is often seen as peripheral or undeveloped areas. Despite their loose texture making them less suitable for construction or agricultural activities, it is this very characteristic that provides players with unique opportunities for expansion and innovation. Taking "Cities: Skylines" as an example, desert tile become ideal zones for planning urban expansion. Although the development potential of these terrains is limited, they introduce new challenges and opportunities to urban planning and development, inspiring players to explore different urban construction strategies.

5. *Stone*: Stone tiles typically represent rugged or barren game areas suitable for constructing defensive structures or extracting resources. Rock tiles in simulation and management games often indicate regions with abundant resources but higher development difficulty. For example, in the island-building simulation game "The Survivalists," rock tiles are essential locations for gathering stones and crafting tools, playing a vital role in the island's development and self-sufficiency.

6. *Wood*: Wood tiles are the primary source of wood and wild resources in simulation and management games. For example, forests in "Life is Feudal: Forest Village" provide resources and play a crucial role in maintaining ecological balance. Proper forest management is vital for the long-term sustainable development of villages.

7. *Water*: Water tiles like rivers and lakes are vital components of agriculture and ecosystems in simulation and management games. For example, in the "Farming Simulator" series, water tiles play a crucial role in irrigation and agricultural production. Players need to plan water sources wisely to support crop growth and the development of animal husbandry. Lakes and rivers in "Stardew Valley" are important places for fishing and crop irrigation, making them essential for farm management.

4.3   Tile Map Editing Methods

The uniqueness of the QMBS lies in the fact that players only need to provide a short description of no more than 40 characters to generate the desired terrain. In addition, players can use a map brush to personalize specific areas or select preset map layouts to create a more perfect effect. Here are detailed descriptions of various map editing functions:

Brush Editing Mode: Players can experience more intuitive and free editing fun in this mode. They can select any of the seven essential terrain elements as a "brush" on the map editing interface and then click on any area of the tile

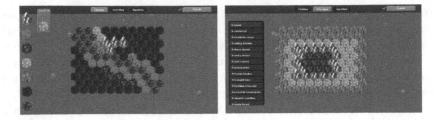

Fig. 3. The Brush Editing Mode (left) and the Preset Mode (right)

map to change the terrain. This method gives players more creative space and flexibility, allowing them to create unique map landscapes like artists painting on canvas, whether the layout of mountains and rivers or the distribution of forests and grasslands; precise implementation can be achieved through brush editing, as shown in Fig. 3(left).

Preset Mode: This mode is suitable for players who want to quickly create terrain with specific features. In this mode, players can choose from multiple preset terrains such as "dense forest" or "spectacular mountains." Once selected, the entire 10×10 tile map will immediately transform into a new map matching the selected preset. This method simplifies the complex detail editing process and ensures that the generated map matches the player's expectations in style and characteristics, as shown in Fig. 3(right).

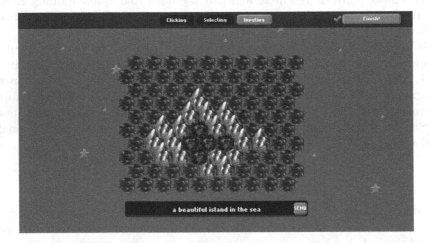

Fig. 4. Text Input Editing Mode: Players can input their descriptions, and subsequently, the system will autonomously generate corresponding maps.

Text Input Editing Mode: Players can succinctly describe their desired map features in the game interface's input field. Using a concise sentence of no more than 40 characters, such as "blue sea golden sand" or "emerald green grassland," players can outline their ideal map. This word limit encourages players to think carefully and clarify their needs, expressing them in a concise text. After the description is complete, click the "Generate" button, and the QMBS system will generate the corresponding map based on the description and display it to the player, as shown in Fig. 4.

4.4   LLM Rule

Foundation Models. When implementing the QBMS model, we primarily focused on utilizing existing large-scale language models to generate game maps and explore their potential in map editing and enhancing player experience. Among the various options of large pre-trained models, we decided to adopt mature models available in the market rather than retraining or fine-tuning open-source models like GPT-2, LLaMA, and PandaLLM.

According to a Comprehensive Performance Evaluation Report of Large Language Models conducted by Tsinghua University, ChatGPT has displayed remarkable superiority in semantic comprehension, output articulation, and generalization capabilities. It possesses a vast knowledge base and performs exceptionally well in role-playing and specific scenario simulations. ChatGPT has also introduced the GPT Builder tool, which allows users to create custom GPT assistants through pre-written language descriptions. For non-traditional applications like QBMS that require generating spatial information content, ChatGPT is capable of generating the desired content more accurately and reliably. Therefore, in the specific implementation of QBMS, we have chosen ChatGPT as the preferred model.

Rules Understanding. In developing the QMBS system, our core task is to ensure that LLMs can accurately understand and respond to user requests. Specifically, this means generating terrain matrices that meet specific standards based on user instructions. To achieve this goal, we employed the GPT Builder tool. This tool enabled us to articulate the core principles of terrain generation and to create customized GPT models. This ensures that the LLM can generate terrain data according to user-defined dimensions, constituent elements, and format standards. Through continuous experimentation and adjustment, we ultimately formulated effective and stable prompts.

The design of GPT Builder is user-friendly, with a clear and straightforward workflow that mainly includes two steps: model construction and model validation. In the model construction step, developers can input detailed rule instructions through the control interface on the left side, allowing for fine adjustments to the model's internal logic. In the model validation step, the real-time preview interface on the right side gives developers a window to view the output effects of the model instantly. Additionally, GPT Builder offers the functionality of model saving and editing, which means that even after the model has been used, developers can still make necessary modifications and improvements.

Here are detailed prompts for this step:

As a sophisticated map generator, you can create corresponding text tile maps based on detailed descriptions. The map is presented as a 10 × 10 text matrix, where each character precisely represents a specific terrain type, forming an overhead view of the tile map.

In this matrix, the available terrain attributes and their meanings are as follows:

Desert: Symbolizes sandy terrain, such as deserts or dunes.

Hamlet: Represents residential houses or villages, indicating the presence of buildings or human settlements in that area.

Wood: Represents trees or forests, indicating that the area is covered with woodlands or greenery.

Stone: Symbolizes stones or rocks, indicating rocky terrain.

Grassland: Represents grassland, fields, meadows, or uncultivated wasteland.

Mountain: Represents mountains or highlands, indicating a rugged terrain.

Water: Represents aquatic environments, including rivers, lakes, and other similar features.

The generated tile map will be presented as a 10-row by 10-column text array, where each character accurately depicts the terrain feature at the corresponding position. There is no need for spaces or separator symbols between these characters to maintain visual cleanliness and clarity. Please ensure that the output contains only 100 characters and that the character types are limited to seven types above.

Before creating the map matrix, you need to analyze the content of the text description thoroughly and decide which elements should be included in the map, such as mountains, rivers, forests, etc. Also, consider how these natural features should be represented on the map, for example, the direction of the mountains or the flow of the rivers. Then, based on these characteristics, output a 10 × 10 text matrix to represent the tile map.

GPT Builder will adjust the model based on the prompt words. If we input "a forested area" to describe the terrain, GPT will output the content as shown in Fig. 5.

4.5 Data

According to previous research [30], providing diverse examples is crucial for a more accurate understanding of intent and familiarity with specific rules in the generation task. To achieve this, we have created a collection of examples featuring various terrains to enhance GPT's comprehension and standardize its output format. These examples are organized in a CSV file, following the format of "prompt words" and "output," and uploaded to GPT Builder for learning

4.6 Unity-Based Map Generation Plugin

The implementation of the QMBS relies on the Unity3D engine, and its core functionality is achieved through the interaction of three main components: the User

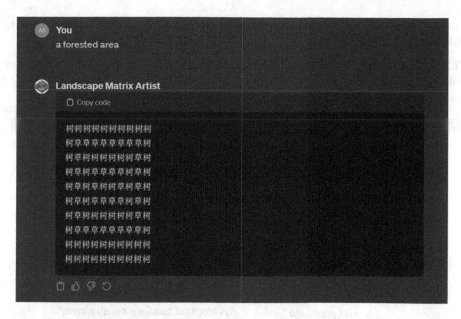

Fig. 5. The output of the customized GPT model when the prompt "a forested area" is input

Interaction Module, the Customized GPT-4 Model, the Map Drawing Module, and the Tiles Database. The following is a detailed organization and description of each module in the QMBS:

User Interaction Module: The crucial part of this module is the text input module, which is responsible for receiving player input regarding the terrain in the form of text descriptions. These descriptions may include terrain features, the layout of map elements, or specific style requirements. To help players refine their requirements, this module limits the length of the text input to 40 characters. Once the player input is complete, the terrain description text is sent to OpenAI's API interface via UnityWebRequest and processed by our customized GPT-4 model.

Customized GPT-4 Model: Our customized GPT-4 model parses the text to extract terrain elements and spatial layout features when receiving descriptive text input. The model then generates a 10×10 text matrix densely packed with information to represent the generated tile map. This text matrix provides detailed records of the terrain's spatial positions and the tiles' attributes. Once the text matrix is generated, the information is transmitted to the map drawing module via the API interface for visualization processing.

Map Drawing Module. This module loads the appropriate tile sprites from the tile database based on the tile position information and type attributes recorded in the text matrix to allow players to see the generated map. The module then sets the corresponding tile types at the respective positions in the tilemap, ultimately achieving the visual display of the entire tilemap.

Tiles Database: This database contains specific tile sprites for seven types of tiles, consistent with those used by large language models. The map drawing module can access the block data to draw the block.

Through the collaborative work of these modules, the QMBS effectively transforms the terrain text descriptions provided by players into visualized maps, as shown in Fig. 6.

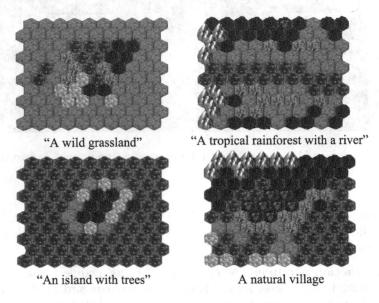

"A wild grassland"   "A tropical rainforest with a river"

"An island with trees"   A natural village

Fig. 6. Some examples of tilemap generated using the QBMS

5   Conclusion

This study proposes an innovative design approach that integrates procedural content generation (PCG) with the player's gaming experience by translating the player's natural language inputs into rules for generating game content. Using the combination of PCG and LLM, we empower players to intuitively and in real-time participate in and adapt game content creation. This type of interaction dramatically enhances players' creative freedom and deepens their gaming experience.

Our research highlights the great potential of the LLM in the field of game design, introducing a novel approach to the creation of game elements. This interactive model, which involves the player directly in the game design process, takes game creation and experience to a new level and opens up possibilities for future game development.

Acknowledgments. This work was partly supported by Shenzhen Key Laboratory of next generation interactive media innovative technology (No: ZDSYS202 10623092001004)

References

1. Ashlock, D., Lee, C., McGuinness, C.: Search-based procedural generation of maze-like levels. IEEE Trans. Comput. Intell. AI Games **3**, 260–273 (2011)
2. Stanley, K., Cornelius, R., Miikkulainen, R., D'Silva, T., Gold, A.: Real-time learning in the NERO video game. In: Proceedings of the AAAI Conference on Artificial Intelligence and Interactive Digital Entertainment, vol. 1, pp. 159–160 (2005)
3. Melotti, A., Moraes, C.: Evolving roguelike dungeons with deluged novelty search local competition. IEEE Trans. Games **11**, 173–182 (2018)
4. Kartal, B., Sohre, N., Guy, S.: Generating Sokoban puzzle game levels with Monte Carlo Tree search (2016)
5. Sturtevant, N.: An argument for large-scale breadth-first search for game design and content generation via a case study of fling! In: Proceedings of the AAAI Conference on Artificial Intelligence and Interactive Digital Entertainment, vol. 9, pp. 28–33 (2013)
6. Cardamone, L., Lanzi, P., Loiacono, D.: TrackGen: an interactive track generator for TORCS and speed-dreams. Appl. Soft Comput. **28**, 550–558 (2015)
7. Epstein, M.: How 'no man's sky' composes completely original music for every player. Digital Trends (2016)
8. Fredericks, E., DeVries, B.: (Genetically) improving novelty in procedural story generation. In: 2021 IEEE/ACM International Workshop on Genetic Improvement (GI), pp. 39–40 (2021)
9. Macedo, Y., Chaimowicz, L.: Improving procedural 2D map generation based on multi-layered cellular automata and Hilbert curves. In: 2017 16th Brazilian Symposium on Computer Games and Digital Entertainment (SBGames), pp. 116–125 (2017)
10. Yahya, N., Fabroyir, H., Herumurti, D., Kuswardayan, I., Arifiani, S.: Dungeon's room generation using cellular automata and Poisson Disk Sampling in roguelike game. In: 2021 13th International Conference on Information & Communication Technology and System (ICTS), pp. 29–34 (2021)
11. Summerville, A., et al.: Procedural content generation via machine learning (PCGML). IEEE Trans. Games **10**, 257–270 (2018)
12. Volz, V., Schrum, J., Liu, J., Lucas, S., Smith, A., Risi, S.: Evolving Mario levels in the latent space of a deep convolutional generative adversarial network. In: Proceedings of the Genetic and Evolutionary Computation Conference, pp. 221–228 (2018)
13. Ping, K., Dingli, L.: Conditional convolutional generative adversarial networks based interactive procedural game map generation. In: Advances in Information and Communication: Proceedings of the 2020 Future of Information and Communication Conference (FICC), vol. 1, pp. 400–419 (2020)
14. Park, K., Mott, B., Min, W., Boyer, K., Wiebe, E., Lester, J.: Generating educational game levels with multistep deep convolutional generative adversarial networks. In: 2019 IEEE Conference on Games (CoG), pp. 1–8 (2019)
15. Gutierrez, J., Schrum, J.: Generative adversarial network rooms in generative graph grammar dungeons for The Legend of Zelda. In: 2020 IEEE Congress on Evolutionary Computation (CEC), pp. 1–8 (2020)

16. Bontrager, P., Togelius, J.: Learning to generate levels from nothing. In: 2021 IEEE Conference on Games (CoG), pp. 1–8 (2021)
17. Irfan, A., Zafar, A., Hassan, S.: Evolving levels for general games using deep convolutional generative adversarial networks. In: 2019 11th Computer Science and Electronic Engineering (CEEC), pp. 96–101 (2019)
18. Guzdial, M., Riedl, M.: Toward game level generation from gameplay videos. arXiv preprint arXiv:1602.07721 (2016)
19. Blizzard Entertainment: Warcraft III: Reign of Chaos (2002)
20. Entertainment, B., Entertainment, W. & Others Starcraft ii. *Blizzard Entertainment.* (2010)
21. Zhang, B.F.: Exploring the Attractive Factors of Mobile Tower Defense Games (2018). https://api.semanticscholar.org/CorpusID:116323950
22. Zhong, X., Xu, J.: Measuring the effect of game updates on player engagement: a cue from DOTA2. Entertain. Comput. **43**, 100506 (2022)
23. Rutherford, K.: This is how a garden grows: cultivating emergent networks in the development of Stardew Valley. Indie Games Digit. Age **8**, 123 (2020)
24. Medler, B:. Visual game analytics. In: Game Analytics: Maximizing the Value of Player Data, pp. 403–433 (2013)
25. Thorn, A.: Making a 2D game. In: Moving from Unity to Godot, pp. 105–160. Apress, Berkeley, CA (2020). https://doi.org/10.1007/978-1-4842-5908-5_4
26. Halpern, J.: Developing 2D Games with Unity. Apress, Berkeley, CA (2019). https://doi.org/10.1007/978-1-4842-3772-4
27. Chapman, A.: Is Sid Meier's civilization history? Rethink. Hist. **17**, 312–332 (2013)
28. Duncan, S.: Minecraft, Beyond Construction and Survival. Carnegie Mellon University (2011)
29. Mukherjee, S.: Age of empires. In: How to Play Video Games, vol. 1, pp. 157–164 (2019)
30. Todd, G., Earle, S., Nasir, M., Green, M., Togelius, J.: Level generation through large language models. In: Proceedings of the 18th International Conference on the Foundations of Digital Games (2023). https://doi.org/10.1145/3582437.3587211

Enhancing Pokémon VGC Player Performance: Intelligent Agents Through Deep Reinforcement Learning and Neuroevolution

Gian Rodriguez⬀, Edwin Villanueva⬀, and Johan Baldeón⁽✉⁾⬀

Pontificia Universidad Católica del Perú, Lima, Peru
{gianp.rodriguezp,ervillanueva,johan.baldeon}@pucp.edu.pe
https://www.pucp.edu.pe/

Abstract. Competitive Pokémon battles demand deep strategic thinking and real-time decision-making, posing challenges for players seeking to optimize their performance. This paper presents a novel approach utilizing Deep Reinforcement Learning and Neuroevolution to develop AI agents that excel in the complex Video Game Championships (VGC) format. We address the limitations of existing research by focusing on VGC double battles and their evolving rules. Our intelligent agents learn through game experience, offering competitive challenges to human players and suggesting optimal moves in an intuitive interface. Additionally, we present a tool that leverages the agent's knowledge to promote the use of underutilized Pokémon, fostering gameplay diversity and enriching the experience for both novice and experienced players. This research demonstrates the potential of AI-powered assistance in enhancing player experience and strategic decision-making within complex competitive games.

Keywords: Intelligent agents · Deep reinforcement learning · Neuroevolution · Agent-based gaming · Pokémon battles · Game AI

1 Introduction

The realm of online multiplayer gaming, particularly in the eSports sector, has undergone a significant transformation, where video games have evolved into competitive platforms that demand profound strategic thinking and skill from players. At the core of this gaming landscape is the concept of players controlling agents within the game, allowing them to select their agents before engaging in a match [13]. In this paper, we delve into the world of the highly popular Pokémon video game and its competitive arena, which offers a plethora of resources and tools to aid players in refining their competitive prowess [10].

Pokémon battles stand out for their unique characteristics, featuring simultaneous, real-time moves rather than the conventional turn-based style. This distinctive complexity gives rise to a diverse array of strategies, gameplay levels, and metagame theories, rendering it a game of remarkable intricacy [5]. The crux

X. Fang (Ed.): HCII 2024, LNCS 14730, pp. 275–294, 2024.
https://doi.org/10.1007/978-3-031-60692-2_19

of the challenge lies in calculating the optimal sequence of moves to secure positional advantages each turn, ultimately leading to victory. The intricate nature of Pokémon battles has led players to either rely on established strategies or utilize damage calculators, which, while beneficial, can be time-intensive [4].

In recent years, artificial intelligence (AI) agents leveraging deep reinforcement learning have achieved superhuman performance in tackling challenging classic games [12,14,16] , opening up new avenues for addressing previously insurmountable problems [11]. Pokémon battles, with their partially observable states, atomic turns, and stochastic elements, present a captivating AI challenge distinct from traditional games [15]. However, existing research predominantly focuses on single battles, overlooking the more intricate double battles, particularly within the Video Game Championships (VGC) format, where rules undergo annual evolution [4].

The absence of agents operating within the VGC 2022 format poses a significant constraint, impeding players from experimenting with new teams or strategies against a diverse array of opponents. As the metagame evolves and converges around dominant strategies, Pokémon that are less favored remain underutilized. Fostering diversity in gameplay is crucial for player engagement and enjoyment, particularly for newcomers seeking a more varied gaming experience.

This research endeavor aimed to address the challenges players encounter in simplifying team construction and strategy development for the VGC 2022 format. The primary objective was to develop an intelligent agent that excels in VGC 2022, serving as a competitive adversary for human players, assisting in strategic decision-making, and advocating for the utilization of less popular Pokémon.

The article investigates various machine learning approaches for building Pokémon game agents. Additionally, a software tool was developed based on the best performing agent to help the user choose strategic moves and use less popular Pokémon. The results indicate successful selection and development of intelligent agents tailored for this intricate environment, with agents adept at optimizing their actions in battle. Key software components have been devised to enhance communication with the game environment and augment user comprehension. Furthermore, a recommendation system has been established, empowering players to make informed decisions during matches. Ultimately, this project equips users with tools to foster diversity in gameplay and bolster their journey towards becoming adept and strategic Pokémon trainers.

2   Related Work

The realm of online multiplayer gaming, particularly in eSports, has undergone a significant transformation, where video games have evolved into competitive platforms that demand profound strategic thinking and skill from players. Central to this gaming landscape is the concept of players controlling agents within the game, enabling them to select their agents before engaging in a match.

In this context, the Pokémon video game and its competitive scene stand out, offering a wealth of resources and tools to assist players in refining their competitive abilities.

Pokémon is one of the most popular video games in the world. Most people are familiar with the basics, such as catching Pokémon and leveling them up to make them stronger. However, unknown to most is the extensive competitive scene that exists behind Pokémon battles. There are forums, websites, damage calculators and databases, all with the purpose of helping players improve their competitive skills [10].

Pokémon battles are renowned for their unique characteristics, featuring simultaneous, real-time moves rather than the traditional turn-based style. This distinctive complexity gives rise to a diverse array of strategies, gameplay levels, and metagame theories, making it a game of remarkable intricacy. The core challenge lies in calculating the optimal sequence of moves to secure positional advantages each turn, ultimately leading to victory. The intricate nature of Pokémon battles has led players to either rely on established strategies or utilize damage calculators, which, while beneficial, can be time-intensive.

Recent advancements in artificial intelligence (AI) have seen agents leveraging deep reinforcement learning achieve superhuman performance in tackling challenging classic games, opening up new possibilities for addressing previously insurmountable problems [1–3,6–8]. Pokémon battles, with their partially observable states, atomic turns, and stochastic elements, present a captivating AI challenge distinct from traditional games. However, existing research predominantly focuses on single battles, overlooking the more intricate double battles, particularly within the Video Game Championships (VGC) format, where rules undergo annual evolution [9].

3   Motivation and Objectives

The absence of intelligent agents capable of operating within the VGC 2022 format poses a significant constraint, impeding players from experimenting with new teams or strategies against a diverse array of opponents. As the metagame evolves and converges around dominant strategies, Pokémon that are less favored remain underutilized. Fostering diversity in gameplay is crucial for player engagement and enjoyment, particularly for newcomers seeking a more varied gaming experience.

This research endeavor aimed to address the challenges players encounter in simplifying team construction and strategy development for the VGC 2022 format. The primary objective was to develop an intelligent agent that excels in VGC 2022, serving as a competitive adversary for human players, assisting in strategic decision-making, and advocating for the utilization of less popular Pokémon.

Specific objectives and corresponding outcomes encompassed the selection of a machine learning-based method, the proposal of an aid tool for strategic moves, and the implementation of a tool to promote the use of less popular

Pokémon. The results indicate successful selection and development of intelligent agents tailored for this intricate environment, with agents adept at optimizing their actions in battle. Key software components have been devised to enhance communication with the game environment and augment user comprehension. Furthermore, a recommendation system has been established, empowering players to make informed decisions during matches. Ultimately, this project equips users with tools to foster diversity in gameplay and bolster their journey towards becoming adept and strategic Pokémon trainers.

4   Methodology

The methodology employed in this research aimed to enhance Pokémon VGC player performance through the utilization of intelligent agents developed using deep reinforcement learning and neuroevolution. The process involved a series of steps encompassing the development, evaluation, and validation of these agents within the Pokémon VGC 2022 format. The following sections outline the key components and procedures utilized in this study:

4.1   Software Component Development

- **RE.1.1**: A software component was created to establish connectivity between the intelligent agent and the online gaming environment of Pokémon VGC (See Fig. 1).
- **RE.1.2**: Another software component was designed to extract supplementary information from the game environment.
- **Tools**: Python, GitHub, Sublime Text, WebSocket.
- **Methods**: Syntax analyzer.

4.2   Candidate Agent Development

- **RE.1.3**: Candidate methods based on machine learning were defined for the development of Pokémon VGC 2022 format game agents.
- **RE.1.4**: Candidate agents were developed to operate within the Pokémon VGC 2022 format. In Fig. 2, you can see the command line interface with the record of the interactions that the intelligent agent is carrying out, in the first column, you can see the number of battles, in the second column, the number of the turn in which the has acted for that battle, in the third column, the reward received for the action generated in that turn, in the fourth column, the historical reward, and finally, in the fifth column, the date and time in which the agent has acted. Likewise, it is observed that the agent receives a reward of -9999 when performing illegal actions, to teach it not to perform them in certain states.
- **Tools**: Python, GitHub, Sublime Text, NumPy, TensorFlow, Keras.
- **Methods**: Machine learning.

Fig. 1. Connecting a random agent to a battle using the Battle Module, which allows the user to directly confront this agent.com.

Fig. 2. Training the intelligent agent for the case of deep reinforcement learning method using Double Deep Q-Learning algorithm.

4.3   Agent Evaluation and Selection

– **RE.1.5**: Candidate agents operating in the Pokémon VGC 2022 format were evaluated to determine the most suitable opponent for human players.

- **RE.1.6**: The selected agent was evaluated against human players to validate its satisfactory performance in the Pokémon VGC 2022 format.
- **Tools**: Python, Sublime Text, WebSocket, IA-PUCP Servers.

Figure 3 shows the evolution of the average, maximum and minimum reward obtained by the neuroevolution method using the NEAT algorithm based on 6 genomes, where the rewards obtained have been limited to a range between 10,000 and −10,000, which are sufficiently indicative of whether the agents have carried out a satisfactory action or vice versa. Within the last 200 generations carried out after 5 d of training, it is observed that the maximum reward (NEAT MAX) reaches the maximum limit in more than 50% of the generations indicated above, while there are several generations in which the minimum reward (NEAT MIN) reaches 5000, which indicates that in certain scenarios that are repeated between each battle, the 6 genomes perform too many satisfactory actions; However, there are other scenarios in which the maximum reward (NEAT MAX) decreases too much, which indicates that there is great difficulty on the part of the 6 genomes to perform any good action.

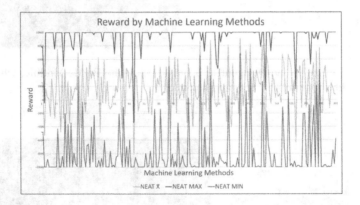

Fig. 3. Evolution of the average, maximum and minimum reward obtained by the neuroevolution method using the NEAT algorithm based on 6 genomes.

Figure 4 shows the comparison of the evolution between the rewards obtained by the neuroevolution method using the NEAT algorithm (NEAT $\bar{X}$) and the deep reinforcement learning method using the Double Deep Q-Learning algorithm. Where it is seen that both methods perform satisfactorily or cause difficulty in certain scenarios, likewise, it is seen that the performance of the deep reinforcement learning method is a little more stable, that is, it presents fewer peaks concerning neuroevolution.

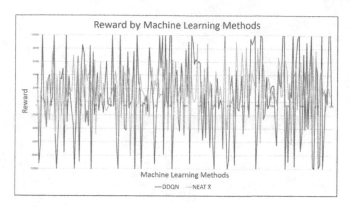

Fig. 4. Evolution of rewards obtained by the neuroevolution method using the NEAT algorithm and the deep reinforcement learning method using the Double Deep Q-Learning (DDQN) algorithm.

Figure 5 shows the trend of the reward obtained using the Double Deep Q-Learning algorithm, where the linear evolution indicates a positive trend until reaching a reward slightly greater than 1000.

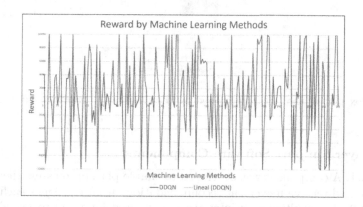

Fig. 5. Linear evolution of the reward obtained using the Double Deep Q-Learning (DDQN) algorithm.

Figure 6 shows the trend of the reward obtained using the NEAT algorithm, where the linear evolution indicates a positive trend until reaching a reward slightly greater than 2000.

Additionally, in Fig. 7, using a box plot, it is easier to see that the reward obtained by the NEAT algorithm is slightly higher compared to the Double Deep Q-Learning algorithm, and a negative outlier value of −8000 is also observed, which It is claimed that there are situations in which all genomes present difficulties as mentioned above.

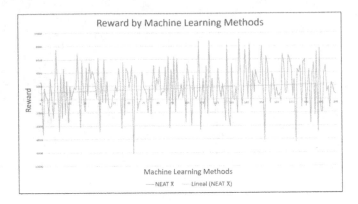

Fig. 6. Linear evolution of the reward obtained using the NEAT algorithm.

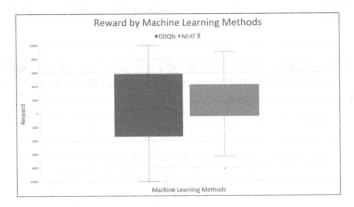

Fig. 7. Box plot of the reward obtained by the Double Q-Learning and NEAT algorithms.

4.4   Player Support Software Components

- **RE.2.1**: A component was developed to enable players to assess their performance and receive movement recommendations from the agent each turn.
- **RE.2.2**: An intuitive help interface was created for users to visualize their performance and agent recommendations seamlessly (See Fig. 11a, Fig. 11b and Fig. 13).
- **Tools**: Python, GitHub, Sublime Text, WebSocket.
- **Methods**: Syntax analyzer, Usability in interfaces.

For the development of the component, the websocket of the Pokémon Showdown! web simulator was used to automatically obtain updates on the status of the battle, for this purpose syntax analyzers developed have also been used to interpret the JSON strings that the aforementioned web simulator sends on a recurring basis.

A report is delivered that aims to constantly inform the user of the status of the battle through the Analysis Module; this is done through the command line interface of the operating system. The tags that are present in the report are listed below.

- **[INFO]**: Indicates the login status of the user or agent in the web simulator and the phases of the battle.
- **[ACTION]**: Indicates the recommendation made by the comprehensive genetic algorithm for the team preview and the intelligent agent for the battle turns.
- **[REWARD]**: Indicates the reward obtained for the actions performed by the user in the web simulator.
- **[COLOR]**: Indicates the colors in hexadecimal coding that represent the elemental types associated with the recommended movements. Table 1 presents the list of colors used in the software component.
- **[ERROR]**: Indicates if there was an error when starting the battle using the module, the messages are as follows: Incorrect user or password!, The team does not comply with the rules of the format!

In Fig. 8 we can see a model of the aforementioned report, where the lines indicating the key are repeated n times according to the number of turns in the battle, except that the first instruction indicates a wait for the user. At the end of the battle, the name of the winning user will be indicated and also a counter that indicates whether the application user has won or lost the battle.

```
          [INFO]     Iniciando sesión…
          [INFO]     ¡Sesión iniciada con éxito!
          [INFO]     Buscando una batalla en formato gen8vgc2022
          [INFO]     ¡Batalla en curso!
          [INFO]     Vista Previa del Equipo
          [ACTION]   ['Pokémon 1', 'Pokémon 2', 'Pokémon 3', 'Pokémon 4']
        ┌ [INFO]     Turno: ? / Action: forceSwitch / Action: Wait
   n    │ [REWARD]   [????, ????]
 veces ─┤ [ACTION]   ['Movimiento 1', 'Objetivo 1', 'Movimiento 2', 'Objetivo 2']
        └ [COLOR]    ['#??????', '#??????', '#??????', '#??????', '#??????', '#??????']
          [INFO]     Ganador: ???
          [INFO]     W: 1 L: 0
```

Fig. 8. Model of the report that the Analysis Module delivers to the player.

The unit tests for receiving the report can be seen in Fig. 9. Which follows the model presented in Fig. 8. Where the states before starting a battle, the recommendation for the team preview, and the recommendations from turn 1 along with the rewards obtained and the colors associated with each movement that the Pokémon must perform.

Table 1. Table of colors in hexadecimal coding using the RGB model that represents the movements associated with some type.

Type	Hexadecimal color
Normal	#A8A77A
Fire	#EE8130
Water	#6390F0
Electric	#F7D02C
Grass	#7AC74C
Ice	#96D9D6
Fighting	#C22E28
Poison	#A33EA1
Ground	#E2BF65
Flying	#A98FF3
Psychic	#F95587
Bug	#A6B91A
Rock	#B6A136
Ghost	#735797
Dragon	#6F35FC
Dark	#705746
Steel	#B7B7CE
Fairy	#D685AD

Figure 10 shows the start of a battle between an agent using the aforementioned model against a human whose pairing was random.

Figure 11a shows the recommendation made by the intelligent agent through the Analysis Module for the equipment preview stage. In Fig. 11b, after continuing with the recommendation received in Fig. 11a, the recommendation for turn 1 is now displayed, including the performance obtained by the previous action, which is -1826 (the human opponent has a slight advantage).

Figure 12 shows the status of turn 2 after continuing with the recommendation received in Fig. 11b.

Finally, in Fig. 13 we can see the recommendation for turn 2 and, most importantly, the historical performance obtained by following the previous recommendation, which is a positive value, obtained by adding the -1826, received initially, with 2647, received by the action on turn 1, so the positive value of 821 is obtained (slight advantage for the intelligent agent).

4.5 Team Building and Feedback

- **RE.3.1**: A software component was devised for constructing the team utilized by the agent in Pokémon VGC 2022 battles.

Fig. 9. Reception of the report, by the player, through the Windows Command Prompt.

Fig. 10. Starting a battle between the intelligent agent and a human through random pairing.

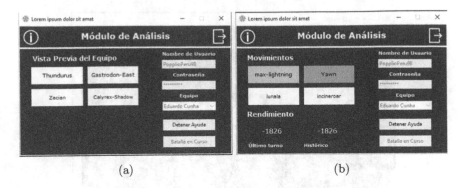

(a)   (b)

Fig. 11. (a) Recommendation received through the Analysis Module for the equipment preview. (b) Recommendation and performance received through the Analysis Module for turn 1.

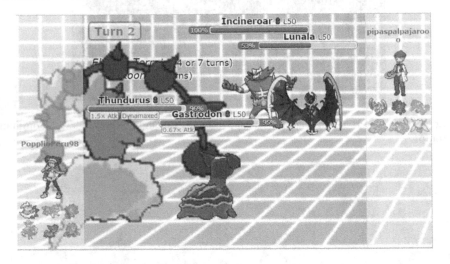

Fig. 12. Turn 2 state, where the intelligent agent now has a slight advantage.

- **RE.3.2**: An interface was established to facilitate users in intuitively building the team employed by the agent in battles (See Fig. 14).
- **RE.3.3**: A software component was developed for the agent to diagnose weaknesses in the team during training.
- **RE.3.4**: An interface was created for users to receive feedback on potential improvements to the team (See Fig. 15).
- **Tools**: Python, GitHub, Sublime Text, WebSocket, IA-PUCP Servers.
- **Methods**: Syntax analyzer, Usability in interfaces.

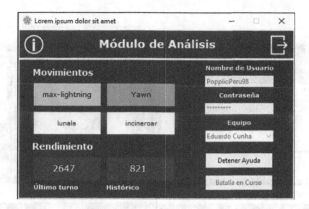

Fig. 13. Recommendation and performance received through the Analysis Module for turn 2.

By following this comprehensive methodology, the research aimed to enhance the gaming experience of Pokémon VGC players by providing intelligent agent support and tools for strategic decision-making and team optimization within the competitive landscape of the VGC 2022 format.

5 Results

This project successfully addressed the challenges faced by players in simplifying team building and strategy development for the VGC 2022 format. The study aimed to develop intelligent agents that excel in the VGC 2022 environment, serving as competitive opponents for human players, providing strategic guidance, and promoting the use of less popular Pokémon. The key findings of the research are as follows:

5.1 Effectiveness of AI Agents

- The developed AI agents demonstrated remarkable learning capabilities and optimization of actions within the VGC 2022 format.
- Through deep reinforcement learning and neuroevolution techniques, the agents adapted to the complex and dynamic nature of Pokémon battles, showcasing superior performance.

In Fig. 16, you can see the list of the 8 opposing teams that both algorithms have faced during their evaluation, which correspond to the teams that have been used by the players who have obtained the first 7 and eleventh places in the Pokémon World Championship developed on the third weekend of August 2022.

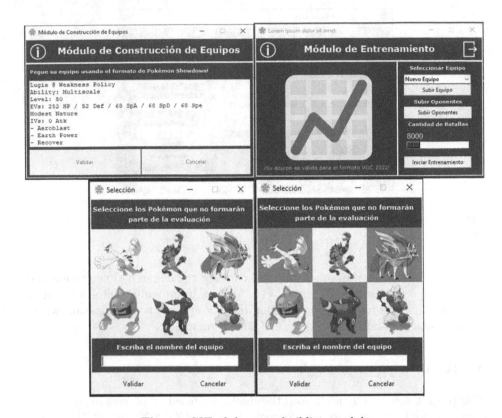

Fig. 14. GUI of the team building module.

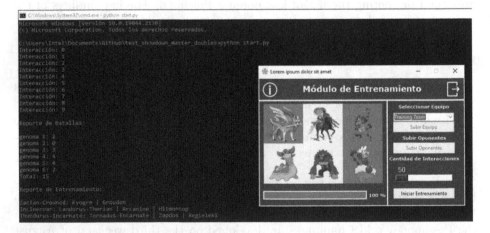

Fig. 15. GUI of the module for receiving feedback on potential improvements to the team.

Fig. 16. Opponent teams used during the evaluation of the Double Deep Q-Learning and NEAT algorithms.

Table 2 shows the position table obtained by the DDQN algorithm against the 8 teams mentioned above after 10 interactions with each one. Table 3 shows the position table obtained by the NEAT algorithm against the 8 teams mentioned above after 10 interactions with each one carried out by the 6 genomes. It is worth noting that unlike the position table presented for the DDQN algorithm, the battles carried out entirely by the algorithm are counted, since the DDQN algorithm receives support from a random agent according to the value of the exploration factor, which gives it a certain advantage.

In Fig. 17, you can see the radial graph of the reward obtained using the DDQN algorithm with respect to the 8 opposing teams, where it is validated that the algorithm presents a slight advantage with respect to teams 2, 6 and 7, and a disadvantage compared to team 4.

In Fig. 18, you can see the radial graph of the reward obtained using the NEAT algorithm with respect to the 8 opposing teams, where it is validated that the algorithm presents a greater disadvantage in general with respect to the 8 teams, but there is a slight advantage over team 4.

Therefore, it is validated that, after 5 d of training, the NEAT algorithm using 6 genomes presents a slight improvement compared to the DDQN algorithm, using 219 inputs in the input and output layer, with 4 hidden layers, 219, 111, 54 and 38 in each respectively. Since in the position table, it can be seen that the NEAT algorithm, which does not receive any support at the beginning of its training, is presenting an improvement that is reflected in the linear trend; However, the DDQN algorithm, despite receiving help from a random agent that fills its memory with random actions, has seen less improvement, this is reflected

Table 2. Position table of results obtained by the DDQN algorithm.

DDQN			
W	L	T	R
6	4	0	740.80
8	2	1	4402.20
6	4	2	−351.30
5	5	3	1215.50
6	4	4	1593.90
8	2	5	3751.10
8	2	6	4164.80
6	4	7	781.90

Table 3. Table of results obtained by the NEAT algorithm.

NEAT X̄			
W	L	T	R
30	30	0	−234.78
25	35	1	−501.35
19	41	2	−2070.17
30	30	3	2.85
27	33	4	−1479.28
28	32	5	−185.33
23	37	6	−1263.48
22	38	7	−994.88

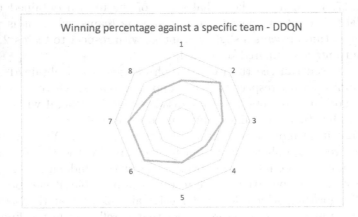

Fig. 17. Radial graph of the reward obtained using the DDQN algorithm with respect to the 8 opposing teams.

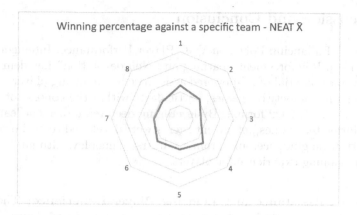

Fig. 18. Radial graph of the reward obtained using the NEAT algorithm with respect to the 8 opposing teams.

in the position table where the random agent has supported in DDQN decisions up to 50% of the time; However, it does not present a greater improvement compared to the DDQN that has started without support from the beginning.

5.2 Functionality and User Experience of Software Components

- The software components designed to aid players in strategic decision-making and team evaluation proved to be effective and user-friendly.
- Players could assess their performance, receive recommendations from the agent for each turn, and visualize their progress through an intuitive interface, enhancing their overall gaming experience.

5.3 Impact on Promoting Diverse Gameplay

- The tools implemented in the research project significantly contributed to promoting diversity in gameplay within the VGC 2022 format.
- By encouraging the use of less popular Pokémon and providing feedback on team weaknesses and improvements, the tools empowered players to explore new strategies and enhance their skills as Pokémon trainers.

The research outcomes were supported by data analysis, visualizations, and examples that illustrated the effectiveness of the developed AI agents and software components. The project not only enhanced player performance but also contributed to a more engaging and varied gaming experience for Pokémon VGC players. The results highlighted the successful integration of intelligent agents, machine learning techniques, and user-centric design principles to address the evolving challenges in competitive Pokémon battles, ultimately benefiting both experienced players and newcomers seeking a competitive edge in the VGC 2022 format.

6   Discussion and Conclusion

The project "Enhancing Pokémon VGC Player Performance: Intelligent Agents Through Deep Reinforcement Learning and Neuroevolution" has demonstrated the significant potential of AI-powered assistance in enhancing player experience and learning in competitive games, particularly within the context of Pokémon battles in the VGC 2022 format. By leveraging deep reinforcement learning and neuroevolution techniques, intelligent agents were developed to optimize actions, provide strategic guidance, and promote diverse gameplay, ultimately elevating the overall gaming experience for players.

AI-Powered Assistance in Enhancing Player Experience: The integration of intelligent agents into the gameplay environment has shown promising results in assisting players to make informed decisions, optimize their strategies, and adapt to dynamic battle scenarios. The AI-powered assistance not only enhances player performance but also fosters a deeper understanding of game mechanics and strategic thinking, contributing to a more engaging and rewarding gaming experience.

Importance of User-Centered Design: Central to the success of the AI tools developed in this research is the emphasis on user-centered design principles. By prioritizing user experience, feedback mechanisms, and intuitive interfaces, the tools effectively support players in their decision-making processes, providing relevant recommendations and insights tailored to individual gameplay styles. This user-centric approach ensures that the AI tools are not only effective but also engaging and accessible to a wide range of players.

Ethical Considerations of AI in Competitive Gaming Environments: As AI technologies continue to play a significant role in competitive gaming environments, it is crucial to address ethical considerations surrounding their use. Transparency, fairness, and accountability in AI algorithms are essential to maintain a level playing field for all players. Additionally, ensuring that AI-powered assistance complements rather than replaces human decision-making is vital to preserve the integrity and skill-based nature of competitive gameplay.

Conclusion: In conclusion, the research project has made significant contributions to the field of HCI in games by showcasing the potential of AI-powered assistance in enhancing player performance and learning in competitive gaming environments. By developing intelligent agents through deep reinforcement learning and neuroevolution, the study has demonstrated the effectiveness of AI tools in optimizing gameplay strategies, promoting diversity, and improving user experience.

Future Directions: Moving forward, future research in this line of work could explore advanced AI techniques, such as multi-agent systems and ensemble learning, to further enhance the capabilities of intelligent agents in competitive gaming. Additionally, investigating the long-term impact of AI-powered assistance on player skill development, engagement, and enjoyment could provide valuable insights for designing more personalized and adaptive gaming experiences. By continuing to innovate at the intersection of AI and HCI in games, researchers can unlock new possibilities for enhancing player experiences and shaping the future of competitive gaming environments.

Acknowledgements. This project has received financial support from the Pontifical Catholic University of Peru (CAP project PI0762).

References

1. Abukhait, J., Aljaafreh, A., Al-Oudat, N.: A multi-agent design of a computer player for nine men's morris board game using deep reinforcement learning. In: 2019 6th International Conference on Social Networks Analysis, Management and Security, SNAMS 2019, pp. 489–493 (2019). https://doi.org/10.1109/SNAMS.2019.8931879

2. Aljaafreh, A., Al-Oudat, N.: Development of a computer player for seejeh (a.k.a seega, siga, kharbga) board game with deep reinforcement learning. In: Procedia Computer Science. vol. 160, pp. 241–247 (2019). https://doi.org/10.1016/j.procs.2019.09.463

3. Arun, E., Rajesh, H., Chakrabarti, D., Cherala, H., George, K.: Monopoly using reinforcement learning. In: IEEE Region 10 Annual International Conference, Proceedings/TENCON, pp. 858–862 (2019). https://doi.org/10.1109/TENCON.2019.8929523

4. Barros, P., Sciutti, A.: All by myself: learning individualized competitive behavior with a contrastive reinforcement learning optimization. Neural Netw. **150**, 364–376 (2022). https://doi.org/10.1016/j.neunet.2022.03.013

5. Chen, K., Lin, E.: Gotta train'em all: learning to play pokemon showdown with reinforcement learning (2018). https://cs230.stanford.edu/projects_fall_2018/reports/12447633.pdf

6. Czech, J., Willig, M., Beyer, A., Kersting, K., Fürnkranz, J.: Learning to play the chess variant crazyhouse above world champion level with deep neural networks and human data. Front. Artif. Intell. **3** (2020). https://doi.org/10.3389/frai.2020.00024

7. Gu, S., Chen, T., Li, J., Wang, W., Liu, H., He, R.: Deep reinforcement learning for real-time strategy games. In: Proceedings of the AAAI Conference on Artificial Intelligence, vol. 33, pp. 1286–1293 (2019)

8. Hu, J., Zhao, F., Meng, J., Wu, S.: Application of deep reinforcement learning in the board game. In: 2020 IEEE International Conference on Information Technology,Big Data and Artificial Intelligence (ICIBA), vol. 1, pp. 809–812 (2020). https://doi.org/10.1109/ICIBA50161.2020.9277188

9. Huang, D., Lee, S.: A self-play policy optimization approach to battling pokémon. In: 2019 IEEE Conference on Games (CoG), pp. 1–4 (2019). https://doi.org/10.1109/CIG.2019.8848014

10. Khosla, K., Lin, L., Qi, C.: Artificial Intelligence for Pokemon Showdown. Ph.D. thesis, PhD thesis, Stanford University (2017). https://docplayer.net/63514819-Artificial-intelligence-for-pokemon-showdown.html
11. Llobet Sanchez, M.: Learning complex games through self play-Pokémon battles. B.S. thesis, Universitat Politècnica de Catalunya (2018). http://hdl.handle.net/2117/121655
12. Mnih, V., Kavukcuoglu, K., Silver, D., Graves, A., Antonoglou, I., Wierstra, D., Riedmiller, M.: Playing atari with deep reinforcement learning (2013). https://doi.org/10.48550/ARXIV.1312.5602
13. Reis, S., Reis, L.P., Lau, N.: Vgc ai competition - a new model of meta-game balance AI competition. In: 2021 IEEE Conference on Games (CoG). IEEE (Aug 2021). https://doi.org/10.1109/cog52621.2021.9618985
14. Silver, D., et al.: Mastering the game of go with deep neural networks and tree search. Nature 529(7587), 484–489 (2016). https://doi.org/10.1038/nature16961
15. Simões, D., Reis, S., Lau, N., Reis, L.P.: Competitive deep reinforcement learning over a pokémon battling simulator. In: 2020 IEEE International Conference on Autonomous Robot Systems and Competitions (ICARSC), pp. 40–45 (2020). https://doi.org/10.1109/ICARSC49921.2020.9096092
16. Tesauro, G.: Programming backgammon using self-teaching neural nets. Artif. Intell. 134(1–2), 181–199 (2002). https://doi.org/10.1016/s0004-3702(01)00110-2

Towards Semi-Automated Game Analytics: An Exploratory Study on Deep Learning-Based Image Classification of Characters in Auto Battler Games

Jeannine Thiele⬤, Elisa Thiele⬤, Christian Roschke⬤, Manuel Heinzig⬤, and Marc Ritter$^{(\boxtimes)}$⬤

Faculty of Applied Computer and Biosciences University of Applied Sciences Mittweida, Technikumplatz 17, 09648 Mittweida, Germany
{jeannine.thiele,elisa.thiele,christian.roschke,manuel.heinzig, marc.ritter}@hs-mittweida.de

Abstract. With the growing interest in player profiles and game analytics, semi-automated annotation can provide data which can serve as a source of information for enhancing game strategies and the overall gaming experience. This study proposes a tooling-based workflow to tackle this subject while using the mini game *Chicken Dinner* in *Heroes Charge* as an example. It includes the implementation of a Deep Learning network in *MATLAB*, which runs the classification process for a semi-automated annotation. To accomplish this, several game play videos were recorded and split into individual frames. After a manual selection, these serve as training and testing images for the network. The outcomes of this research include a reproducible workflow that enables a partial annotation for auto-battler games, as well as a system that facilitates such annotation for the *Chicken Dinner* mini-game in *Heroes Charge*. The conclusion indicates that semi-automated annotation of digital game play is possible. This study shows an approach to semi-automated annotation and presents promising prospects for future research and applications.

Keywords: Game analytics · Semi-automated annotation · Transfer learning · Neural networks · Team lineups · Video annotation · Image classification

1   Introduction

Data-driven game design and player profiling have gained more importance in today's game development and e-sports business, for optimizing game design and enhancing the overall gaming experience. Therefore, this research focuses on facilitating the annotation of game characters on a digital battlefield during mobile gaming sessions. This topic is crucial in the context of understanding the players' behavior, in genres like sports simulations, strategy games and survival

X. Fang (Ed.): HCII 2024, LNCS 14730, pp. 295–306, 2024.
https://doi.org/10.1007/978-3-031-60692-2_20

shooters. It gains insights into player strategies, supports game balance assessments [1], and facilitates the creation of personalized gaming content. Additionally, in the competitive gaming area, insights into hero selections are essential for improving e-sports dynamics. This study presents an approach that allows third party users to dive deeper into the game statistics, to improve their personal game strategy or get to know more about the game mechanics, alongside the developers. The research's broader context underscores its significance in the realm of data-driven game design, ultimately shaping player satisfaction and contributing to the sustained success of mobile games.

2   Concept and System Architecture

The main objective of this study was to develop and implement a workflow to facilitate semi-automated game annotation by automatically identifying game characters (referred to as heroes in this research) represented on extracted images from video snippets. This also involved identifying specific properties like the level of these heroes, developing a workflow for the annotation process, and displaying all the collected information while minimizing the amount of human interaction required.

2.1   Featured Auto-Battler Game: *Chicken Dinner*

These investigations are carried out on the example of the auto battler game *Chicken Dinner*. This mini game is part of the tactical adventure RPG *Heroes Charge* [2] from the company *uCool Inc.*, whose deep overall auto battler combat system engages players in the long run. The mobile game is composed of a growing number of mini-games, various battlefields, and quests which grants a wide experience for the players with arbitrary parameterization and tuning opportunities.

Chicken Dinner is a recurring event in which the players must collect and level up heroes to protect their crystals to win the game. Each round starts with six players. All of them must buy and place heroes on the battlefield strategically. Only the starting budget and the rewards received in the current game are available to purchase heroes. Therefore, a shop offers a random selection of heroes in each round which can be refreshed for a fee (referred to in-game as crystal energon), but only contains stronger heroes as the game progresses. In addition, the success of a team of heroes is influenced by factors such as power-up items, team formation, group advantages (which you get from characters of the same races and groups), rarity of the heroes, and their star level (usually three heroes of the same star level merge to create a stronger hero of the next level) as well as all these factors of the opponent's team.

The main goal is to survive wave after wave and compete against the other players and computer-controlled teams by strategic decision making while choosing, upgrading and expanding the number of a teams specific characters. Each game consists of a maximum of 30 waves starting by usually buying and placing

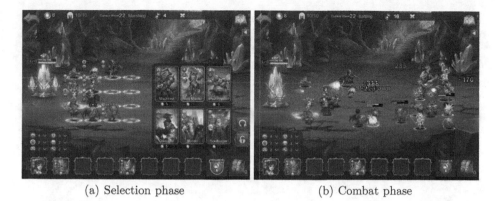

(a) Selection phase   (b) Combat phase

Fig. 1. Game play screenshots showing samples of the two different game phases.

one to three heroes. Computer opponents must always be fought in wave 1, 2, 10, 15, 20, 25, and 30. In the other rounds you compete against other players.

Each player has to defend his mighty purple crystal starting with 100 energy points being decreased while loosing a wave against an opponent. Players are removed from the game when their crystal energy reaches zero. Furthermore, each player starts the game without heroes and with an equal set of the game currency with a choice of three different upgrade options. This means everyone can only rely on their own tactics and knowledge instead of general player success such as overpowered heroes or purchased advantages.

This secluded game environment offers fair conditions and asks for the experience of the gamer for a victorious outcome. Because of these points, it's interesting to analyze different player profiles and get to know more about the different approaches and their outcomes. Also due to its separate game environment, recurring structure, and equal conditions for all players, regardless of their general success, efforts and playtime spent in *Heroes Charge*, it is particularly suitable for analysis.

Division into Game Phases. In the project, the game videos are divided into selection and combat phases. In addition, the course of the game is considered in so-called waves, which are defined in the game itself. A game usually lasts between 20 and 30 waves with each wave consisting of a *selection* and a *combat phase*. All interactions between the player and the game take place in the selection phase (see Fig. 1(a)). The results of the combat phase can also be derived there. This phase includes actions such as buying and selling heroes, placing heroes on the field, distributing items, and improving crystal levels. In the combat phase, the assembled team fights autonomously against an opposing team (see Fig. 1 (b)). The player has no influence on the action and is just an observer of the battle.

Selection of Relevant Data for Annotation. By reviewing the start and end pictures of the selection phases of a game, the current wave, the reward points before and after the purchase of hero cards, the number of heroes, the position and identity of the heroes, group combinations, the hero cards in the substitution bench, the crystal level and the crystal energy can be detected. In this research, it was decided to focus on the automatic recognition of the heroes and their position, because this aspect was considered to be the most interesting based on gaming experience. Other aspects such as group combinations and the number of heroes can also be derived directly from the identification of the heroes and their position. To put the information into a meaningful context, the current wave is noted as well.

Image Classification of Heroes. Image classification is the process of categorizing images into predefined classes or labels based on their content [3]. Using this approach breaks down the task of recognizing the heroes and their positions into smaller, simpler tasks. In concrete terms, this means for this project that cutouts are extracted from the images of the selection phases, each of which showing a hero (or containing an empty spot). All heroes and empty positions are therefore classes, thus a trained neural network can find a suitable class for the content of the image patches. By then including the original position of the patches, the identity and the position of the hero can be obtained. In addition, textual information given in numbers like gained energon crystals and the current wave number can be extracted by common OCR techniques like *Tesseract* [4].

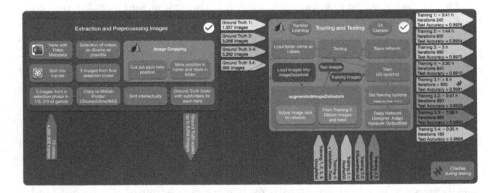

Fig. 2. Overview of the image classification workflow for hero recognition in *Chicken Dinner* from video footage starting with the extraction and pre-processing of images to the training and testing of different setups summarizing the results of various training sessions.

Fig. 3. Visualization of the indexing of hero characters on the battlefield on the player side. To address each position, a combination of numbers representing the rows and letters representing the columns have been used.

2.2 Methods and Tools

In order to develop a semi-automated annotation of *Chicken Dinner* game sequences, an experimental approach was applied. In addition, many different tools such as *Snapmotion*, *MATLAB* and a spreadsheet editor were combined. *Snapmotion* is an app for *Apple* devices that extracts images from videos. It was used to export training and test images from the recorded game videos but is of course also necessary for the annotation workflow. The integrated software development environment *MATLAB* [5] was utilized to semi-automate the game play annotation. In this study, it performs transfer learning on pre-trained image classification networks like *GoogLeNet* [6] (see Fig. 2) and was used to build several applications around it. This includes live scripts for image splitting, renaming, and the annotation output. Furthermore, a workflow for semi-automated annotation was created. The spreadsheet editor was used to create tables such as a hero register, which includes all game characters with their characteristics and group affiliations, and the table that provides an overview of the available video footage and their metadata.

2.3 Requirements and Preparations

The training of a deep learning network demands large data sets of relevant images. Therefore, 73 game play videos of *Chicken Dinner* lasting more than 30 h (4,595,908 frames) in total were recorded in compliance with predefined recording criteria. Furthermore, a table that contains information and meta data about each video was compiled to create more clarity and facilitate the selection of relevant videos. The selected video footage was divided into single images (see Fig. 3) by using the tool *Snapmotion*. The extracted images were then further processed by segmentation into hero positions (see Fig. 4).

In order to get an overview of the possible focal points of an annotation and the necessary procedure, game annotations were carried out manually on sample

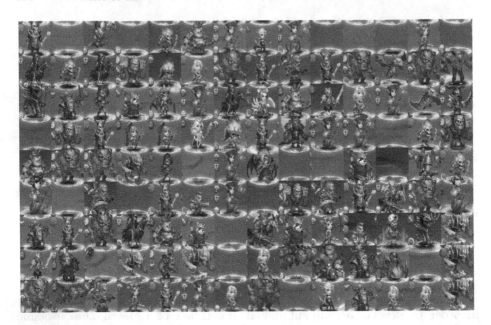

Fig. 4. A compilation of 126 randomly extracted hero patches visualizing the variability of the training images with different environmental and lighting conditions.

snippets yielding specific annotation tables. In addition, a hero register was created that includes all heroes, their characteristics and group affiliations as well as a group register that contains all groups, their advantages and group members. These registers make it possible to easily retrieve additional information about classified characters during the annotation process.

3   Implementation

This section will give deeper insights into the workflow that was used to implement the semi-automated *Chicken Dinner* game annotation in *MATLAB* by using pre-trained neural Networks.

3.1   Extraction and Preparation of Training Images

The recorded game play videos have been separated into images by extracting every eighth frame using the program *Snapmotion*. In order to retrieve relevant and heterogeneous image patches, three keyframes are retrieved each from three different selection phases. Using a *MATLAB* live script 16 image patches from every keyframe were extracted showing the positions a hero is located at or could be placed on the battlefield annotated in a chess board like manner. In order to get a set of training data, a folder for every hero and empty positions was created resulting in 54 folders. Overall 6,864 images had been saved and labeled. More

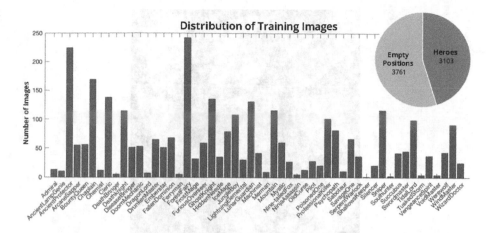

Fig. 5. The bar chart shows the distribution of training images across the 53 different hero classes. In addition the pie chart displays the ratio of images displaying empty positions compared to image patches containing heroes.

than half of them contain image patches from empty positions. The remaining 3,103 images of heroes are not evenly divided into all types of heroes as shown in the diagram (see Fig. 5).

3.2 Image Processing with *MATLAB*

The images were uploaded to the workspace by using the *ImageDatastore* container. The images were separated into training and testing data where 20% of each sub-folder was reserved for the testing of the created hero classifiers. To fit in a pre-trained network, the images had to follow a specific size. For most networks, the size had to be 224×224 px. Therefore, the images had been resized by using a *MATLAB* resize command or an *AugmentedImageDatastore* supporting automated image augmentation via affine transformations (see Fig. 6) reducing over-fitting during the training processes [7].

3.3 Transfer Learning for Pre-trained Networks in *MATLAB*

In the development of this image classifier, the best results were accomplished by performing transfer learning on the pre-trained network *GoogLeNet*. Other pre-trained networks had been tested as well but this chapter will focus on *GoogLeNet* and its transferability to other networks.

We use *MATLAB's Deep Network Designer* to perform transfer learning with a pre-trained network by changing the output size to the number of the requested 54 classes including a class for every hero and a none-class for all the empty positions. The adjusted network was saved to the workspace and loaded into our live script by additionally using training options like *stochastic gradient*

Fig. 6. Example of 8 augmented and affine transformated training images.

descent with momentum [8] and an initial learning rate of 0.001 performing 30 epochs for each training process.

The infographic (see Fig. 2) provides information about the different training settings tested. Such as the use of different sizes of training image sets and the different pre-trained networks.

3.4   Test Stage

In order to evaluate the performance and accuracy of the classifier trained, unseen test patches were used (refer to 3.2). Those data were classified by the newly trained classifier. A confusion chart shows the distribution of the recognized objects.

Fig. 7. The *Chicken Dinner* hero *Chaplain* in its different evolutionary states (from left to right as a one, two, and three star level hero).

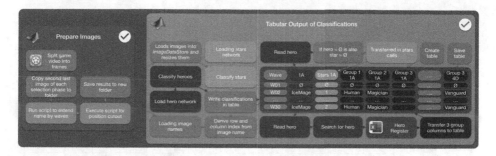

Fig. 8. Infographic showing the workflow to create the annotation table of hero positions, evolutions, and affiliations by using the results of the hero classification within the process of semi-automated annotation.

3.5 Recognizing the Level of Evolution of Characters

An additional classifier specialized in recognizing the heroes level of evolution also referred to as star level was trained to collect more semi-automated game play information. For the procurement of training and testing data images from the data pool for hero recognition have been chosen (some of each star level of every hero (according to availability)) and manually divided into three different classes (one star, two stars, and three stars). The different star levels can be recognized, for example, by the size of the heroes and the color of the glowing ring surrounding them (see Fig. 7).

The training setup was derived from the setup of the hero classifier. Several options like different pre-trained networks and initial learning rates have been tested. The best results have been reached by transfer learning *ResNet50* with an initial learning rate of 0.01. This training took about 15 minutes for training 30 epochs with 30 iterations each on a *Apple MacBook Pro M2 with 24 GB RAM*. The described procedure for testing the hero classifiers (3.4) achieved a result of 85.71% accuracy.

3.6 Classification Output: Creating an Annotation Table

To use the classifications for game play annotation, they have to be displayed in an informative way. Therefore, an annotation table in *MATLAB* was created that was meant to display the heroes, their positions, groups, and star level for every wave of a game play video. In order to fill the table with game play information heroes and star levels have to be classified. First, an image from every selection phase of the video was extracted with several *MATLAB* live scripts extending their names by the corresponding wave number being split into battlefield positions. We classify these image patches by using our classification output method while adapting to the network input size required. These hero and star level classification results were written into the table by extracting specific parts of their image names. The procedure described is also shown in more detail in Fig. 8.

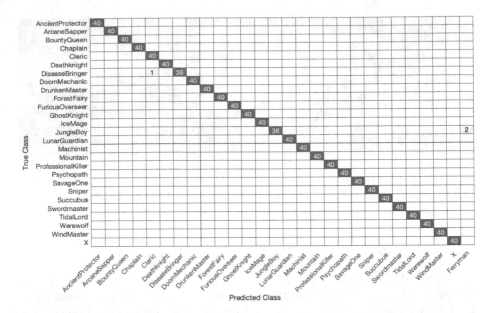

Fig. 9. Confusion chart showing the results of an attempt in which half of the different classes were tested with 40 images each. The checked classes are those from which the most sample images have been collected.

4   Evaluation

To evaluate the performance of the trained model, the 27 classes containing the highest number of images were selected. The folders of these classes were manually reduced to 40 images each, to ensure an equal set of testing data. These images haven't been used as training data before. As shown in the confusion chart (see Fig. 9), the classifier performed very well on these images with only three misinterpreted heroes resulting in a 99.72 percent accuracy. It could be expected that a further test with all hero classes would result in a slightly worse accuracy as the classifier didn't have as much training data from those missing classes.

Furthermore, the accuracy of the semi-automated annotation was tested. Its performance on recognizing heroes and their evolution stages in the images of each wave and writing this data down in the according document was evaluated on a sample video lasting 28 min and 32 s (6,420 frames). For consistency, it was ensured that this video only included heroes from the trained model. All heroes and empty positions were correctly identified for this example. The evolution level recognition chose the right hero classes in 72.05 percent of all cases. Overall, the semi-automated annotation achieved a 95.89 percent accuracy in this example. A shortened version of the table can be seen in Fig. 10. To visualize the semi-automated annotation results, the cells containing correct annotations have been colored in green while false ones are shown in orange. Furthermore, the data that the blue cells are containing was filled in semi-automated based on correct annotations.

5 Summary and Future Work

The achievements of this exploratory study include workflows and applications for *Chicken Dinner* annotation based on the game footage and extracted images. Specifically, this means that with the input of *Chicken Dinner* images (of each wave) and a few user inputs, a game annotation can be automatically generated. This includes information about the hero's lineup, their level (one to three stars), and group affiliation (see Fig. 8). In addition, several neural networks for recognizing heroes and their levels were trained. Also, insights into the design and execution of such training were gained, and many workflows, for example for game recording, image processing, and the procuring of training images, have been defined.

The developed workflow for annotating team lineups in *Chicken Dinner* allows to get deeper insight into different game strategies and the importance of specific heroes and their groups. Helping other players to develop their ideal strategies, but also supporting developers in understanding deeper game mechanics to improve their projects. Furthermore, the approaches that were worked on

Wave	1A‑H	1A‑S	1A‑G	1B‑H	1B‑S	1B‑G	1C‑H	1C‑S	1C‑G	1D‑H	1D‑S	1D‑G	2A‑H	2A‑S	2A‑G	2B‑Hero	2B‑Star Level	2B‑Groups	2C‑H	2C‑S	2C‑G	2D‑H	2D‑S	2D‑G	3A‑H	3A‑S	3A‑G	3B‑H	3B‑S	3B‑G	3C‑H	3C‑S	3C‑G	3D‑H	3D‑S	3D‑G	4A‑H	4A‑S	4A‑G	4B‑H	4B‑S	4B‑G	4C‑H	4C‑S	4C‑G	4D‑H	4D‑S	4D‑G
1	X	X		X	X		X	X		F	1	T	X	X		X			C	1	B	X	X		X	X		X	X		X	X		X	X		X	X		X	X		X	X		X	X	
2	X	X		X	X		X	X		F	1	T	X	X		TidalLord	1	Elemental	C	2	B	X	X		X	X		P	1	U	X	X		X	X		X	X		X	X		X	X		X	X	
3	X	X		X	X		X	X		F	1	T	X	X		TidalLord	1	Elemental	C	1	B	X	X		X	X		P	1	U	X	X		X	X		X	X		X	X		X	X		X	X	
4	X	X		X	X		X	X		F	1	T	X	X		TidalLord	2	Elemental	C	1	B	X	X		X	X		P	1	U	X	X		X	X		X	X		W	1	L	X	X		X	X	
5	X	X		X	X		X	X		F	1	T	X	X		TidalLord	2	Elemental	C	1	B	X	X		X	X		P	1	U	X	X		X	X		X	X		W	1	L	X	X		X	X	
6	X	X		X	X		X	X		F	1	T	X	X		TidalLord	2	Elemental	C	2	B	X	X		X	X		P	1	U	X	X		X	X		X	X		W	1	L	X	X		X	X	
7	X	X		X	X		X	X		F	1	T	X	X		TidalLord	2	Elemental	C	2	B	G	1	U	X	X		P	1	U	X	X		X	X		X	X		W	1	L	X	X		X	X	
8	X	X		X	X		X	X		F	1	T	X	X		TidalLord	2	Elemental	C	2	B	G	1	U	X	X		P	1	U	X	X		X	X		X	X		W	1	L	X	X		X	X	
9	X	X		X	X		X	X		F	1	T	X	X		TidalLord	2	Elemental	C	2	B	G	1	U	X	X		P	1	U	X	X		X	X		X	X		W	1	L	X	X		X	X	
10	X	X		X	X		X	X		F	1	T	X	X		TidalLord	2	Elemental	C	2	B	G	1	U	X	X		P	1	U	X	X		X	X		X	X		W	1	L	X	X		X	X	
11	X	X		X	X		X	X		F	1	T	X	X		TidalLord	2	Elemental	C	2	B	G	1	U	X	X		P	1	U	X	X		X	X		X	X		W	1	L	X	X		X	X	
12	X	X		X	X		X	X		F	1	T	X	X		TidalLord	2	Elemental	C	2	B	G	1	U	X	X		P	1	U	X	X		X	X		X	X		W	1	L	X	X		X	X	
13	X	X		X	X		X	X		F	1	T	X	X		TidalLord	2	Elemental	C	2	B	G	1	U	X	X		P	1	U	X	X		X	X		X	X		W	1	L	X	X		X	X	
14	X	X		X	X		X	X		F	1	T	X	X		TidalLord	2	Elemental	C	2	B	G	1	U	X	X		P	1	U	X	X		X	X		X	X		W	1	L	X	X		X	X	
15	X	X		L	1	L	X	X		F	1	T	X	X		TidalLord	2	Elemental	C	2	B	G	1	U	X	X		P	1	U	X	X		X	X		X	X		W	1	L	X	X		X	X	
16	X	X		L	1	L	X	X		F	1	T	X	X		TidalLord	2	Elemental	C	2	B	G	1	U	X	X		P	1	U	X	X		X	X		X	X		W	1	L	X	X		X	X	
17	X	X		L	1	L	X	X		F	1	T	X	X		TidalLord	2	Elemental	C	2	B	G	1	U	X	X		P	1	U	X	X		D	1	U	X	X		W	1	L	X	X		X	X	
18	X	X		L	1	L	X	X		F	1	T	X	X		TidalLord	2	Elemental	C	2	B	G	1	U	X	X		P	1	U	X	X		D	1	U	X	X		W	1	L	X	X		X	X	
19	X	X		L	1	L	X	X		F	3	T	X	X		TidalLord	2	Elemental	C	1	B	G	2	U	X	X		P	2	U	X	X		D	2	U	X	X		W	2	L	X	X		X	X	
20	X	X		L	1	L	X	X		F	3	T	X	X		TidalLord	2	Elemental	C	1	B	G	2	U	X	X		P	1	U	T	2	E	D	2	U	X	X		W	1	L	C	2	B	X	X	
21	X	X		L	1	L	L	1	L	F	1	T	X	X		X			C	2	B	G	2	U	X	X		P	2	U	T	3	E	D	2	U	X	X		W	2	L	X	X		X	X	
22	X	X		L	1	L	L	1	L	F	1	T	X	X		ProfessionalKiller	1	Undead	C	2	B	G	2	U	X	X		P	1	U	T	3	E	D	2	U	X	X		W	2	L	X	X		X	X	
23	X	X		L	1	L	L	1	L	F	3	T	X	X		ProfessionalKiller	1	Undead	C	2	B	G	2	U	X	X		P	1	U	T	3	E	D	2	U	X	X		W	2	L	X	X		X	X	
24	X	X		L	1	L	L	1	L	F	1	T	X	X		ProfessionalKiller	1	Undead	C	2	B	G	2	U	X	X		P	2	U	T	3	E	D	2	U	X	X		W	2	L	X	X		X	X	

H - Hero
S - Star Level
G - Groups
X - Elements of none class, i.e. empty position

▮ - correct classification
▮ - automatically filled and correct
▮ - incorrect classification

Fig. 10. Shortened table visualizing the checked semi-automated annotation results. The cells have been minimized in order to provide an overview about the annotation results. Representative the position 2B is shown in its full size.

could be transferred to other games in subsequent research or further developed concerning player profiling.

In summary, this study successfully developed a semi-automated annotation technique for hero placements in the mobile game *Chicken Dinner*, which can provide valuable insights into player strategies and game balance. The significance of this study lies in its contribution to data-driven game design, enhancing player satisfaction, and supporting the sustainable success of mobile games. In addition, the workflow and applications developed in this study can serve as a model for analyzing team lineups in other games, expanding the impact of the research on the gaming industry.

References

1. Sahibgareeva, G.F., Kugurakova, V.V.: Game balance practices. Program Systems: Theory and Applications **13**(3), 255–273 (2022)
2. Wang, W., Zhang, R.: Improved game units balancing in game design through combinatorial optimization. In: 2021 IEEE International Conference on e-Business Engineering (ICEBE), pp. 64–69. Guangzhou, China (2021). https://doi.org/10.1109/ICEBE52470.2021.00022
3. Bi, Y., Xue, B., Zhang, M.: Genetic Programming for Image Classification. Volume 24. Springer Cham (2021)
4. Smith, R.: An overview of the tesseract OCR engine. In: Ninth International Conference on Document Analysis and Recognition (ICDAR 2007), Curitiba, Brazil (2007). https://doi.org/10.1109/ICDAR.2007.4376991
5. Smith, E.: MATLAB. In: Introduction to the Tools of Scientific Computing. TCSE, vol. 25, pp. 185–210. Springer, Cham (2020). https://doi.org/10.1007/978-3-030-60808-8_9
6. Szegedy, C. et al.: Going deeper with convolutions. In: 2015 IEEE Conference on Computer Vision and Pattern Recognition (CVPR), pp. 1–9. Bosten, MA, USA (2015). https://doi.org/10.1109/CVPR.2015.7298594
7. Kaur, T., Gandhi, T.K.: Deep convolutional neural networks with transfer learning for semi-automated brain image classification. In: Machine Vision and Applications 2020, vol. 31, 20. (2020). https://doi.org/10.1007/s00138-020-01069-2
8. Yanli, L. et al.: An improved analysis of stochastic gradient descent with momentum. In: 34th Conference on Neural Information Processing Systems (NeurIPS 2020), Vancouver, Canada (2020). https://doi.org/10.48550/arXiv.2007.07989

An Affect-Aware Game Adapting to Human Emotion

Panagiotis Vrettis(✉) ⓘ, Andreas Mallas ⓘ, and Michalis Xenos ⓘ

Computer Engineering and Informatics Department, Patras University, Patras, Greece
{vrettis,mallas,xenos}@ceid.upatras.gr

Abstract. The vision of affect-aware video games outlines games that can dynamically react to the emotion of the player. In this paper, we designed and developed a game that incorporates an emotion recognition system that follows this principle, aiming at adapting gameplay elements based on the player's current emotion. The game's design employs the user's emotion as an implicit form of input method (in contrast to explicit methods in other works) by adjusting multiple in-game parameters ranging from more easily distinguishable such as audio and visual changes to more subtle such as journal entries, emotionally themed hints/presentation, and ending quotes. An exploratory study aimed at exploring the viability of the system with 22 participants showed promising results regarding game satisfaction while also indicating that the game achieved its design goal of utilizing user emotion as an implicit input method. Finally, results suggest that visual and audio changes were the most easily perceived by the users, with other changes being less noticeable.

Keywords: Affective Computing · Affect-Aware Games · Adaptive Games · Implicit Interactions

1 Introduction

It could be argued that video games are at the forefront of technological innovation, allowing state-of-the-art technologies to be available and affordable to the end users. The field of Human-Computer Interaction (HCI) focuses on the interactions between the player and the game, including the input methods, which is an area that has seen great strides recently. The first video game only used a mechanical telephone dialer that later gave way to specialized dedicated controllers with buttons and control sticks as inputs [1]. In the last decades, additional input devices grew in popularity that incorporated accelerometers, gyro sensors, body tracking, and input combinations like tangible tools with multi-touch interfaces [2]. In the academic field, there is ongoing research in input methods for video games, with studies using head movement and facial expressions as input methods [3, 4], and others use more "passive" inputs such as a brain-computer interface-controlled video game that uses consumer-grade electroencephalography (EEG) hardware [5] or an adaptive game that uses EEG [6].

Lankes et al. [7] developed a game that uses facial expressions as an explicit input method and states that "...the player is forced to reproduce specific facial expressions to

X. Fang (Ed.): HCII 2024, LNCS 14730, pp. 307–322, 2024.
https://doi.org/10.1007/978-3-031-60692-2_21

progress in the game" and the facial expressions are not a representation of their actual emotions but an explicit input method where the users manipulate their expressions based on the game state. One could argue that this contrasts with the vision of affect-aware video games where the game can dynamically react to the recognized current emotion of the player [8, 9] and thus indicating an implicit nature of the emotions as game input.

Nacke et al. [10] categorizes affect video game input as directly or indirectly controlled by the user, with Facial Emotion Recognition (FER) input being a direct control of the game as the players can willingly change their facial expressions as a game input. This distinction is rational, but regarding the direct input, it only states the possibility of direct control and not the actual usage.

The type of adaptation the game incorporates might influence a game input, even if characterized as being directly controlled. Robinson et al. categorized the mapping of the input to the actual changes that occur in-game in two categories [11]. The first is the "action" category that corresponds to changes that "control direct actions or game mechanics", and the second is the "context" category that refers to changes that affect "the mood or context of the game".

We argue that FER, even though characterized as a direct control input, can function as an implicit input -similar to the distinction [12] made between implicit and explicit biofeedback and comparably to how the term "implicit" is used in research in the field of context-aware systems [13, 14]- in the sense that the user's emotions are not -by game design- actively and intentionally adjusted by the user as an input for the game when incorporated into a game with context-based input mapping. Additionally, Robinson et al., in a systematic literature review of affective gaming [11], concluded that the incorporation of facial expressions for context-based mappings is an opportunity for innovation, indicating the novelty of this approach.

In this paper, we designed, developed, and performed an exploratory study on the viability of a game that incorporated an emotion recognition system that follows the previous principles. Additionally, we examined the use of FER as an implicit input method while also examining the noticeability of context-based input mappings based on their type.

2   Related Work

The term affective computing was coined by RW Picard in her 1997 book of the same name and is described as "...computing that relates to, arises from, or deliberately influences emotions" [15]. Affective computing applications can support research on human emotions, as well as lead to significant advancements in cognitive theory. Such applications utilize select modalities from a plethora of possible input types in an attempt to give machines empathy.

The most common modalities are vision-based, often taking advantage of human facial features and other physiological emotional responses [16]. Those modalities encompass inputs associated with computer vision, and as such require the appropriate techniques to obtain. More specifically, methods akin to head tracking, eye tracking, body gesture recognition, and machine learning are capable of substantially enhancing human-to-computer communication.

The Facial Action Coding System (FACS) [17] has been used extensively in computer vision algorithms for emotion evaluation [18]. More modern approaches target more than one modality (multi-modal), and through research have shown better results than their unimodal counterparts [19, 20].

The impact of affective computing also extends to the field of video games. Computer games of all genres are very much tied to their individual sets of inputs. These inputs are the communication bus between player and game, and therefore, removing an existing one or adding a new one, can affect the player's experience. In fact, incorporating the player's affective data into a game can have a variety of benefits.

In our context, the expression adaptive games refer to a game that can adapt or be adapted beyond the limits of predefined settings through an intelligently acting engine [21]. Adaptive games are oftentimes directly associated with affective computing, considering they tend to utilize techniques associated with the latter to adjust themselves.

One increasingly common class of adaptive video games are the ones that aim to adjust their difficulty to maximize the player's takeaway from the game. This is accomplished by a method called "Dynamic Difficulty Adjustment" (or DDA), and typically uses the player's stress as a metric to reduce the difficulty, and bring the stress to an acceptable level, where the player is neither bored (low difficulty), and neither stressed (high difficulty) [22].

Several studies have used real-time anxiety evaluation to suit the challenge rating of a game to the player's needs [23]. One noteworthy use case is the application of the player's affective state in educational games, where the utmost goal is the absorption of knowledge by the player. Indeed, by evaluating the player's emotional state using suitable sensors (biosensors, a camera, etc.), rather than postulating their state as a hardcoded value, the learning quality can be amplified.

More specifically, researchers at La Trobe University compared an adaptive game that used DDA, with a standard difficulty game, and found that despite having no effect on the player's motivation to learn (both games resulted in the same amount), the adaptive game resulted in a consequential increase in learning outcomes [24].

Reidy et al. in their work managed to increase players' feeling of competency and feeling of being challenged, by implementing DDA in a virtual reality (VR) game for cognitive training [25]. Difficulty adjustment is not the only form of adaptability in games. As a matter of fact, the claim that all parameters in a game can in some way conform to an individual player's preferences is quite plausible.

For example, VR games that are used to guide the player through some sort of program (e.g., fitness), could benefit greatly from adjusting to each player, possibly increasing the outcomes of said program. Ouriel Barzilay and Alon Wolf [26] developed a VR game that coaches patients with neuromuscular issues through biomechanical exercises, in order to recover their neuromotor abilities. The game adapted to each user, by calibrating itself based on calculations made by an artificial neural network that used the user's biometric data during a standard task to train itself, and then recommended user-specific tasks to them. Improvements up to 33% were achieved in some exercises.

To carry out this type of adaptation, a plentitude of techniques has been tested, such as machine learning, decision trees, and neural networks. These are used to build player-specific models, based on which the adaptation is performed.

It should be mentioned that with the approach taken in our work, we aim to further bridge the gap that currently exists between human emotions and games. Previous studies have primarily detected emotions with traditional methods (EEG, temperature, skin conductivity, etc.), with examples where stress and anxiety or the player's positive/negative affective state have been used as inputs to dynamically adjust difficulty [27], and with some games attempting to elicit fear in players for whom fear was not detected in the context of a horror game by monitoring their pulse rate [28].

Dworak et al. suggested a theoretical model for adjusting in-game parameters by reading biofeedback signals so as to conform game aspects to the player's emotional state [29]. Despite the usefulness of such a model, the design details remain ambiguous, with its usability seemingly only viable in simple repetitive video games.

In contrast, our modus operandi aspires to meticulously design game mechanics that conform to all the basic human emotions [30] (with a smaller emphasis on surprise), which we recognize using FER, rather than more traditional sensors.

3 Emotion Recognition

For the purposes of this paper, we created a game that utilizes the player's emotions as additional input. To achieve that, we first trained an artificial neural network that receives frames containing a face and identifies the associated emotion. Next, we developed a computer software that supplies the aforementioned neural network with processed images from a computer camera feed and writes the predicted emotion and the prediction certainty in a file. That file is used by a game we designed to apply the player's emotion to a large variety of in-game parameters.

3.1 Choosing the Camera as a Sensor

The motivation for choosing the camera as an Automated Emotion Evaluation (AEE) sensor is that, beyond the fact that it facilitates the experiment process since the participating user does not need any specialized device (e.g., a biosensor), the comfort of the user is ensured, as opposed to sensors that require physical contact, and inevitably reduce their comfort level and, by extension, the quality of the experience. At the same time, the field of AEE using a camera is interesting and is something that -to the authors' knowledge- has not been attempted before in this type of use case. Finally, it is worth mentioning how easy it is to install the emotion recognition system on the participants' premises since it allows for several alternatives for a camera input device (e.g., using a smartphone camera via specialized free software, laptop, etc.), requires a simple installation procedure, and has a very low computational cost.

3.2 Neural Network Specifications

After experimenting with various model architectures (neural or otherwise), a Convolutional Neural Network (CNN) was used, which is notably applied in visual imagery analysis [31]. This type of architecture enables feature extraction, classification, and emotion recognition without the incumbency of extensive input preprocessing before training (end-to-end).

After extensive testing of various architectures, transfer learning was used for increased accuracy and input size, and reduced file size by implementing pre-trained weights from the VGG16 model [32].

As a dataset, we chose the extensively used Rohit Verma's publicly available "fer2013" [33] image set, which includes 7 emotions. It is important to note that due to the low resolution of the dataset images and the fact that they were received from open sources such as stock images, the performance of our model might be increased with the use of a higher quality non-open source dataset.

To partially circumvent this issue, we made use of the TensorFlow[1] library upscale capabilities to increase our training images to 150×150 pixel resolution (originally 48x48 pixel). Increasing the resolution enabled us to implement a larger input layer in our model and therefore allowed for a larger input frame. The benefit of the extra information in our input is crucial, as it refines our intent of focusing the frame on the subject's face while retaining the maximum amount of data possible.

To guarantee that the model could be used in any modern system -without requiring high-performance hardware specifications- we kept the number of parameters as low as possible while preserving the model's accuracy, a major goal in our work.

In the end, the result is more than sufficient for our use case. We chose the four emotions that were appropriate for our use case (happy, sad, surprised, angry) and trained our model on the respective data resulting in a CNN model capable of facial emotion recognition (FER) on an input frame of size 150×150 pixels, with an accuracy of 85.4%.

3.3 Emotion Recognition Software

Having trained our FER model, we needed some type of software to use it. To accomplish this, we designed a simple application that runs inside the Windows command line, without the need for any user input. This app runs completely independently of the game, and its function is to appropriately process images from the camera feed, hand them over to the input of the neural network for inference, and write the predicted emotion and certainty percentage to a JSON (JavaScript Object Notation) file. A set of steps is followed to produce the desired result, as the raw images generated by the camera are not in a suitable form for the model. The procedure followed by our software is presented in Fig. 1.

---

[1] https://www.tensorflow.org/.

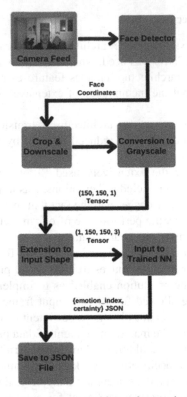

Fig. 1. Emotion recognition software pipeline.

4 Adaptive Game

We designed and developed a first-person perspective 3D game, that follows the concept of "escape room" experiences and is a fusion of exploration, subtle storytelling, and puzzle-solving. The engine used is Unity3D[2] (version 2020.3.0f1), with all code written in C#. It's worth noting, that to accomplish our goals regarding in-game sound effects and music, we used the Wwise platform[3] (version 2021.1.4.7707) as a sound engine.

As previously mentioned, the purpose of our game is to incorporate the player's emotional state in a variety of ways that influence the player's experience during a playthrough. We, therefore, needed a design that highlights the usefulness of emotions as a complementary input. While numerous approaches were brainstormed, we made the decision to incorporate mechanics that -to our knowledge- have never been attempted before and span all individual parts of the game. Some of those original ideas revolved around the previously explored dynamic difficulty adjustment and a horror game that adapted to the player's feeling of fear, but those were dismissed in favor of more extensive and innovative approaches.

---

[2] https://www.unity.com/.

[3] https://www.audiokinetic.com.

To combat potential issues concerning the detection of the player's face (and therefore inference of emotion) we keep the player informed by notifying them with a message in the game's UI, prompting them to make sure their camera can clearly see their face, and only when conditions allow for clear detection the message disappears. The system stores the data regarding the periods in which a face was not detected (if any) and compares it to the periods that the player's emotion would be needed as input; if during these periods the face was undetected, that data is deemed invalid, but that was not the case for any participant.

4.1 Game Design

Titled "One More Time with Feeling", it's an exploration game where the player moves between different areas of the world by solving puzzles. The game can be divided into 6 respective levels, most of which require the player to solve the level's unique puzzle to progress. One prime goal was to enhance player immersion by embracing player-world interactivity by allowing the player to interact with most game-objects, such as opening and closing doors and windows by dragging their mouse in a lifelike motion, examining objects by rotating them around and using devices like keypads by clicking on their buttons. The storytelling part of our game is designed to be subtle. Narrative information is given to players in the shape of notes they can collect and read, and through cassette tapes they can play (voiced-over) to discover story information in conjunction with riddle hints. Those pieces of narrative content can act as stimuli that, in turn, elicit different emotional responses from player to player.

Given that many of the puzzles in the game require items to be examined or placed in the correct slot, players are equipped with an Inventory graphical user interface (GUI) where they can access all items they have gathered. By selecting an item, they get a description based on the knowledge level they have on said item, with the level increasing when the player examines the item (rotates it around in front of them) or finds a different one that contains information about the first. This allows the character to have a potentially higher level of information than the player, preventing instances where the latter can't solve a puzzle due to lacking some encyclopedic knowledge. Some of the items can also be used from the inventory, mainly to place them in slots, such as inserting a tape into a cassette player.

Most of the puzzles contain riddles that need to be unraveled to solve the puzzle itself. Hints given to the player in various forms like text and audio can be easily forgotten, and it's crucial to prevent the player from backtracking or resorting to notetaking. To alleviate that, the player can use a different GUI that functions as a Journal. There, the character automatically "writes" entries concerning information discovered by the player and "thoughts" that the character has, the tone of which is affected by the player's emotion.

4.2 Mechanics Influenced by Emotion

Our novel approach to an adaptive game is defined by the connection between the player's emotional state and that of the character. A set of in-game parameters are affected by this connection, with each one aiming to explore an entirely distinctive kind of modulation.

In total, we count 5 in-game changes that are affected by the player's emotion (dynamic music, adaptive graphical content, journal entry tone, level and riddle setup, ending setup), some of which occur in real-time, while others follow different strategies. All those 5 changes are part of the context-based mapping incorporated in our game, as they target primarily environmental changes of a variety of subtlety.

One of the most prominent ways the game adapts is the music. We designed a dynamic music system, which changes the track according to the corresponding emotion. To accomplish this, we wrote 3 sets of music pieces, with each set containing one track per emotion (happy, sad, angry). The first set applies to levels 2 and 3 (Fig. 2, a), and the music changes if a different emotion is detected by a check that occurs every 10 s to avoid perpetual changes. The second set is used in levels 4 and 5, with the music track selected only once, upon the player entering the level 4 room.

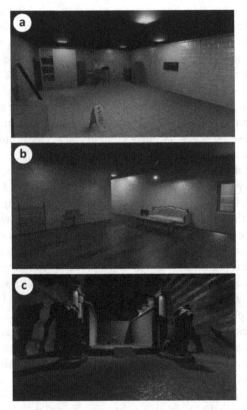

Fig. 2. Images from levels of the game, (a) level 3, (b) level 4, (c) level 6.

This is part of the emotion-based setup level 4 undergoes, as described below. The last set is utilized as a part of the ending setup (also described below), with the track chosen according to the most commonly occurring emotion throughout the playthrough. These last 3 pieces of music are different from the other sets, as they're more melodic and less repetitive, in contrast to the ambient and looping nature of the others. Regarding the type of music, a few works included in the book "Handbook of Music and Emotion: Theory, Research, Applications" [34] were consulted, especially the chapters of Gabrielsson, Alf, and Erik Lindström [35].

The second emphatic adaptation occurs in the game's graphical content. In our game, the majority of wall and floor materials (shading and texturing of an object) are designed to modulate themselves to reflect the player's emotion. In a similar way to music, some changes happen in real-time (10-s detection intervals), while others only take place once. The change is in the form of a shift, that happens gradually until the new material is completely present. Each object can have a distinct set of 3 materials (one per emotion). To represent the player's emotional state through those materials, we used as foundation the emotion-color associations like the ones referenced in the work of Niels A. Nijdam [36]. As environment objects aren't made of single colors, we needed to convert those associations to image textures. Those associations do not provide enough information for us to pick an image, so certain assumptions had to be made. Those materials are designed to reflect each emotional state, with angry state materials appearing more damaged, while sad state materials appear darker and somber (Fig. 3). The happy state materials are the default ones and represent the default form of the environment.

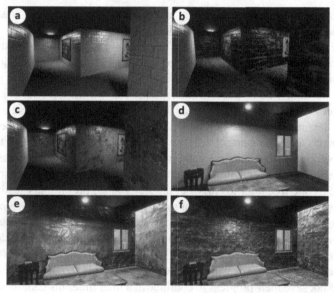

Fig. 3. Material variations for two of the levels: (a), (b), and (c) are the happy, sad, and angry state materials of the first level, respectively. In the same order, (d), (e), and (f) are of the third level.

As hinted above, level 4 (Fig. 2, b) undergoes a setup according to the player's emotion on entry. Besides the material and music changes, the core element of this setup is the puzzle. The riddle the player needs to solve is different for each emotion and is written in a way that reflects it. The happy version mentions a party, the sad one hints at a soldier's funeral, and the angry one revolves around some sort of bestial transformation. The hints are also placed in slightly different locations inside the level.

The ending in level 6 (Fig. 2, c) is adapted to the most occurring emotion throughout the playthrough. The first alteration is to the game-objects. The pillars around the temple are more damaged if the angry emotion was the most prominent and completely broken if the sad emotion was the most prominent. The music played is also selected from a set of 3. Finally, when the player finishes the game, a quote associated with their emotion appears, in an attempt to empower that emotion (rather than have them change it, necessarily).

Lastly, the game's Journal mechanic is also affected by emotion. This is by far the most subtle change taking place and relates to the tone of the writing of each Journal entry. More specifically, each entry that isn't associated with a puzzle has two different versions based on the detected emotion the moment it's written: for a happy emotion, the entry is clear and concise, while for any other emotion, the entry is more panicky and verbose. This is done to convey the player's emotion through the character.

5 Methodology

An exploratory study aimed at exploring the viability of the system was conducted with 22 participants, 3 females, and 19 males, aged between 13 to 58 (M = 33.6, SD = 12.9). The initial design was to conduct the study in a laboratory, but due to covid restrictions that would limit the number of participants. For the reason mentioned above, the participants were recruited online by registering in a participation form, giving them two options, the first was to play on their premises, and the second was to arrange a play session in a lab. Most users opted for the first option and were given a user manual with detailed instructions on how to download, setup, play and then complete the questionnaire after the game. Users opting for the second option had to complete fewer steps before playing since the game was already downloaded and installed on a lab's computer, with all other actions being identical. The participants were requested to set aside at least one free hour to carry out the study since preliminary testing revealed that the game takes an average of one hour to complete. Considering the game's reliance on the player's emotions as input, it is critical to minimize factors that could interfere with the player's emotions (other than the game itself). Participants were also instructed to keep any distractions to a minimum during the study (avoid using other devices, having their phones on silent, etc.). The game was designed to be played in a single session, and players could not save their progress to continue at a later time; instead, they could only pause for a brief break if necessary. All participants signed a consent form (online or printed) for their user's data and had the option to consult a "puzzle solutions" document in case of experiencing difficulties progressing through the game.

After they experienced the game, they completed a custom questionnaire. The questionnaire comprised two parts, one focusing on game satisfaction and the other on the user's perception of the emotion recognition element of the game. For evaluating game satisfaction, core subscales of the GUESS scale [37] relevant to the game were identified and utilized (Usability/Playability, Play Engrossment, Enjoyment, Audio Aesthetics, Personal Gratification, and Visual Aesthetics subscales). A custom subscale to examine which type of game changes were identified by players during gameplay was developed, with an additional item inquiring whether the participants used the system as an explicit input method.

6 Results

This section presents the results of the exploratory study conducted with the 22 participants and is divided into two parts. The first part presents the results regarding game satisfaction by utilizing core subscales of the GUESS scale, and overall, the results were positive, with no subscale having low scores. The second part presents the results regarding the emotion recognition aspect of the game.

6.1 Game Satisfaction Results

Reliability analysis for each subscale was carried out by calculating Cronbach's α for the participants (n = 22), and all subscales had acceptable reliability. Specifically, the Usability/Playability subscale consisted of 11 items ($\alpha = 0.889$), the Play Engrossment subscale consisted of 8 items ($\alpha = 0.884$), the Enjoyment subscale consisted of 5 items ($\alpha = 0.889$), the Audio Aesthetics subscale consisted of 4 items ($\alpha = 0.903$), the Personal Gratification subscale consisted of 6 items ($\alpha = 0.878$), and the Visual Aesthetics subscale consisted of 3 items ($\alpha = 0.763$).

Having acceptable reliability, all the items per subscale were averaged to obtain an average score for each subscale [37] and the results are presented in Table 1. The Audio and Visual Aesthetics subscales had the highest scores (Mean > 6), indicating that the dynamic nature of the audio and visuals of the game -based on the user's emotion- does not seem to influence the user experience in a negative way. The Play Engrossment subscale obtained the lowest score (Mean = 4.74), and although it is marginally above the baseline (Mean = 4.5), it indicates that there were mixed opinions regarding the immersion the users felt during the game, something that can also be ascertained by the highest Std. Deviation value among subscales (SD = 1.369).

Finally, high scores were observed for the Usability/Playability, Enjoyment, and Personal Gratification subscales, with scores exceeding a Mean score of 5.5, indicating that the users did not find particular problems with the usability of the game, while at the same time, most of them reported high levels of enjoyment and personal gratification.

6.2 Results Regarding the Emotion Recognition Aspect of the Game

The users that participated in the exploratory study of the game were informed beforehand that the game adapts to their emotions, but they were unaware of what aspects of the game this adaptation influences. To examine if the participants tried to influence the emotion recognition part of the game, the questionnaire item "I tried to influence the emotion recognition, actively and on purpose" had 4 participants answering yes and 18 no. These results indicate that most of the participants -even though they knew that the game adapts to their emotions- did not attempt to fake an emotion to see how it would influence the game.

Table 1. Average score of each subscale regarding user satisfaction.

Subscale	Mean	SD
Usability/Playability	5.77	0.80
Play Engrossment	4.74	1.37
Enjoyment	5.84	1.11
Audio Aesthetics	6.12	0.91
Personal Gratification	5.78	0.92
Visual Aesthetics	6.27	0.61

Table 2 presents the results of the custom questionnaire items related to the emotion recognition system of the game, focusing on the participants' perception of the adaptive nature of the game to their emotions. Questionnaire items 1 and 2 -regarding the audio and visual changes- have the highest scores, both being near the baseline, with all other items (3, 4, 5) being lower. What these results demonstrate is that alterations based on the user's emotion to the visual and audio aspects of the game are the most likely to be detected by the user, while other, more subtle changes (journal entries, emotionally themed hints/presentation, and ending quotes) are potentially less noticeable. Overall, the scores indicate that the mechanics that were influenced by the users' emotions are perceptible to users, with only 2 of them reporting that they did not notice any changes (answering 1 to all 5 items).

Table 2. Questionnaire item results regarding emotion recognition.

Item	Mean	SD
I noticed a change in the music	4.55	1.84
I noticed a visual change in the material of the walls and floor	4.18	2.24
I noticed a change of tone in the journal entries	3.64	1.99
I noticed a room with emotionally themed hints and presentation	3.73	1.80
I noticed that the ending quote was associated with an emotion	3.73	2.10

6.3 Discussion

To offer a sense of perspective concerning the scores achieved by the game regarding game satisfaction, Table 3 presents a comparison between the mean scores per subscale of our game with the mean scores of the GUESS scale (with data gathered during the scale's validation [37]). The authors of the GUESS scale mention that the scale was distributed to participants who chose to evaluate commercial video games (console and computer games) that they liked (which was corroborated by the high scores that they achieved). The genres included in the scale's evaluation covered a wide variety of the most popular game genres. As Table 3 shows, the mean scores in all the examined subscales are comparable to the GUESS validation scores, which indicates that -despite incorporating a novel game mechanic that adapted game elements based on the player's emotions- the game did not detract from the player's game satisfaction, scoring high across all subscales even when compared to popular commercial video games. Specifically, our game has higher mean scores at 3 out of 6 subscales examined (in usability/Playability, Visual and Audio aesthetics). Given that the findings for the emotion detection element of the game revealed that the visual and aural changes were the most noticeable by the players, it is reasonable to assume that the adaptive nature of the game may have favorably influenced the players' ratings in this area.

Table 3. Comparison between the mean scores per subscale of our game with the mean scores of the data gathered during the GUESS scale validation.

Subscale	Our Game Mean Scores	GUESS Validation Mean Scores
Usability/Playability	5.77	5.74
Play Engrossment	4.74	4.89
Enjoyment	5.84	6.23
Audio Aesthetics	6.12	5.91
Personal Gratification	5.78	5.89

7 Conclusion and Future Work

The paper presents a game that incorporates an emotion recognition system, aiming at adapting gameplay elements based on the user's current emotion. The game design utilizes the user's emotion as an implicit form of input method (in contrast to explicit methods in other works) by adjusting multiple in-game parameters ranging from more easily distinguishable such as audio and visual changes, to more subtle such as journal entries, emotionally themed hints/presentation, and ending quotes.

An exploratory study with 22 participants, that examined users' level of satisfaction in the game, in conjunction with their perception of the emotion recognition aspect of the game, was conducted. Regarding game satisfaction, the users scored above average on all subscales, indicating that all aspects of the game examined (Usability/Playability, Play Engrossment, Enjoyment, Audio Aesthetics, Personal Gratification, and Visual Aesthetics) were very well received by the participants with almost all subscales achieving noticeably high scores apart from the results of the Play Engrossment subscale which indicated mixed opinions in regard to the immersion the users felt during the game. The results in half of the subscales examined are favorable, even compared to the evaluation of popular commercial video games. Concerning the emotion recognition aspect of the game, 82% of the participants stated that they did not explicitly attempt to influence the emotion recognition system of the game, indicating that the game achieved its design goal of utilizing user emotion as an implicit input method. This result shows that a FER-based input method, when mapped with a context-based input mapping, can result in an implicit game input. Regarding the users' perception of the adjustments the game made based on their emotions, the results indicate that visual and audio changes were the most easily perceived by the users, with other changes being less noticeable. The high scores in the subscales Usability/Playability and Visual and Audio Aesthetics, in conjunction with the perception of the participants that the Audio and Visual changes of the adaptive system were more prominent, could suggest that utilizing the player's emotion as input might have positively influenced the players' satisfaction. Overall, the results of this work are promising and could indicate the viability of affect-aware systems based on the user's emotion in the field of video games as well as affect-aware computing in general. Future work could include a more comprehensive user evaluation involving additional participants that will further corroborate the findings of this work.

References

1. Thorpe, A., Ma, M., Oikonomou, A.: History and alternative game input methods. In: 2011 16th International Conference on Computer Games (CGAMES), pp. 76–93 (2011). https://doi.org/10.1109/CGAMES.2011.6000321
2. Speelpenning, T., Antle, A.N., Doering, T., van den Hoven, E.: Exploring How Tangible Tools Enable Collaboration in a Multi-touch Tabletop Game. In: Campos, P., Graham, N., Jorge, J., Nunes, N., Palanque, P., Winckler, M. (eds.) Human-Computer Interaction – INTERACT 2011: 13th IFIP TC 13 International Conference, Lisbon, Portugal, September 5-9, 2011, Proceedings, Part II, pp. 605–621. Springer Berlin Heidelberg, Berlin, Heidelberg (2011). https://doi.org/10.1007/978-3-642-23771-3_45
3. Ilves, M., Gizatdinova, Y., Surakka, V., Vankka, E.: Head movement and facial expressions as game input. Entertain. Comput. 5, 147–156 (2014). https://doi.org/10.1016/j.entcom.2014.04.005
4. Taheri, A., Weissman, Z., Sra, M.: Exploratory design of a hands-free video game controller for a quadriplegic individual. In: Augmented Humans Conference 2021, pp. 131–140. Association for Computing Machinery, New York, NY, USA (2021). https://doi.org/10.1145/3458709.3458946
5. Ewing, K.C., Fairclough, S.H., Gilleade, K.: Evaluation of an adaptive game that uses EEG measures validated during the design process as inputs to a biocybernetic loop. Front. Human Neurosci. 10, 223 (2016). https://doi.org/10.3389/fnhum.2016.00223
6. van Vliet, M., Robben, A., Chumerin, N., Manyakov, N.V., Combaz, A., Van Hulle, M.M.: Designing a brain-computer interface controlled video-game using consumer grade EEG hardware. In: 2012 ISSNIP Biosignals and Biorobotics Conference: Biosignals and Robotics for Better and Safer Living (BRC), pp. 1–6 (2012). https://doi.org/10.1109/BRC.2012.6222186
7. Lankes, M., Riegler, S., Weiss, A., Mirlacher, T., Pirker, M., Tscheligi, M.: Facial expressions as game input with different emotional feedback conditions. In: Proceedings of the 2008 International Conference on Advances in Computer Entertainment Technology. pp. 253–256. Association for Computing Machinery, New York, NY, USA (2008). https://doi.org/10.1145/1501750.1501809
8. Kołakowska, A., Landowska, A., Szwoch, M., Szwoch, W., Wróbel, M.R.: Emotion Recognition and Its Applications. In: Hippe, Z.S., Kulikowski, J.L., Mroczek, T., Wtorek, J. (eds.) Human-Computer Systems Interaction: Backgrounds and Applications 3, pp. 51–62. Springer International Publishing, Cham (2014). https://doi.org/10.1007/978-3-319-08491-6_5

9. Szwoch, M., Szwoch, W.: Emotion Recognition for Affect Aware Video Games. In: Choraś, R.S. (ed.) Image Processing & Communications Challenges 6. AISC, vol. 313, pp. 227–236. Springer, Cham (2015). https://doi.org/10.1007/978-3-319-10662-5_28

10. Nacke, L.E., Kalyn, M., Lough, C., Mandryk, R.L.: Biofeedback game design: using direct and indirect physiological control to enhance game interaction. In: Proceedings of the SIGCHI Conference on Human Factors in Computing Systems, pp. 103–112. Association for Computing Machinery, New York, NY, USA (2011). https://doi.org/10.1145/1978942. 1978958

11. Robinson, R., Wiley, K., Rezaeivahdati, A., Klarkowski, M., Mandryk, R.L.: "Let's get physiological, physiological!": a systematic review of affective gaming. In: Proceedings of the Annual Symposium on Computer-Human Interaction in Play, pp. 132–147. Association for Computing Machinery, New York, NY, USA (2020). https://doi.org/10.1145/3410404.341 4227

12. Kuikkaniemi, K., Laitinen, T., Turpeinen, M., Saari, T., Kosunen, I., Ravaja, N.: The influence of implicit and explicit biofeedback in first-person shooter games. In: Proceedings of the SIGCHI Conference on Human Factors in Computing Systems, pp. 859–868. Association for Computing Machinery, New York, NY, USA (2010). https://doi.org/10.1145/1753326.175 3453

13. Mallas, A., Xenos, M., Katsanos, C.: A Descriptive Model of Passive and Natural Passive Human-Computer Interaction. In: Kurosu, M. (ed.) Human-Computer Interaction. Theoretical Approaches and Design Methods: Thematic Area, HCI 2022, Held as Part of the 24th HCI International Conference, HCII 2022, Virtual Event, June 26–July 1, 2022, Proceedings, Part I, pp. 104–116. Springer International Publishing, Cham (2022). https://doi.org/10.1007/978-3-031-05311-5_7

14. Serim, B., Jacucci, G.: Explicating "Implicit Interaction": an examination of the concept and challenges for research. In: Proceedings of the 2019 CHI Conference on Human Factors in Computing Systems. pp. 1–16. ACM, Glasgow Scotland Uk (2019). https://doi.org/10.1145/ 3290605.3300647

15. Picard, R.W.: Affective Computing. MIT Press, Cambridge, MA, USA (1997)

16. Bailenson, J.N., et al.: Real-time classification of evoked emotions using facial feature tracking and physiological responses. Int. J. Hum. Comput. Stud. **66**, 303–317 (2008). https://doi.org/ 10.1016/j.ijhcs.2007.10.011

17. Hjortsjö, C.-H.: Man's face and mimic language. Studen litteratur, Sweden (1969)

18. Richardson, S.: Affective computing in the modern workplace. Bus. Inf. Rev. **37**, 78–85 (2020). https://doi.org/10.1177/0266382120930866

19. Comas, J., Aspandi, D., Binefa, X.: End-to-end facial and physiological model for affective computing and applications. In: 2020 15th IEEE International Conference on Automatic Face and Gesture Recognition (FG 2020), pp. 93–100. IEEE, Buenos Aires, Argentina (2020). https://doi.org/10.1109/FG47880.2020.00001

20. Siddharth, Jung, T.-P., Sejnowski, T.J.: Multi-modal approach for affective computing. In: 2018 40th Annual International Conference of the IEEE Engineering in Medicine and Biology Society (EMBC), pp. 291–294. IEEE, Honolulu, HI (2018). https://doi.org/10.1109/EMBC. 2018.8512320

21. Streicher, A., Smeddinck, J.D.: Personalized and adaptive serious games. In: Dörner, R., Göbel, S., Kickmeier-Rust, M., Masuch, M., Zweig, K. (eds.) Entertainment Computing and Serious Games, pp. 332–377. Springer International Publishing, Cham (2016). https://doi. org/10.1007/978-3-319-46152-6_14

22. Zohaib, M.: Dynamic Difficulty Adjustment (DDA) in computer games: a review. Adv. Human-Comput. Interact. **2018**, 1–12 (2018). https://doi.org/10.1155/2018/5681652

23. Liu, C., Agrawal, P., Sarkar, N., Chen, S.: Dynamic difficulty adjustment in computer games through real-time anxiety-based affective feedback. Int. J. Human-Comput. Interact. **25**, 506–529 (2009). https://doi.org/10.1080/10447310902963944

24. Sampayo-Vargas, S., Cope, C.J., He, Z., Byrne, G.J.: The effectiveness of adaptive difficulty adjustments on students' motivation and learning in an educational computer game. Comput. Educ. **69**, 452–462 (2013). https://doi.org/10.1016/j.compedu.2013.07.004

25. Reidy, L., Chan, D., Nduka, C., Gunes, H.: Facial electromyography-based adaptive virtual reality gaming for cognitive training. In: Proceedings of the 2020 International Conference on Multimodal Interaction, pp. 174–183. ACM, Virtual Event Netherlands (2020). https://doi.org/10.1145/3382507.3418845

26. Barzilay, O., Wolf, A.: Adaptive rehabilitation games. J. Electromyogr. Kinesiol. **23**, 182–189 (2013). https://doi.org/10.1016/j.jelekin.2012.09.004

27. Obaid, M., Han, C., Billinghurst, M.: "Feed the Fish": an affect-aware game. In: Proceedings of the 5th Australasian Conference on Interactive Entertainment, pp. 1–6. Association for Computing Machinery, New York, NY, USA (2008). https://doi.org/10.1145/1514402.1514408

28. Araki, H., Ikeda, T., Ozawa, T., Kawahara, K., Kawai, Y.: Development of a horror game that route branches by the player's pulse rate. In: Proceedings of the 23rd International Conference on Intelligent User Interfaces Companion, pp. 1–2. Association for Computing Machinery, New York, NY, USA (2018). https://doi.org/10.1145/3180308.3180322

29. Dworak, W., Filgueiras, E., Valente, J.: Automatic emotional balancing in game design: use of emotional response to increase player immersion. In: Marcus, A., Rosenzweig, E. (eds.) Design, User Experience, and Usability. Design for Contemporary Interactive Environments: 9th International Conference, DUXU 2020, Held as Part of the 22nd HCI International Conference, HCII 2020, Copenhagen, Denmark, July 19–24, 2020, Proceedings, Part II, pp. 426–438. Springer International Publishing, Cham (2020). https://doi.org/10.1007/978-3-030-49760-6_30

30. Jack, R.E., Garrod, O.G.B., Schyns, P.G.: Dynamic facial expressions of emotion transmit an evolving hierarchy of signals over time. Curr. Biol. **24**, 187–192 (2014). https://doi.org/10.1016/j.cub.2013.11.064

31. Valueva, M.V., Nagornov, N.N., Lyakhov, P.A., Valuev, G.V., Chervyakov, N.I.: Application of the residue number system to reduce hardware costs of the convolutional neural network implementation. Math. Comput. Simul **177**, 232–243 (2020). https://doi.org/10.1016/j.matcom.2020.04.031

32. Simonyan, K., Zisserman, A.: Very Deep Convolutional Networks for Large-Scale Image Recognition (2014). https://doi.org/10.48550/ARXIV.1409.1556

33. Dumitru, Y.B., Goodfellow, I., Cukierski, W.: Challenges in Representation Learning: Facial Expression Recognition Challenge. https://kaggle.com/competitions/challenges-in-representation-learning-facial-expression-recognition-challenge (2013)

34. Juslin, P.N., Sloboda, J.A.: Handbook of Music and Emotion: Theory, Research, Applications. Oxford University Press, Oxford (2010)

35. Gabrielsson, A., Lindström, E.: The role of structure in the musical expression of emotions. In: Handbook of Music and Emotion: Theory, Research, Applications, pp. 367–44. Oxford University Press (2010)

36. Nijdam, N.A.: Mapping emotion to color (2009)

37. Phan, M.H., Keebler, J.R., Chaparro, B.S.: The development and validation of the game user experience satisfaction scale (GUESS). Hum. Factors **58**, 1217–1247 (2016). https://doi.org/10.1177/0018720816669646

DanceFree: A Somatosensory Dance Game Based on 3D Dance Animation Generation Algorithm

JunFan Zhao[1]([envelope]), MingYang Su[1], QiHui Zhou[1], Xiang Luo[2], JiDa Li[1], JingYing Zhang[1], and Xiu Li[1]

[1] Tsinghua Shenzhen International Graduate School, Shenzhen, GuangDong, China
zhao-yf17@tsinghua.org.cn
[2] Tencent, Shenzhen, GuangDong, China

Abstract. As an art form with a long history, dance is very popular in culture, entertainment and other fields. With the rapid development of motion capture and graphics rendering technology, traditional dance forms have also ushered in digital transformation. Dance games, as a game type with dance as the core gameplay, not only provide players with opportunities for physical exercise, but also promote social interaction and bring players a unique entertainment experience. Restricted by the high production cost of dance animation, most dance games contain only a small amount of pre-produced dance content during the development process, making it difficult to satisfy players' diverse preferences and demand for new content. With the continuous development of artificial intelligence technology, efficient production of 3D dance animation has become possible. This technological advancement not only enables development teams to quickly update game content, but also enables players to realize user-generated content in the game. In order to explore the prospects of AI technology in dance games, we developed a somatosensory dance game based on 3D dance animation generation technology. This game contains a rich variety of dance animation database and allows players to freely create personalized game levels. We hope that by introducing AI technology into dance games, players can freely enjoy the charm of dance art in the game.

Keywords: Somatosensory Dance Game · Artificial Intelligence · User-Generated Content

1 Introduction

Dance is an ancient form of art that expresses emotions, tells stories and passes on culture through body movements and rhythms. At present, dance is also regarded as a way of physical exercise and fitness, which widely present in people's daily lives. With the iterative development of 3D graphics technology, motion capture and hardware, dance has begun to play an increasingly important role in games, movies and other fields. Advances in technology allow dance to be presented in a realistic way in the virtual world. Motion capture accurately records dance movements, 3D graphics technology brings the dancer and its dance to the virtual world, giving players an in-depth artistic experience.

Although various dance-related games have a large audience around the world, the high cost of producing 3D dance animation, its most important component, still limits the development of dance games. Based on the current production process and prior experience of 3D dance animation, if you want to finally present an well-made dance animation in the game scene, you must at least go through several processes such as choreography by choreographers, dancer motion capture, data cleaning and repair, animation model nesting and rendering. To be more specific, a one-minute original dance animation requires tens of thousands of dollars, a large number of technicians, expensive motion capture venues, and nearly half a month to produce. The high production cost not only limits the efficiency of creators to produce high-quality game content, but also limits the space for user-generated content.

At present, research on the digitization of dance focuses more on the innovation of interaction modes and content itself. Researchers are committed to allowing players to interact using virtual reality devices or somatosensory devices to obtain a more realistic dance experience. At the level of content innovation, researchers are more concerned about the empowering effect of digital dance on education and cultural communication. However, only a few studies have focused on how to how to address the cost issues that dance encounters during the digitization process.

The rapid development of artificial intelligence (AI) technology provides technical support for the production of dance animations, and the introduction of a series of generative models such as GAN, Transformer, Diffusion, etc. makes AI approaching or even surpassing human beings in the fields of Natural Language Processing (NLP) and Computer Vision (CV). Using AI to generate 3D dance animation is the most appropriate way to reduce costs and expand user-generated content space.

The purpose of this study is to explore whether the application of AI technology can provide players with a better game experience. To this end, we developed a somatosensory dance game based on 3D dance animation generation algorithm, which contains a database of AI-generated dance animations and a game mode that supports custom dance levels. In the game, players need to follow the rhythm of the music and correctly perform the corresponding dance poses to get points, the more accurate the player's poses, the higher the score. The game is based on the Unity engine and utilizes the Kinect device for somatosensory interaction.

On the whole, this study innovativeness is twofold as follows:

1. AI algorithm is utilized to efficiently generate a large number of 3D dance animations and populate the game with them as game content, verifying that AI can assist the development of dance games.
2. Using AI to realize user-generated content for dance games, allowing users to define game content according to their own interests.

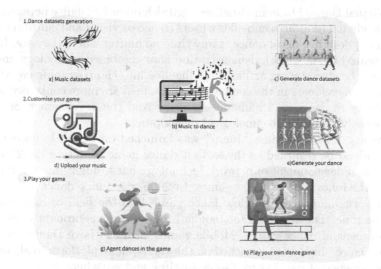

Fig. 1. In DanceFree, players can not only play a large number of rich game content based on the initial dance database, but also upload music to produce dance animation to define their own game content.

2 Background

2.1 Development of Dance Games

The essence of games is the simulation of real life. For dance games, exquisite dance animation and gorgeous scenes are necessary elements. Therefore, limited by the development of various technologies, dance games have not appeared in the public's view until the 21st century. In serious games, dance elements are more often used as art forms or cultural carriers to help players learn better; while in commercial games, dance elements are more often used as part of the game mechanism to provide players with a better entertainment experience.Numerous research in the field of serious games have attempted to digitize dance in a variety of ways, introducing non-heritage dance to users in the form of virtual museums and serious games (Fig. 1).

Some researchers are committed to preserving intangible cultural heritage dances through digital methods. "The i-Treasures" [15,16]project not only digitizes songs and handicrafts, but also digitally records traditional dances. The digital research on Pulus folk dance [17] records dance movement data related to its culture, and is aimed at Open to the public.

In addition, some researchers are more interested in making intangible cultural heritage dance reach more users in a low-threshold form [19]. The Terpsichore [18] project combines information technology with narrative, focusing on promoting the digitization of intangible culture related to traditional dance, and providing economically feasible solutions to cover a wider user group.

The Virtual Dance Museum visualizes digital-human folk dance performances in multiple virtual interfaces and allows users to access visual and cultural (music and costume) descriptions of dance at any time no matter where they are. Living Archive created a dance work demonstration that combined technology and the human body by introducing artificial intelligence into choreographic creativity.

Moreover, developers in the commercial game field are more concerned about the scalability of dance as a game mechanism. And the development of dance games is closely related to technological development.

In January 1998, the game "Jump" was launched on the PS1 console platform, which can be regarded as the earliest dance game. Entering the 21st century, the rapid development of network technology has brought more new possibilities for the innovation of dance games. In 2005, the online dance social game "Audition" was launched, bringing dance game into the field of online games for the first time. The arrival of the mobile Internet era has brought more room for development of dance games. Mobile games such as "Love Dance OL" and "Tiantian Dance" have been launched on the smartphone platform, realizing the gaming experience of dancing to a song anytime and anywhere.

While the Internet has advanced, somatosensory technology has also continued to evolve. Somatosensory games that emphasize body movement are naturally compatible with dancing behaviors in the real world. Dance games have become one of the most imaginative categories of somatosensory games. In 2009, a game called "Just Dance" developed by Ubisoft was launched on the wuii platform. With the support of somatosensory equipment, players can actually dance solo, duet or even group in the game.

Overall, only few studies have paid attention to the application of artificial intelligence technology in dance games, whether in the field of serious games or commercial games.

2.2   3D Dance Animation Generation Algorithm

3D dance animation generation technology can be divided into two categories: synthetic and generative. Among them, the synthetic approach mainly generates time-stable dance animation by splicing dance clips. The synthetic method can only rely on the existing dance database, cannot generate new dance animation and has poor diversity.The generative approach, on the other hand, generates dance animations directly through neural networks, which performs better in terms of diversity, but is limited by the model's ability to model over long periods of time, making it difficult to generate time-stable dance animations.

Synthetic Approach. The synthetic approach was derived from the classical motion graph search algorithm, The core idea is to rely on the dance database to build an motion graph, and then select the motion fragments in the motion graph that best match the music characteristics based on the music, and splice all the motion fragments.

In the traditional motion graph search method, the core idea is to use the transfer cost of the motion as the edge in the graph, and synthesize a dance by finding and splicing the motion sequence with the smallest sum of transfer costs. Arikan [3] and Kovar [2] formally introduced the notion of graph-based motion synthesis by defining the problem as finding paths in a pre-constructed motion graph. The study by Kim [1]. extended the framework to deal with rhythmic motions by introducing constraints involving motion beats and rhythmic patterns. More complex music-dance matching constraints were developed for path finding in motion graphs [4] [5]by many researchers Manfrè [6] articulated this problem using Hidden Markov Models (HMMs), which allow for an efficient solution to the problem using dynamic programming or beam search algorithms.

However, due to the lack of methods for researchers to grasp the relationship between music and dance, most of the dances generated by traditional action graph search algorithms lack aesthetics and fail to match the style and rhythm of the music. The development of deep learning has helped researchers better find a deeper relationship between music and movement.

In 2020, Kang [7] proposed a music-driven dance movement synthesis system. This system includes a deep learning-based embedding framework for movement music and a graph search-based movement synthesis framework. In 2022, Ho [8] focused on optimizing the rhythm matching and graph search parts of dance music based on Chen's work. They proposed the concept of dynamic graph search, that is, searching only in the columns of movements that best match the music style, which reduces the search cost.

Overall, the synthetic approach benefits from the quality of the dance database and can produce stable long-duration dance animations, but it is also limited by the dance database, which makes it difficult to produce new dance movements, and lacks diversity in terms of the style of the input music.

Generative Approach. The core idea of generative approach is all about converting music into movements encoded in a low-dimensional potential space, and then recovering the corresponding dance movements from the potential space by decoding.

If focusing on the broad field of motion generation, networks such as CNN, RNN, and Transformer have been applied. These approaches can correlate cross-modal features and extract meaningful representations from complex and diverse real-world data, generating motion sequences that better meet the needs of complex cross-modal alignment. However, it is after 2019 that people are formally focusing on cross-modal transformations for music and dance.

Lee [9] proposed the first 2D music-to-dance generation framework that uses VAE to model dance units and GAN networks to generate dance sequences. Li [10] and others used two Transformer structures to process music information and action information respectively in 2020, fused the processed information together and predicted the action at the next moment. Li [11] proposed AI-Choreographer, improves upon previous work, while retaining the dual-channel Transformer for music and dance, they added a cross-modal Transformer to model the distribution between audio and action. Li [12] proposed a new method,

DanceFormer. Instead of defining the output as a long dance sequence, they define it as output keyframes and transition curves.

Overall, generative approach can generate dance animations that match the music style and perform better in terms of diversity, but are limited by the model's ability to model long duration, making it difficult to generate long-duration dance animations.

Table 1. Summary of dance animation generation algorithm. DL meas deep learning.

Researcher	Time	Method	DL	Contribution
Kovar [2]	2002	Synthetic	✗	Motion graph-based
Kim [1]	2003	Synthetic	✗	Use music rhythm to constrain dance animation generation
Shiratori [4]	2006	Synthetic	✗	More complex music-dance matching constraints are introduced
Ofli [5]	2011	Synthetic	✗	Introduce HMM model
Kang [7]	2021	Synthetic	✓	Combine deep learning with motion graph search methods
Ho [8]	2022	Synthetic	✗	Dynamic motion graph is introduced
Lee [9]	2020	Generative	✗	Generate 2D dance animation using GAN
Ren [13]	2020	Generative	✗	Graph convolutional networks are used to optimize 2D dance animation production
Li [10]	2020	Generative	✗	Use Transformer to produce dance animation
Li [11]	2021	Generative	✗	A cross-modal Transformer is introduced to model the distribution between music and action
Li [12]	2021	Generative	✗	Generate excessive curves between motion keyframes rather than directly output dance animation
Gong [14]	2021	Generative	✗	Realized the generation of dance based on text and music

3   Method

DanceFree is a dance somatosensory game developed based on the Unity engine and 3D dance animation generation algorithms. DanceFree has a built-in database of 154 songs with initial dance animations, which are all generated by AI. It provides three modes for players to play. In Teaching Mode, the player can pick any dance from the dance animation database and follow the avatar to complete the learning of the dance; in Dance Mode, the player needs to control the avatar in the game world through body movement, and score points by striking the correct dance poses at the rhythm points; in Customization Mode, the player can upload the music to invoke the AI to generate the dance animation, and then the player can play his/her own created dance levels in the Dance Mode (Fig. 2).

Fig. 2. Players need to dance with the lead dancer and pose as correctly as possible to get a higher score.

3.1 Dance Animation Database

Select Appropriate Generation Algorithm. As mentioned in the previous section. Synthesized approach are more advantageous in terms of generation duration of dance animation, and generative approach are more advantageous in terms of generation diversity. Dance games have higher requirements for the duration of dance animation generation. The generated dance animation should be basically equivalent to the duration of the music. In addition, the construction of custom modes also requires high diversity of dance animations. The algorithm should be able to ensure that players can generate completely different dance animations using the same song.

Therefore, instead of choosing a particular generative or synthesized approach, we chose the latest comprehensive approach available, FineDance [20]. This method is divided into two parts: clip generation and retrieval synthesis, which is a new approach that combines generative and synthetic approaches. In the clip generation part, the network generates a large number of diverse dance fragments; in the retrieval synthesis part, the generated dance clips are constructed into a motion graph, and a graph search is performed to generate a time-stable dance animation.

Specifically, the clip generation part consists of a music-dance unified feature extraction network to map music clips and dance clips into a same feature space, and a 3D dance animation clips generation network based on the Diffusion model, which receives input musics and generates dance animations with matching styles and rhythms.

The retrieval synthesis part is a long-time animation synthesis method based on dynamic motion graph search. The existing dance database and the newly generated dance animation of each music clip form a dynamic action graph, and the music-dance unified feature extraction network is used to find the most matching dance animation for the input music, while considering the coherence of the movements between animations, completing the continuous splicing of animations, and finally outputting a long-time stable dance animation.

Build Database. In the end, we use FineDance algorithm to build an initial dance database of 154 dance songs in 12 styles for players to experience (Fig. 3).

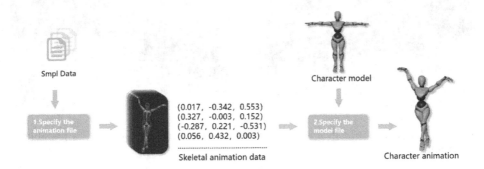

Fig. 3. We developed a blender plugin to efficiently convert AI-generated dance data into FBX files for the game engine.

3.2 An Introduction to Dancefree

Somatosensory Interaction. The interaction of the game is based on Kinect V2.0, a motion-sensing input device developed by Microsoft, which can capture human movement, facial expressions and voice commands without any handheld controller, thus providing a new way of interaction. As a traditional art, dance should be better promoted and passed down through games. Dance games should not be like traditional video games, where players need to sit in front of the computer. Dance games should encourage players to move, exercise, and dance in the real world.

In DanceFree, the player's upper body movements in the real world will be fully projected in the virtual world, controlling the avatar to pose accordingly. In this way, the player can control the avatar to pose correctly to gain points or reach the level goal to pass the game.

Teaching Mode. In order to let players learn the dances in the dance animation database better and master each dance move precisely. We have carefully split the dance animations in the database. We first cut the whole dance into dozens of dance clips of a few seconds according to the rhythm of the music, and then arrange a virtual character as the lead dancer in the game scene to present these dance animations in order. After the lead dancer finishes a segment, the player needs to imitate the lead dancer's moves and complete them correctly three times before learning the next move. The UI shows the name of the dance the player is learning, the number of times the current move has been completed correctly, the number of completed moves, and the accumulated learning time. We think it will be too difficult for the player to play a dance level made up of dances they are not familiar with, and we want the player to learn more about dance genres such as street dance and Chinese classical dance through this dance game, so we develop the Teaching Mode (Fig. 4).

Fig. 4. In the Teaching Mode, players need to follow the lead dancer and correctly complete each dance segment. The UI helps the player understand their learning progress more clearly.

Dancing Mode. In Dancing Mode, players are free to choose multiple dance songs for combination challenges. The system will automatically generate levels based on the player's choices. Similar to the game "OhShape", at each rhythm point of the music, a shadow will be generated to move towards the player, and the player needs to pose correctly in order to get the score, the more the player's pose matches with the correct pose, the higher the player's score will be. In addition, each pose the player poses will have a corresponding rating, according to the accuracy of the player's posture, divided into bad, normal, good, excellent four levels, each time the player moves, there will be a corresponding UI to remind the player's performance (Fig. 5).

Fig. 5. In Dancing mode, players need to strike the right pose at the rhythm point in order to score points.

Customization Mode. The 3D dance animation generation algorithm not only significantly reduces the development cost of the game but also provides the important function of player-generated content, which is one of the major features of DanceFree compared to other dance games. In DanceFree's Customization Mode, players only need to upload their favorite songs according to the system's guidelines, and the system will call the algorithm to generate the corresponding dance animation, and generate the corresponding level content according to this animation. In addition, the player's customized dance animation will be saved in the game's dance database, and the player will be able to play the customized level over and over again in Dancing Mode (Fig. 6).

Fig. 6. In the Customization Mode, players can upload their favorite music to customize the content of the game.

4   Experiment

To validate the effectiveness of our work, we conducted two experiments. A total of 36 participants took part in our experiments, including 18 males and 18 females. Of these participants, 10 have more than five years of dancing experience, 10 have ance experience, and the remaining 16 participants have not learned any dance.

4.1   Can AI-Generated Dance Animations Replace Real Dance Animations?

To assess whether AI-generated 3D dance animations can replace motion-captured animations as the core content of a dance game, we invited participants to play dance levels based on motion-captured animations and levels based on AI-generated dance animations. Then they are required to evaluate both types of levels. Specifically, we selected ten dance animations from the FineDance dataset and synchronized them with corresponding music to create dance animations. Players are given the choice to select three songs and sequentially complete levels composed of motion-captured animations and levels composed of AI animations. Participants were asked to evaluate the animations on authenticity, artistry, style

Table 2. Experiment 4.1 results

	Authenticity		Artistry		SM		RM		Enjoyment	
	M	SD	M	SD	M	SD	M	SD	M	SD
Motion Capture	4.89	1.12	4.21	1.98	3.99	2.03	4.09	1.01	3.11	1.65
AI Generate	4.11	1.7	4.02	1.01	4.01	1.99	4.13	1.57	3.2	1.42

Note: M=Mean; SD=Standard Deviation.

matching(SM), rhythm matching(RM), and level enjoyment using a Likert scale ranging from 1 to 5 (Table 2).

As shown in Table 2,When AI-generated dances are part of the level content, players still perceive that their authenticity and artistry are not as good as that of real dances, which may be because AI-generated dances have some warped frames, and the deep learning network has not yet grasped the deep relationship between music and dance. But in terms of rhythm matching, style matching, and level enjoyment, AI-generated dance is even slightly better than real dance. We think this may be because the game always generates frozen dance poses at rhythmic points, and players do not watch the full, smooth dance animation. But it also proves that the dance animation resources produced by AI is enough as game content for players to play.

4.2   Can Customization Mode Provide Players with a Better Gaming Experience?

To validate whether Customization Mode can provide players with a better game experience, we invite 36 participants to take part in an experiment. We used the Game Experience Questionnaire (GEQ) to assess the players' game experience, the questionnaire is presented in the form of a Likert scale ranging from 1 to 5.Participants are first asked to play three songs specified by the system and then complete the questionnaire. Afterward, they are allowed to choose three songs they personally like and create custom levels in the Customization Mode to play. Subsequently, they fill out the questionnaire once again.

As shown in Table 3, players clearly preferred the custom mode, especially in terms of immersion and positive emotions. We think this is because the gameplay is the same in both modes, but the customization mode allows players to play dances generated from their favorite songs, which makes it more fun for players. In addition, in terms of Challenging indicators, the game experience brought by the two modes is not very different. We believe that this is because the game mechanics of the two modes are basically similar, and the skills players need to understand and learn are also the same, so it will not show too much difference. We also conducted semi-structured interviews with some players, and a portion of them mentioned that the custom mode provided them with greater freedom. They expressed disinterest in the songs specified by the system, as they had not heard them before. Watching AI-generated dance animations synchronized with their favorite songs and dancing along with them was described as very exciting.

Table 3. Experiment 4.2 Results

Items	Questions	Specified Content		Customize Content	
		M	SD	M	SD
Immersion	I think this game is interesting	3.03	1.91	4.37	1.23
	I was impressed with the game	3.77	2.01	4.78	1.4
Flow	I forget everything else while playing the game	3.89	1.54	4.12	1.7
	I'm totally in the game	3.01	0.97	3.56	0.82
Competence	I feel a sense of accomplishment	2.94	0.70	3.87	0.66
	I have skills	3.41	1.21	3.99	1.47
Positive Emotion	I feel satisfied	3.50	1.48	4.15	0.56
	I feel good	3.51	2.21	4.09	0.77
Negative Emotion	I feel boring	2.19	0.76	1.97	1.08
	I feel tired	2.89	1.11	2.04	1.63
Challenging	I find the game challenging	3.19	1.46	3.23	0.94
	I put in a lot of effort	2.41	1.95	2.93	2.07
Restlessness	I feel depressed	3.18	1.44	2.28	1.88
	I feel restless	1.76	0.95	1.24	0.87

Note: M=Mean; SD=Standard Deviation.

The experimental results validate that our developed custom mode enhances the players' gaming experience.

5   Conclusion

With the development of technology, dance elements with cultural connotations are more and more often applied in games. Commercial games represented by JustDance are popular all over the world, and many players learn to dance and strengthen their bodies through dance games; many researchers also pay more and more attention to enhancing the dissemination and preservation of dance culture by digitalization. However, few developers and researchers have tried to use AI technology to solve the problems of high production cost and small space for player customization of dance animations in dance games.

In order to solve this problem, we introduced 3D dance animation production technology into the field of dance games, and explored and made some contributions in the research field of AIGC-enabled game production.

Specifically, we developed DanceFree, a somatosensory dance game based on 3D dance animation generation technology. We first borrowed AI technology to efficiently generate a large number of initial dance libraries with various styles to ensure players' initial game experience. Compared with traditional dance games, we can expand the dance database faster and at a lower cost, and continue to update the game. In addition, we have opened a custom mode to players. By leveraging the excellent generation capabilities of AI, players can upload any music they like, and DanceFree will generate corresponding dance game content for players. Compared with the fixed dance music database of traditional dance games, We provide space for players to generate their own content. In terms of gameplay, we followed the somatosensory interactive gameplay of most dance games. Players complete the correct dance moves to pass the game and gain scores. We conducted two experiments to verify the validity of our work, and the results showed that 1) AI-generated dance animations are sufficient to replace real dance animations as part of the game content. 2) AI-based customization modes can give players a better experience.

Due to the limitations of the development team's ability and cost, we will not be releasing this game to the market for the time being. However, in the future, we will continue to research the combination of AI technology and dance games, and strive to realize innovation in the gameplay mechanism, explore more possibilities of AI-enabled game development, and bring players a brand new game experience.

Acknowledgments. This work was partly supported by Shenzhen Key Laboratory of next generation interactive media innovative technology (No: ZDSYS-20210623092001004)

References

1. Kim, T., Park, S., Shin, S.: Rhythmic-motion synthesis based on motion-beat analysis. ACM Trans. Graph. (TOG). **22**, 392–401 (2003)
2. Kovar, L., Gleicher, M., Pighin, F.: Motion graphs. Seminal Graph. Papers: Push. Bound. **2**, 723–732 (2023)
3. Arikan, O., Forsyth, D.: Interactive motion generation from examples. ACM Trans. Graph. (TOG). **21**, 483–490 (2002)
4. Shiratori, T., Nakazawa, A., Ikeuchi, K.: Dancing-to-music character animation. Comput. Graph. Forum. **25**, 449–458 (2006)
5. Ofli, F., Erzin, E., Yemez, Y., Tekalp, A.: Learn2dance: learning statistical music-to-dance mappings for choreography synthesis. IEEE Trans. Multimed. **14**, 747–759 (2011)
6. Manfrè, A., Infantino, I., Vella, F., Gaglio, S.: An automatic system for humanoid dance creation. Biol. Inspired Cogn. Architect. **15**, 1–9 (2016)
7. Chen, K., et al.: Choreomaster: choreography-oriented music-driven dance synthesis. ACM Trans. Graph. (TOG). **40**, 1–13 (2021)
8. Au, H., Chen, J., Jiang, J., Guo, Y.: Choreograph: Music-conditioned automatic dance choreography over a style and tempo consistent dynamic graph. In: Proceedings of the 30th ACM International Conference On Multimedia, pp. 3917–3925 (2022)
9. Lee, M., Lee, K., Park, J.: Music similarity-based approach to generating dance motion sequence. Multimed. Tools Appl. **62**, 895–912 (2013)
10. Li, J., et al.: Learning to generate diverse dance motions with transformer. ArXiv Preprint ArXiv:2008.08171. (2020)
11. Li, R., Yang, S., Ross, D., Kanazawa, A.: Learn to dance with aist++: Music conditioned 3d dance generation. ArXiv Preprint ArXiv:2101.08779. **2** (2021)
12. Li, B., Zhao, Y., Zhelun, S., Sheng, L.: Danceformer: music conditioned 3D dance generation with parametric motion transformer. Proce. AAAI Conf. Artif. Intell. **36**, 1272–1279 (2022)

13. Ren, X., Li, H., Huang, Z., Chen, Q.: Self-supervised dance video synthesis conditioned on music. In: Proceedings of the 28th ACM International Conference on Multimedia, pp. 46–54 (2020)
14. Gong, Y., Chung, Y., Glass, J.: Ast: audio spectrogram transformer. ArXiv Preprint ArXiv:2104.01778 (2021)
15. Dimitropoulos, K., et al.: A multimodal approach for the safeguarding and transmission of intangible cultural heritage. The case of i-Treasures. IEEE Intell. Syst. **33**, 3–16 (2018)
16. Cozzani, G., Pozzi, F., Dagnino, F., Katos, A., Katsouli, E.: Innovative technologies for intangible cultural heritage education and preservation: the case of i-Treasures. Personal Ubiquit. Comput. **21**, 253–265 (2017)
17. Aristidou, A., et al.: Virtual Dance Museum: The case of greek/cypriot folk dancing. In: Proceedings of the Eurographics Workshop on Graphics and Cultural Heritage (Aire-la-Ville, Switzerland, Switzerland, 2021), Hulusic V., Chalmers A.,(Eds.), GCH. **21** (2021)
18. Aristidou, A., Shamir, A., Chrysanthou, Y.: Digital dance ethnography: organizing large dance collections. J. Comput. Cult. Heritage (JOCCH). **12**, 1–27 (2019)
19. Andreoli, R., et al.: A framework to design, develop, and evaluate immersive and collaborative serious games in cultural heritage. Journal On Computing And Cultural Heritage (JOCCH). **11**, 1–22 (2017)
20. Li, R., et al.: FineDance: a fine-grained choreography dataset for 3D full body dance generation. In: Proceedings of the IEEE/CVF International Conference on Computer Vision, pp. 10234–10243 (2023)

Author Index

X. Fang (Ed.): HCII 2024, LNCS 14730, pp. 337–338, 2024.
https://doi.org/10.1007/978-3-031-60692-2

Printed in the United States
by Baker & Taylor Publisher Services